HISTORY AND THEORIES OF PSYCHOLOGY

HISTORY AND THEORIES OF PSYCHOLOGY

A Critical Perspective

Dai Jones
Field Chair of Psychology,
Cheltenham and Gloucester College of Higher Education

and

Jonathan Elcock
Senior Lecturer in Psychology,
Cheltenham and Gloucester College of Higher Education

A member of the Hodder Headline Group
LONDON

Co-published in the United States of America by
Oxford University Press Inc., New York

First published in Great Britain in 2001
by Arnold, a member of the Hodder Headline Group,
338 Euston Road, London NW1 3BH

http://www.arnoldpublishers.com

Co-published in the United States of America by
Oxford University Press Inc.,
198 Madison Avenue, New York, NY10016

British Library Cataloguing in Publication Data
A catalogue record for this book is available from the British Library

Library of Congress Cataloguing-in-Publication Data
A catalogue record for this book is available from the Library of Congress

ISBN 0 340 74116 3 (hb)
ISBN 0 340 74117 1 (pb)

1 2 3 4 5 6 7 8 9 10

Production Editor: James Rabson
Production Controller: Iain McWilliams
Cover Design: Terry Griffiths

Typeset in 10 on 12pt Palatino by Phoenix Photosetting, Chatham, Kent
Printed and bound in Great Britain by MPG Books Ltd, Cornwall

What do you think about this book? Or any other Arnold title?
Please send your comments to feedback.arnold@hodder.co.uk

CONTENTS

PREFACE

The nature and aims of this book are detailed in the introduction. Here, we want to take the opportunity to thank all those involved in helping its production. We would like to thank our students for acting as guinea pigs for some of the ideas and material contained within, particularly those studying the modules Psychology and Social Issues and History and Theories of Psychology. We would also like to thank Jo Shutt for allowing us to make use of material collected for her final year project, which comprises part of Chapter 6. A number of authors have been important in shaping our ideas, but we would particularly like to acknowledge Graham Richards for his support in our development of a critical, historical curriculum, and for his support in the preparation of the book proposal. In acknowledging support, we would like to thank our friends and families for their forbearance during times of stress, and our college for giving us the freedom to develop these ideas within the curriculum and for their practical support and encouragement in producing the book. Particular thanks go to our publishers for taking a chance on unknown authors, and for putting up with more than one missed deadline. Finally, our thanks to Kali Gagen for her support and patience in proof-reading the manuscript. As usual, any errors and omissions are the sole responsibility of the authors.

Dai Jones
Jonathan Elcock
April 2001

INTRODUCTION

This book is intended in part as a history of Psychology, but not as a complete history – the coverage given is partial and truncated. (In the current volume, we follow the convention of Richards (1996), in using 'psychology' to refer to the subject matter of psychology, and using 'Psychology' to refer to the discipline that studies that subject matter.) A large number of histories of Psychology are available, varying in scope of coverage, and in the approaches taken by the authors. For the current volume, we have decided on a limited coverage of the historical development of the discipline, allowing space for a greater discussion of contemporary Psychology than is normally the case. Thus rather than presenting a detailed history of Psychology, and concluding with a chapter describing contemporary Psychology, we present an overview of the history of Psychology, and give detailed coverage of issues of debate within contemporary Psychology. The choice of historical material has been directed by our interests, and also to highlight the central argument of the book, that the development of the discipline has been, and continues to be, contingent on a wide range of factors. Having said that, we believe that the presentation of the history of Psychology given here is both valid and valuable, for the reasons given below.

In addition to being a history of Psychology this book is a resource for critical Psychology. A major focus of the book is on investigating a number of issues and debates within contemporary Psychology. In doing so, we draw on a wide range of sources and arguments, including those within the discipline and from related disciplines such as philosophy and sociology. We also consider the variety of contexts within which the discipline has developed and is currently developing. Examining the history of Psychology provides a framework for the approach to critical Psychology that the book adopts. Thus we start by considering how Psychology has been shaped in the past by a variety of factors, and then show how similar forces are operating on the contemporary development of the discipline. This book is therefore more than a history of Psychology. As suggested in the preceding paragraph, the book is a combination of a critical history of Psychology, and a critical look at current issues in Psychology. We believe that the history of the discipline provides an important resource for critical psychologists, in that it provides a rich set of material for the practice of metatheory. In the remainder of this introduction, we shall justify this by defining some of the terms used, and drawing together our arguments. This, we hope, will prepare you for the approach we are taking to the book. Over the course of the book as a whole, we hope to provide plenty of evidence as to the validity and value of the approach.

What Is Critical Psychology?

Different psychologists use the term 'critical Psychology' in many different ways. Before looking at the value of studying history as a resource for critical Psychology, it is important to be clear what sense of the term we are using. Here, we will review some approaches to critical Psychology. What unites these different approaches is a degree of rejection of mainstream Psychology, so we will start by considering what 'mainstream' Psychology is.

Fox and Prilleltensky (1997) describe mainstream Psychology as a view of Psychology as a science conducted by objective researchers and practitioners who uncover the truth about human behaviour. This form of Psychology, they argue, is that which is most often taught in institutions, and practised by applied and research psychologists. This view holds the practice of Psychology to be value free, and unaffected by what might be termed extradisciplinary concerns.

In contrast, there are a number of positions, described as critical Psychology, that reject this view of Psychology as an objective science conducted in isolation. Critical Psychologies variously emphasize the influence of a range of factors in shaping the development of the discipline, the reflexivity of the discipline itself, and the sociopolitical consequences of psychological theory and practice. We will discuss these various forms of critical Psychology in two coarsely defined groups: political critical Psychology, and metatheoretical critical Psychology.

An important aside here is to note the debate around the identification of internal and external factors. In a naïve view, it is possible to identify discrete factors influencing the development of the discipline, some of which are internal to the discipline, and others of which are external to the discipline, these factors having largely discrete effects. It seems more reasonable to say that there is a range of factors influencing the discipline, which vary in the degree to which they are identified as important to Psychology. Further, these forces act interactively and reflexively.

Political critical Psychology is concerned with developing a Psychology that has themes of social justice, the welfare of communities, and altering the status quo of society in general and Psychology in particular (Fox and Prilleltensky 1997). Such critical Psychologies discuss the nature of mainstream Psychology in these terms, with an emphasis on achieving change. Examples of this kind of critical Psychology include feminist Psychology and many forms of discursive Psychology.

What we (cautiously) term metatheoretical critical Psychology has a more academic concern, and is less concerned with effecting change, although the work of political critical psychologists is an important resource. Metatheoretical critical Psychology is particularly concerned with assessing the adequacy of theory, method, and practice within Psychology. This approach aims to encourage a stronger appreciation of the strengths and weaknesses of particular approaches and theoretical positions in Psychology, and emphasizes the need for contextual and integrative interpretation. Writing as lecturers, we see this as not only a more realistic approach to the subject matter of the discipline, but also as a valuable intellectual approach in its own right.

Approaches To History

A number of approaches to history have been identified, for example, by Richards (1996), which will be briefly summarized. Old style histories tended to have a narrow, intellectual focus, tracing the chronological development of the discipline. They were largely celebratory (or Whiggish, or progressivist), describing development as a progressive process of finding the truth. Such histories generally overlooked the wider context in which the discipline developed. Such an approach might be described as internalist (in contrast to externalist, but see above). In such histories, the progressive development of the discipline occurred in intellectual and cultural isolation, and so was (implicitly) immune to contamination by outside forces. Presentist histories are histories in which the author's theoretical position represents the truth, and are generally written to show previous theories as a developmental process leading to this true position. Such histories fail to accept that the present theoretical orthodoxy may be no more valid than previous orthodoxies, which were themselves viewed as the true position by the presentist historians of the time.

Recently, a number of alternative approaches to history have been adopted. Particularly interesting are revisionist and anti-revisionist histories, and what might be called new history, all of which are discussed below. These histories share, to varying degrees, a rejection of the progressivist and internalist approach, but the presentist approach is harder to avoid – it is clearly impossible to write history from anything other than the present. Even so, it is important to avoid the trap of discussing contemporary theories as largely true.

There are a number of reasons why we might want to study history. Briefly, and looking, for now, at the study of history in its own right, we can identify:

1 Interest
2 Understanding

One way to appreciate the nature of the discipline is to examine how it got to be the way it is. Thus we can look at the questions that have been asked about psychological issues, and the ways in which the questions have been addressed, as a way of understanding current work in Psychology.

3   Learning the Lessons

In Psychology, theories come and go, as do methodologies. By studying the history of Psychology, we can learn the lessons of the past. If we are replacing previously accepted theories or methodologies with new ones, we have to address the difficulties that led to the rejection of the old, for example, introspection was criticised as being subjective, so any replacement had to not be (overtly) subjective. More importantly, however, sometimes theories or methodologies are revisited, and when they are accepted anew it is important to improve on any previous weaknesses, as is currently the case in neuropsychology. Relatedly, previous theories or methodologies may have been rejected prematurely, and with hindsight the values of those theories can be seen, for example, the work of Bartlett.

4   Critical Understanding

Understanding how psychology got to be the way it is is all very well. However, studying history offers far more than this. In particular, by studying history we can benefit from hindsight, and use this perspective to examine the way in which the development of theories in Psychology is dependent on a range of factors, most of which have little to do with the subject matter itself.

Having looked at the types of history that are pursued, and looked broadly at the reasons for studying history, it is important to consider the roles that history can play. Historical accounts are not neutral, and involve some degree of selection of focus and choice of interpretation. Mainstream Psychology is often seen as being supported by a certain type of history – the traditional, celebratory, history that serves to justify the status quo, making it seem the inevitable consequence of a progressive development. Clearly, such histories are necessarily intellectual.

Just as mainstream Psychology is supported by traditional histories, so is political critical Psychology supported by critical histories, most notably those written from a feminist perspective. However such histories, in seeking to challenge the mainstream, run the risk of being revisionist. For example, Leon Kamin and Stephen Jay Gould have both been accused of revisionism (Harris 1997), for *The science and politics of IQ* and *The mismeasure of man* respectively.

Critical histories need not necessarily be revisionist. Harris describes the programme of the new history of Psychology that tries to be more contextual, more inclusive, and avoidant of the problems of celebratory and revisionist histories. This kind of history, with an emphasis on social context and political concerns, is of great value to political critical psychologists. Of particular interest to us as metatheoretical critical psychologists is the question, what role can history play in supporting our work?

History As Metatheory

In looking at the value of history to metatheoretical critical Psychology, we shall consider two particularly good examples of Harris's new history –

Danziger's (1990) *Constructing the subject*, and Herman's (1995) *The romance of American psychology*. Danziger's book focuses on the way in which Psychology has created its own subject matter, and particularly on the way in which much of what is now accepted as a necessary component of psychological research is a social construction. As such, this historical approach provides valuable insights into the nature of methodology within Psychology, as a counterpoint to the orthodox presentation of current methodology as the right way of conducting psychological research. Herman's book focuses on the role of psychologists in the pursuit of political and cultural authority, and the impact of this pursuit on the nature of theories produced. Rather than presenting Psychology as a tool of authority, however (as revisionist histories might do), she emphasizes the reflexive relationship between the discipline of Psychology and the sociopolitical context within which Psychology is studied and practised.

Both books are good examples of the use of history for the purpose of critical understanding, as described previously. They show how the current orthodoxy in Psychology is the result of a range of contingent factors, rather than some inevitable outcome. These books look at single issues. A similar approach, applied more widely, is used in Richards's (1996) *Putting psychology in its place*.

A critical understanding of the development of contemporary Psychology is fundamental to our metatheoretical critical Psychology, and critical histories are essential in providing this understanding. However, we take the approach further. Having used a historical perspective to demonstrate the factors underlying development and acceptance of theoretical positions, we can use the same techniques to consider issues of debate in present day Psychology, showing that the same forces are in operation in the ongoing development of the discipline – clearly this involves a rejection of the view of contemporary theories as true. We feel that this approach to the study of Psychology is valuable and powerful, both in terms of developing a clearer view of the nature of Psychology, and in terms of promoting critical engagement with the discipline in students. To quote Harris (1997), 'through historical awareness, it will be easier to critically view what is taking place today'.

ABOUT THE AUTHORS

It is conventional in introducing a text to give a little background information about the authors, either to satisfy the curiosity of the reader or to convince the reader of their credentials. While both are valid purposes, we believe the provision of background information plays a more important role. As stated above, and as will be emphasized in later chapters, any history, and indeed any piece of writing, is necessarily partial, and will necessarily be influenced by the positions of the authors. In order to take account of this, it is necessary to provide information about the authors to enable the reader to judge how the authors' position has influenced the writing. Here, therefore, we will introduce ourselves and attempt to explain how our views have influenced our writing.

We are both lecturers in Psychology at Cheltenham and Gloucester College of Higher Education (CGCHE). I (Dai) am currently, and Jonathan was formerly, course leader for the undergraduate programme in Psychology. My background was originally in computer science, moving into Psychology via an MSc in cognitive science and research in artificial intelligence and cognitive linguistics. I joined CGCHE as a postgraduate student in Psychology before accepting a position there as a full-time lecturer. In studying cognitive Psychology, I was struck by the reliance of conventional cognitive Psychology on particular philosophical positions, and particular modelling techniques and assumptions. My interest was in how such positions and assumptions came to adopted, having concluded for myself that alternatives were more plausible. In particular, I am connectionist rather than symbolic in my approach to cognitive modelling, and this position has a reflexive relationship to my positions regarding philosophy of mind, and the metaphors underlying cognitive Psychology. Considering such issues necessarily leads to a degree of intellectual metatheoretical criticality. In addition, although my expertise is in the cognitive domain, I am of course influenced by my political beliefs, which are to the left of centre. A combination of concern about the uses Psychology is put to in support of antithetical (to me) political positions, and a nascent metatheoretical criticality, has led me to a broader criticality. Pursuing this interest introduced me to a range of valuable historically based critical material, which hinted at the value of history for metatheory.

My (Jonathan) background is more conventionally psychological than Dai's. I came to Cheltenham and Gloucester the year before the full Psychology degree began. Although my background was more cognitive than social that year (1992) the original course leader was internally promoted, leaving me as both course leader and without a social psychologist. After a year where I taught traditional social psychology I rapidly developed an interest in the, then new to me, challenges to social psychology that discourse analysis presented. That led me towards social constructionism and critical Psychology, two areas that seemed much more consonant with my general views on politics and how things work than mainstream Psychology. For me history is a part of the solution to the puzzle 'just why are things constructed as they are?'

BOOK ORGANIZATION

As the title suggests, the book is in two parts. The first part, comprising eight chapters, gives an overview of the history of Psychology. Starting with a survey of approaches to history and the philosophy of science, the following chapters give a partly chronological, partly topical, coverage of the development of Psychology. Thus we trace the factors influencing the founding of Psychology as a particular kind of discipline, and the subsequent rapid and early development of a range of different approaches in academic Psychology, up to 1945. We then look at the concurrent development of applied Psychology, and more closely at the relationship between the psychoanalytic movement and disciplinary Psychology. We finish this time period by looking at the relationship between Psychology and wider society, looking at the reflexive relationship between the two, before going on to look at postwar developments in social and cognitive Psychology. This part of the book will be of particular interest to those interested in the history of Psychology, but as discussed above, the emphasis will not be on tracing the chain of events, but rather on identifying the contextual factors influencing the ongoing development of the discipline.

The second part of the book, comprising seven chapters, looks at a range of issues in contemporary Psychology. In general these chapters can be read in isolation, although there are links between some – these are highlighted in the text. We start by looking at the relationship between Psychology and minorities, including an appropriate historical perspective. We then examine the nature and role of contemporary Psychology, and the tensions operating within the discipline. In part, this chapter marks out the territory to be traversed by later chapters. We then consider current debates around folk Psychology and advocate a closer examination of the content of people's everyday psychologizing – a topic sadly overlooked by much academic Psychology, which leaves a gap to be filled by popular psychology. Following this, we look at methodological issues in contemporary Psychology, and conclude by considering the major branches of modern Psychology, cognitive, and social. In each of these, we critically examine orthodox positions and assess alternative views. The range of issues considered are those that most interest or concern us as authors – different authors would have chosen a different set of issues.

Throughout the book, the intention of each chapter is to act as an introduction to a particular area, rather than as a complete coverage. The intended audience is advanced undergraduate students, who already have some knowledge of the nature of Psychology. To this end, the coverage is intended to be accessible, to favour breadth over depth, and to emphasize arguments and debates rather than description. This means that some readers, particularly colleagues, may find the coverage to be incomplete, and lacking depth. We apologize for this, but we believe it to be a necessary consequence of our audience design. It is expected that having read these introductions to particular topics, the reader will go on to do further reading in the area. To facilitate this, each chapter concludes with a selection of recommended further reading.

FURTHER READING

Benjamin, L. (ed.) 1997: *A history of psychology: original sources and contemporary research*, 2nd edn. Boston: McGraw Hill.

Brennan, J. 1998: *Readings in the history and systems of psychology*, 2nd edn. Upper Saddle River, NJ: Prentice-Hall.

Danziger, K. 1990: *Constructing the subject: historical origins of psychological research.* Cambridge: Cambridge University Press.

Fox, D. and Prilleltensky, I. 1997: *Critical psychology: an introduction.* London: Sage.

Goodwin, C.J. 1999: *A history of modern psychology.* New York: John Wiley.

Gould, S.J. 1996 revised: *The mismeasure of man.* London: Penguin.

Gross, R. 1995: *Themes, issues and debates in psychology.* London: Hodder and Stoughton.

Herman, E. 1995: *The romance of American psychology.* Berkeley: University of California Press.

Leahey, T.H. 2000: *A history of psychology.* Englewood Cliffs, NJ: Prentice-Hall.

McGhee, P. 2001: *Thinking Psychologically.* Basingstoke: Palgrave

Richards, G. 1996: *Putting psychology in its place.* London: Routledge.

Valentine, E. 1992: *Conceptual issues in psychology,* 2nd edn. London: Routledge.

1

HISTORY AS METATHEORY

INTRODUCTION

The purpose of this chapter is to construct the foundations underpinning our critical approach to Psychology. In many ways it is the most abstract chapter of the book. In the remaining chapters we aim to use history as metatheory and in order to do this we need to understand some of the ways that the sciences, including Psychology, can be seen as social activities. Thus in this chapter we intend to review the ways that science can be regarded, the ways in which history of science can be studied and come to a position that allows us to develop a critical approach to Psychology using history. To some extent we acknowledge that this review is limited and we do not to go deeply into the complex philosophical arguments that surround the topic. At the end of the chapter is an annotated bibliography that should guide interested readers towards this fascinating literature.

In developing an approach to history we also develop an approach to science, science as a social activity. To some extent these notions are intertwined, so the bulk of this chapter will explore investigating science as a social activity.

GENERAL ISSUES WITH APPROACHES TO HISTORY

Harris (1997) suggests that there are three ways of writing histories of Psychology; celebratory histories of Psychology, revisionist histories of Psychology and finally critical histories of Psychology.

Without wishing to denigrate the considerable scholarship of many of the early works in the history of Psychology, the majority of them were celebratory histories and suffered two major defects. The first is the *presentist* bias, the tendency to write a history to justify the current status quo, also known as *Whig history* after the tendency to believe that history was inevitably progressive and so the current state of affairs must be the most advanced. The second was a tendency to be *internalist*, that is little attention was paid to the various influences from outside of the discipline and was concentrated on the history of theoretical change within the discipline as if it was only driven by empirical and theoretical change.

One possible reason for this was the need for Psychology, or the 'new Psychology' as proponents called it, to represent itself as a coherent discipline with both an intellectual history rooted in western philosophy and a scientific approach that rendered it both separate and superior to other approaches.

While scholarly works on the history of Psychology did not always suffer from these problems the majority of students' first acquaintance with the history of Psychology, often in the first chapter of an introductory textbook, almost certainly suffers from these biases in their most extreme form. While there may be a pedagogical reason for treating the history of the discipline in this way, Richards's (1996) book has demonstrated that it is possible to write successfully for introductory students in a more complex and meaningful way than many other contemporary textbooks.

The second type of histories that Harris identifies are revisionist histories, including examples such as Thomas Szasz's work on anti-psychiatry, Leon Kamin's (1974) book *The science and politics of IQ* and Steven Jay Gould's (1981, revised 1996) *The mismeasure of man*. All of these books, although coming from different ideological perspectives, offer a passionate and articulate account of the failing of some area of Psychology. All of the works were part of a current debate within Psychology and the social policy areas connected to aspects of Psychology. They are a useful corrective to the notion that Psychology stands outside of political and cultural frameworks. However, they share one flaw with celebratory histories. They tended towards a heroic view of history, by suggesting that a particular cadre of psychologists represented all of Psychology. Harris also maintains that the authors of these histories judge past scientists to be in error by the standards of today, and that in the case of Kamin and Gould see malicious intent, on the part of psychologists, whenever there is social injustice.

The final type of history that Harris identifies is critical history, the main point of which is to be a history focused more on social context and political power as well as intellectual history and the beliefs of a few leading figures. Like Harris, we believe that this focus enables a more nuanced understanding both of the past and present consequences of holding particular positions in Psychology.

In developing a critical historical approach to Psychology we believe it is necessary to develop an approach to understanding science as a social activity. In the next, major section approaches to science are reviewed in order to understand that approach. At the end of the chapter we return to the history of Psychology, in order to sketch an approach to understanding historical change in Psychology.

APPROACHES TO SCIENCE

At various points in the history of Psychology there has been great controversy over whether this discipline can, or should be, a science. Wündt divided his system of psychology between a limited scientific project, part of the *Naturwissenshaft*, and a larger cultural project not amenable to scientific methods, part of the *Geistewissenshaft*. With the rise of Humanistic Psychology, and the criticisms that this attracted from more orthodox psychologists, Maslow (1966) wrote a book calling for more use of experiential rather than experimental methods. More recently a number of different social constructionist psychologists (for example, Harré, K. Gergen, Kitzinger and Edwards) and feminist psychologists (for example, Holloway, Kitzinger, M. Gergen and Josselson) have called for a variety of different ways of doing Psychology. We return to all of these debates in their contexts in later chapters. Psychologists have, in the main, seen the discipline as either a science or an aspiring science and some of the debates within Psychology have depended on what type of science Psychology should be. For this reason it is important to examine the debates around science with the aim of discussing an approach to science that enables a critical historical perspective.

Logical Positivism and Popperian Anti-Positivism

The modern style of scientific explanation can be linked to a much larger movement in the history of western thought which includes the rise of Protestantism and the associated rise of rationalization, British empiricist philosophers, Descartes's philosophy and later the Enlightenment and modernity. These topics form the substantive topic of the next chapter but the major point is that these developments were not themselves isolated and abstract from cultural conditions.

One foundational figure that can be highlighted is Isaac Newton, who defined the scientific enterprise as the search for a small number of mathematical laws from which the regularities of nature could be deduced. In Newton's scheme there was no need to provide precise mechanisms by which his three laws of motion and theory of gravity operated. The fact that they could be used to predict the motion of planets and moons was sufficient.

Comte codified a more extreme version of this marking the beginning of positivism. As Giddens (1974) and May (1997) have remarked, positivism as now used by many sociologists has been stripped of its original meaning and is now used as a term of abuse, to be hurled at anyone who tries to quantify social issues. It is necessary to rescue the term from what may be its current sense in order to understand its impact on science. In the positivist philosophy of science three functions were assigned to science: *description, prediction* and *control*.

Description was for positivists the basic goal of science, to remain as close to observation as possible and not to indulge in hypothetical explanations. Under this scheme scientists would closely observe natural events, discover the underlying regularities and propose scientific laws that summarize these descriptions. These scientific laws were not seen as theories or hypotheses but as no more than accurate summary descriptions.

Prediction flows naturally from these descriptions. The scientific laws proposed would allow for the prediction of future events provided that these mathematical summaries were accurate.

Control comes from the ability of, for example, engineers to create objects according to these scientific laws, thus intervening in the natural order.

This scheme is of course impoverished when it comes to explanation. An attempt to save the *logical-positivist position,* as positivism became known as it melded with developments in logic and mathematics, was made by Hempel and Oppenheim. The Hempel-Oppenheim approach to explanation was that scientific explanations could be regarded as logical arguments. The events to be explained, the *explanandum,* could be deduced from the *explanans,* the relevant scientific laws and observed initial conditions. A key feature here is that what is to be explained must be separated from its explanation.

Hempel was aware of at least one of the problems with the logical positivist scheme of science and came up with the famous 'paradox of the raven' to illustrate the problem of drawing generalizations (1946).

Imagine that you are an ornithologist attempting to confirm the hypothesis that all ravens are black. Obviously finding a black raven would, to some degree, confirm the hypothesis, and finding a white raven would irrefutably disconfirm the hypothesis. Hempel's paradox begins with the claim that the hypothesis can be simply restated as 'All non-black things are non-ravens'. Logically this restatement appears to be the same as the original hypothesis. This rewording is a *contrapositivist* and contrapositives of any statement are identical in meaning to the original wording. This is where the paradox begins. 'All non-black things are non-ravens' is a lot easier to test. Sitting at your chair you can see a number of things that are not black and are not ravens which help confirm the hypothesis all ravens are black. It is a lot easier than going to all the places where ravens usually dwell and observing them there. However, the same evidence can be used to support different hypotheses, the hypothesis 'All ravens are white' has as its contrapositivist 'all non-ravens are non-white': thus a red herring would provide confirmation of both hypotheses. This is clearly absurd. The solution is a set of rules known as Nicod's criterion after the philosopher Jean Nicod. In terms of black ravens these can be stated as:

1   Sighting a black raven makes the generalization more likely.
2   Sighting a non-black raven disproves the statement.
3   Observations of black non-ravens and non-black non-ravens are irrelevant.

The logical-positivist scheme has had a number of impacts on Psychology, not least that at the time that Psychology began to assert its disciplinary identity the main approach to science was logical-positivism. Some of the anti-metaphysical pronouncements of the behaviourists can be linked to the positions of the logical positivists. However, even during this era there were Psychologists, for example, those developing the techniques of factor analysis and the testing of mental and other attributes, whose work cannot be judged as an attempt to follow the strictures of logical positivism.

However, by the time that the Hempel-Oppenheim model had been proposed logical-positivism was in trouble, not least from events in physics and the reactions to these events in philosophy.

The anti-positivist philosopher, Popper, proposed an argument in favour of falsifiability as an alternative to positivism. Popper compared the logical-positivist position of science to a bucket into which the wine of knowledge was presumed to flow pure and simple from patiently and industriously gathered facts. The problem that Popper highlighted is that it is possible to find empirical facts to support even the most ridiculous claims. Popper's solution to this dilemma is that scientific theories must be able to make predictions that are in principle falsifiable. The issue is whether it is more important to look for confirming instances or non-confirming instances and with Popper's proposal it becomes more important to develop experiments, or search for observations, that are a test of a hypothesis because they may disprove it.

What Popper gives us is a way of judging scientific theories. Scientific theories should give us hypotheses that are open to refutation. A theory that provides too many limits on the observations it accepts, or in the face of disconfirming evidence a theory that alters to make it less testable is a poor theory. Popper's scheme is often described as the norm for good science. Scientists in their professional pronouncements sound like good Popperians, although as a study by Gilbert and Mulkay (1984) shows, scientists may well talk very differently amongst themselves.

There are a number of points to be made at this stage. The first is that many psychologists still talk like logical-positivists rather than good Popperians. For example, some still talk of finding empirical laws of human behaviour. This may explain the well-recorded publication bias in journals, that journals are more likely to report significant results than results that reject the experimental hypothesis, despite the fact that those well-designed studies that reject a hypothesis are more informative under Popper's scheme than those studies that confirm an experimental hypothesis.

The second is that Popper's philosophy had a direct impact on a Psychologist called Peter Watson, who developed a number of experimental tasks to test whether or not people reasoned according to Popper's logic. Summarizing a very dense literature it appears that people suffer from a number of biases when reasoning. One of these, a confirmation bias, suggests that most people look for confirmatory evidence rather than evidence that may refute a hypothesis. This work has developed into a Psychology of scientists, which attempts to model the cognitive processes of science; while it may be interesting it is an approach far removed from the one we are taking in this book.

The third, and most important from our perspective, is that neither of these views of science, even in their more complex formulations, will suit our purposes within this book.

In the logical-positivist version incorrect past theories would be incorrect because of either errors or biases by previous generations of scientists, or because previous scientists had no (technological) way of making the necessary observations. Under this scheme our book would be a cautionary tale, cataloguing errors and discussing biases, with the occasional lauding of new discoveries that allow the psychologist to see things more clearly. All of the time we would be using the current state of psychological knowledge as the gold standard of a comparison.

The Popperian view may at least prevent us from this presentist bias, with the knowledge that the current theories may be refuted at any time, even in the publication lag between the writing and the reading of these words. However, in a Popperian view we would be looking for those critical experiments and observations that disconfirmed old theories and cleared the way for new ones. This would be very much a celebratory account of the heroic efforts of those pioneers who came up with the experiment, or decided to search for the observation that proved critical.

Alternatives to Popper

Popper's thesis has a number of critics. The main point of many of these criticisms is that the rarity of the crucial experiment is seen as a determinant of a change in scientific theory.

Conventionalism

Critics of Popper, such as Pierre Duhem, make the argument that theories evolve by convention, on the basis of such factors as simplicity, parsimony, elegance, and not merely on the basis of their ability to withstand falsification. Duhem (1954) argues that not only are crucial experiments rare but that they are impossible. The reason for this is that an experiment can lead to an adjustment in the general formulation of a theory rather than a wholesale discarding of the theory. For example, the theory of evolution by natural selection has undergone a number of changes. When Darwin first proposed the theory he suggested a 'blending' of inherited characteristics from both parents. With greater understanding of genetic mechanisms it becomes clear that some characteristics can be wholly inherited from a parent. The Duhem-Quine hypothesis certainly has more explanatory value than just Popperian falsification and the two sets of principles can be seen to work together in the official rhetoric of science.

Following from falsification most scientists would agree that:

1 In order to be considered scientific a theory must be stated so that it can be falsified by a finite set of observations.
2 A scientific theory can only be falsified and *never* proved to be correct.

Consistent with conventionalism, however, most would also agree:

3 Theories change over time so that additions can appear to original formulations, as well as replacements for some parts of theories, as long as the reformulated theory still makes predictions that leave it open for falsification.
4 If a particular hypothesis from a theory does not receive support that is no reason for discarding the whole theory.
5 That if a theory is repeatedly not supported it needs to be either altered or discarded.

However:

6   That a hypothesis is supported does not prove a theory, because another, better, theory may be waiting in the wings, able to account for all the existing results yet also able to make new predictions.

This formulation appears to be the current position of many working scientists, including psychologists. As the example drawn from cognitive Psychology research suggests, it can be applied to theoretical change within Psychology and it does provide some space that allows for an account of how and why theories change. However, without disputing the usefulness of the formulation for scientists, it remains a largely internal account. By this I mean that both the evidence and the conventions are accounts that separate science from other cultural activities. The problem of having a way of examining scientific theories without using current formulations as the most accurate one, albeit a temporary and liable change theory, remains.

Kuhn and Paradigms

Thomas Kuhn's (1962) book *The structure of scientific revolutions* has had a profound impact on how many philosophers, historians of science and working scientists understand the way that science operates, particularly at times of change in science. Kuhn divides scientific activity into two phases, 'normal science' and much rarer moments when a revolutionary paradigm shift occurs. In Kuhnian terms a paradigm is a world view shared amongst the great majority of working scientists in a particular discipline. In a phase of normal science there is a consensus amongst working scientists over what constitutes the proper problems and methods for their discipline. Some types of observation and experiment would yield data that are regarded as illegitimate as they are either tackling problems that are not part of the discipline or they are obtained using methods that are constructed as unscientific. During the revolutionary phase there is argument amongst the scientists of a particular discipline about both methods and problems that the discipline should tackle. During the revolution it is not strictly scientific criteria that decide the outcome. Instead cultural factors are also important, including the receptiveness of policy makers towards a shift in problems being tackled, the availability of funding for particular research projects and the current cultural *Zeitgeist*. For example, Kuhn suggests that amongst the processes that lead to a resolution of a paradigm is a generational shift. Proponents of a new paradigm tend to be younger; they will produce more doctoral graduates who share the paradigm of their tutors. Proponents of the established paradigm tend to be older, their viewpoints becoming marginalized as they near retirement.

The Kuhnian viewpoint is hotly contested but has had one, maybe paradoxical, result. Proponents of a view, at least in the social sciences, that is seen as in some way different, claim that this viewpoint is a new paradigm. This rhetoric amongst proponents of change is in danger of changing the meaning of the term paradigm, in much the same way that using positivist as a term of abuse has changed the meaning of that term. Commenting, ironically, on this situation, as part of a larger critique of the current values of social science, Rex Stainton Rodgers draws an analogy between theories in the social sciences and washing machines. Both have a built in obsolescence and a need to be replaced at regular intervals.

For Psychology the Kuhnian approach, even when accepted, has had a confusing legacy. Kuhn believed that Psychology and the other social sciences were preparadigmatic since there was no one agreed paradigm and both methods and theories are still being contested. Some commentators on Psychology, however, do believe that Psychology has had a series of paradigms, starting with Wündt's experimental introspection, moving through to behaviourism and now with cognitive Psychology as the paradigm. In accounting for Psychology as a series of paradigms it is necessary to use a conceptual shoe horn and ignore those aspects of the discipline that do not fit. In Chapter 12 we will explore Danziger's view that the metalanguage of dependent, independent and intervening variables has played the role of Kuhnian paradigm across a number of sub-disciplines within Psychology since the late 1930s.

SCIENCE AS SOCIAL ACTIVITY

The most important influence on the approach to science taken in this book comes from the field known as the sociology of scientific knowledge (SSK). Danziger, Farr and Richards are three of the proponents of this viewpoint as it applies to the practices of Psychology that have influenced both our approach to Psychology and the history of Psychology.

As with feminism, SSK has had both an influence on the way that science is understood and the way that some researchers within Psychology work. Derek Edwards (1997), Jonathan Potter (1996) and Mike Michael (1997) all use SSK within their social constructionist psychologies. However our purpose in pursuing this line is to provide the basis for our account of Psychology not to use it as part of an argument for a particular part of Psychology. In Chapter 15 we attempt to provide an account of the social constructionist movement within Psychology examining, amongst other things, the role of SSK within that movement.

SSK, of course, has its own history, Jonathan Potter's (1996) book offers a good summary of those developments tailored towards an audience of psychologists. In this section, as in the earlier sections of this chapter, the summarized account we give is an attempt to explain our position and not to provide an exhaustive review. Potter also poses a number of questions that need to examined by those who adopt the science as social activity approach. One of those, the *tu quoque* critique, will be examined at the end of this section.

The majority of work within SSK has concentrated on sciences like physics and biology, rather than the social sciences. Danziger suggests two possible reasons for this; one being that the interdependence between Psychology and social knowledge is obvious, the other that such an approach may undermine the scientific status of psychology. In agreement with Danziger it appears that the second reason may be what prevents psychologists seeing their own discipline in this way. However, the fact that most work within SSK has been concerned with other sciences is beneficial, as it becomes clear that the approach does not only apply to disciplines like Psychology. SSK is concerned with science as a social activity. In common with an earlier sociology of science there is an interest in the ways that aspects such as funding decisions, institutional organization, career moves of particular scientists are still important but this is not the main focus of SSK. Instead the focus is on the practices that help construct scientific knowledge.

Karin Knorr-Cetina's (1983) ethnographic study of laboratory practice suggests that instrumentation is fundamental to scientific claims and procedures, but that this process is far from a mechanical application of 'correct' procedures. Instead in the day to day activity of science there are ad hoc processes for deciding which observations count and which are, for example, errors caused by a particular staining process. Instruments themselves are products such that any particular result depends upon a series of prior results, where prior results become the basis for certain technological procedures. These prior results were themselves decided on a social nexus of usage, interpretation, criteria of adequacy, decisions on what counts as proper functioning of an instrument and so on.

The next set of studies are all linked in that they consider the *rhetoric* used by scientists. Before examining these it is worth briefly talking about rhetoric. Rhetoric is a term that until recently was only used as a term of abuse, *mere rhetoric* being compared with either reality or with a logically justified argument. In using the term here, however, we mean the argumentative language used by scientists (and others) when justifying a particular knowledge claim. This usage within Psychology can be traced to Billig.

Nigel Gilbert and Michael Mulkay (1984) studied the accounts of scientists who conducted work on the chemical storage of cellular energy. The materials they analysed included technical reports and the interview statements of a group of biochemists that included a Nobel Prize winner. Gilbert and Mulkay identified a number of features of these scientists' discourse, including the notion that scientists use two different kinds of explanation, an empiricist repertoire and a contingent repertoire. The empiricist repertoire is the impersonal rhetoric used by scientists in their technical reports. The focus is on the method based, data driven account of findings and theoretical choices. This can be seen as the official story of how science operates in a Popperian fashion, the production of factual knowledge through the operation of rule based formal procedures. However scientists also use a contingent repertoire, an appeal to insight or biases, personal motives and thoughts, where conclusions and theory may give rise to, rather than follow from, the empirical work that surrounds them. The contingent repertoire was used in interviews to account for why a particular research programme was found to be interesting, or to provide a human interest story about how a particular finding was reached. It was also used as a way of dismissing how things went wrong for rivals, especially when explaining findings that were now discredited.

The existence of these two repertories is acknowledged by researchers, Gilbert and Mulkay give examples culled from the spoof contrasts pinned to laboratory or departmental noticeboards. Robert Sternberg in *The psychologist's companion* (1993) notes in his tips for writing journal articles:

> ... there just isn't room for these autobiographical details. Therefore, journal articles are usually written in a manner that bears little resemblance to the way the research was actually conducted. This difference is not dishonesty: Professionals simply know how the system works.
>
> (Sternberg 1993:178)

The important lesson for us as writers from Gilbert and Mulkay's work is the need to be aware of both types of account, and not to treat either as the single truth.

Celia Kitzinger (1987) considers the use of rhetoric in sociological and psychological studies of homosexuality. She separates her analysis into five themes (which she describes as neither exhaustive or mutually exclusive) which are:

1 The 'up the mountain' saga.
2 The rhetoric of scientific method.
3 The mythologizing of expertise.
4 The utility account,

and finally:

5 Textual persuasion and literary effects.

Two aspects of Kitzinger's analysis will be examined further, the 'up the mountain' saga and the mythologizing of expertise. The up the mountain story, which according to Kitzinger was given this name by Rorty (1980), is the oft told story of a long and arduous uphill journey towards a golden age of knowledge at the peak; and away from the quagmire of ignorance in the valley below.

> Its function is to illustrate the superiority of contemporary over past research findings: in its less gracious version, all previous researchers are presented as fundamentally inadequate scientific investigators, who perpetuated elementary methodological or theoretical crimes; in its most gracious form present-day scientists may be dwarfs standing on the shoulders of giants, but can see further for all that.
>
> (Kitzinger 1987: 8)

Kitzinger in her detailed and entertaining account of rhetoric in research goes on to illustrate that even, or especially when past (social science) research is seen as having a poor track record, it is still possible to justify the need for yet more social scientific research. This is often united with a call to be more impressively objective and impartial than the social scientists who came before.

Kitzinger (1987) begins her section on the mythologizing of expertise with the notion that 'scientific expertise brings with it the power to define reality.' Of all of the accounting strategies open to scientists and social scientists it is the myth of the unbiased, neutral scientific expert that credits scientists with access to knowledge denied to ordinary mortals. As Kitzinger shows, using examples from research on homosexuality, there is a sharp juxtaposition between 'scientific' and 'lay' concepts, which serve to reinforce the status of the scientific. Examples that Kitzinger uses include:

> 'Stereotypes often depict ... but current research shows ...' (Peplau and Gordon 1983: 227); 'It is a popular myth that ... but the data indicate ...' (Hedblom 1973).
>
> (Kitzinger 1987: 10)

Kitzinger shows how this account is used in conjunction with the 'up the mountain' story as a way of denigrating previous researchers falling prey to stereotypes and Mary Crawford (1995) notes a similar process in research on gender and language. Another aspect of this account is the way that potential personal bias is countered in the rhetoric of researchers, as researchers contrast their role as ordinary person and scientist:

> Initially, I became aware of my own biases, established them and looked beyond them for the facts.
>
> (Ettorre 1980: 13)

This type of accounting, which is widespread not only amongst scientists but others who need to acknowledge potential accusations of bias made by others, is called 'stake inoculation' by conversation analysts. What the work of authors on the rhetoric of science gives us is an appreciation of the complexity of accounts by scientists. What it cannot give us is a way of 'reading through' the rhetoric to the reality beyond.

The final aspect of SSK work that is examined is Latour and Woolgar's (1979, 1986) delightfully heretical account of how reality is constructed in the laboratory, involving the processes of *inversion* and *splitting*.

One characterization of splitting and inversion comes from Woolgar (1988):

(1) document
(2) document   →   object
(3) document   object   [independent existence]
(4) document   ←   object
(5) deny (or forget about) stages 1–3

The first stage is that scientists possess a series of documents. These include past research findings, but more importantly current observational ones such as tapes, transcripts, marks on paper, various machine produced observations. At this stage scientists may also work to produce more of these documents. These documents are then used to project the existence of a particular object, stage two. This is where much of the 'work' of science is done, in deciding which observations are interesting, and which count as the documents that support the existence of a particular object. The third stage is splitting. The object's existence is assumed to be separate from the documents that originally supported it. The fourth stage is inversion where the relationship between the object and the documents is inverted. Now the existence of the object is used to explain why particular documents have been created. Finally the process by which the object was knowledged into being is forgotten about or denied.

Seeing science as a social activity is for us a crucial aspect of our account of Psychology. In doing so we are not suggesting that Psychology is merely a social construction, that needs to be replaced by a more realist account of human beings. The sociology of scientific knowledge gives us a set of tools that we can use to give an account of Psychology.

Investigating science as a social activity means that we examine things differently from either a logical positivist, Popperian, contextualist or Kuhnian standpoint. There has to be agnosticism towards whether a particular set of research findings are some true reflection of reality, because our only grounds for doing so would be some other set of research findings. This does not mean that we cannot criticise a particular approach, but we do this by looking at the consequences of that approach, not whether or not it is the truth. By combining this level of analysis with (some) feminist analysis we are also sensitive towards issues of power in a wider societal setting and this, we believe, allows for a more nuanced account compared with a focus only on particular research groups.

Tu quoque

One argument used against the position that science is a social activity, and other varieties of social constructionism, is the *tu quoque*, or you too, argument. A potential critic entertains the notion that science, or knowledge production in general, is a social activity but points out that this position is also a social construction, in an apparent belief that this undermines the argument.

There are a number of possible responses to the *tu quoque* argument that are worth considering.

One position is a variation of the theme of critical realism, from the work of Roy Bhaskar (1991). Bhaskar suggests that we need to differentiate between two issues. We have the scientist's account of some phenomenon, and we have the question of why the account takes the form that it does. In saying that the account is socially constructed we are not saying that the phenomenon itself is a construction, as it exists in a realm that is transfactual or intransitive. It is not feasible in this scheme to give as an explanation for the account of a particular phenomenon that it is the way that it is simply because that is what the phenomenon is like. No modern philosopher of science would take that position, but this constructionism with a realist boundary has at least one problem.

The first is what phenomena should be taken as 'transfactual', and the nature of boundary conditions between these. Some would posit that only some phenomena from the natural sciences such as dinosaurs, DNA, electrons are transfactual, while many of the phenomena from the social sciences are not. Other would argue that phenomena such as social class and patriarchy are transfactual, while others such as attention deficit disorder and schizophrenia are not. Yet others would argue that conditions that have a biological basis, such as Alzheimer's Disease (AD), are transfactual, but that the ways that people with AD are treated is constructed.

The second, given that we only have accounts to work, is why does it make any difference to us if we take something to be transfactual or not. As we cannot have access to this intransitive realm it seems better to remain agnostic towards it.

This is not to say that this position is a simple social constructionist position. It is, obviously, not possible to *create* any construction of a phenomenon, although some postmodernist writing appears to suggest that it is, because such constructions are social. As Bruner (1995) points out despite the apparent peril of relativism, or solipsism that this position entails, the peril never seems to quite materialize. For him the peril does not arise: he is interested in those aspects of meaning making that relate to the domain of ordinary living and the psychologist needs to proceed from a notion that meanings are infused with the perspective of a particular person. Hereto we are attempting to explain the accounts given of psychological phenomena by particular people, who happen to be psychologists, and in keeping that focus we do not fall into a metaphysical morass of relativism.

PSYCHOLOGY AND SCIENCE

Studying science as a social activity enables an analysis of the various constructive practices that exist within science and helps with an analysis on the various influences upon science. However, with Psychology there is one final reflexive twist, the way that Psychology affects psychology.

With most scientific disciplines there are cases of how the construction of a particular fact has changed across history. For example, the same dinosaur fossils have been used as the evidence for two very different types of dinosaur, one being the small brained, slow moving creature that was inevitably replaced by quick-witted mammals and the other being the well-adapted creature which was only displaced as the dominant phylum by an accident of history. Similarly, as Steven Jay Gould (1991) demonstrates, the fossils of the Burgess Shale were at the time of Walcott shoehorned into a categorization system that demonstrated they were ancestral versions of modern groups. Later Harry Whittington successfully revised this classification to demonstrate that most of the animals in the Burgess Shale have no modern descendants. Naturally both constructions are constrained by the evidence to hand, but changes in how evolution is constructed – from an inevitable climb towards progress, to a much more complex history of contingent change – enable different constructions of the meaning of that evidence. No one would argue that our species constructions of these animals have any effect of the fossil remains themselves. The same cannot be said of Psychology.

As Graham Richards has consistently argued, and shown (for example, 1989, 1996, 1997) the discipline of Psychology has a profound effect on our psychology. To use two of his examples, no one had an IQ score until circa 1914 and no one had an Oedipus complex prior to Freud. Ian Hacking (1995) similarly traces various constructions of split personality, from double consciousness, fugue states, multiple personality disorder (MPD) and now (DSM-IV, 1994), dissociative identity disorder (DID). As Hacking says 'the symptoms, diagnosis, aetiology and social role of the condition have all changed' in the 150 years since double consciousness was first reported.

It is for this reason that Psychology needs to be treated differently from the other sciences and it is for this reason that Danziger's suggested split between human kinds and natural kinds is adopted here. This is not the same as suggesting that Psychology is any more (or less) socially constructed than any other discipline, nor is it the same as suggesting that Psychology is in some way less (or more) scientific than any other discipline. Finally it provides no basis for trying to divide Psychology into different sub-disciplines by virtue of whether they are more or less scientific.

Change in Psychology

Richards (1997) in the résumé of his book *Race, racism and psychology* offers a summary of his approach to the historical process of change in Psychology which is useful for our purposes here. Richards shows two premises:

1   Psychology as a discipline is a product of the 'psychologies' of those within it; thus psychology is necessarily reflexive in character.
2   Psychologists represent specific constituencies in the discipline's host societies, and until the mid-twentieth century these were predominantly white, male and middle- or upper-class. While there has always been a degree of heterogeneity within this group this was a restricted sample of the constituencies in society as a whole.

These are useful, and not a reduction to the individual heroic figure, as they highlight the complex interpolation between the actor and their social context. It is especially worthy of note that we see the psychology of the actor itself as a social product.

Given these premises, change in Psychology has necessarily been determined by more than any 'objective' knowledge gains, including changes in the psychological character of the discipline's practitioners, in the light of changed sociohistorical circumstances, and the broadening of the psychological constituencies represented in the discipline. Given that psychological knowledge affects people's psychologies there is a further reflexive twist as the disciplines previously produced 'knowledge' affects the practitioners' psychologies.

Richards points out three consequences that immediately follow from these premises.

1 As Psychology is one of the social arenas in which the psychological issues affecting a host society are formulated, discussed and (temporarily) resolved, the historical changes within the discipline both reflect and help constitute the change itself.
2 The psychological issues facing a particular constituency can only be addressed within Psychology in a fashion, which is satisfactory for the members of that constituency only, insofar as it is itself represented with the discipline.
3 Conversely, excluded constituencies can only be considered, by the discipline at the time, in terms of their psychological significance for those included.

We believe that in giving a reading of the history of particular notions in Psychology, suggesting reasons for how they came into being and tracing the consequences of them, we can gain some leverage on understanding some of the current issues within Psychology. It is this focus on consequence, rather than intention, that keeps the spectre of relativism at bay, and it is because we believe that Psychology affects psychology that we feel the enterprise is worthwhile.

FURTHER READING

Bhaskar, R. 1997: *A realist theory of science*. London: Verso.

Crawford, M. 1995: *Talking difference. On gender and language*. London: Sage.

Edwards, D. 1997: *Discourse and cognition*. London: Sage.

Gilbert, G.N. and Mulkay, M. 1984: *Opening Pandora's box: a sociological analysis of scientists' discourse*. Cambridge: Cambridge University Press.

Gould, S.J. 1991: *Wonderful life: the Burgess shale and the nature of history*. Harmondsworth: Penguin.

Harré, R. 1993: *Social being*. Oxford: Blackwell.

Harris, B. 1997: Repoliticizing the history of psychology. In *Critical psychology: an introduction*. D. Fox and I. Prilleltensky (eds), London: Sage Publications.

Kitzinger, C. 1995: *The social construction of lesbianism*. London: Sage Publications Ltd.

Knorr-Cetina, K. 1983: The ethnographic study of scientific work: towards a constructionist interpretation of science. In K. Knorr-Cetina and M. Mulkay (eds), *Science Observed*. London: Sage.

Kuhn, T.S. 1962: *The structure of scientific revolutions*. Chicago: University of Chicago Press.

Latour, B. and Woolgar, S. 1979: *Laboratory life: the social constitution of scientific facts*. Beverly Hills, CA: Sage.

Michael, M. 1997: Critical social psychology: identity and de-prioritization of the social. In T. Ibanez and L. Iniguez (eds) *Critical social psychology*. London: Sage.

Potter, J. 1996: *Representing reality: discourse, rhetoric and social construction*. London: Sage.

Richards, G. 1996: *Putting psychology in its place*. London: Routledge.

Robinson, D.N. 1995: *An intellectual history of psychology*. London: Arnold.

Sternberg, R.J. 1993: *Psychologist's companion: a guide to scientific reading for students and researchers*. Cambridge: Cambridge University Press.

2

THE FOUNDING OF PSYCHOLOGY

S.J. Gould, writing about natural history and baseball, discusses the power-ful allure of origin myths (Gould 1991). For example, while baseball has obvi-ous links with other stick and ball games, from rounders to cricket, it also has an official but mythical foundation story. According to this story baseball was founded in 1839, by Abner Doubleday, who interrupted a marbles game behind a tailor's shop in Cooperstown, New York. Doubleday went on to draw a baseball diamond, explained the rules of the game and gave it the designation of base ball. There is no need to push this analogy any further, except to say that any attempt to distinguish a single instance when Psychology was founded would lead to little more than an origin myth.

Yet while there has always been psychology (though not always with that name attached) and there have often been scholars who speculated about its nature, there has not always been Psychology. In this chapter we are con-cerned first with the discourses that have arisen around the founding of psy-chology, and second with the intellectual and cultural conditions that enabled Psychology, as a discipline and, in the early twentieth century, as an institution within society, to develop. From these starting points we will con-sider the ways that Psychology developed up until the end of the nineteenth century.

ORIGIN MYTH PART ONE: THE MYTH OF WÜNDT

Many introductory textbooks begin the history of Psychology as a scientific discipline with the foundation of Wündt's laboratory in 1879, although occa-sionally 1876, the date that William James began to teach physiological Psychology using a small demonstration laboratory at Harvard is given as a foundation date instead. There are good reasons for using the period from 1873–81 as a starting place, a period during which Wündt published *Grundzüge der Physiologisehen Psychologie* (Principles of physiological psy-chology) and established *Philosophische Studien* (Philosophical studies) a jour-nal dedicated to publishing the results from his laboratory. However, these

OLSON LIBRARY
NORTHERN MICHIGAN UNIVERSITY
MARQUETTE, MICHIGAN 49855

reasons, as Danziger points out, are to do with the way that a community of psychologists was assembled, than the foundation of the laboratory per se. In the origin myth the date is important because it marks the origin of Psychology as a science, rather than as part of philosophy, which was often dismissed as armchair speculation. The appeal towards a point of origin coinciding with experimentation, which Farr depicts as part of a positivistic approach to the history of psychology, can even be seen starkly within the discourses around the origin of social Psychology. Here many introductory social Psychology textbooks (e.g. Baron and Byrne 1998) use Triplett's experiments on the effects of competition as the origin of social Psychology.

The experiment, and the experimental laboratory, are depicted as important because of the way that Psychology has constructed itself as a science, and specifically an experimental science like physics or chemistry. This has an allure to this day as we shall discuss later (see especially Chapters 1 and 15) and, given that so much of the effort of Psychology lecturers in introductory courses is to convince undergraduates that Psychology is a science, this myth continues to serve an important role.

In part the origin myth can be explained because Boring's *History of experimental psychology* (1950) is often erroneously referred as a history of Psychology. As a history explicitly of experimental Psychology it is appropriate to begin with the community of psychologists that first used that model of investigative practice. However the way that Boring's work has been assimilated into introductory textbooks, often just called the first history of psychology, lends credence to the notion of a definite starting point.

While Wündt stands out as a good founder figure because of the allure of this being a scientific psychology, the assumption that his method involves introspection, and the fact that he saw *Physiologischen Psychologie* as only a part of the enterprise of psychology make him a founder who is almost embarrassing. Sometimes Wündt's fall from grace is explained in terms of a battle between two different systems of psychology, structuralism and functionalism. Wündt's structuralism lost out to James's functionalism in the USA, introspection was discredited and so-called better methodologies found.

There are a number of features of this account that are worth examining in some depth. We will examine, before moving on to the other part of the origin myth, the notion that there is a lineage of intellectual tradition of psychology that stretches back to the ancient Greek philosophers.

One reason why it has been difficult to appreciate Wündt is that it has not until recently been acknowledged that *Physiologischen Psychologie* was only a part of psychology; the second part, albeit as a distinct component rather than a synthesis, was *Volkerpsychologie* (roughly translatable as 'psychology of the people'). For Wündt, Psychology was to be about the study of the human mind. Part of the conditions for human minds is that they exist within communities, and for Wündt, in order to study processes such as language and memory, as well as practices that make up cultures, it was necessary to study communities of people. This precluded a laboratory based natural science approach to those aspects of the discipline in favour of an approach that would investigate people within cultures. *Physiologischen Psychologie* was limited to studying only the 'lower' mental processes, the immediate objects of conscious awareness.

Some of the reasons for this rejection may have been methodological, but the more important reason may be the limited scope of the natural science aspect of Wündt's project. By focusing on the immediate objects of conscious awareness Wündt limited scientific psychology. This study of psychology involved various methods, the introspective reports, which were largely limited to judgements of size, intensity and duration of physical stimuli and occasionally judgements about whether or not physical stimuli were simultaneous or successive were one aspect of method. Wündt also invested much importance in reaction time studies which did not contain even this somewhat curtailed and limited amount of introspection.

However, as we discuss in this chapter, the objects that psychologists would soon be studying were much more varied than this project. The limited objects of study of this psychology may account more fully for why Wündt was repudiated.

Another part of the difficulty that Wündtian psychology faced was that Titchener, who created the term structuralism, systematically misrepresented Wündt's views in the USA, where, perhaps oddly given the number of early US psychologists who obtained their doctorates at Leipzig, he had come to be seen as the champion of Wündt. The far greater difficulty probably surrounds Wündt's very limited project for an experimental psychology. Wündt believed strongly that it was not possible to explore mental phenomena beyond basic sensory processes using any form of introspection:

It is true that the attempt has frequently been made to investigate the complex functions of thought on the basis of mere introspection. These attempts, however, have always been unsuccessful. Individual consciousness is wholly incapable of giving us a history of human thought, for it is conditioned by an earlier history concerning which it cannot of itself give us any knowledge (Wündt 1916: 3).

ORIGIN MYTHS PART TWO: AN UNBROKEN LINEAGE

The second part of this discourse is the way that thinkers from before the founding of Psychology are described. It is within this part of the discourse that, mainly within introductory textbooks, there is a Whiggish aspect to the history of psychology. This part of the discourse reinforces the idea that psychology has a history as long as any other science, with the ancient Greek philosophers being seen as concerned with the same problems and ideas as current psychologists. Indeed it is only possible to re-present the past in this way by taking a Whig approach, where people are praised, or condemned, to the extent that their ideas fit in with modern conceptions of Psychology.

That is not to say that there is no value in investigating a history of ideas, but it is to say that in order to do so with any sensitivity it is necessary to appreciate that the psychological ideas were only a small part of much larger systems of philosophy or theology. And as Danziger demonstrates so effectively in *Naming* the *mind* (1997) those systems have radically different understandings about people. More fruitful approaches may lie in Richards's history of psychological language and in Danziger's work on more recent innovations in psychological language. Perhaps in keeping with the general spirit of this book in studying changes in language, we are studying changes in collective phenomena, with all of the implications about the effects of cultural setting, rather than studying great men of history. However this must be tempered with the realization that what scholars write about in their time may not be what is important to the population as a whole. Widespread availability of printed materials is a relatively recent phenomenon, and, of course, the broadcast media are a twentieth-century phenomenon. However, despite these caveats, it is possible to draw some conclusions about how psychology has changed since written records began.

The work of Danziger shows that most of the discourses and terminological tools that are available to us as modern psychologists have brashly modern roots; attitude, intelligence, motivation are all terms of late nineteenth- or early twentieth-century origin. As the work of Halperin (1992) demonstrates, describing sexuality as either a part of identity or a reason for general behaviour is very rare before the nineteenth-century. Richards (1989) and, with a somewhat different goal in mind, Gregory (1981) have demonstrated that as technologies change so do our analogies to what happens within the human mind. Indeed Richards's work, somewhat like the work on emotion by Stearns (1995), suggests ways that descriptions of external phenomena become, over time, psychological descriptions of internal phenomena. Finally, and writing for a slightly different purpose than we are, Robinson (1995) shows that writing on psychology, often by theologians and philosophers, reflects current concerns of the societies that they are writing in. All of these make us suspect that modern academic psychology is also a cultural product with concerns that, to varying extents, reflect modern social concerns.

At the same time there is no point in dismissing earlier philosophical systems because they have influenced the way that academics write about psychology. It may be that we can be seen as both having our cake and eating it. We wish to assert that there is something different about modern Psychology compared with those writing about psychology that occurred in (often) theology and philosophy. However we do not want to give prominence to one single event that led to this modern psychology. Hopefully our reasons for doing so will become clear.

INTELLECTUAL AND SOCIAL CONDITIONS

Modern Psychology is rooted in the intellectual and social conditions of the nineteenth-century, with intellectual concerns rooted in the social conditions of the time. In this extensive section we review these concerns and the intellectual responses to them.

The only extensive work on psychological language was done by Graham Richards in 1989, although Danziger in *Naming the Mind* (1997) devotes some space to explaining the lack of continuity between ancient traditions of (what Richards somewhat clumsily calls) self-reflexive language and the modern traditions of Psychology. The basic claim is that nothing which amounts to modern psychological language can be found until the late seventeenth century. Richards goes on to claim that it is changes in technologies that opened the way for these changes in expressions.

It is worth reflecting on these claims for a second or two. They are buttressed by the idea that psychological categories are not what philosophers call natural kinds, because if they were then even if naming systems had changed people would still be able to talk about the same things. Rather they play both a descriptive and normative role. Creating a psychological category allows people to understand their subjectivity in a different way. For example, Danziger describes at length Aristotle's divisions of different kinds of reason. The first point to note is that there was no division between objective and subjective that we have become so used to in modern language. There were, however, other divisions and categories that we are not so familiar with, but we will just concentrate on one of them.

This the division between *psyche* and *nous*, which was translated into the Latin *intellectus*. *Psyche* can be defined as those aspects of humanity that we share with other animals and *nous* as those things that are peculiar to humans. *Nous* referred to those things: classically logical inference, conceptual thinking and abstraction that humans could do, but also referred to the rational order of the world. It was simultaneously the way that humans could rationalize and the features of the world that were patterned rationally. For a human to use *nous* it is not only a way of finding the best means to an end but also simultaneously finding the best, the most aesthetic and the most moral end. It is difficult to even contemplate what this means given our much more instrumental way of understanding what intelligence and reason is about.

Having examined just one of the differences between ancient and modern understanding of persons including the self, it is worth quickly tracing modern notions of self.

In English this can be traced approximately to the mid-1600s. Today there are scores of words that are compounded with self. Before the 1600s there are very few examples of self words, and the majority of them refer to self-harm, or the self as sinner who has to learn to become as one with the divine plan. Our current notions of the encapsulated individual are essentially modern constructs.

It was in Britain in the 1700s that a new moral philosophy began to emerge. This has its importance for our story in that it was moral and mental philosophy that Psychology replaced as an academic subject in the universities of the USA, as a means to answering questions about what people were essentially like. Psychology, despite the fact that the majority of its categories are now less than a hundred years old, built upon the moral philosophy of the 1700s. The fact that any of the psychological categories that were written about at this time are still important is possibly because early eighteenth-century Britain can be seen as the prototypical modern society and the problems of that society are still, to some extent, the problems of modern society. That a moral discipline is eventually replaced by a scientific discipline is a Victorian transformation. This is discussed, especially in the context of the USA, in further depth in Chapter 3.

The notion of a self as a moral agent is a necessary condition of modern psychology, but by itself this change does not harbinger a scientific psychology. So it is to one of the most revolutionary changes in scientific thinking of the nineteenth-century that we now turn in understanding the intellectual conditions that allow for Psychology.

The Theory of Evolution by Natural Selection

Following Graham Richards's analysis, the theory of evolution by natural selection and its popularization by Herbert Spencer (1855) stands out as one of the most important intellectual and social changes that paved the way for a science of psychology.

Acting as both a sign of the secularization of knowledge that characterized the Victorian era and as one of significant events that helped foster that secularization, Darwin's *Origin of species* (1859) was important in providing an integrating framework for the budding discipline of Psychology.

Darwin proposed natural selection as the mechanism that could explain the evolution of organisms scientifically. All current organic life had evolved from previous forms of life, across vast expanses of time, with those animals more suited to the prevailing ecological conditions surviving more readily, and producing more offspring than those animals less well-suited. The mechanism was blind to future events, reacting to current conditions, and through some form of inheritance (the genetic mechanism not being available to Darwin who favoured some form of blending of characteristics from both parents) various legacies would be left in their descendants. At the time, and especially given the lack of knowledge about genetics, natural selection was attacked as being an insufficient mechanism by itself to account for the variety in life. Evolution did not sweep away earlier ideas associated with the assumed supremacy of British civilization, but rather some of these were assimilated into the framework, and eventually would become Social Darwinism.

What the theory of evolution did do was to place humans into a zoological framework. Humans were descended from primates and thus could no longer be seen as semi-divine. Ironically, at the same time, the older theological notion of a great chain of being was retained, with the idea that there was a progression in evolution from lower to higher animals, with, unsurprisingly, the human species seen as the highest animal of all. While there is nothing within the *Origin of species* to warrant such a claim, the prevailing cultural mores, with white European males seeing themselves as the epitome of all that is civilized and rational, led many people to seeing themselves as the most evolved of all creatures on earth. Richards (1997), amongst others,

THE FOUNDING OF PSYCHOLOGY 31

shows how this scientific racism was used. For the time being it is sufficient to note that the notion of progress was retained and recast into an evolutionary framework.

Also popularized within this broader evolutionary framework, although like the notion of inevitable progress not an essential part of Darwin's theory, was the idea popularized by the German biologist, Ernst Hackel, that each individual recapitulates in their development, as an individual, the evolutionary stages that their species had passed through. This idea was often summed up as 'ontogeny reflects phylogeny' and was itself compounded with social Darwinist ideas and thus women, the lower classes and non-white peoples could (sometimes at best) be seen as juvenile members of the human species.

Second the idea of there being variation within species was important both to evolutionary theory and to the fledgling discipline of Psychology. If variation occurred in physiological traits it was assumed that it could also occur in psychological traits. The work of Galton, which had a major influence on the British statistical tradition and ultimately the investigative practices of much modern Psychology, was concerned with measuring variation in psychological traits. The notion that these traits were inherited led to the next concern, that of degeneration.

The notion of degeneration also became popular, especially in a context where the working classes were seen to be deficient because of their inherited psychological and physiological traits. If, as it is claimed with the human species, natural selection is suspended because of advances in medicine and the technology of healthy living (for example, adequate uncontaminated water supply, food, heating, housing, etc.) then unfit organisms can survive and reproduce. Thus, the quality of the population may decline as the usual evolutionary mechanisms are subverted. Perhaps oddly, the 'civilized' Europeans were also thought to have degenerated in some psychological functions, especially with regard to perceptual processes, compared with primitive peoples. As a further twist to this, upper-class women were constructed as being at a more juvenile evolutionary level than their male counterparts while also suffering from this civilized level of degeneracy.

These concerns, which all reflected the concerns of the ruling classes, the main constituency represented in those who would become the first few generations of psychologists, led to a number of concerns about human nature.

The evolutionary framework led to speculation about how much the human mind retained of its animal origins. This stimulated both an interest in comparing humans with lower animals and the concept of instinct. Instinct, which before the Darwinian revolution was a concept used to refer to innate patterns of behaviour implanted into the human soul by God, now became natural inherited capacities that are part of the human species' biological inheritance. This biological instinct concept, which would later be pushed beyond reasonable limits both inside and outside the discipline of Psychology, rested on a tautology that plagues some personality theories to this day. Thus a person may be tidy because of an instinct for tidiness, the evidence being that such an instinct exists since (many) people are tidy. Those who are not tidy obviously lack the inheritance of the tidiness instinct. This type of theorizing can get out of hand with as many as 5,000 instincts being named, including instincts for social conventions such as politeness.

The focus on variation within species focused attention on the variation within the human species, this in turn leading to Francis Galton's studies of individual differences and to various statistical procedures, correlation but later regression and factor analysis, for analysing them.

The child, as an early stage in the development of the adult, became a focus for study due to the interest that recapitulation aroused. Thus as well as learning about development of adults we may also be able to understand the evolution of the human species through looking at children. Although there are a variety of frameworks through which we understand children, this evolutionary developmental framework retains its influence today (see, for example, Morss [1995]) although recapitulation is now a discredited doctrine.

The notion of degeneration provided a framework of understanding for a host of social issues within Victorian societies, such as crime, madness, idiocy and alcoholism. This idea would have a profound impact on social policy up until the second half of the twentieth century and probably still has an impact upon discourses about social policy to the present day.

The idea that civilization was a continuance of progressive evolution in a social sphere led to the idea that if civilized values are removed then people de-evolve into a more primitive form. This had an impact on Le Bon's theories of crowd mentality as well as informing discourses around alcohol and other drugs. Again this idea still has an impact upon discourses about crowd and other social behaviours.

The notion of higher and lower animals led to the notion that the human brain can be divided into higher and lower aspects and functions. Thus the cortex became the site where it was postulated that higher mental functions, reasonable thought, language and ethics resided, whereas more primitive functions, such as aggression or sex, were assumed to be in the more primitive parts of the brain. The long and unresolved debate between investigating whole brains and localization of function may have its roots in this concern.

Evolution in general gave a framework for bringing the study of humans into a natural science framework. Psychology has had aspects that have rejected evolutionary concerns and at times has had aspects when all Psychology has been explained within a natural selection framework: the picture today is somewhat muddled. Across the discipline some researchers pay little heed to possible biological constraints, whereas elsewhere especially, for example, in research on children and on individual differences broad acknowledgement is made of biological factors, whilst evolutionary psychologists appear to be trying to explain everything in terms of their reading of evolutionary theory. That these positions can coexist may have something to do with the model of investigative practice used within most of psychology. In the next section we concentrate on models of investigative practice.

Models of Investigative Practice

The theory of evolution by natural selection, together with the prevailing social conditions, led to a number of concerns for the first generations of psychologists, and some of these concerns still inform Psychology today. The second half of the nineteenth century is also important in terms of types of investigative practice used within Psychology. Three broad models, the laboratory experiment, the clinical interview/case study and the British statistical tradition of investigative practice all have nineteenth-century roots, and given the way that Psychology has tended to construct and define itself through its methodologies these have also continued to have an influence upon the discipline into the twenty-first century.

Although the laboratory experiment is seen as the gold standard method amongst many Psychologists, the current tradition of experiments, outside of some elements of perception (especially psycho-physics), has at its roots the British statistical tradition, and it is with this that this section will begin.

It is now so commonplace that psychological knowledge claims are made on the basis of groups of participants that it is sometimes difficult to imagine that such a development radically altered the nature of psychology, enabling it to become a discipline that could inform the debates around the various social issues highlighted earlier in the chapter.

Much of this development, so at odds with the Wündtian approach, can be traced to the interest in social statistics that predates the beginnings of Psychology as an intellectual discipline. Interest in using descriptive statistics of crime, suicide and poverty were established in Europe and the USA by the middle of the nineteenth century. Statistical societies, which campaigned for social reform, utilized these official statistics in their campaigns and were active across a number of countries. These statistical societies began to circulate their own questionnaires rather than just rely upon the official statistics that were available. G. Stanley Hall, using the model of a municipal statistical office in Berlin, used questionnaires in his study of the content of children's minds, which while the subject of his investigation may at first glance appear quite Wündtian (sharing a concern with the content of mind) the method and substance of his investigation has much more to do with using mass data, encouraged perhaps by this general popularity of descriptive statistical inquiry.

The statistical tradition has its roots in the work of the Belgian statistician Quételet. As part of understanding the regularities and patterns in the statistical data with which he was working on and social indices such as crime, he invented the idea that these patterns could be attributed to the average individual, or differences between average individuals in different groups. Thus if there were different rates of crime, these could be seen as varying with the average propensity to crime across different groups. If crime rates varied with such factors as age, sex or even climate, then this could be seen as due to the influence of those factors upon crime. In continental Europe there were strenuous arguments against making inferences about individuals based upon the average individual. In England things took a different turn with H.T. Buckle who argued that such statistical regularities could be used as evidence about individual actions. This sort of thinking, which still underlies the use of inferential statistics within psychology, has the dual assumptions that individuals can be freely aggregated into groups and that knowledge about a group can tell us significant facts about individuals. This dual focus is the level of analysis that Psychology, as a theoretical discipline works at.

There were other important factors at work within Britain. Darwin supplemented his own observations on the emotions of children and people from other cultures with knowledge gained in a questionnaire survey on emotional expression. Francis Galton, Darwin's cousin and the founder of eugenics, used the questionnaire method in his study of mental imagery and its inheritance. Those, and there were many, within the discipline of psychology who used the evolutionary framework outlined above may have been particularly interested in looking at the distribution of psychological concepts across populations. That Galton and Darwin also used the method for investigations that have some significance to psychology could only help to legitimate the methodology.

Galton's interest in the inheritance and distribution across the population of human abilities led to a methodological strategy that rested on these developments in statistical analysis. The Victorian self-improvement movement meant that people had an interest in their own abilities, with a view to improving them, and this enabled Galton to open a laboratory at the International Health Exhibition and a later one elsewhere. People could, upon paying a small fee, be tested on a whole range of abilities, including olfactory discrimination, reaction time, motor behaviour and mental imagery. This enabled Galton to sample over 9,000 people on a whole range of measures.

The British statistical tradition founded by Galton and Pearson, while rooted in the earlier work of the Belgian statistician Quételet and earlier interest in descriptive statistics, has led to a predominance of quantitative experimental psychology. Galton's statistical methods enabled him to investigate heredity and to quantify the amount of variation within populations. They also enabled him to compare one population with another.

The Clinical Experiment

The clinical experiment came into Psychology through medicine. There are a few features of this model of investigative practice that have found their way into modern psychology. The first is the name 'subject' for the participants in psychological research. Early French investigators, including Binet, were using hypnosis as a tool of psychological research, and referred to those that they did their investigations upon as *sujet*, a term that had come into medical usage at least by the eighteenth century to refer to patients who would be the object of medical care. The term originates by referring to corpses as subjects for medical dissection, a usage still current, and passed into more general usage through the habit of referring to patients who were to undergo surgery as subject. The usage also implies a power relationship. The subjects of hypnotic experiments were often females with a preexisting patient–doctor relationship with the experimenter, and thus there was a huge status difference between the subject in an experiment and the experimenter. This contrasts with Galton's research above where he referred to his participants as 'applicants' although the fact that they were willing to pay him to be measured on a range of tests also implies that his expertise was recognized. These power relationships still exist today, with participants of research, most often referred to as subjects, having an inferior status to the experimenter. That the experimenter hopes that their use of a laboratory has removed 'confounding variables', such as social relationships, is one of the ironic aspects of many modern psychological investigations. The continued use of the word subject, with a history that implies a passive recipient of another's intentions only serves as a reminder of one of the adages of discourse analysis: that words that we choose when we are writing and talking about things may carry with them more meanings than we could possibly know.

The Laboratory Experiment

The ways that laboratory experiments were conducted in the mid- to late nineteenth century have left the least enduring legacy on current investigative practice. For Wündt there were four conditions of the perfect laboratory experiment.

First, perfect experiments can be carried out on one's own. Where experimenters are necessary they are only necessary insofar as they supply the experimental subject with stimuli. Ideally a machine could do this task.

Second, the presence of another person impairs one's ability to think and observe. As we shall discuss later, part of the controversy that arose between Wündt and the generation of German psychologists that repudiated his ideas was the way that they carried out interrogation experiments by asking the subjects of experiments what they were thinking.

Third, the cognitive and moral authority of the experimental subject needs to be preserved. Wündt was particularly critical of the hypnosis experiments because for him hypnotism was a state in which the person had no ability to exercise their own free will. For Wündt the very act of taking away a person's free will was immoral, whatever the aims of experimenter, or other person such as a medical doctor, in that relationship, except in his words, for those cases that are explicitly sanctioned by law. Wündt was also suspicious of those forms of investigative practice in which an experimenter interrogates an experimental subject because the cognitive authority of the experimental subject is undermined.

Finally Wündt was concerned that the ideal psychological observer, the subjects in experiments, needed to be themselves trained psychologists. Wündt was thus hostile to both applied psychology, which used as its subjects people not trained as psychologists, but also the psychological survey, which undermines the cognitive authority of the subject by restricting their range of responses.

Of course this needs to be understood in the context that Wündt's experimental psychology was not the whole of psychology, with his *Völkerpsychologie*, as part of the *Geiteswissenschafenten*, roughly the human rather than natural sciences, being important to study the higher processes of the mind. Indeed Wündt refers to experimental psychology as the nursery school (*Vorschule*) for the psychologist. Finally we do not discuss Wündt's methodology for studying *Völkerpsychologie* for two reasons. One is to do with the organization of this book, since it falls someway out of the time period we have set for ourselves in this chapter. Second, it is because, despite the number of dissertations that he supervised (some 186 according to Kusch) and that he often chose what his students would do, he never supervised a *Völkerpsychologie* thesis, which may lead to the conclusion that he believed that he was the only psychologist at Leipzig to have got out of the nursery.

The German University System

Given the issues that psychologists so rapidly turned their attention to, it is slightly puzzling that Wündt's *Physiologischen Psychologie* is in anyway seen as foundational. Insofar as he retains some importance, beyond what Richards calls the 'psychological' fact that for most psychologists Leipzig in 1879 is the birthplace of Psychology, it is probably due to the German university system. The German university system is very old. Leipzig university, for example, was founded in 1409, and like other medieval universities the university system in the German states it provided for training for law, medicine and the church. When the University of Berlin, originally established in 1696 was re-established in 1809 it had a novel feature, research or *Wissenschaft*. The German university system was the first that allowed students to complete degrees by research alone, the degree of Doctor of Philosophy. Within the German university system a number of novel fields of studies established themselves, often within the arts faculties, including linguistics, physiology, botany, chemistry and of course psychology.

The Doctor of Philosophy degree (a title betraying its roots in arts faculties) and the new fields of study attracted many foreign students. For example, the historian Sokal (1981) estimates that around 10,000 US citizens studied in Germany for PhDs between 1865 and 1914. After World War One many British universities began offering this degree, perhaps in the hope of gaining US graduate students, but by this time universities in the USA were also offering their own PhD programmes so there was little uptake.

While *Wissenschaft* was an important feature of the modern German university there was debate amongst German intellectuals about two different types of *Wissenschaft: Naturwissenschaft* and *Geisteswissenschaften*. This corresponds approximately to the distinction between natural sciences and the human and social sciences. For Wündt psychology was neither a pure natural science nor a pure human science, rather different aspects of psychology fitted into the *Naturwissenschaft* and the *Geiteswissenschaften*. This can in part be explained by Wündt's reaction to the work of Kant, who disputed whether a natural science of mind was possible because of the problematic status of introspective thought. Thus Wündt's natural science of psychology would not look at the higher functions of mind and for these a *Geiteswissenschaften* approach would be taken.

Many early US psychologists obtained their initial training in Psychology under Wündt. Boring published a list of these experimental psychologists: G.S. Hall (Clark), J.McK. Cattell (Columbia), H.K. Wolfe (Nebraska), E.A. Pace (Catholic University), E.W. Scripture (Yale), F. Angell (Stanford), E.B. Titchener (Cornell), L. Witmer (Pennsylvania), H.C. Warren (Princeton), H. Gale (Minnesota), G.T.N. Patrick (Iowa), G.M. Stratton (California), C.H. Judd (Chicago), G.A. Wawney (Beloit). (Boring 1950: 347)

As well as this influence, at least in terms of the prestige of graduate studies for the scholars concerned, on experimental psychology, Wündt also had an influence on non-experimental social psychology and here at least some of his concerns remain with us. Farr (1996) has shown, that in addition to this list of experimental psychologists who attended Leipzig University, G.H. Mead, whom we discuss at length in Chapter 7, and W.I. Thomas, the Chicago sociologist, who may have been responsible for the introduction of the concept of social attitudes into Psychology, also studied under Wündt. According to Blumenthal (1973) his influence on linguistics was also profound with many linguists attending his lectures on the psychology of language including de Saussure, renowned for his semiology and work on signs. Farr also presents evidence that Wündt's *Völkerpsychologie* influenced Durkheim, Vygotsky and Freud (whose *Totem and Taboo* is a rejoinder to Wündt's writings on the 'totemic age'). Thus while Wündt's direct influence on experimental psychology may be symbolic and institutional rather than at the level of theory, his influence on alternative forms of psychology is certainly worth noting.

It is however the history of experimental psychology that has become conflated with a history of psychology and it is worth pursuing the thesis that Wündt's influence here is fairly small. For this let us turn to the situation in Germany and how Wündt's natural science of psychology fared in its home soil.

The 'Image-less Thought' Controversy

The details of this controversy unfold at the end of the period, up until 1900, of the main bulk of this chapter. The controversy arises out of the methodological and theoretical writings coming out of the Psychological Institute of the University of Würzburg between 1900 and 1907.

That Wündt was repudiated, to use Danziger's term, by psychologists outside Germany may have been due to the very different notions about the status of Psychology outside Germany. However, and in keeping with the thesis that Wündt's status as a founder of Psychology is mythical, he was also rapidly repudiated within Germany. The major figures, followers of

Kusch who will be referred to as Würzburgers, (although their institutional location may have been Bonn, Munich and Köningsberg as well as Würzburg), belong to the generation of psychologists that immediately follow Wündt. The major figures in this controversy are: Külpe (1862–1915). who was the director of the Würzburg Institute from 1896–1909, Ach (1871–1946), Bühler (1879–1963), Marbe (1869–1953), Messer (1867–1937), Selz (1881–1943) and Watt (1879–1925). This repudiation is often referred to as the image-less thought controversy, although as the work of Kusch demonstrates there was much more to it than that. It is also glossed as a demonstration that introspection is a poor methodology because different laboratories obtained different results, whereas the debate at the time was theoretical rather than empirical.

According to Kusch there are four sites of technical dispute between the Würzburgers and Wündt and beyond these technical issues there was an intertwining of a number of social and cultural issues, some involving the relationship of psychology to other disciplines but others with much broader cultural issues in-turn-of-the twentieth-century Germany.

The first of these technical disputes involved the discovery of three new kinds of mental contents. Wündt has claimed that there were three irreducible forms of mental contents, sensations, feelings and presentations. To this traditional trio the Würzburgers added situations of consciousness, awareness and thoughts.

Second the Würzburgers challenged the psychological theory of judgements, in which thinking consisted of forming judgements and drawing inferences. This challenge happened in two forms. One involved a reinterpretation of what mental representations of judgements meant, while for others this whole question was mistaken and instead some thought psychologists took as their research question the issue of what people experience when they think.

The third was the idea that there were determining tendencies that linked presentations and thoughts in a goal oriented fashion, the goal being the solving of some form of problem or task. This was part of the Würzburgers' rejection of associationism, and while Wündt also rejected associationism, unlike his US champion Titchener, the solution that the Würzburgers gave was also part of their attack on the limitations of only having three forms of mental contents.

Some of the Würzburgers were very critical of Wündt, claiming that he used 'feelings' in situations where there should be further analysis.

Finally the Würzburgers claimed that it was possible to use retrospective reports of thought processes provided that these reports were collected in a controlled experimental setting. The prototypical experiment here would have a subject do some task and then have the experimenter ask them about the contents of their mind between hearing the problem and providing the solution. As the Würzburgers expanded their studies it was no longer feasible for them to use only trained psychologists as subjects in these studies, although there was considerable variation in the amount of training that these lay subjects would receive.

Even this short sketch should give an indication that there is much more going on here than the idea that different laboratories using introspectionist methods gave different results. Many of the areas that the Würzburgers were investigating would for Wündt belong to *Völkerpsychologie* and thus were not seen as being open to the natural science method. Wündt doubted that the interrogative method, as he called it, that the Würzburgers used could give reliable and valid results because of the power of the person asking the questions and the possibility of leading the subject through the questioning.

Kusch (1999) also draws attention to the way that the laboratories at Leipzig and Würzburg were being organized and suggests that the more egalitarian organization at Würzburg mirrored their more egalitarian theory of mind. The strictly hierarchical organization at Leipzig fitted in with the strict division that Wündt had between lower and higher mental processes. Intertwined around this debate was a further debate about the place of Psychology within the academe. For Wündt the study of the higher processes of mind were not amenable to experimental study, and no part of psychology was reducible to physiology. As we have already discussed, the Würzburgers did not believe this: provided that their experimental methodology was used, *all* of psychology could be a natural science, and some processes would be reducible to physiology.

The second issue was the scope of psychology. For Wündt psychology needed to be a purely theoretical science, as it was not yet possible to start applying such a young science. The Würzburgers were self-consciously developing thought psychology in such a way that it could be applied to problems in education and psychiatry. With thinking as its central concern it may have appeared obvious that education, teaching children to think and psychiatry, helping people no longer able to think properly, would be areas to which thought psychology was directly relevant. As part of this Külpe suggested that Psychology should be located within the medical faculty rather than the philosophy faculty.

The third issue was the relationship between Psychology and philosophy. Wündt deemed that Psychology was a discipline that was separate from Philosophy but he wanted it to remain within philosophy departments, at least at this period in the history of Psychology. Part of the reason for this is that Wündt was worried that psychologists would otherwise rapidly become people who just did experiments for no good reason, and this fits in with the conception of Psychology as a theoretical discipline. Another reason may have been Wündt's plan for his career, to develop a limited experimental discipline of Psychology, a metaphysics and finally a social psychology that would be part of the research tradition known as *Geiteswissenschaften* rather than a natural science. The final reason was Wündt's belief that philosophy needed to learn from Psychology, and that Psychology should be the most fundamental of the disciplines that make up the *Geiteswissenschaften*.

Beyond those issues, but also intertwined with them were larger cultural issues. Wündt in his social philosophy maintained that the collective had primacy over the individual. In his ethical philosophy he opposed the individual's right to happiness preferring the notion of the collective good, and in his political philosophy he insisted that the state came before the individual citizen. Wündt believed, and perhaps with good reason, that the Würzburgers thought psychology was a much more individualized psychology, and in some of their writings the Würzburgers did not agree with all of Wündt's collectivist ethics and politics.

There was no decisive end to this controversy within the timeframe that we have decided to limit ourselves to within this chapter. Indeed the controversy continued within German and Austrian Psychology until 1933. The Gestaltists who fled the Nazi regime in the 1930s had a more collective approach to psychology than the behaviourists in the USA. What the controversy does show is that Wündt, despite his many achievements which we hope we have highlighted within this chapter, is a very curious figure for a founding father.

SUMMARY AND CONCLUSIONS

Wündt is important to the founding of Psychology, not least because it is now a psychological fact to several generations of psychologists that he was the founder figure. He also began a tradition of the experimental laboratory based investigative practice that is still part of the panoply of methods that psychologists use. Wündt's direct influence on theories within psychology may be small, but the recent rediscovery of Vygotsky and G.H. Mead, who independently adopted parts of his system of *Völkerpsychologie* has had some influence on the broad social constructionist movement, while he may have had an enduring legacy within linguistics.

The treatment of Wündt also gives us some lessons in how histories are constructed. He has been regarded as a founder figure in two ways. First the foundation of a laboratory was seen as the time when a science of psychology began, often a move in histories informed by positivism that appear to search for a sharp distinction between metaphysics and science. Second he was the first of many figures whose ideas are reputedly overthrown by revolutionary new ideas that help us climb up the mountain of knowledge. So, on close examination, Wündt's introspection appears to be no more than the verbal reports that many cognitive psychologists ask of their research participants which cause us to be, justifiably, wary in treating any claims of historians of a discipline as value free.

Psychology, in our reading, arose not because of the actions of any single person but because of a nexus of social and intellectual conditions. As the next chapter illustrates, the types of psychology that emerge within societies depended initially upon the needs of those societies.

FURTHER READING

Danziger, K. 1990: *Constructing the subject: historical origins of psychological research.* Cambridge: Cambridge University Press.

Danziger, K. 1997: *Naming the mind: how psychology found its language*. London: Sage.

Farr, R.M. 1996: *The roots of modern social psychology, 1872–1954*. Oxford: Blackwell.

Gould, S.J. 1991: *Bully for brontosaurus*. London: Penguin Books.

Gregory, R.L. 1981: *Mind in science*. London: Penguin Books.

Kusch, M. 1999: *Psychological knowledge: a social history and philosophy*. London: Routledge.

Richards, G. 1989: *On psychological language*. London: Routledge.

Robinson, D.N. 1995: *An intellectual history of psychology*. London: Arnold.

3

THE EARLY DEVELOPMENT OF PSYCHOLOGY

This chapter looks at the early development of academic Psychology, from around 1880 to 1939. Initially, it considers the major theoretical movements in the discipline, which are usually characterized as the 'schools' of Psychology. Coverage of the development of the early schools is the traditional approach to histories of Psychology, and the set of schools has become quite formalized: structuralism, functionalism, behaviourism, and Gestalt. The first three of these are American, and Gestalt had some influence in the USA, so the set of schools clearly reflects an American dominance in the writing of disciplinary histories. Indeed, the identification of schools can be seen as an American phenomenon. Gestalt apart, European Psychology tended not to be easily characterized into discrete movements. In part, this may be because European Psychology lacked the critical mass that American Psychology quickly established, but the notion of schools should be seen as a construct of historians. Celebratory historians, seeking to support the perception of an independent scientific discipline, needed to emphasize unity and progress. The identification of discrete schools with a shared theoretical orientation, and of the replacement of one school by another in a process of intellectual Darwinism, is a mechanism that allowed this. In fact, the construction of unified schools hid a considerable degree of disagreement, and the development of the discipline was more gradual than is suggested by the traditional story of replacement. Despite this, we follow this broad outline in considering theoretical developments in academic Psychology, while pointing out disagreements and continuities.

An aspect of Psychology's early development that is often overlooked is the development of methodology in Psychology. When covered, it is usually to show that Wündtian introspection was rejected in favour of the more rigorous scientific methods of American functionalism and behaviourism, and that Gestalt failed because its methodologies were not scientifically rigorous. In fact, the development of methodology in Psychology is intertwined with theoretical and practical developments in the discipline, and with the social contexts within which the discipline developed. While today there is considerable orthodoxy in the discipline about suitable methodology, in its early development there were three distinct models of psychological research that could have been adopted. In the second part of the chapter we look at the development of methodology, and at some of the factors influencing methodological choices.

For the most part, this chapter concentrates on the development of academic Psychology, although applied Psychology is considered when relevant. A fuller discussion of the development of applied Psychology is given in Chapter 4. This chapter does not consider the development of psychoanalysis – the relationship between Psychology and psychoanalysis is a complex one, and so is discussed in Chapter 5. This chapter concentrates on developments in American Psychology, since it was the American model of Psychology that became dominant in the western world, and particularly the Anglophone world, following World War Two. However, the development of American Psychology, and of Psychology's methodology, was shaped in part by developments in the UK, Germany, and Russia, and these will be discussed where relevant.

The organization of material around the early development of Psychology is difficult. The development of academic Psychology is closely intertwined with the development of applied Psychology and with the development of methodology, and this three-way relationship is embedded in a range of social and intellectual contexts. In order for a discussion of this development to be accessible, it is necessary to introduce some artificial divisions. In this text, we discuss theoretical and methodological developments here, but with some consideration of the impact of the drive towards application and the social and intellectual contexts. In Chapter 4 we discuss the development of applied Psychology, featuring other developments, and social and intellectual contexts, where relevant. Finally, in Chapter 6 we summarize the role of social and intellectual contexts in shaping the nature of both academic and applied Psychology. While this approach leads to some overlap between chapters, we feel that restating the intricate relationships is preferable to overlooking them. We also feel that the social context is sufficiently important to warrant a dedicated chapter rather than only including that material piecemeal in other chapters. Chapter 6 thus acts as a kind of capstone to the discussion in Chapters 3 and 4.

THEORETICAL DEVELOPMENTS IN PSYCHOLOGY

Boring (1950) describes how Psychology came to America as a new separate discipline in the late nineteenth century, taking form in the USA as an offspring of German experimental Psychology and British evolutionary biology. He thus provides a creation myth for Psychology in the USA, just as Wündt represented a creation myth for Psychology as a whole. However, as we shall see, the development of Psychology in the USA was directly shaped by a number of intellectual and societal trends in the USA. In considering this development, therefore, we shall first look at forerunners to Psychology in the USA.

Forerunners of American Psychology

The first insight we can make is that there was already a form of psychology in the USA – as there was elsewhere – before Wündt, although it was not identified as a separate discipline. This is clearly indicated by the way in which early psychologists described their project as 'new Psychology', as opposed to, of course, old psychology. Traditional histories have shown the new Psychology as a dramatic departure from the old, but considering the nature of both old and new Psychology we can see continuities as well as differences.

Just as the new Psychology stemmed in part from philosophy (see Chapter 2), so too did the old psychology. In the case of old psychology the philosophical tradition of choice was Scottish common sense realism. This was in part a reaction against associationism, though there were areas of similarity, and adopted a pragmatic compromise position between rationalism and empiricism. The common sense realists identified a number of innate powers, or faculties, which they believed should be investigated in an empirical, non-reductionist way. In part, the movement was an attempt to reconcile philosophy and Protestantism. In identifying innate faculties, the realists were adopting a practical orientation, believing that the faculties could be trained to influence personality. The link with religion was achieved by emphasizing the development of those faculties associated with the moral guidance of the church.

Common sense realism had a major impact on intellectual thought in the USA because the early universities were religious foundations, generally being linked to the Protestant faiths. Scottish academics, reconciling philosophy with Protestantism, were influential in the development of these universities, and in developing their curricula. A distinctive feature of the curriculum in such institutions was a compulsory course in mental and moral philosophy which dominated American university education until the growth of secular universities following the Civil War. The philosophy taught on these courses can be seen as a reaction against secular continental philosophies, and emphasized the consistency of Christianity with philosophy and logic. The mental and moral philosophy movement adopted the faculties of the common sense realists, and out of this developed 'faculty psychology'. Faculty psychology was seen as a science of the soul, wherein introspection revealed the soul. The role of psychology was to identify the faculties, and then moral philosophies were to show how faculties should be used and developed.

Closely associated with faculty psychology was the pseudo-science of phrenology. Phrenology adopted similar faculties to faculty psychology, and claimed that each faculty was located in its own organ within the brain. Phrenology enjoyed wide popularity in the first half of the nineteenth century, particularly in the USA, and was important in popularizing the notion of a science of mind, and in pioneering a functionalist approach, since the faculties were discussed in terms of the functions they performed. In Europe phrenologists attempted to be scientific, but it took a slightly different form in the USA. American phrenology was mainly driven by the Fowler brothers, who proselytized widely. They minimized the scientific content and emphasized instead the practical value of the subject. This practical orientation fitted with American views of the improvement of the individual, and the Fowlers strongly advocated the potential for individual change through phrenology. They also linked phrenology with religion and morality, fitting it with the prevailing intellectual climate. While phrenology was discredited in the second half of the century, we can see strong similarities between the programme of American phrenology and later functionalist applied Psychology.

Early histories of disciplinary Psychology portrayed mental and moral philosophy as dogmatic and opposed to new scientific and intellectual thinking, the purpose being to champion the new Psychology as a revolutionary approach sweeping aside superstition. In fact, this account is wrong in two ways. First, mental and moral philosophy was not as anti-scientific as portrayed, and had incorporated European evolutionary thinking into its overall framework. Second, the new Psychology was in some senses a continuation of mental and moral philosophy by other means. Certainly the new Psychology replaced the mental and moral philosophy curriculum in the secular universities, and was taught alongside mental and moral philosophy at the old universities. However, the approach taken to the new Psychology followed the agenda set by the old, and most early textbooks for Psychology were structured around the topics of mental and moral philosophy. The new Psychology incorporated the German experimental methods, and adopted a secular and more rigorously scientific approach, but the concerns addressed by the new Psychology were the same. These included a view to practical application and the explanation of mental function, but also included a distinctively American moral project. As we shall see, these concerns were to endure throughout the development of American Psychology.

The Development of 'new Psychology'

The new Psychology in the USA was to take a rather different form from continental Psychology. While Wündt was establishing a Psychology of consciousness, following from Kantian idealism, in the USA new Psychology quickly became a Psychology of adaptation. In part, this reflects the influence of British biology identified by Boring. The fusion of evolution and Psychology prompted two fundamental questions, which Leahey (2000) describes as the 'species question' and the 'individual question'. The species question asks what differences there are in the mental and behavioural capacities of different species, while the individual question asks how the individual adapts to their environment, effectively the study of learning. The two are interrelated, in that if there are few differences between species, then all species can be described by similar laws of learning, whereas if there are great differences, then there must be different laws of learning for different species. Early psychologists were to concentrate on the individual question, focusing on how individuals adapt to their environment.

Psychology of adaptation had its roots in nineteenth-century Britain, and particularly in the psychology of Herbert Spencer, first introduced in *Principles of psychology* (1855). Spencer integrated associationism, physiology, and Lamarckian evolution, later revising his system to incorporate Darwinism. Spencer's associationism suggested that the mind was initially a blank slate waiting for the formation of associations, and was in opposition to the old faculty psychology. As Darwinian thought became more widely accepted associationism became ascendant, and adaptational Psychology was widely adopted in the USA and Britain. Spencer's reception in the USA was helped by his formulation of social Darwinism, which as we shall see in Chapter 6 had a great appeal in American society. British adaptational Psychology reached its apogee with the work of Galton, whose studies of individual differences and development of statistical methods reflected his adaptational approach.

While human Psychology adopted an adaptational approach to the individual, comparative Psychology adopted a similar approach to animals, addressing the species question rather than the individual question. Given the widespread commitment to an adaptational view of mind, comparative psychologists saw their task as being the investigation of animal minds, and comparing mindedness across species. Again, the initial development of this form of comparative Psychology was in Great Britain, where Darwin had considered the expression of emotions in animals. Romanes extended Darwin's project, investigating the nature of intelligence in a range of animals. His aim was to trace the evolution of mind, influenced by the notion of a chain of being, with humankind as the pinnacle. This comparative project combined faculty psychology with associationism, and introduced an objective behavioural method: since animals could not introspect, it was necessary to infer mental processes from behaviour. Romanes used an anecdotal method, collecting observational reports and attempting to construct plausible narratives about mental life in animals. To do so he analogized to his own reasoning and was prone to attribute complex thought processes, which prompted debate within the field. C. Lloyd Morgan argued that such inferences should be no more complex than necessary, and also distinguished between objective and projective inferences. Objective inferences would generate hypotheses that could be tested scientifically, whereas projective inferences falsely analogized to subjective human mental states and were unscientific. Despite Morgan's warning, projective inferences continued to be used, and led to perceived absurdities in anthropomorphizing human qualities on to animals. These excesses were to lead to a rejection of the possibility of mindedness in animals.

American comparative psychologists rejected the anecdotal method, preferring instead experimentation and laboratory control. While this increased rigour, it also led to warnings that such studies lacked ecological validity, a charge which Köhler was later to use against Thorndike's work. The question of ecological validity is a recurring one in Psychology, for example Neisser has raised it in regard to cognitive Psychology. There is clearly a trade off between rigour and validity, but generally Psychology has suggested that experimental rigour is necessary in the initial stages of collecting data and developing theory, while validity can be checked later. Notably, such checking of validity has tended not to occur. The question of ecological validity is addressed more fully in the second part of the book.

Psychologists addressing the individual question tended to believe that there were only quantitative, rather than qualitative, differences between species. Findings from comparative Psychology suggesting that behaviour was a sufficient source of evidence to infer mental function, and that animal behaviour could be explained without recourse to consciousness, lent support to a trend away from mentalistic explanations of human actions to behaviouralistic explanations. This trend will be examined in the next section.

While adaptational Psychology had roots in British evolutionary and comparative Psychology, the nature of new Psychology in the USA owed much to the development in the 1870s of the philosophy of pragmatism, by Peirce, James and Wright. This philosophy was a synthesis of the work of Bain, Darwin and Kant. Bain had previously incorporated associationism, physiology and behaviour into a psychological system that emphasized the role of beliefs in directing action. With the addition of evolutionary thinking, the pragmatists suggested that beliefs are engaged in a struggle for survival, and that learning was a matter of consolidating the fittest beliefs. From Kant, the pragmatists took the notion that beliefs need not be true, and those that achieve desired ends – which they called 'pragmatic beliefs' – have value. For the pragmatists then, philosophy should concentrate on the adaptational value of beliefs to an organism. This new approach to the individual question would be adopted by American Psychology, and it also anticipated the increasing concentration on behaviour, since beliefs have value only in the extent to which they guide behaviour.

Pragmatic philosophy had a number of formulations. As a basis for adaptational Psychology, the most important formalization was to be that of James. James was concerned to rescue free will within Psychology and set limits on the scope of determinism, and also wished to promote Psychology as a source of morally beneficial knowledge. His *Principles of psychology* (1890) was essentially a psychological formulation of pragmatism, and was to set the agenda for functionalist Psychology for years to come. The pragmatism outlined in *Principles* was more expansive than that of Peirce, emphasizing that ideas had to be meaningful to people's lives. Against Peirce's narrow scientific view, James suggested that ideas had to be weighed against the breadth of human experience, allowing for consideration of emotion and ethics.

The central argument of *Principles* was to emphasize the functions of consciousness over its content, these functions being characterized in adaptational terms. James also suggested that the formation of associations can be directed by consciousness, which allowed for free will, and emphasized that Psychology needed to be a practical subject that could make a difference to people's lives. *Principles* helped establish Psychology as a natural science in America, although James was equivocal about the importance of the scientific method, as illustrated by his allowance of free will and of morality. The emphasis on Psychology as a natural science and at the same time the defence of free will is not the only paradox in *Principles*. The James-Lange theory of emotion, for instance, suggested that behaviour causes consciousness, and hence that consciousness might be unimportant to Psychology. This conflicted with James's views on free will, but was to help lead American Psychology away from the study of consciousness.

From Mentalism to Behaviourism

The early development of the new Psychology saw a shift from investigating the contents of consciousness to considering its function, and an emphasis on the practical application of Psychology. In both of these, the new Psychology reflected its inheritance from the old. Another shift was to come, however, which Leahey (2000) describes as a shift from mentalism to behaviourism. While the new adaptational Psychology began by considering consciousness as its source of evidence using introspection as the chosen methodology (mentalism), we have seen that pressure was building to deny the importance of consciousness and to concentrate on behaviour as the main source of evidence (behaviourism). In this section we shall trace this shift during the period 1890 to 1912, showing that when behaviourism arose as an identified school of Psychology, the discipline had already adopted a behavioural orientation. This shift was driven in part by a desire for application and by the wider social context. These effects are discussed more fully in Chapters 4 and 6.

In theoretical terms, the shift from mentalism to behaviourism is apparent in the development of motor theories of consciousness. The earliest major example of such a theory was Münsterburg's action theory, which attempted to remove consideration of will by explaining behaviour as automatic motor responses to stimuli. This was very much influenced by an increasing acceptance of reflex theories, derived from physiology. For Münsterburg behaviour was the result of associations between incoming sense nerves and outgoing motor nerves, with these associations being formed without the intervention of consciousness. The existence of consciousness was accepted, but it was seen as an awareness of behaviour rather than an agent of behaviour, and hence as epiphenomenal. In Münsterburg's theory, the contents of consciousness were determined by three factors – external stimuli, overt behaviours, and internal physiological changes. Consciousness consisted entirely of passive awareness of these three factors, and had no other role. Given Münsterburg's theory, Psychology must be physiological, and applied Psychology must explain actions as the outcome of environmental circumstances, rather than the result of conscious thought.

With increasing support for motor theories came the view that consciousness was irrelevant to the project of Psychology, and that behaviour should be the main source of evidence. This was reinforced in the 1890s with Dewey's formulation of instrumentalism, which provided a pragmatic view of consciousness, and Dewey's work on the reflex arc. His 1896 paper 'The reflex arc concept in psychology' set the foundations for a functionalist Psychology by rejecting the associationist formulation of the reflex arc as a discrete sequence of stimulus, sensation and response. Dewey accepted that these events occurred, but conceived of them as coordinated behaviours combining to allow the organism to adapt to the environment. Sensation to Dewey was a form of behaviour that interacted with other concurrent behaviours. This move allowed him to account for differences in sensation in terms of a stimulus's relationship with other behaviours occurring at the same time. Dewey's system removed the need to explain differential responses to stimuli in terms of consciousness focusing attention. Although conscious experience may occur, this was solely the result of interacting behaviours, and it was the behaviours that Psychology needed to focus on.

Dewey's work was foundational to functionalist Psychology. The shift from content to process had been gathering pace since James, and introspection was being increasingly devalued as a methodology. The acceptance of motor theories, which characterized consciousness as epiphenomenal, suggested that there was no value in studying consciousness. Instead, experimental psychologists began investigating the relationship between stimuli and people's responses to them, rather than investigating the conscious events stimuli produced. The questions being asked in psychological research were now of the form 'how are responses determined by stimulus conditions?', with an emphasis on objectively measured behaviour rather than introspective reports. This new approach to Psychology focused on learning, seen as being the means by which organisms adapt to the environment.

Although this shift was widespread, albeit gradual, there were those who maintained a commitment to the old style of new Psychology. Most notable amongst these was Titchener. Titchener identified the trend to functionalism, and in his 1898 work *Postulates of a structural psychology* he attempted to defend Psychology as the science of consciousness. In this, he described his own system of Psychology, which he termed 'experimental' Psychology, as the study of structure analogous to the study of morphology in biology. However, he also described a form of Psychology which he termed 'functional' Psychology, as the study of function analogous to physiology in biology, and a form of Psychology he termed 'genetic', analogous to ontogeny in biology. His description of functional Psychology closely matched the emerging trend, and psychologists following the approach adopted the term 'functionalism' to describe their project. Titchener's preferred system became known as 'structuralism', and during the first decade of the twentieth century functionalism and structuralism often seemed to be in competition.

In analogizing these two systems of Psychology to biology, Titchener was attempting to show that structuralism should logically precede functionalism. He recognized the growing appeal of functionalism, but claimed that before functionalism was possible, it was necessary to complete the task of the Psychology of content. However, while many agreed with Titchener's analogy, most disagreed with the primacy given to structuralism, arguing that the mind is not like a physical system, and that functionalism should, if anything, precede structuralism. The tide of opinion was running against Titchener, in part because of the opportunities for application and professionalization that functionalism offered, and soon Titchener was isolated. Titchener's main legacy was the establishment of rigorous laboratory training as an essential part of undergraduate training in Psychology. Functionalism itself faced problems during this period however. For many, consciousness maintained a role in directing learning, but it became increasingly paradoxical to argue that reflexive nerve processes are unaffected by consciousness but that learning was. The solution to the paradox was to jettison the concept of consciousness as interesting to Psychology.

By 1905, functionalism was the dominant approach within American Psychology. A prime mover in establishing functionalism was Angell, who argued that unlike in biology, mental functions produced structures as needed during perception. This reverse of Titchener's analysis implied that the structure of the mind was transient, and outside the province of a scientific Psychology. Functionalism was seen as a logical progression from old psychology, and content Psychology was now presented as a temporary interruption. Given the physiological basis of behaviour suggested by functionalism, functional Psychology was seen to be allied to biology rather than philosophy, which in itself was of value to psychologists attempting to establish Psychology as an independent discipline separate from philosophy. The functional approach was also far more applicable than introspective Psychology, the same investigative framework being suitable for pedagogy, mental hygiene and developmental Psychology.

The changes in academic Psychology up to 1910 were supported by changes in philosophical positions. The idealism underlying content Psychology was replaced by pragmatism or instrumentalism, which both denied a special role for consciousness. Consciousness was increasingly seen as a motor response indistinguishable from behaviour, and by 1911 Angell was suggesting that Psychology should be 'a general science of behaviour'. This was supported by the development of new fields of Psychology, for example individual difference Psychology, which had no use for introspection. The time was ripe for an alternative framework to be introduced.

Behaviourism

Behaviourism is conventionally presented as a revolutionary break from the past. However, as we have seen, it is perhaps best characterized as the logical culmination of changes occurring in the discipline over the preceding 15–20 years. As so often in the historiography of Psychology, the shift to behaviourism has been exaggerated by disciplinary historians as a way of strengthening the approach's claims to validity. In this section we look at the development of behaviourism, and show that its claimed dominance of American Psychology was both less complete than usually presented, and a gradual process of acceptance.

Behaviourism, as a distinct school in Psychology, was originally formulated by Watson in his 1913 paper 'Psychology as a behaviourist views it', often termed the 'behaviourist manifesto'. Watson had started his academic career as a comparative psychologist, particularly investigating learning in rats, and had been impressed by the work on motor conditioning conducted by the Russian comparative psychologist Bekhterev. He published his manifesto while he was head of Psychology at Johns Hopkins, and in it expressed dissatisfaction with the current state of Psychology, including its methods, the language used, and the tasks it set itself. While his main target was Titchener's structuralist approach, he also attacked functionalism for not having discarded consciousness entirely. Having set out his reservations, he then went on to propose an alternative approach to Psychology. He rejected the philosophical concerns of previous approaches, since these were of no practical value, and adopted a strong positivist stance to psychological investigation. He also presented Psychology as an adjunct to biology, whose task was to correlate psychological functions with biological structures, and explain these correlations in physiological terms. He concentrated on the individual question, suggesting that just as genetics was a biological universal in adaptation, so learning was a behavioural universal in adaptation. Given this, he presented the rat as a convenient 'behaving organism' that could be used to investigate these universal laws. He also identified a need for greater methodological uniformity and rigour, concentrating on behaviour as the sole source of evidence.

For Watson, then, Psychology was a purely objective, experimental natural science, whose goal was to 'predict and control behaviour'. This clear statement was attractive after the obfuscations of previous systems. Its immediate impact was quite limited, mainly attracting younger psychologists, but Watson was to prove an effective proselytizer following publication of his manifesto. As part of this, Watson applied his approach to the study of emotional development in children, most famously in the 'Little Albert' study. This classic study is usually presented as a success for behaviourist principles, Watson being able to induce fear of a white rabbit in an infant through conditioning. However, Harris (1979) has reinterpreted the paper, and shows that there were problems with both the methodology and with the analysis of the results. Further, Watson himself made fairly weak claims in the original publication, but these claims became exaggerated over time as the paper was added to behaviourism's origin myth.

In 1920 Watson was forced to leave academia following a divorce scandal, but he continued to proselytize widely with magazine articles, radio broadcasts, and popular books. He is famous for applying behaviourist principles to advertising, although it has been suggested that he did no more than use existing techniques and claim they were behaviourist. However, his formulation of behaviourism was not very successful, his main impact being through his advocacy of the general approach and through his linkage of basic and applied Psychology. Behaviourism in the 1920s faced stiff competition from mental testing and Gestalt, which received more attention in US textbooks than is usually recognized, but came to dominate experimental Psychology from the 1930s onwards. There are a number of reasons for this, including the proselytizing mentioned above, the introduction of Pavlov's work to the American audience, the development of operationism, and the work of the neobehaviourists.

Pavlov is often mentioned with Watson in descriptions of the foundation of behaviourism, but in fact his main work on conditioning did not become widely known in the USA until his work was translated into English in the mid-1920s, and he undertook tours of the USA in 1927 and 1929. Pavlov was aware of Thorndike's methodological developments, and was also influenced by Darwin and the Russian physiologist Sechenov. In 1863 Sechenov had explained psychological events as reflex actions in the cortex, mediated by excitatory and inhibitory neural processes, and Pavlov adopted this explanatory framework in his own work. Pavlov's formulation of classical conditioning clearly fitted with Watson's behaviourist programme, but was to prove more convincing than Watson's own formulation.

One of the problems identified with a positivist approach to science was of how to avoid discussing unobservable factors. This problem was addressed in physics by Bridgman in 1927, who developed the approach of operationism. He distinguished between observable and theoretical (unobservable) events, and suggested that the problem of discussing theoretical events could be solved if they were defined in terms of measurement, since any meaningful theoretical event would have observable consequences. The notion of producing operational definitions of theoretical events was to prove fruitful for a Psychology of behaviour, and experimental methodologies in modern Psychology still rely on such definitions, as will be discussed in Chapter 12.

As the behaviourist approach increased in popularity it fragmented into a number of distinct formulations, most notably those of Tolman, Hull and Skinner. A comparison of their systems highlights the considerable diversity that the term behaviourism both encompassed and obscured, particularly in terms of theoretical complexity. What these later behaviourists (sometimes termed 'neobehaviourists') shared was their belief in the existence of consistent laws of behaviour across species, in the centrality of learning to understanding behaviour, and in the practical application of Psychology.

Chronologically, Tolman was the first of the neobehaviourists to develop a new system for behaviourism. His 'purposive behaviourism', initially developed during the 1920s, was an attempt to reintroduce purpose into behaviour. Tolman was influenced by links to Gestalt Psychology, particularly Koffka, and his system is often seen as less reductionist than other approaches to behaviourism. Tolman was attempting to explain the behaviour of organisms as wholes, and to do so introduced the concept of field, borrowed from Gestalt, into a behaviourist framework. He introduced purposiveness by claiming that behaviour was directed towards adaptational goals rather than being reactive, although 'purposive' in this sense is meant descriptively rather than causally. Tolman's final innovation was the introduction of 'intervening' variables, hypothetical factors intervening between stimulus conditions and behaviour, the most famous of which was the 'cognitive map' of the environment which Tolman suggested organisms developed. Intervening variables reintroduced mentalistic concepts, and because of this Tolman is sometimes cited as a forerunner of cognitive Psychology. However, this mentalism was seen as subjective, and limited the wider impact of Tolman's system.

A more successful formulation was provided by Hull, who was for many years the most successful proponent of behaviourism. As with Tolman, Hull adopted a hypothetico-deductive system in experimentation, involving successive stages of formulating hypotheses to account for phenomena, testing the hypotheses, and revising them on the basis of the results. Hull produced many PhD graduates who followed this system, and his lasting legacy was to establish this as the norm in psychology investigation. Hull's system was based on a set of postulates, which provided complex algebraic formulations to account for behaviour. He borrowed Tolman's concept of intervening variables, but not as mentalistic constructs. For example, reaction potential was described by a mathematical function predicting the probability that a response will occur at a given time, which incorporated a number of factors including drive and habit strength. Hull's methods and formal theory were similar to natural sciences, particularly physics, and hence had an appeal for psychologists wishing to present their subject as a true science. Until the early 1950s, Hull was the dominant experimental psychologist in the USA. However, the system's complexity was not justified by its empirical base, and had limited success in moving beyond learning. These, together with continuing disputes over the interpretation of data, helped fuel growing suspicions that behaviourism was a flawed system.

While Hull was for a long time the most prominent of the neo-behaviourists, he was to be overtaken by Skinner. Skinner's system was a combination of Pavlovian classical conditioning and Skinner's own operant conditioning. He rejected intervening variables as 'explanatory fictions', as he was later to reject cognitive Psychology. He also rejected physiological Psychology, believing that behaviour could be explained without recourse to physiology. Skinner took a largely atheoretical approach, and was particularly concerned with the development of a behavioural technology, as indicated by his work on education and programmed instruction. His impact has been obscured by the success of cognitive Psychology, but he was very effective in convincing people of the importance of an experimental analysis of behaviour, and also found his approach applied far more widely than any previous behaviourist.

Ultimately, behaviourism was to fail as a theoretical approach. As the approach developed, it became clear how difficult it would be to describe complex behaviours in terms of a sequence of simple learnt associations, and in addition the strong environmentalism of the approach was coming under attack from developments in the study of instincts. The development of the cognitive approach, which will be discussed in Chapter 8, displaced behaviourism as the most prominent theoretical framework within Psychology. However, behaviourism had a number of enduring effects, most prominently methodological. The behaviourists established operationism, the hypothetico-deductive approach, and standardized experimentation as the norm in Psychology investigations, and provided a new technical language. The term 'methodological behaviourism' is sometimes used to describe the use of the experimental method in modern Psychology.

Gestalt Psychology

Gestalt Psychology developed in Germany at the same time as behaviourism was developing in the USA. It is often presented as an exclusively German school of Psychology that only became known within the USA with the displacement of Jewish psychologists to the USA during Nazi rule. Furthermore, it is claimed that Gestalt Psychology had no impact in the USA because it was not sufficiently scientific. This presentation often coincides with the presentation of behaviourism as a revolution, and for the same reasons. Histories that celebrate behaviourism also tend to present Gestalt as an inferior and unwelcome competitor. We shall see however that Gestalt Psychology had some appeal within the USA, and had an influence on the development of American Psychology both during and after behaviourism's ascendancy.

As with American Psychology, Gestalt was a product of the intellectual and social contexts within which it developed, which are described in Chapter 6. Summarizing briefly, Gestalt Psychology arose in Germany from 1910, at a time when Europe faced considerable social turmoil. The old social order that valued an intellectual elite was under threat from urbanization and industrialization, and the continent was soon to be engulfed by war. Part of the threat to established culture was perceived to come from reductionist Psychology that attempted to eliminate consideration of human values. The Gestaltists presented an approach to Psychology that was holistic rather than reductionist, in part to defend their culture from this threat. Given their desire to maintain consideration of human values, the Gestaltists necessarily retained consciousness as an object of investigation. In addition to this social context, the Gestaltists were working in an intellectual context that had been galvanized by advances in physics, with the development of quantum theory. Within the premier natural science, Albert Einstein, Max Planck and others were rejecting a mechanistic Newtonian view of the universe and replacing it with a universe based on fields of forces. While Anglophone

Psychology continued to look for linear cause and effect explanations in Psychology, the Gestaltists attempted to apply the latest approaches in physics to Psychology. As Richards (1996) observes, the adoption of sophisticated theory from physics left the Gestaltists in no doubt about the scientific credentials of their project. Indeed, they were attempting to contribute to a unified discourse in the physical sciences. They felt little need to adopt a narrowly specified scientific methodology, and emphasized theory development rather than data collection. As we shall see, this was to be a disadvantage in the USA.

The Gestaltists followed a tradition of holistic thought in German-speaking Psychology (see Ash 1995). For some time, it had been observed that in form perception certain forms resist decomposition into more basic elements. The most famous illustration is that of Von Ehrenfels, whose 1890 paper 'On Gestalt qualities' described how a musical melody may be played in a range of keys or on different instruments, but remains recognisably the same melody. The melody has a 'form quality' that does not depend on constituent elements. This observation posed a serious challenge to reductionist Psychology, and suggested that the brain is actively involved in perception. Carl Stumpf argued that direct experience had primacy over reduction to elements, a view that was to shape the Gestalt project. Stumpf became Director of the Psychological Institute at Berlin, and while there he directed the PhDs of two of the founders of Gestalt, Koffka and Köhler, and introduced them to his system of phenomenology. Another important influence was Oswald Külpe, leader of the Würzburg school, who directed the PhD of Wertheimer and also worked with Koffka.

Wertheimer moved to Frankfurt in 1910 where he worked with Koffka and Köhler. Their collaboration was to prove fruitful, and in 1912 Wertheimer published 'Experimental studies on the perception of movement', an investigation of the phi phenomenon. This paper is usually considered to be the foundation of Gestalt Psychology. The three's collaboration at Frankfurt was to be brief, Koffka leaving in 1911 and Köhler in 1913, but they continued to work together. The system of Psychology they sketched out was rationalist and anti-reductionist, and relied heavily on the systematic experimental introspection favoured by the Würzburg school. Initially they focused on issues in perception, but soon extended their work into thinking, problem solving and learning. Their fundamental insight was that form qualities determine the characteristics of constituent parts, rather than the other way round, which was explained by describing perception as the resolution of fields of forces, including physiological, perceptual, and environmental. They identified the general principle of Prägnanz, that psychological phenomena are organized in the most meaningful way, and several laws of Prägnanz describing specific organizing principles.

Gestalt Psychology was introduced to America by Koffka, in a 1922 *Psychological Bulletin* article entitled 'Perception: an introduction to Gestalt theory', which he followed up with a campus tour in 1924 and an address to the APA in 1925. In 1927 he accepted a full-time position in the USA. Koffka was more successful in advertising Gestalt Psychology than is commonly acknowledged. Murchison's (1930) *Psychologies of 1930*, a survey of then current systems of Psychology, devoted as much space to Gestalt as to behaviourism, and Woodworth's (1931) *Schools of contemporary psychology* described Gestalt as 'a strong and valuable addition to the varieties of psychology' (p. 125). Tolman's purposive behaviourism was clearly influenced by his association with Koffka. During the 1920s and early 1930s Gestalt Psychology flourished, extending into cognition and learning with the work of Wertheimer, Köhler, Von Restorff, and Duncker. It was also adopted by Lewin in his pioneering work in developmental and social Psychology. The range of work based on Gestalt ideas during this time shows that rather than being solely a theory of perception, as it is often presented, the Gestalt Psychologists believed that they were providing a complete system for Psychology.

The demise of Gestalt as a school is indicative of the importance of social and intellectual context on the development of Psychology. This demise was triggered by the rise to power of the Nazi party in Germany. It is often suggested that the Nazis deliberately destroyed German Psychology, although this is a mistake. The Nazis removed Jewish academics, including Wertheimer and Lewin, from their positions, and they emigrated to the USA. Köhler followed in protest against the Nazi policy. This left Gestalt Psychology without their major figureheads in Germany, and those Gestaltists who remained, for example Metzger, reformulated their theories in support of Nazi ideology. This process is described in more detail in Chapter 6. In the USA, the leading Gestaltists continued their work, and continued to have some influence. However, all three had positions at institutions that did not offer postgraduate study. The consequently limited opportunities to train doctoral students severely restricted the growth of the school. It has been suggested that the Gestaltists' failure to obtain positions at leading universities reflected the low esteem in which American colleagues held them. However, during the Depression of the 1930s there were limited opportunities for academic psychologists, and the fact that they were able to find positions probably indicates high esteem rather than low.

Both Wertheimer and Koffka died early, in 1941 and 1943 respectively. Only Köhler was left to proselytise for Gestalt, which he continued to do up to his retirement in 1958. In addition, Gestalt Psychology did not fit well with the social and intellectual context in the USA, with its emphasis on concrete ideas and practical application. The theoretical and philosophical orientation of Gestalt contrasted with the empirical and pragmatic mindset prevalent in US Psychology. Ultimately, the insights of Gestalt were assimilated into mainstream American Psychology, while the overall theoretical framework was rejected. Despite Gestalt's failure as a complete system for Psychology, it had a considerable influence on later Psychology. The influence of Gestalt can be seen in the social and developmental Psychology of Lewin, the social Psychology of Asch, and Festinger's social cognition. Köhler was made president of the APA in 1959, and his presidential address called on American psychologists to incorporate Gestalt insights. Simon (1992) suggests that cognitive Psychology can be seen as a combination of behaviourism and Gestalt, and cognitive theories of perception and problem solving clearly show the influence of Gestalt theory. It has also been suggested (Palmer 1995) that connectionist approaches to cognitive science represent a return to Gestalt principles. Finally, Wittgenstein's later work on the philosophy of Psychology was frequently inspired by Gestalt principles. It is interesting to speculate on what the nature of contemporary Psychology would be if Gestalt Psychology had continued to develop.

METHODOLOGICAL DEVELOPMENTS IN PSYCHOLOGY

This section looks at the early development of models of investigative practice in Psychology. By investigative practice, as opposed to applied practice, we mean the methods with which psychologists construct studies for the advancement of knowledge, hence 'pure' research rather than application. We shall describe the three major models of investigative practice extant around 1900, and show how methodological diversity became methodological orthodoxy. Although we concentrate on pure research, we will see that the methods adopted in pure research were strongly influenced by applied practice, and by social context.

Competing Models of Investigative Practice

Given that the development of experimental Psychology is usually credited to Wündt, we shall start by considering the methods suggested by Wündt for an experimental, scientific Psychology. Wundt was reacting against Kant's claim that scientific psychology was impossible, and to do so drew on earlier developments in psychophysics. Psychophysics extended on previous work in physiology by investigating subjective experience of stimulus magnitude as a function of objectively measured magnitude, finding that there was a non-linear relationship between stimulus magnitude and perception. To do so, psychophysicists asked respondents to give estimates of stimulus magnitude, using newly developed procedures of constant stimuli, limits, and average error. Wündt extended this model of investigative practice into Psychology by asking respondents to report on conscious experiences in response to stimuli, thus seeking to identify component elements of conscious experience.

Wündt's method of asking respondents to report conscious experience was a form of introspection. However, introspection as a form of self-observation presented certain difficulties for a scientific Psychology, since the introspector could be relying on memory of experience, rather than reporting experiences as they happened. To get around this, Wündt distinguished between 'self-observation' and 'inner perception'. Self-observation consisted of a post hoc report of experiences, which could potentially be contaminated by memory effects. Inner perception, on the other hand, consisted of observers responding immediately to precisely controlled stimuli, reporting conscious experiences according to a limited number of criteria. A period of training was necessary for observers to ensure that they responded without bias and that they were familiar with the criteria. This distinction between self-observation and inner perception was critical for Wündt's method, but was lost in translation into English. Both phrases were translated as 'introspection', and English readers assumed the more familiar self-observation was being referred to – at least, English histories described the method as such, perhaps in order to discredit the method and emphasize the superiority of home-grown methods.

A notable feature of the Wündtian method was that the experimenter's role was subordinate, being mainly to present stimuli. Experimenters and observers frequently swapped roles, and complete data was recorded for each observer individually. The focus of research was on finding universal features of human consciousness, the assumption being that each person's consciousness was constructed out of the same basic elements. As will become apparent on reading Chapter 6, this view fitted the intellectual context in Germany at the time, and given this view each individual's report was valuable.

Wündt believed that his methods were scientific provided they were restricted to investigating limited sensory and perceptual processes. However, others wished to delve deeper into consciousness, and so extended Wündt's notion of introspection. A notable example of this was Külpe, who founded the Würzburg school. Külpe elaborated on the introspective method, taking it closer to self-observation, but he attempted to get round memory effects by introducing 'fractionation' – complex events were split into sub-tasks, and observers reported on each sub-task in turn. Wündt's American students adopted methods closer to Külpe than to Wündt himself – as we shall see, Wündt's strict specification of method was not widely adopted. However he was instrumental in establishing Psychology as an experimental discipline, and later psychologists did adopt the notion of control of stimuli and variation of conditions. For instance, Ebbinghaus used these features of the experimental method in his studies of memory and of the formation of associations between ideas.

While Wündt was establishing Psychology as an experimental science in Germany, a different approach to scientific Psychology was developing in France. Here the focus was on investigating abnormality, and Psychology arose out of a medical context. Whereas in Germany the major areas of investigation in Psychology were perception and universal elements of consciousness, in France the major areas were mental health and the investigation of brain pathology. This difference in focus reflected differences in the social and intellectual contexts in the two countries: Germany had a university system dedicated to the advancement of pure knowledge, whereas in France intellectual activity was often situated in applied settings. These differences necessarily led to differences in methodology.

French investigations into the psychological bases of abnormality took place mainly in clinical settings, with medical patients being used as participants in Psychology experiments. This led to a method where the experimenter had control of the investigation, with the participant in a subordinate role. The goal of the experiment was to investigate abnormal mental states, pursued through intensive investigation of individuals. Unlike German Psychology, experimenters were not trying to investigate universal characteristics of the mind, but rather were focusing on an individuals' abnormal operations.

This clinical method, with a focus on identifying individuals' mental operations, was to be extended beyond clinical settings, although the term 'clinical method' persisted. For instance, Binet used such intensive individual investigations in his identification of educational sub-normality, and Piaget used the method in identifying thought processes in children. The approach was criticised for a lack of objectivity, but defenders pointed to the richness of the data produced. However, this data was specifically related to individuals, and the method was not suitable for mass testing and the identification of group averages. This is clear in the development of intelligence testing. Binet's original tests were designed to give a rich picture of a child's capabilities, applied according to the clinical method. However, as we shall see in Chapter 4, they were developed in a way that would allow group testing, and the rating of individuals in comparison to a group. The basis of this development was the third model of investigative practice that we shall look at.

While both the German and French models of investigation focused on the individual, in Britain an alternative approach was developing that would allow the investigation of the distribution of characteristics, and of differences between groups. This approach is mainly associated with Galton, who introduced group measurement and the use of statistical methods, based on the work of Quételet. Galton shared a widespread concern with the degeneration of the population, and was a leader of the eugenics movement. He realized that in order to establish the basis of degeneration, and to suggest interventions, it would be necessary to measure variation in populations and to identify hereditary traits. Galton developed methods which would allow the quantification of the degree and nature of variation, the investigation of the extent to which heredity operated, the description and comparison of populations, and the identification of the place of an individual in a population. His methods depended on the measurement of a large group on a particular scale, which could then be used to identify a distribution of measures across a group. Given two groups who were believed to differ, their group scores could be compared, and given an individual, their score could be compared to other scores in a group.

Galton's method concentrated on groups rather than individuals, and offered the promise of practical expertise which would be attractive to paternalistic managers. Thus the method could be used to decide whether on a particular measure, such as intelligence, males differed from females, or some individuals were inadequate compared to the wider population. Following Galton's work, successive statisticians concentrated on refining the statistical techniques underlying the method, including correlation and factor analysis. A major development was that of Fisher in 1925, who introduced methods of difference testing, and the testing of the null hypothesis. A major perceived advantage of this approach was that the methods of investigation and analysis were neutral regarding the measures being taken, as long as numerical data was available. This fitted in with positivist approaches in Britain and the USA, with an emphasis on data rather than theory, and encouraged the development of new methods of measurement. An important effect of the use of such statistical methods on scores from groups of participants was to create an idealized 'average' participant. Psychology was to become the scientific investigation of such hypothesized average 'individuals', rather than investigating individuals themselves.

Towards Methodological Orthodoxy

The development of Psychology in the USA went hand in hand with the development of methodological orthodoxy – a certain model of investigative practice developed which was to become accepted as the norm in Psychology. This model is that which is taught as part of undergraduate courses, where it is normally presented as if it was the obvious and only way to conduct investigations in psychology. However, we shall see that the adoption of this approach over others depended on a range of social, practical and intellectual factors. Fundamentally, this model was adopted because it best fitted what most psychologists in the USA wished Psychology to be, a practical discipline that offered a technology for social control.

The mainstream approach to investigation that emerged was a synthesis of experimentation, statistical analysis, and US intellectual commitments. Wündtian experimentation provided a model for laboratory based investigation focusing on the control of extraneous factors and systematic variation of conditions. The British statistical tradition emphasized the measurement of psychological variables, a focus on investigating groups rather than individuals, and the use of statistical methods to investigate differences and relationships. In line with intellectual developments in the USA, the measurements taken were to be objective measurements of overt behaviour, mental events being seen as unsuitable for such measurement. 'Behaviour' here is used in the broadest sense, including, for example, performance on intelligence tests or measures taken using questionnaires.

Danziger (1990) has investigated the historical development of this orthodox methodology in depth. He shows that within US Psychology, the method had its basis in the application of psychology to education. In the late nineteenth and early twentieth centuries, the US education system was going through massive expansion. Managers of education, facing the need to control this expansion, called on the expertise of early psychologists. What was needed were methods for measuring children's performance and of comparing the conditions that produced those performances. Testing groups of children on a set of measures and comparing group means offered an efficient technology for administrators in effecting educational change. This approach soon spread to other areas of applied Psychology, and only a little more slowly to academic Psychology. As we shall see in Chapter 6, academic psychologists shared some of the vision for Psychology as a technology for change, and readily adopted methodologies that would allow this. American psychologists, both applied and academic, desired a certain kind of knowledge product, and the methodology developed in educational Psychology seemed to offer the means of producing this kind of knowledge. The kind of knowledge desired was a result of the generally accepted view of the nature of individuals, and hence of what it was that Psychology needed to explain.

German Psychology in the same period offers an interesting counterpoint. As stated above, German psychologists were attempting to describe universal features of the mind, their intellectual context being shaped by an emphasis on community rather than on individualism. Chapter 6 compares the social and intellectual contexts of the USA and Germany. One of the effects of these differing contexts was that German psychologists had a different view of what the project of Psychology was, and used different methods to produce different knowledge products.

The Impact of Methodological Choice

There were a number of effects of the adoption of the methodology described here. As new statistical techniques were developed, new possibilities for decision making opened up. Relatedly, as the aspirations of psychologists grew, new techniques were developed to meet these aspirations, an example of which was the development of factor analysis as a tool for psychometrics. The development of such techniques led to an extension of measurement, fitting in with an empiricist perspective of collecting data first, and theorizing later (one of the criticisms of Gestalt from American psychologists was that there was too much theory, and not enough data). In general, the methodology adopted to conduct a piece of research will shape the nature of the research, and the knowledge produced. At the earliest stage, the requirements of the methodology will shape the research questions asked, and the way in which the questions are addressed. The methodology will shape what kind of results the research will produce, and hence what kind of conclusions can be drawn.

A notable feature of the methodology described above is that it enshrines, and lends support to, a particular Anglo-American view of human nature, and of the nature of individuality. Individuals, in this model, are best described numerically on a range of scales – thus an individual has a certain level of intelligence or a certain type of personality. This leads to a form of reductionism, whereby the richness of individuality is reduced to a small set of measures. A person's attitude to a certain topic is no longer a complex set of possibly contradictory beliefs, but rather a single number derived from a questionnaire.

These latter two points, that methodology shapes knowledge production, and that methodologies reflect conceptions of the individual, are apparent in a number of current debates about methodology in Psychology. In social Psychology, researchers adopting a 'new paradigm', qualitative approach are questioning the traditional quantitative approach. The knowledge produced using each of the two approaches is very different, in the latter case attempting to describe an 'average' individual, and in the former attempting to describe an actual individual. A similar effect can be found in the debate within cognitive neuropsychology between group studies and case studies. Group studies fit better with the orthodox view of what appropriate research in Psychology is, whereas case studies mark a return to the French clinical tradition. Again, the knowledge produced by the two approaches differs in some important respects.

The observation that the orthodox methodology is particularly suitable to describing individuals as numbers suggests further insights. The notion of describing individuals quantitatively allows the comparison of individuals to some established norm, where the norm is some range of scores around the mean of a group. This in turn suggests the identification of undesirable individuals, and possible interventions. In addition, a quantitative experimental approach allows the easy evaluation of interventions – for example, give two sets of children two different forms of instruction, and compare scores on a test of knowledge. We have previously discussed the suitability of the methodology to application, and we shall see further examples in Chapter 4. In the context of the present discussion, it is important to note that the approach described here was particularly suitable for the advancement of a certain kind of Psychology, a Psychology that hoped to offer practical expertise. The methodology allowed the development of applications of Psychology, which created openings for the professional practice of Psychology. Such a methodological approach was an important factor in advancing the goal of professionalizing the discipline of Psychology.

CONCLUSION

In this chapter, we started by considering the early development of theories of Psychology in the United States. We showed that American Psychology developed differently from the Psychology of Wündt, and looked at the causes of these differences. First, we considered the forerunners of the new Psychology in America, showing that the new experimental Psychology was as much a progression from previous psychological discourse as it was a replacement for that discourse. Second, we looked at the development of adaptational Psychology as the dominant approach in America, in contrast to the content Psychology of Wündt and Titchener. We showed that adaptational Psychology was derived from British evolutionary and comparative Psychology, and was closely associated with the development of the philosophy of pragmatism. Fundamental to adaptational Psychology was an increasing consideration of the functions of consciousness rather than its contents. Third, we showed that as well as a shift to considering function, there was a shift from mentalism to behaviourism, emphasizing the study of behaviour as the principal domain of Psychology. This initially began with the development of functionalism, America's first native Psychology, but culminated in the rejection of consciousness and the establishment of behaviourism as the dominant school of experimental Psychology in America, although other approaches continued. The common theme in this consideration is an emphasis on showing the continuity of psychological thought in America, rather than the artificial identification of revolutionary shifts that characterize traditional histories. We ended this part of the chapter by considering the development of Gestalt Psychology, and its often overlooked influence on the development of Psychology in the USA.

In the second part of the chapter, we considered the development of methodology within Psychology, continuing the discussion introduced in Chapter 2. We saw that early Psychology used a range of competing models of investigative practice, but that over time an orthodox methodology developed. We showed how the development of this orthodoxy was the result of a range of social, intellectual, and practical factors, and considered the impact of the methodology on the development of theory and practice within Psychology. A fuller discussion of the impact of methodological choice, from a contemporary perspective, is given in Chapter 12.

FURTHER READING

Ash, M. 1995: *Gestalt psychology in German culture 1890–1967*. Cambridge: Cambridge University Press.

Benjamin, L. (ed.) 1997: *A history of psychology: original sources and contemporary research*, 2nd edn. Boston: McGraw Hill.

Danziger, K. 1990: *Constructing the subject*. Cambridge: Cambridge University Press.

Leahey, T.H. 2000: *A history of psychology*, 5th edn. Upper Saddle River, NJ: Prentice-Hall.

Morawski, J.G. (ed.) 1989: *The rise of experimentation in American society*. New Haven, CT: Yale University Press.

O'Donnell, J.M. 1985: *The origins of behaviorism: American Psychology 1870–1920*. New York: New York University Press.

Richards, G. 1996: *Putting psychology in its place*. London: Routledge.

4

THE DEVELOPMENT OF APPLIED PSYCHOLOGY

In this chapter we trace the early development of applied Psychology, with particular reference to the USA. As discussed in the previous chapter, the distinction between theoretical and applied development is largely an artificial one, as the two proceed in tandem and inform each other. We shall see examples of this in the present chapter. We separate the material in this artificial way to make the coverage more easily understood, but we recommend that this chapter be read in conjunction with Chapters 3 and 6.

While it may sometimes seem as if the development of scientific Psychology created an opportunity for the first time to assess individuals and apply intervention strategies, such practices were established before the discipline of Psychology developed. This is most evident in the case of psychiatric practice, but was also the case in education. What the new discipline provided was improved technologies for existing practice, which were then extended to new opportunities for practice through the development of methodology and measurement techniques. We trace this development here.

We begin the chapter by looking at the particular circumstances in the USA that drove the development of applied Psychology. We then consider forerunners to applied Psychology, showing that the idea of applying the study of mind to improving the human condition was not new when psychology became established. Following this, we look in some depth at the development of mental testing, and then briefly discuss the development of the main areas of application, namely educational, industrial and clinical Psychology.

AMERICAN PSYCHOLOGY AND APPLICATION

In considering the growth of applied Psychology, it is necessary to recognize the social and intellectual context of the USA in the late nineteenth century. This was characterized by economic and population growth, western expansion, technological innovation, and industrialization. There was a view of America as the home of pragmatic individualism – despite great poverty and injustice – bolstered by Spencer's formulation of Social Darwinism. In this context, Psychology offered the appeal of marketable expertise as a technology for social change – provided the theories were suitable. Theory development occurred in the context of this demand, and also of the general acceptance of Social Darwinist principles. This social context encouraged the development of adaptational Psychology, as described in Chapter 3, and particularly of the functionalist school.

Functionalism facilitated a view of psychology, and a body of theories, that encouraged application. This context had a direct impact on the development of mental testing, which we shall consider shortly. However, it should be noted that an opposing force at the start of the twentieth century was the dawn of the 'progressive era' , which espoused a rejection of Social Darwinism (only partly accepted) and a tackling of social injustice. Psychology played a part here too, particularly in the programme of progressive education. This progressive context can be seen reflected in the development of behaviourism, strongly environmentalist and confident of being able to effect change through the application of behaviourist principles. However, by the time behaviourism developed, individual difference Psychology had already taken root, leading to a dissociation between academic, behaviourist Psychology and applied, individual difference Psychology in later years.

There have been ongoing tensions between views of Psychology as a pure science and of Psychology as an applied discipline from the start of the century, particularly in the USA. This is illustrated, for example, by Boring's *History of experimental psychology* (1950), intended to bolster pure scientific research, and by the establishment of groupings of experimental psychologists such as Titchener's 'experimentalists' and, more recently, the American Psychological Society in response to a perceived applied bias on the part of the APA. The roots of these tensions can be seen in part in the early pressures towards application faced by the early psychologists.

The existence of pressures towards finding applications of psychology is illustrated by Scripture's 1895 introductory text, which explicitly linked experimental procedures to possible applications. In 1900, Dewey gave a presidential address to the APA warning of the dangers of engaging in pure laboratory research, without application to 'the conditions of life' .

Goodwin (1999) identifies a number of pressures that drove Psychology towards application. These pressures were societal, institutional and financial. Social pressures stemmed from the American faith in the power of science as a means of life improvement, driven by the impact of technological advances such as the telephone and electric lighting. This faith, together with the American view of their society as allowing individuals to succeed by their own efforts, led to the development of pragmatism, which emphasized application. In addition, the societal changes created by industrialization and urbanization created movements for reform, such as the Progressive movement, which viewed Psychology as a suitable technology to inform reformist practices. These forces did not compel psychologists to develop applicable theories. Rather, psychologists were members of the society, and shared the society's concerns. For the most part, psychologists were eager to develop theories and methods suitable for application. It is perhaps not a coincidence that the main resistance to functional, applicable Psychology came from Titchener, an English émigré less steeped in the surrounding societal context than his peers.

Some of the reasons why psychologists were eager to develop applications for their new science stemmed not from their eagerness to reform society, but rather from the institutional contexts they found themselves in. Psychology was initially seen as a branch of philosophy, and most early academic psychologists found themselves within departments of philosophy. Within these departments concerns were raised about the cost of equipment and space needed for psychological research, and psychologists found they needed to justify this cost by showing the utility of their discipline. A good example can be seen in the career of Robert Yerkes, a comparative psychologist at Harvard who found himself under pressure to produce work of more immediate human relevance. Beyond justifying costs however, psychologists believed themselves to be pursuing a new natural science, not just pursuing philosophy by other means, and found themselves constrained by departmental policies that emphasized philosophy over Psychology. Psychologists felt that they should be given an independent identity within universities, and demonstrations of practical utility were a valuable way of justifying the institutionalization of the discipline. As we shall see in Chapter 6, a similar effect occurred in Germany, where the encouragement of applied Psychology by the Nazis led directly to Psychology's independence from philosophy.

Pressure also came from the more mundane concerns of earning a living. Although academic Psychology expanded rapidly in the USA, the number of individuals completing PhDs in Psychology grew more rapidly. For most, the favoured occupation was working in an academic psychology laboratory, but the supply of candidates outstripped demand. In order to pursue Psychology and make a living, many psychologists had to offer their services to institutions, businesses and individuals. Even when people found suitable laboratory positions, academic salaries were often so low that psychologists found themselves supplementing their income by engaging in applied work. Not all psychologists were happy with what seemed to be a compromise of their interests, but as applied Psychology developed it became an increasingly attractive occupation.

FORERUNNERS OF APPLIED PSYCHOLOGY

In this section we look briefly at phrenology, suggesting that this discipline created an expectation that a science of mind could lead to application. We then look in more depth at the development of Galtonian Psychology, which was to provide the basis for the main methodological approach adopted within both applied and theoretical Psychology.

Phrenology (literally, 'the study of mind') was a discipline popular at the start of the nineteenth century that purported to provide a scientific explanation of mind. Developed by Gall, it was predicated on the Scottish common-sense notion of independent mental faculties. To phrenologists, these faculties were localized in specific 'organs' of the brain, and an individual's endowment of a particular faculty directly corresponded to the size of the organ. Further, the size of the organ was reflected in the shape of the skull, large organs leading to bumps on the surface of the skull, and small organs leading to depressions. An individual could be described by 'reading the bumps', measuring the shape of the skull in different areas to give an assessment of strong and weak faculties. With hindsight there were a number of problems with this. The particular problems that led to charges of phrenology being only a pseudo-science were that the number of faculties was arbitrary (for example, 27 for Gall, 37 for Spurzheim), and that findings that contradicted the theory were explained away, rather than leading to modification of the theory. As an example of the latter, Descartes's skull was shown not to have the expected bump corresponding to rationalism – the response was to claim that Descartes was overrated. Interestingly, similar problems can be seen in Psychology. In both personality measurement and intelligence testing, there is debate over the number of factors that need to be considered, for example, Eysenck's two-factor theory of personality versus Cattell's sixteen factors versus the 'big five' . During the early development of intelligence testing, scores were sometimes 'estimated', and rated according to eminence.

The term phrenology was coined by Spurzheim, rather than Gall. Spurzheim was an early follower of Gall, who fell out with him over the number of faculties to be included in the system of phrenology. He was to prove a successful proselytizer of phrenology, touring Europe, Great Britain and the USA to advertise the system. In the USA, Spurzheim particularly impressed the Fowlers and Wells, who established the firm of Fowler and Wells (described by Bakan (1966) as the antecedent of the Psychology Corporation) to provide phrenological services, including the publication of popular books. Phrenology continued in the USA into the twentieth century, the Institute of Phrenology staying in business until 1912. In the USA, phrenology was very much an applied discipline, using phrenological examinations to predict such things as an individual's ability or suitability for employment. Phrenology popularized the notion in the USA of an applied science of the mind, both in institutional settings and for the broader public.

Ultimately, phrenology failed because of doubts about the validity of the theory and about its scientific basis. However, the market for mentalistic expertise created by phrenology was readily embraced by the mental testing movement that developed at the start of the twentieth century. The development of the mental testing movement depended on the work of Francis Galton in Britain during the latter half of the nineteenth century. Galton, a cousin of Charles Darwin, was a committed hereditarian who looked for evidence of the variability of characteristics that was necessary for evolution to operate. Fundamental to this exercise was the use of measurement, to identify how characteristics vary amongst individuals in a population. Galton therefore developed a range of measurements of both physical and mental characteristics, believing that mental characteristics were inherited in the same way as physical characteristics. This belief in the inheritance of mental characteristics was first justified in his early work on the familial lineage of 'distinction', which culminated in the book *Hereditary genius* (1962). He followed this with more quantitative work, based on the laws of deviation from the mean developed by Quételet. Quételet had shown that numerical measures of physical characteristics conformed to a normal distribution. From this Galton reasoned that any inherited characteristic followed such a distribution, and when he found that scores on a Cambridge mathematics exam also followed a normal distribution, he concluded that intellectual ability must be inherited also. There are a number of flaws of reasoning here, particularly in assuming that only inherited characteristics would show a normal distribution. However, his conclusions were widely accepted.

Following on from this, and work on the familial incidence of eminence, Galton developed an interest in the relative influences of nature and nurture. He initially investigated this using a questionnaire distributed to members of the Royal Society, the first recorded such use of a questionnaire, and then developed the method of twin studies. These twin studies compared monozygotic and dizygotic twins, and thus represent an early use of control groups in psychological research. He came to strongly hereditarian conclusions, consistent with his earlier belief, and this led to his advocacy of a programme of positive eugenics, whereby the 'best' people would be encouraged to breed. In order to advance his eugenic programme Galton believed it was important to be able to identify the best scientifically, and so he conducted a large-scale programme of anthropological measurement which allowed the collection of large sets of physiological data. To make sense of this data, he developed the concepts of correlation and regression to the mean, and encouraged Pearson to develop mathematical procedures to calculate an index of correlation.

Galton is famous for applying quantitative measures to any phenomenon of interest. However, unlike Darwin and later Cattell, who relied on Baconian induction, Galton started with a problem and looked for means of addressing the problem in quantitative terms, in some senses anticipating the development of the hypothetico-deductive method, although he was happy to induce conclusions having gathered sufficient data. His lasting contributions to Psychology were largely methodological, by showing the value of physical and mental measurement using test batteries, showing the relevance of the normal distribution, introducing the concepts of correlation and regression, making systematic use of questionnaires, and introducing the control group through twin studies. These advances, developed in the service of a programme of eugenics, were assimilated into mainstream methodology, and were important to the development of a functional science of behaviour.

In Europe, Galton's individual Psychology ran counter to the goal of finding the universal features of the human mind, although some work on individual differences was conducted in Britain and Austria. In the USA however, due in part to the less rigid American university system, individual difference Psychology quickly grew, and by World War One accounted for over half of research papers presented at APA meetings. In the American social context, Galtonian individual Psychology fitted the goals of developing a technology for social change. The main conduit for Galton's ideas was Cattell, who met with Galton in Britain, having previously been taught by Wündt and Hall. Cattell was galvanized by Galton's approach, and brought anthropometric testing and British statistics to the USA. These ideas were adopted by Jastrow, notable mainly as a popularizer of Psychology, who strongly advocated the use of Galton's methods and arranged a public anthropometric testing laboratory at the Chicago Expo of 1893. The idea of individual testing and comparison would not have been new to an American public used to applied phrenology.

THE MENTAL TESTING MOVEMENT

As described earlier, mental testing has its origins in the work of Galton, whose work was introduced to the USA and widely popularized by Cattell. Cattell was a product of an education steeped in mental and moral philosophy, and Protestant values. He was also strongly influenced by Baconian inductivism – a belief that if you collect enough data, significant patterns will emerge. This is in contrast to the dominant position in experimental psychology, of deductivism, whereby theories are developed and then later tested against data. Inductivism, while marginal to experimental Psychology, has been important, if only implicitly, in the development of individual difference Psychology. Cattell was a hereditarian, although he accepted some degree of environmental influence, and was a believer in eugenics, offering his children $1,000 apiece to marry the child of a professor. Given this, his commitment to individual difference Psychology is unsurprising.

Cattell followed the well-worn path to Germany, but stopped at Cambridge on the way back. During his time in Britain, he met Galton and was impressed by the range of procedures Galton had developed for measuring individual differences. On his return to the USA in 1889 he was made Professor of Psychology at the University of Pennsylvania, where he refined Galton's procedures to develop a battery of tests he called 'mental tests and measurements' – the first use of the term – which he believed would be useful 'to training, mode of life or indication of disease' (Cattell 1890). He further refined these tests following a move to Columbia, developing a battery that consisted largely of sensory and reaction time tests.

Cattell's tests inspired similar efforts from others, for example Sanford extended Franz Boas's anthropometric tests to schoolchildren and Wolfe advocated the use of mental tests in the school system. At the Chicago Expo in 1893 Jastrow and Boas collaborated in running a testing laboratory, with Boas administering physical anthropological measurements and Jastrow administering extensions of Cattell's mental tests, having taken suggestions from Galton. Following the expo, Cattell, Jastrow, Sanford, Baldwin and

Witmer collaborated on the development of a battery of physical and mental tests for administration to college students. Reporting to the APA in 1897, the group recommended the application of anthropometric tests and the Columbia mental tests, and rejected tests of complex mental processes. This in part reflects American Psychology's aversion to consideration of mental processing – Münsterberg criticized the inclusion of any mental tests, claiming that 'psychical facts' could not be measured.

While Galton and Cattell's tests relied on physical and sensory/perceptual measurements, an alternative approach was to measure more complex mental phenomena, an example being the completion tests devised by Ebbinghaus in the mid-1890s to measure the effect of five-hour school sessions. This basic strategy was adopted by Binet to develop tests of ability for the identification of children needing remedial education. The Binet test (later the Binet-Simon scale) consisted of a graded series of tasks and problems, categorized by the abilities of a 'normal' child at a particular age. The level of test attained by a child was their 'mental level' , later mistranslated as 'mental age', with a range of consequences.

Binet's tests, developed out of the French clinical tradition, seemed to fit well with the project of individual difference Psychology. However, they were initially rejected by American psychologists. Cattell cautioned that it was hard to be sure that they measured real psychological phenomena, a criticism that can still be applied today (see, for example, Richards 1996). Sharp (Sokal 1997) observed that the individual tests were independent from each other, and hence they were useless. This finding would not concern Binet, who believed that intelligence was multifaceted and changeable, and his scale was only usable in a specific educational context. However, American psychologists wanted tests that would reliably classify individuals in the same way, which would later lead to an acceptance of unitary views of intelligence.

At Columbia, Cattell introduced mental testing of incoming students, which he later correlated with academic achievement. He found that test results did not correlate with achievement, suggesting that his tests were not measuring intellectual ability. This led to disillusionment with the use of such tests. Scripture and Jastrow both abandoned their use, and Witmer focused on clinical applications. The tests continued to find applications in specialized applied tasks, and were used in investigating racial and gender differences and in promoting eugenics. Apart from popularizing such testing, Cattell's enduring influence on Psychology came from his proselytizing of applied Psychology, through the publication of the *Psychological Review* and editorship of *Science*, the establishment of the Psychological Corporation, and membership of the American Association for the Advancement of Science and the National Academy of Sciences. However, the primary tool of mental testing came to be a modification of Binet's tests, initially developed by Goddard.

Goddard graduated with a PhD from Hall's programme at Clark. After a short period teaching, he set up a research programme at a school for the 'feeble minded'. Initially, he used tasks similar to Cattell's, but on a tour of similar European institutions he came across Binet's tests. He translated the scales, and found they compared well with the observed abilities of his children. Goddard gave precise technical definitions to the terms 'idiot' (mental age (MA) 1–2) and 'imbecile' (MA 3–7), and invented the term 'moron' (MA 8–12). This development of a technical language helped legitimize the professionalization of Psychology. Goddard's claim (shared by others) was that morons damaged society, but could only be identified by carefully trained professionals – psychologists. Thus the concerns of Social Darwinists also created a marketplace for Psychology, a symbiotic relationship that certainly did not damage the development of applied Psychology, and by extension the nature of applied Psychology.

Goddard's translated scales quickly gained popularity in the USA, but it soon became apparent that the purpose to which they were being put was somewhat different from that envisaged by Binet. Goddard believed that intelligence was inherited and unchangeable, and recent advances in genetics led him to believe that feeble mindedness was caused by a single recessive gene. In support of this, he published the Kallikak case study. This view led Goddard to adopt a eugenicist stance, and he recommended that the feeble minded should be institutionalized or sterilized.

Goddard had a clear view that portions of USA society were unfit. However, he was also concerned – as many were – that the increasing number of immigrants were importing further mental deficiency. Largely this was because the 'old' immigrants were from northern and western Europe, while the 'new' immigrants were largely from southern and eastern Europe – anathema to the existing, predominantly WASP population. Few middle-class Americans at the time really believed in the sentiment that the USA was a haven for the poor and oppressed of other lands.

An immigration centre was established on Ellis Island in 1892, and one of its tasks was to screen out the mentally defective. However, there was concern that this was not succeeding – enter Goddard with his tests. He claimed that his tests could pick out defectives with over 90 per cent accuracy, a reflection of his naïve faith in the tests. Even when his research assistants expressed doubts about the tests' validity, Goddard persisted. The expansion of mental testing at Ellis Island led to a large increase in deportations on the grounds of mental deficiency, by 350 per cent in 1913 and 570 per cent in 1914.

Although Goddard made use of the Binet-Simon scale, it was not entirely suited to American purposes. The next stage in the development of testing in the USA came from Terman, who joined the faculty at Stanford, where he built the Psychology department into one of the country's finest. His main contribution to mental testing was the revision of the Binet scales, and their standardization – an important step in the development of psychometrics. In 1916 he produced the Stanford-Binet scale, which quickly dominated the American market and remains the gold standard amongst IQ tests. The scale included the first use of the term IQ, based on the German Stern's earlier use of the concept of a 'mental quotient'. This change fitted in with Terman's view of intelligence as unitary – Binet never believed intelligence could be measured with a single number – and helped to fix and legitimize the concept. The ability to produce a seemingly valid, interval level measurement of intelligence was important in expanding the range of applications of the concept. It also fitted in with the desire for tests that could be used to categorize individuals according to a single, easily obtained measure. Terman used his scale to identify both the feeble minded and the gifted, believing that by identifying and nurturing the gifted a meritocracy could be achieved. Terman had a vision of a stratified democracy, wherein one's opportunities depended on one's abilities as measured by the IQ test.

Although Terman's test proved useful, the need for it to be administered on individuals restricted its applicability. With the advent of World War One Robert Yerkes, facing institutional pressure to produce useful Psychology, persuaded the US army of the value of mass psychological testing. This involved a change to testing procedures, since the Binet procedure was designed for individual administration. During the period 1917–18, Yerkes and his team tested 1.7 m recruits using new group tests, the Army Alpha and Beta, described in Gould (1996). The War ended in 1918, with the testing having made no real contribution, but the mass programme had an important effect in legitimizing testing, and thus Psychology, particularly through the production of large scale tests which could be sold to industry. Yerkes, Terman and others saw this form of testing as leading to the establishment of psychology as a 'science of human engineering'.

Although mental testing initially concentrated on measuring intelligence, the development of such tests brought together all the elements necessary for the extension of testing to other areas. The statistical and methodological procedures used to standardize tests, apply them to groups, and compare results, could be used with any psychological phenomenon for which a suitable measurement could be designed. While academic Psychology concentrated on behaviour, individual difference Psychology extended into considering personality, attitudes, and psychopathology. This led to increased opportunities for applied Psychology in education, industry and clinical practice.

PSYCHOLOGY'S FIRST MARKET – EDUCATION

It is often suggested Psychology's first area of application was education (for example, Danziger 1990), and the links between Psychology and education were to prove important in establishing Psychology and shaping both its theories and its methodology. Much applied educational Psychology today depends on mental testing, but even before the development of such tests psychologists were using their expertise to guide educational practice. This was particularly the case in the USA and France, though the particular form of the relationship differed in the two societies. In the USA, Psychology provided ideas to guide the reform of general education, while in France Psychology's roots in abnormal clinical practice shaped its application to education. Even in Germany, where applied

Psychology was very slow in developing, the psychology which was applied was pedagogical.

The rapid application of Psychology to education reflected a perceived crisis in education, and a desire to enhance the professional status of teaching by basing it on scientific theories. For Psychology, the chance to apply expertise to education provided a suitable area for the legitimization of the discipline as a socially useful science. In most areas, opportunities for the application of psychology were constrained by a lack of support from policy makers and by a lack of institutional links. In education however, previous links between old psychology and education set a precedent for the use of psychological expertise. Once Psychology had legitimized its usefulness to education, it was then able to argue for its application in other areas.

The application of the new Psychology to education in the USA began with the work of G. Stanley Hall, who started the child study movement. Hall was a confirmed evolutionist, influenced by Spencer and taught by James at Harvard. The PhD he completed at Harvard is often considered to be the first Psychology doctorate awarded in America. Following this he went to Leipzig, claiming to have been Wündt's first American student, although this is incorrect (Benjamin, Durkin, Link, Vestal and Accord 1992). While in Germany he toured German laboratories, and was introduced to recapitulation by Haeckel. On his return to the USA however he had difficulty in finding employment. His response was to investigate the application of psychology to education, for which he toured schools in Germany, France and Britain. This work led to invitations to lecture on pedagogy to local teachers at Harvard and at Johns Hopkins. The success of these talks led to Hall being offered a part-time lectureship and then a chair at Johns Hopkins, titled Professor of Psychology and Pedagogy.

Hall's position at Johns Hopkins gave him an opportunity to shape strongly the development of American Psychology. He established the first true research laboratory in America, soon followed by other universities, and taught Cattell, Dewey, Jastrow and Sanford. His success led to an offer to become President of the newly instituted Clark University, which he established on the lines of European research universities. As President, he became the great organizer of American Psychology, establishing the APA. His work concentrated on psychology and pedagogy from an evolutionary perspective. At Clark he established summer schools for local teachers and published the journal *Pedagogical seminary*. His research made extensive use of questionnaires – he often claimed to be the originator of the technique, but Galton used them first – and was strongly influenced by his views on recapitulation. This commitment led to him identifying different stages of the lifespan, associating each with different stages in the development of the species. His prescriptions for teaching and training over the lifespan differed according to each stage, and were shaped by his analogy with phylogenetic development. He advocated school reform, arguing that schools should be made more child centred.

Hall's child study movement was essentially conservative, concentrating on the collection of data to profile the development of children. In this, Hall was joined by Cattell and Sanford, who used anthropometric testing to collect data on children. Alternative approaches were developed by Dewey and by Witmer. Dewey saw the mind as an instrument of adaptation, and believed that schools should help the mind's adaptation to the environment through appropriate education. He established a laboratory to investigate the learning processes of children, with an emphasis on active engagement in learning. He began the progressive education movement, designed to guide the reform of school education, but his wider aim was to achieve a progressive society, using understanding of the scientific laws of behaviour to plan society as a whole on a rational basis.

While Dewey's emphasis was on the reform of education of normal children, Witmer adopted a clinical approach to children's learning. He established a 'psychology clinic', which is often seen as the origin of clinical Psychology but had a greater influence on the development of educational Psychology. Witmer was concerned with therapeutic intervention with children who would today be labelled 'learning disabled'. His clinic took children who had been referred through the school system, and administered anthropo-, opto-, and psychometric tests to arrive at a diagnosis, which was then used in the design of a therapeutic regime. This concern with rehabilitation contributed to the growth of environmentalism and the emphasis on behaviour. However, it was somewhat at odds with other approaches to learning disability, particularly that of Goddard. While Witmer used psychological tests to evaluate the effectiveness of interventions, Goddard used them to confirm existing social diagnoses of feeble mindedness. The contrast between Witmer and Goddard is an interesting example of how the approach taken to research affects psychological theory. Goddard applied his tests in fixed institutional settings with no attempt to effect change, and found that feeble mindedness was a stable characteristic. Witmer however used a range of methods to achieve rehabilitation, and found that feeble mindedness was caused at least in part by environmental factors, and could be remediated by environmental interventions. Despite the success of Witmer's interventions, Goddard's hereditarian approach prevailed in mental testing and individual difference Psychology. Witmer's approach was largely assimilated into education departments, but had an enduring influence on the child guidance movement.

Psychology's application to education soon extended beyond prescriptions for education and assessment of the feeble minded. With the increasing urbanization of American society and the extension of compulsory universal education, educational administrators soon turned to psychologists for help in shaping education to the needs of an industrial society. For administrators, the descriptive data collected by Hall was insufficient. What was needed was comparative data on the performance of groups in different conditions, that could be used to evaluate alternative educational practices. The emphasis in this approach was on the measurement of outcomes, rather than the investigation of mental processes, and this required a shift in methodology. This shift in methodology, designed for a particular application, was soon extended to other applied areas and to academic Psychology (Danziger 1990).

The form of application required by educational administrators demanded investigative practices that produced statistical knowledge, and particularly information about average performance in different conditions. For administrators, information about individuals was only useful for the purposes of categorization, for which an individual's performance was compared to the group average. Whereas previous individualistic Psychology such as Binet's had investigated individuals' styles of functioning, termed typology, this new approach of comparing performances against an average required that mental processes must be the same for all members of a group. The methodology demanded that there could not be qualitative differences between individuals, only quantitative. This was in part a consequence of the dominant view of what mental tests were measuring, but the application of the methodology lent support to the view. It was of course possible to find individual differences in scores on a test, and these findings could be used to confirm that there were quantitative differences. However, the findings could also be explained in qualitative terms – one individual's functioning style may be less successful than another's. Such explanations were not pursued because of an a priori commitment to being able to categorize individuals on a continuous scale.

The desire to compare an individual's performance to a group average required the establishment of norms of performance. Testers were measuring against set criteria, which were determined by the area of application and by the requirements of the sponsors of the test. These criteria were of course socially determined, by existing views of which criteria were important and which were not. For example, an intelligence test may value linguistic and mathematical ability rather than artistic and creative ability. Such a decision is shaped by the values of the society within which the test is designed, rather than any necessary primacy of those skills.

Having developed a range of mental tests, and norms of performance, the focus of research and application became distributions of scores rather than individuals. Initially such research was correlational, identifying which factors are linked, but the development of techniques for the experimental manipulation of groups and of relevant statistical tests gave administrators the ability to compare different practices. In particular, to evaluate a particular educational technique the investigator could create a treatment group, which received the new technique, and a control group which did not. The scores of these two groups could then be compared. The results of such investigations apply to the particular groups in the particular contexts of the tests, but soon psychologists went beyond this to make claims about general psychological processes and phenomena, based on statistical estimates of population, rather than sample, characteristics. Although developed for a particular application, this approach had a limited impact on applied Psychology, partly because it was often difficult to organize such studies in institutional settings and partly because much applied work was concerned with categorization. However the approach came to dominate academic

Psychology, based on the assumption that the results of such research revealed universal laws of human behaviour.

INDUSTRIAL PSYCHOLOGY

The development of mental testing opened a wide range of opportunities for the application of psychology to business, as phrenology had been. However, before mental testing became established there was a significant amount of work done in the area of industrial Psychology. A number of individuals were influential in this work, including Walter Dill Scott, who advocated the application of psychology to advertising, arguing that psychology could be used to influence people through suggestion and appeals to emotion. He also published work on the use of psychology in improving industrial efficiency. More notable was Münsterberg, who had followed James as head of the psychology laboratory at Harvard. Münsterberg was a prolific author, producing some two dozen books as well as a number of articles in popular magazines. Although originally an experimental psychologist, he became increasingly interested in the application of psychology. He produced important work in forensic Psychology, including observations on the unreliability of eyewitness testimony and hypnosis, and on the environmental causes of criminality. He also did early work in clinical Psychology, developing a form of psychotherapy. His main influence, however, was in industrial Psychology, where he applied the results of psychology experiments to a range of problems in business, including employee selection, productivity, and the design of work.

There were a number of other pioneering industrial psychologists in the pre-World War One period. Walter Van Dyke Bingham created a then unique Division of Applied Psychology at Carnegie Institute of Technology (now Carnegie-Mellon University) and re-established the Psychological Corporation after the departure of Cattell. Lilian Gilbreth pioneered time and motion studies with her husband Frank, and later the study of ergonomics. Finally, Harry Hollingworth became famous for defending Coca-Cola against charges of damaging public health with the inclusion of caffeine, and became a popular consulting psychologist in a range of areas. Ironically, Hollingworth always preferred his pure research to his applied work.

During this period, the application of psychology was encouraged by a progressive view of the scientific management of business, including of personnel. However, pre-World War One opportunities for industrial application were limited. Following the War, Yerkes in particular advertised the great success Psychology had achieved in managing personnel problems in the army, particularly through the use of mental testing. This gave a big boost to industrial Psychology, helped by the publication of some influential research such as that identifying the Hawthorne effect (although this has been shown to be a myth, Bramel and Friend 1981). The scope of the discipline increased during this area, for example, through the introduction of personnel counselling, and Witmer's clinical work was to lead to the development of career guidance. Although the basis of industrial Psychology has been criticized for concentrating on the creation of happy automata and deflecting workers from valid concerns about their working conditions (Baritz 1960) business has remained convinced of its value.

CLINICAL PSYCHOLOGY

Clinical Psychology, as currently practised, is a post World War Two development. However, its origins can be traced to 1896, when Witmer created the first psychological clinic. This clinic had a greater effect on the development of educational Psychology and the child guidance movement, and was somewhat at odds with most pre World War One clinical Psychology, but it is sometimes used by disciplinary historians to show clinical Psychology's heritage. Here, we shall look briefly at the Witmer model, and at mainstream clinical Psychology before and after World War Two.

Lightner Witmer replaced Cattell as director of the Psychology laboratory at the University of Pennsylvania in 1892. In 1896, a schoolteacher brought him a child who, despite general competence, had great difficulty with spelling. After thorough examination, Witmer realized that the child had sight problems, and after these problems were addressed the child's spelling improved. Inspired by this, Witmer established a psychological clinic, whose focus was on the diagnosis of and therapeutic intervention in school related problems in children. The clinic proved popular, and achieved considerable success in intervening to help children with learning difficulties. At the end of 1896, Witmer presented a paper to the APA proposing the establishment of a programme for practical work in Psychology, concentrating on therapeutic intervention. In this, he called for the teaching of psychology to doctors and teachers, and for closer relationships between Psychology and medical schools and educational authorities. He also established the journal *Psychological Clinic* and coined the term 'clinical Psychology'. As described previously, his clinical model was to have considerable influence on educational Psychology, and inspired the development of vocational clinics offering career guidance to adolescents and adults, creating career counselling. In combination with ideas from the mental hygiene movement, his clinic formed the model of practice for the child guidance movement.

Despite the range of influences Witmer's clinic had, claims that he founded clinical Psychology are based more on terminology than on actual practice. Mainstream clinical Psychology before World War Two was influenced more by the mental testing movement, with its hereditarian bias, and the mental hygiene movement. The mental hygiene movement created a demand for consideration of mental health, and mental testing provided the tools to achieve this. However, clinical Psychology found itself in a difficult position. In considering mental health, there was some overlap with the practice of psychiatry, which was growing in influence following World War One. In professional practice, psychiatrists were concerned about encroachment from clinical Psychology, and established stronger links with universities, traditionally a strength of the psychologists. In the face of such competition, the clinical psychologists looked to the APA to support them, but the APA was at that stage more concerned with promoting academic Psychology. The clinicians found themselves concentrating on the administration of mental tests, sometimes within companies or as consultants, and sometimes as low status workers within hospital clinics dominated by psychiatrists.

During the inter-war period applied psychologists, and clinical psychologists in particular, tried several times to achieve increased recognition within the APA, by obtaining associate membership. Full membership however remained the preserve of those who had published scientific research, which most clinical psychologists did not do. Another concession was the creation of a section for clinical psychologists within the APA. However, tensions remained. In 1930 a group of applied psychologists established the Association of Consulting Psychologists (ACP), and in 1938 the clinical psychologists left the APA and merged with the ACP to form the American Association for Applied Psychology. One of the things the clinicians had looked to the APA for was the establishment of a profession of psychologist, but a rather weak attempt at introducing certification for testers failed, since it had no legal force. The attempt to establish professional status was not helped by the number of untrained individuals offering psychological services.

The depression helped to establish the need for professional status for Psychology, mainly because a lack of academic posts meant many more psychologists were becoming involved in applied work. However, before World War Two clinical psychologists remained in a very weak position. This position was to change very quickly following the War with clinical psychologists finding themselves valued, in demand and having professional status. During the War psychologists were in great demand by both the military and business, in areas including selection, training and morale. Given the great demand for psychological services, and the need for efficient management of these services, psychologists established a central agency, the office of Psychological Personnel, to place psychologists in appropriate posts. This office began the reunification of Psychology, which was to lead to the re-creation of the APA along federal lines, giving equal status to its various constituents, including academic and applied psychologists. One of the goals of this new APA was to be the advancement of Psychology as a profession. In part, the organizers had their minds on Psychology's role in the reconstruction of postwar society.

As well as establishing Psychology as a profession, the War had the effect, as had World War One earlier, of showing the value of Psychology to society. It also created greatly expanded job opportunities for applied psychologists in general, and clinical psychologists in particular. The greatest effect was in the creation of demand for psychotherapy. Large numbers of servicemen returning from the War were facing problems in recovering from their experiences and readjusting to civilian life. There were not sufficient psychiatrists to cope with this demand, and in any case psychiatry was mainly concerned with abnormality, and no one wanted to claim that the large numbers of veterans with adjustment problems were abnormal. In order to provide the necessary services, the Veterans' Association (VA) established guidance centres, which included the provision of counselling. This provision was to form the basis of the profession of counselling Psychology. For more serious cases, the VA established training courses in clinical Psychology. Now, however, clinical psychologists were involved in the provision of therapy and diagnosis, not just in administering tests. The training provided by the VA courses defined modern clinical Psychology. The acceptance of widespread counselling and therapy was helped by the veterans' experiences of Psychology during their service. During the War psychologists did more than reactively provide remedial services. As part of their work on morale, they were proactively involved in helping to maintain the mental health of soldiers, through the provision of training and publications. At the War's end, most returning servicemen had had experience of psychological services, and had been convinced of their value. For American Psychology then, the War had the effect of establishing Psychology as a profession, and of changing the social role of psychologists.

CONCLUSION

We opened the chapter by considering some of the social contexts that encouraged the growth of applied Psychology in the USA. These included a general expectation on the part of society, and of psychologists as members of that society, that science should produce socially useful knowledge outcomes. In addition, there were particular institutional pressures that led psychologists to actively apply their findings, including the need to justify the cost to universities of Psychology departments, a desire to establish a distinct identity from philosophy, and the need of psychologists to earn a living or to supplement their incomes.

We then looked at some of the antecedents of applied Psychology. We saw that before the new Psychology was established in the USA, phrenology had positioned itself as a science of the mind that could be used to improve the human condition, creating an acceptance of the possibility of this. Notably, phrenology enjoyed success in the USA for somewhat longer than in Europe, where there was less concern with self-improvement. We also looked at the work of Francis Galton in the development of mental testing, and of methods for application of such tests and for analysing the results. We saw that Galton was in part motivated by a need to select fit and unfit individuals as part of a programme of eugenics. The notion of selection of individuals required the development of particular mathematical techniques, which form the basis of most investigative practice in modern Psychology. Galton's work found limited acceptance in Europe outside of the eugenics movement, but proved appealing to American Psychology, due largely to differing social contexts. Galton probably has a greater claim to foundational status for American Psychology than Wündt, certainly in terms of effect, but early histories of

Psychology barely mentioned him. This could be due in part to the demise of the eugenics movement and his association with it.

After considering Galton, we looked at the development of mental testing, which remains a significant element of applied Psychology. Such testing was very much influenced by Galton, but also by the work of Binet. However, the development of mental tests in the USA was predicated on very different concerns to Binet's original work. While Binet had concentrated on careful assessment of the individual, the tests developed in the USA were concerned with categorizing individuals against a group norm. Binet's intentions were remedial, whereas the American tests were devices for classification. These differences were very much a result of the different contexts in the USA and France, and had important effects on the development of theory. The contrast between Goddard and Witmer, introduced in considering Psychology's links with education, is illustrative of this. In considering mental tests, we also looked briefly at the social uses these tests were put to. The relationship between testing and social policy is considered in more depth in Chapter 6.

In looking at the links that existed between Psychology and education, we saw that education provided an arena for Psychology to legitimize its value as a practical subject. Several trends were identified, including prescriptions for teaching and training, as characterized by Hall and Dewey; remediation of children's school related problems, initially characterized by Witmer, but later to be a major part of educational Psychology; and the use of psychological theories and techniques in guiding educational practice. The methodological developments necessary to enable such use were to have a major impact on investigative practice and by consequence theory development in academic Psychology. More widely, the legitimacy gained through application to education enabled Psychology to claim applicability in other areas.

Psychology quickly applied itself to the problems of business, guided by the progressive ideal of scientific management. As well as the use of mental tests in selection, Psychology was applied to advertising, workplace design and efficiency. Perceptions of the validity of such applications were greatly enhanced by Psychology's role in both World Wars.

While Psychology in general benefited from its contribution to the War efforts, the greatest beneficiary was clinical Psychology. World War One enabled psychologists to establish themselves within psychiatric departments, but in a subordinate role to psychiatrists focused on the administration of tests. The alternative model of clinical practice provided by Witmer was rejected, partly because of a widespread hereditarian view that characteristics were fixed. If this is the case, then psychologists can only classify, not remediate, mental disorders. World War Two established Psychology as a profession and enhanced the status of clinical psychologists. It also created opportunities for psychologists to be involved in the provision of counselling and therapy. The development of clinical Psychology gives a clear indication of the importance of war in the development of Psychology.

A number of the themes in this chapter concern Psychology's relationship with its host society. These are discussed in more detail in Chapter 6. That chapter also gives a comparison between the development of Psychology in the USA and in Germany. We shall see that a differing social context retarded the development of applied Psychology in Germany, until the rise of the Nazi party created a demand for the same kind of expertise that psychologists in the USA were providing.

FURTHER READING

Benjamin, L., Rogers, A. and Rosenbaum, A. 1997: Coca-Cola, caffeine, and mental deficiency: Harry Hollingworth and the Chattanooga trial of 1911. In: L. Benjamin (ed.) *A history of psychology: original sources and contemporary research*, 2nd edn. Boston, MA: McGraw Hill.

Cernovsky, Z.Z. 1997: A critical look at intelligence research. In: D. Fox and I. Prilleltensky *Critical psychology: an introduction*. London: Sage.

Diamond, S. 1997: Francis Galton and American psychology. In: L.L.Benjamin (ed.) *A history of psychology: original sources and contemporary research*, 2nd edn. Boston, MA: McGraw Hill.

Fancher, R.E. 1985: *The intelligence men*. New York: W.W. Norton and Company.

Goodwin, C.J. 1999: *A history of modern psychology*. New York: John Wiley.

Gould, S.J. 1996, revised: *The mismeasure of man*. London: Penguin.

Herman, E. 1995: *The romance of American psychology*. Berkeley, University of California Press.

Journal of the History of the Behavioural Sciences 1997: Historians and the Bell Curve controversies: A Special Symposium 33(2), 127–62.

Leahey, T.H. 2000: *A history of psychology*, 5th edn. New Jersey: Prentice-Hall.

M.M Sokal. (ed.) 1987: *Psychological testing and American Society*. New Brunswick, NJ: Rutgers University Press.

O'Donnell, J.M. 1997: The clinical psychology of Lightner Witmer: a case study of institutional innovation and intellectual change. In: L. Benjamin (ed.) *A history of psychology: original sources and contemporary research*, 2nd edn. Boston, MA: McGraw Hill.

5

PSYCHOANALYSIS AND PSYCHOLOGY

The relationship between psychoanalysis and Psychology is a complex one. At times the two have been identified as one discipline, for example, in the writings about the 'new Psychology' of the 1920s when insights from psychoanalysis, instinct theories and behaviourism were combined. At other times the two have been treated as distinct, most often when comparing the experimental part of the discipline with psychoanalysis. Today the picture is confusing, with it being a psychological fact that many people, both within and outside the discipline, identify Freud as a psychologist. Others view psychoanalysis as nothing to do with Psychology and yet others see the two as perhaps competing disciplines which cover some of the same subject matter but aim towards different ends.

It is perhaps the last formulation that best describes our view. The boundaries between the disciplines may be more porous than many psychologists would wish to admit. All attempts to police boundaries between disciplines have, as one of their purposes, something to say about the way a particular discipline identifies itself. In this respect, popular conceptions of Psychology and the way that practitioners of Psychology see themselves may differ. The boundary seems to be of far more importance to us, as psychologists, than it is to people in general. As with the rest of this book we do not intend to pretend an even handed neutrality. Instead an attempt will be made to highlight our positions and to critically examine these at the same time that we critically examine the intertwining of psychoanalysis and Psychology.

In common with many undergraduate psychology students of my generation what I was taught about psychoanalysis was a quick dismissal of Freud. No mention, that I remember, was made of other depth psychologists and we 'did' Freud in two lectures on the general introduction course. Some five years later when I lectured part-time on an O level in child development psychology, part of the syllabus was to teach students that Freudian theory was unscientific. Later I encountered feminist critiques of Freud, and later still I developed a reading of social constructionist trends in Psychology that led me to be very dismissive of notions of the unconscious. When I first became a higher education lecturer I did not understand why Freud was on the syllabus and, I suspect like many, over identified psychoanalysis with Freud. Yet psychoanalysis continues to have a relationship with Psychology: first, in the way that Freud is used as an antagonist, with his methods and his theorizing attacked and second, in the continuing interest in Freud and psychoanalysis, with the interest by, for example, feminist writers and discourse analysts in using psychoanalytic concepts. Finally, insofar that Psychology takes as its object of study the everyday psychologizing of people, Freud still has a continuing influence on this. If, after, behaviourism, most of the discipline's practitioners became, at least, methodological behaviourists, then after over a century of influence most of the participants in our studies are lay psychoanalysts.

The intention of this chapter is not to give yet another way to attack Freudian psychoanalysis. Instead it is to question the reasons why suspicion has grown up between Psychology and Psychoanalysis. Neither is it our intention to act as apologists for Freud. Insofar as we do, it is as part of an internal argument within a discipline that has too readily dismissed psychoanalytic approaches, while at the same time coopting some of the ideas from psychoanalysis to ensure that Psychology retains a market appeal.

A BRIEF INTRODUCTION TO PSYCHOANALYSIS

Psychoanalysis is a large and complex topic, encompassing a mission to understand human psychology which is linked to therapeutic change and which has been developed into a social theory. There are a multitude of current approaches to psychoanalysis, in some, such as the work of Erikson the role of the Ego is expanded, in others such as Jungian psychoanalysis, the nature of the subconscious is different from Freud's approach. However all of them have at their root Freud's work, and given constraints of space this introduction will concentrate on that.

For the purposes of this chapter we are interested in the ways that psychoanalytic ideas about the development of children have interacted with Psychology, the overlap between personality Psychology and psychoanalysis and the area of clinical application. In this introduction we will review these areas. There are a number of other areas that could be pursued and in particular there is a one area where debate will be delayed until Chapter 15 – the overlap between psychoanalysis and interpretative theories of social Psychology.

The starting point in any introduction to psychoanalysis has to be Freud. While the psychoanalytic movement has diversified considerably since his time and his writing, and there are now schools of thought that have rejected some of Freud's ideas, all of these psychoanalytic theories have their roots in Freud's work. It is also necessary to limit our focus, given that this is one chapter and this topic could easily encompass a book. We hope that the analysis we develop below is at least extendable to other forms of psychoanalysis.

The first and most important of these ideas is that of a dynamic unconsciousness. By this is meant an area of the mind not normally open to conscious awareness that can influence, or direct, the conscious mind and that is in turn influenced or directed by the physical and social environment of which the person is a part. The exact structure of this unconscious arena of mental life is an area of debate between psychoanalysts, and its role in Freud's theory underwent modification as he wrote. For most psychoanalysts it is made up of the residue of infantile experiences, and for many, alongside biological instincts or drives, particularly sexual ones. Early childhood experience, primarily the experiences with their parents up to about age four and five, are seen as being of crucial importance and while details differ on the exact development process for children there is a commonality in the notion that children progress through stages. These lead to the structures of the unconscious that adults have, and once fully formed these become difficult to change.

The basic approach to unearthing this unconscious dynamic mental structure in an adult is through the intense examination of cultural phenomena, from slips of the tongue, dreams, works of arts and the contents of neurosis. For most psychoanalysts the place where this most easily happens is the therapeutic encounter. It is evidence from these encounters that allows for theorizing about processes across peoples as well as being the site at which psychoanalysts can attempt to alter, or ameliorate the effects of, the unconscious dynamics for a particular individual. Much more than most approaches in Psychology the approaches in psychoanalysis are explicitly attempting to create a framework of understanding for human experience. In common with other theories of human nature there is a degree of self-fulfilling prophecy about psychoanalysis, as terms, concepts and ideas have become integrated into our cultural common sense. Our awareness of psychoanalysis has to some extent changed at a fundamental level our psychology, and in this psychoanalysis has been much more successful than any approach within Psychology to date.

The institutionalization of psychoanalysis is also worth commenting upon, especially as it follows a different course in Great Britain and the USA. Within the USA psychoanalysis is the exclusive province of medically trained psychiatrists, who receive their psychoanalytic training following their medical training. Within the UK, while that route is also available for psychiatrists, it is also possible for clinical psychologists to become psychoanalysts. Also within the UK, it is possible for other professionals, such as social workers or mental health nurses, to receive additional training in therapeutic interventions based on, amongst a range of alternatives, psychoanalysis. As counselling and counselling Psychology have proliferated, it is also possible for people to become qualified counsellors, or chartered counselling psychologists, who have at least some background in psychoanalysis.

One aspect of the training of people who become psychoanalysts that is replicated in the counselling approaches is the need for the trainee analyst to themselves undergo psychoanalysis. This has led to some critics of psychoanalysts to call psychoanalysis a cult, and for some criticisms of psychoanalysis to be dismissed as worthless because the authors of those criticisms have not themselves undergone analysis. The cult rhetoric, while appealing in terms of its power to undermine another's position, fails when some account is made of the notion that within all professional training, and to some extent academic study, there is a socialization process. This socialization process has at its root the need for the trainee, or student, to learn to use the discourses that are professed. At worst that process is a little more explicit in psychoanalytic training than in other areas of psychological practice.

Finally this chapter is open to the criticism that it is worthless because neither of the authors have been psychoanalysed. The best that can be said in our own defence is that we are not, as has become common in Freud criticism, going to use *ad hominem* attacks and can only hope that the same convention will apply to our writing.

EARLY POINTS OF DEPARTURE BETWEEN PSYCHOLOGY AND PSYCHOANALYSIS

One of the main arguments that is made later is that as the psychology of peoples was altered by the use of discourses from psychoanalysis, so Psychology needed to change in order to remain relevant to both its undergraduates and to the other consumers of its products. There are, however, some early points of difference between Psychology and psychoanalysis that are worth drawing attention to before the later dynamic is explored in any depth.

There are differences between Freud's scientific project and Wündt's scientific project to understand psychology. Wündt, as outlined earlier, limited his natural science project to immediate conscious experience, while Freud, showing a sensitivity towards this, called his project a 'meta-psychology'. Freud was interested in much more than the immediate contents of the conscious mind and while he still pursued the notion of a scientific discipline it was not to be a science based on the model of physics. Rather, it was to be more akin to biology.

The investigative practices used within psychoanalysis also differed from those available to psychologists. As outlined in Chapter 3, Psychology has at its roots three quite distinct nineteenth-century methodological practices: laboratory studies where trained observers reported on the contents of consciousness; the clinical experiment where physicians intervened in patients psychological processes with hypnosis; and the psychological survey, which used data from a group, or groups, within a population to make claims about individual psychological functioning.

For psychoanalysis the nineteenth-century medical model of clinical interview and clinical experiment was the method of investigative practice. Thus just like in general medicine an analysand presents a set of symptoms. The analyst checks these symptoms, using psychological techniques such as free association and dream interpretation rather than physical techniques, and then intervenes. That the domain of the psychoanalyst's office was both the centre of treatment and data gathering was again based on the prevailing medical model.

Psychology, especially in the USA as outlined in Chapter 3, rapidly became a discipline investigating behaviour rather than mind, a development that began before the advent of behaviourism as investigative practices moved away from the Wündtian laboratory. Psychoanalysis retained, and still retains, its focus on the mind. This may be in part why psychoanalysis continues to inform the discourses that people use about the ways that their minds operate in a way that Psychology has failed to do.

Ironically, given the use of aggregate data within Psychology, its main thrust became a much more individualized discipline than the main thrust of psychoanalysis. It is necessary to understand minds as cultural products in order to understand them. While psychoanalysis, especially under the sway of its own Americanization and some aspects of the psychiatric approach in medicine, also suffered from an individualizing influence, to a large extent it retained an awareness of the cultural setting, at least when practised in the USA and Europe. Psychoanalysis, like Psychology, was not immune to cultural imperialism and (broadly European) ethnocentricity when making claims about people from other cultures. In part, due to the continued awareness that minds are products of a social and cultural environment, psychoanalysis always had more of a potential for cultural critique than Psychology, especially those aspects of Psychology that relied on technological control rather than conceptual understanding to validate knowledge claims.

PSYCHOLOGY COOPTING PSYCHOANALYSIS

Developing a Theory of Motivation

Outside of the narrow focus of Wündt's natural science Psychology, there had been an interest in the 'energy that lies at the root of human behaviour' in the work of William James. In the inter-war period, as the focus of academic Psychology changed in the USA with the rise of the technology of behaviourism, the discipline lost the vocabulary to talk about these internal forces. At the same time, perhaps paradoxically, in the continuing struggle to be a useful discipline attention was turning to problems of the management of organizations.

At the same time there was a surge of interest in psychoanalysis, some of it in the form of new psychology in fields such as education and religious studies, some of it because of the popular accounts of Psychoanalysis being written. As today, some of the undergraduates coming to study Psychology came with an expectation that the academic discipline would provide material consonant with popular understandings of the discipline. At the same time, the popular framework for understanding psychology became influenced by psychoanalytic discourses and in order to give an understandable account of human action it became necessary to adopt some of the notions within everyday understandings of psychology.

Psychoanalytic theories were always more than just a theory of motivation, although the way that psychoanalysis would be re-presented within Psychology would be just that. With the development of a psychology of motivation and later a psychology of personality, the discipline could begin to answer some of the questions that it had been neglecting in its focus on the 'hows' rather than the 'whys' of human psychology. While psychoanalysis undoubtedly has some influence on this change within Psychology it is not the only influence. Within the field of intelligence testing there had been a growing recognition that intelligence in itself did not provide all of the answers that had been hoped for. Intelligence had become a much narrower concept in the early twentieth century than the terms that had preceded it. Indeed Galton, for example, more systematically used the term 'natural ability' rather than intelligence, defined in these terms:

> By natural ability I mean those qualities of intellect and disposition, which urge and qualify a man to perform acts that lead to reputation. I do not mean capacity without zeal, nor zeal without capacity, nor even a combination of both of them, without an adequate power of doing a great deal of very laborious work.
>
> (Galton 1962: 77)

Whatever the understanding of intelligence underlying the work of the intelligence tester, it did not include the notions of zeal nor of the adequate power to do laborious work. Just as in the case of intelligence, one of the forces driving an interest in a Psychology of motivation was education. In business management the problems of how to motivate staff were being introduced and so too in the Psychology of salesmanship. While the psychology of motivation has overlapping marketplaces, and is probably multiply determined, the differences and similarities between it and a psychoanalytical framework are instructive.

Throughout the book we have taken the approach that psychological categories are not ones that sciences such as physics investigate. By concentrating on motivation within this chapter we hope that the notion that psychologists help to create the psychological categories that we use in our everyday reasoning about our own and others' behaviour can be illustrated.

Following Danziger's analysis it is worth considering the word 'motive' itself. While the term has a long history, concentrating upon a single act the abstract form of motive, 'motivation', and the verb form, 'to motivate', are strikingly absent from the English language prior to the late nineteenth century. Even then they were not used in the modern sense. According to Danziger the only references are to the motivation of a turn of events in a novel. Thus, much like attitude, the term 'motivation' is used to describe an aspect of a work of art rather than something about human beings.

In the twentieth century there is an explosion in the usage of these two terms, with the notion that all acts are motivated, and that different people have different, general levels of motivation. In less than a century motivation has changed from an unused category to a part of our cultural common sense, and it is now treated as a natural concept. It is possible to obtain scales that measure an individual's general level of motivation, as well as asking questions about the motivation for a specific event. Questions on 'how to motivate' appear only to be asking for a technical description of what qualities are needed to affect individuals, whereas it is only from the 1920s onwards that this question has even been possible. Such a dramatic change in usage needs an explanation. Psychology plays a major role in that explanation. Even to study motivation would not have occurred to Wündt – his was not a psychology of everyday experience. By 1936 Young was claiming 'All behavior is motivated'. Motivation is one of two categories (personality being the other) that allow Psychology as a discipline to claim special and privileged knowledge about the entire range of human behaviour.

The Growth of Motivation

Troland published the first general textbook with the word motivation in the main title, in 1928. The term became a key word for abstracting services, meaning that interested scholars could find papers on motivation. Introductory Psychology textbooks then began adding a chapter on the topic, and as the concept became more common, so courses were offered on motivation in undergraduate degrees. Thus in 1936 Young could claim that he modelled his text book on an undergraduate course, and that such courses were popular at undergraduate level.

Behind this growth lay several factors. People attracted to the discipline were often drawn by an interest in motives, an interest perhaps fuelled by the popularization of psychoanalysis. Psychoanalytic theories of this time did not use the abstract or verb terms of motive, although they did contain a lot of work on the (unconscious) motives that lay behind behaviours. Ironically, given the marketing reasons to potential students behind the move to studying motivation, Freud is only mentioned as a motivational theorist in order that his claims can be dismissed as unscientific.

Having a psychological category of motivation enabled Psychology to extend its dominion to topics that psychoanalysis would otherwise have dominated. This, in part, explains the reasons why Psychology wants to set itself up as the arbiter of what counts as 'proper' (i.e. scientific) psychological explanation. Psychoanalysis and Psychology are two disciplines with an obvious boundary dispute. By relying on the rhetoric of science (again a modernist move) Psychology dismisses much of psychoanalysis. However, given the huge cultural impact of psychoanalysis, many of the terms from that discipline have been incorporated (after appropriate gerrymandering) into psychological discourse.

The expansion and rationalization of the education system led to the need for a category beyond intelligence to explain differential performance. Despite the early hopes of intelligence testers, there was much that IQ could not explain, for example, why two people with the same IQ would perform differently. It is no great shock that children do not always want to learn, but with a technology of tests of motivation and a group of experts who can help people become motivated (or help teachers to motivate pupils) a new market opportunity was created for Psychology.

Within the applied field of vocational guidance Folsom called, in 1917, for psychologists to rely less on tests of intellect and more on the psychology of interests, motives and character. Psychologists were not the only people giving vocational guidance, and Psychology was not necessarily a discipline that careers advisers studied. However, a growing interest in the psychology of salesmanship, with motivation as a category open to psychologists, made it possible to talk about motivating customers to buy specific products. Within industry there were calls, prompted by high labour turnover, (for example, by Frost in 1920) for psychological input into questions of unwillingness to work and work satisfaction. One other factor is worthy of note is the desire for a technology of social control. In 1923 Perrin made an argument for a psychology of motivation to fill this gap. Scientific social control, as detailed in Chapter 3, had been one of the goals of Psychology.

There were terms in use before motivation that carried at least some of its meanings. For example, the term 'conation' was used during the nineteenth century. However, conation suffered from the company it kept, having been invented by an earlier generation of moral and mental philosophers (for example, Hamilton 1863). As discussed in Chapter 3, psychologists were keen to discredit that recent ancestor of Psychology and so adopting terminology from it may have been difficult. In the 1920s conation was used by McDougal, whose insistence on an instinctive basis won the term no friends within the in vogue behaviouristic Zeitgeist. One of the odder histories to plot is whether naturist or environmental causation is in vogue, as at times both are in vogue in different parts of Psychology. However, in the 1920s when Psychology was pushing itself as a marketable discipline, behaviouristic environmental causation was posited, so that psychologists could intervene in aspects of human nature.

Conation referred to things (for example, will and desire) that had in common objects of inner experience. In contrast, motivation abstracted something (for example, wants and motives) that had commonalities insofar as they were potential objects of manipulation and influence. Of course psychoanalysis based much of its programme on being able to adjust individuals' motives and wants, to help adjust their identity. However, in using the category of motivation Psychology had to bridge the dichotomy between inner experience and what could be measured. Again this can be seen as a direct response to a number of pressures, particularly the need for a meaningful vocabulary for clients, the need to displace psychoanalysis, and the need to remain scientific.

The initial resource for this was the metaphor of energy (for example James 1890). The term 'drive', apparently invented by Woodworth (1918), with some links to the neuro-physiological studies of Sherrington, was eventually what provided the unifying concept in studies of motivation. By 1954 there was even talk of innate drives responsible for cognitive processes. This is an example of the return to a belief in naturalist explanations, coinciding somewhat with the beginning of the end of behaviourism. There is a level of circularity inherent in such explanations – the facts that these drives explain are identical with the facts provided to establish their existence. However, motivation being treated as a natural kind manages to steer an interesting course as an explanation, apparently managing to rescue itself from naturalist explanations, which were out of vogue in 1920s and 1930s America.

Non-Biological Basis to Motivation

In 1938 Murray, head of the Harvard Psychological Clinic, compiled a list of human needs. These needs differed from drives because the biological mechanism was dropped. Over a period of perhaps 50 years the driving force for human behaviour had changed from God given instincts, to biologically inherited instincts, to general biological drives and then to essential human needs. These needs included the needs for acquisition, superiority, autonomy and achievement. Maslow (1954) found this concept of needs crucial to his 'humanistic' psychology, while need for achievement became a major focus of social psychological research between 1953 and 1961, with David McClelland developing the idea that motivation was tied to levels of need of achievement and that this need varied across and within different societies. This would matter little if researchers had not posited these needs as universal features of the human condition, rather than as culturally specific objects. However, what happened instead is that a set of in vogue cultural assumptions become reified as they were used as names of hypothetical forces within the person. These forces were supposedly responsible for producing all actions that could be given the corresponding label.

The effects of this are threefold (whether instinct, drive or basic need is used). These notions act as cultural apologetics; they continue the idea that reasons for human conduct are rooted in the individual rather than in particular social situations; and they allow motivation to continue as a field. What is also ironic is that for a field that claimed to investigate the why of human behaviour only one type of why was ever seen as acceptable.

INTERIM SUMMARY

The treatment of psychoanalysis by psychologists interested in motivation illustrates just how complex, and vexing, the relationship between the two domains can be. One interest within psychoanalysis is what motivates behaviour, and as we have endeavoured to show using Danziger's analysis, this is a very different enterprise to theory of general motivation. Yet by coopting psychoanalytic accounts as if they were providing theories of motivation it is possible for psychologists to judge them, most often as lacking, by the standards of Psychology. At the same time by using a historical analysis we can question, and possibly undermine, the knowledge claims of Psychology. There is a tautology at the heart of motivation theories that has been recognized, in some contexts, since the heyday of instinct theories. The use of aggregate measures to predict lawful regularities in individual behaviour have to some extent disguised this tautology, as has the limited appreciation of operational analysis (discussed in Chapter 12) that is part of the scientific method of Psychology. This epistemological and ontological problem continues to haunt at least some aspects of modern Psychology. In addition, the concept of motivation plays a role in personality theory similar to the unconscious mind in psychoanalytic theory, but in a much more individualistic fashion. Motivation theories have as their root metaphor an energy system, just as with psychoanalytic theories about the unconscious mind. However in Psychology if one fails in a task that is within one's intellectual and/or physical capacity, it is because one is lacking in motivation. The root cause of the failure is the individual, rather than the system of relationships that one is working within and the past experiences that one has had.

At the same time we must recognize the pragmatic success that this manoeuvring by Psychology has had. It allowed for an extension of the domains of human experience that the discipline can claim expertise over and in applications in sports and occupational Psychology has provided professional psychologists with gainful employment. In extending the concept from the workplace to the laboratory, through the Hawthorne studies and then a limited appreciation of some of the social effects of the experimental situation, the idea that some participants in our studies may be motivated to act out of the ordinary, either trying too hard to complete an experimental task, or not hard enough, we have provided ourselves with an ideal concept to explain away some inconvenient findings. That such explanations are only given when results go against our hypotheses might suggest that we are not being the scrupulously unbiased scientists that we claim to be when we attack psychoanalysis on the basis that it is biased and not scientific enough.

COOPERATION DYNAMICS OF SMALL GROUPS

There have been a few examples where the approaches of Psychology and psychoanalysis have been used in a complementary, rather than an antagonistic, way. In keeping with the major theme of the first eight chapters it is fitting that there were clear external pressures on both disciplines.

During World War Two the British found that they had far too few psychiatrists to deal with the mounting number of soldiers requiring psychotherapy. The solution sought was to use group psychoanalysis. It became quickly apparent that the group as a site of therapeutic intervention is very different from the one-to-one situation normally used in psychotherapy. However, despite the difficulties, use of small therapeutic groups was the only option available at the time and this lead to the psychoanalysts involved forming an interest in the dynamics of small groups. Many of the psychiatrists involved in this work at the Tavistock Clinic continued their association after the war. In the USA during World War Two there was also considerable interest in the dynamics of small groups, with Lewin heading a research programme on behalf of the American army. The interest here was improving the effectiveness of the small group under wartime conditions.

Following the War, Lewin went on the found the Group Dynamics Research Centre at MIT. Cooperation between US social psychologists, from the Group Dynamics Research Centre, and British psychologists from the Tavistock Institute of Human Relations, was cemented with the founding of the journal, *Human Relations*.

The combination of group dynamics together with a psychoanalytic interpretation of group phenomena was, however, unique to the Tavistock. The US tradition continued after Lewin's death in 1947, developing upon his ideas with the t-group movement, but it developed without the psychoanalytic framework. Meanwhile in the UK the psychoanalytic study of groups and organizations, with the exception of Jacques at Brunel University, continued outside the British university system. This rare, but not unique, collaboration between a psychoanalytic tradition and a psychological research tradition ultimately made little impact on the mainstream US tradition of social Psychology. However, this work may have had an impact on critical discourse analysis, a theme that is picked up in Chapter 15.

STUDIES IN PREJUDICE AND THE AUTHORITARIAN PERSONALITY

Another site of cooperation between psychoanalytic and more mainstream psychological traditions was the work, centred at Chicago University immediately after World War Two, on prejudice and authoritarianism. This attempt to understand Nazi anti-Semitism was a project that encompassed a whole range of human sciences, not just psychoanalysis and Psychology, although the product of the research that psychologists are most familiar with was *The authoritarian personality* jointly written by Adorno, Frenkel-Brunswik, Levinson and Sanford (1964 [1950]). The inspiration and thinking behind the project was the product of the Frankfurt school of sociology which had been shut down on the orders of Hitler in the 1930s. It was the Frankfurt School, many of whose members were in exile in the USA, that attempted a synthesis between the ideas of psychoanalysis and Marxism.

Some of the roots of this work lie in Freud's work on cultural criticism following World War One and there had been some attempts by European psychologists and psychoanalysts to understand anti-Semitism in the 1930s. The Nazi holocaust undoubtedly pushed the issue to centre stage. Following a conference in 1944, the American Jewish Committee sponsored the 'Studies in prejudice' series of which *The authoritarian personality* is a part. The other works influential within Psychology were Ackerman and Jahoda's *Anti-Semitism and emotional disorder: a psychoanalytic interpretation* and Bettleheim and Janovitz's *Dynamics of prejudice*. While the authors were aware that prejudice needs to be understood within cultural contexts, the decision to focus on the level of the individual was because of the optimistic hope that at an individual level education could help in tackling the issue. However, perhaps due to the individualization of social Psychology in the US context, discussed further in Chapter 7, the comprehensive and complementary nature of the series of work under the 'Studies in prejudice' banner was overlooked, and *The authoritarian personality* is sometimes described as an attempt to wholly explain prejudice through devices such as the Californian *F* (for Fascism) scale.

Perhaps to some extent the fate of this work was influenced by the start of the Cold War, when communism replaced Nazism as a major threat. The authors of *The authoritarian personality* did to some extent cover their Marxist tracks, whereas Ackerman and Jahoda were less restrained in mounting an attack on the culture of the USA as a possible breeding ground for anti-Semitism. However, given the ideological shift to anti-communism in an era that included the notorious McCarthy Anti-American Activities Committee and the first major confrontation by proxy between the USA and the USSR and China in Korea, it is unsurprising that *The authoritarian personality* also suffered from marginalization in the decade after its publication.

CLINICAL PRACTICE COMPETITION

In turning to clinical practice we find the site of both fierce attacks on psychoanalysis and cooperation between psychologists and psychoanalysts. The sites have different historical and geographic localities; in looking at both it is instructive to examine the different constructions of psychoanalysis that were employed.

One of the fiercest critics of psychoanalysis was Hans J. Eysenck. Eysenck was Director of the Maudsley Clinic, and developed a theory of personality that arose out of clinical practice. Eysenck's personality theory, encapsulated within measurements along three axes in the Eysenck Personality Questionnaire, allows for a quantified description of personality. The EPQ was developed on statistical grounds in order to distinguish between normal people and those suffering from an abnormal personality, and through the use of factor analysis it allowed for an exact numerical description. However, it suffers from the usual problem of validity of such measures. There is a continuing argument over the correct factor description to use (three, five or sixteen factors in the current literature), which comes about because within factor analysis choice of factors is ultimately a judgement call not a statistical certainty. However, as has been discussed before, this ability to label a phenomenon with a number appears to be scientific.

At the same time as developing this instrument, and the attendant theory of personality, Eysenck attacked psychoanalysis in terms of its efficacy rate – how many people treated with psychoanalysis got better. In terms of altering symptoms so that the person becomes normal has long been a weakness of psychoanalysis. Part of the reason was Freud's vision of the goal of therapeutic use of psychoanalysis. For example, writing in 1917 Freud states that the final result of psychoanalysis is that the patient 'has rather less that is unconscious and rather more than is conscious in him than he had before'.

Freud's vision of psychoanalysis was never about 'normalizing' the patient and was not to acquiesce to the:

> Demand that the person who has been 'thoroughly analysed' shall never again feel the stirring of passion in himself or become involved in any internal conflict. The business of psychoanalysis is to secure the best possible psychological conditions for the functioning of the ego; when this has been done, analysis has completed its task.
>
> (Freud 1937: 354)

This pessimistic view of analysis, allied with a view that an unhealthy civilization will inevitably result in people having neuroses, is both the reason why psychoanalysis contains within it the potential for subversion and leads to a question, in a clinical context, of what is psychoanalysis actually for. (Given the wide variety of schools of psychoanalysis this vision does not permeate all of them, while some of them take it even further.) The purpose of clinical psychological intervention, however, as part of the larger psychiatric framework, is normalization of the individual; that is, removing symptoms and thereby adjusting patients to behaviours that are expected from them within a given society.

Much of this is a difference in moral visions of the role of the therapist. However, once the question becomes framed within the moral vision of normalization, and the question is answered in terms of how many get better, then psychoanalysis is bound to fail. That psychoanalysis, as a tool of personal exploration, retains its appeal is probably because, to paraphrase Richards, knowing one's score on the EPI, 16PF or whatever, will never give the same amount of insight as understanding ones' unconsciousness a little better.

In writing this I realize that I am beginning to sound like a Freud apologist, but that is not the intention. The goal here has been to show how Psychology has set itself up as the ultimate court in ruling which approaches to understanding psychology count. It is questionable whether the discipline has yet earned the right to do so, and whether or not to do so should be a goal of Psychology.

CONCLUSION

In this chapter an attempt has been made to show just how complex the relationship between psychoanalysis and Psychology has been. Even during the time frame when many psychologists were advocating a complete rejection of unobservable mental phenomena, concepts and notions derived from psychoanalysis still came into the discipline of Psychology. Often these imports were disguised and ironically Psychology became an arena that both borrowed from psychoanalysis and ruled that psychoanalysis was not scientific enough. Outright competition between the disciplines appears to have been more likely when professional boundaries were at stake, while a limited cooperation was plausible when examining some social and cultural phenomena.

At least to some extent it would appear that Psychology's notions about, and its understandings of, psychoanalysis are frozen at the moment when some aspects of psychoanalysis were drawn into the discipline. Much as S.J. Gould notes that most standard textbook treatments of Darwin's theory of evolution begin with an attack on Lamarck, so standard textbook treatments of the areas briefly sketched in this chapter begin with an attack on Freud. Unlike that parallel, however, psychoanalysis is not a dead approach, although its recent impact in the academy has been in areas such as English, cultural studies and social theories rather than Psychology.

It is perhaps fitting, given the potential within psychoanalysis for subversion of the current order, that it is through feminist Psychology that some current understandings of psychoanalysis are once again being bought into Psychology for debate (although given the tendency within Psychology to ghettoize feminist approaches the audience of that debate is admittedly small).

Marie Jahoda, writing in *Freud and the dilemmas of psychology*, noted that Freud did not enjoy an assured place in the history of Psychology. Perhaps today he does, but it is as a straw man to be attacked. She suspected that this might be because the logical positivists judged that psychoanalysis could not be a science. Psychologists may thus wish to distance themselves from psychoanalysis, which also claims to be a science, because of the controversy over its scientific status. However, given the identification of psychoanalysis with Freud, and writing 30 years later after much critical work about Freud, it is probably true that the suspicions that psychologists feel about psychoanalysis are over determined. It may also be that we have internalized these suspicions to such a point that it is difficult for us to conceive of alternative ways of appreciating psychoanalysis. However there is no doubt that psychoanalysis has profoundly affected the discourses that we may use about our own minds, and whatever its limitations it has thus profoundly affected psychology.

FURTHER READING

Ash, M.G. and Woodward, W.R. (eds) 1989: *Psychology in twentieth-century thought and society.* Cambridge: Cambridge University Press.
Benjamin, J.L.T. 1997: *A history of psychology: original sources and contemporary research.* New York: McGraw Hill.
Crews, F.C. (ed.) 1998: *Unauthorized Freud.* London: Viking Penguin.
Danziger, K. 1997: *Naming the mind: how psychology found its language.* London: Sage Publications Ltd.
Dryden, W. and Feltham, C. (eds) 1992: *Psychotherapy and its discontents.* Buckingham: Open University Press.
Frost, S. 1999: *The politics of psychoanalysis.* London: Macmillan.
Goodwin, C.J. 1999: *A history of modern psychology.* Chichester: John Wiley and Sons.

Herman, E. 1996: *The romance of American psychology*. London: University of California Press.

Leahey, T.H. 2000: *A history of psychology*. London: Prentice-Hall International.

Richards, G. 1989: *On psychological language*. London: Routledge.

Richards, G. 1996: *Putting psychology in its place*. London: Routledge.

6

PSYCHOLOGY AND SOCIETY

In collaboration with Joanna Shutt

This chapter considers the early development of Psychology with reference to the societal context within which the discipline developed. In particular, the chapter looks at the relationship between Psychology and society in terms of the impact Psychology had on its host society, but also at the impact the host society had on the development of Psychology. The central argument here is that the societal context within which the discipline develops is an important influence on development, but that the relationship is a reflexive one. This relationship is discussed in other chapters in the book, as part of those chapters' consideration of factors influencing the development of the discipline. However, given the importance of this reflexive relationship we felt it would be valuable to devote a chapter to focus specifically upon it. The argument regarding the reflexive relationship between Psychology and its host society will also be a theme of Chapter 10. Here, we show that in the past Psychology has had such a relationship with its host society. In Chapter 10 we look at the nature of the relationship for contemporary Psychology.

FRAMEWORK

One problem in attempting to illustrate the relationship between Psychology and society during the development of Psychology is that you are immediately faced with decisions. What society or societies should we consider, since societies differ? What areas of Psychology should we talk about, given the diversity of the discipline? And what time period should we consider? It would of course be desirable to answer 'all' to each question, but in a single chapter you have to restrict your coverage. In this section, we shall explain and justify the decisions we have made, while recognizing that readers may have preferred us to make alternative decisions.

The bulk of this discussion will consider the relationship between

Psychology and society in the USA. There are a number of reasons for this. First the area of greatest growth in the early development of Psychology was the United States, and one of the reasons for this was the social context. Given this, the relationship is most clearly seen in the USA. Second, the form Psychology took following World War Two was successfully transplanted to much of the western world, thus indirectly the factors influencing the nature of Psychology in the USA are also important in Europe. Third, there is a greater range of source material available for the USA compared with other societies, as will be apparent from the list of references and further reading.

Although much of the chapter relates to the USA, there will also be a discussion of the relationship between Psychology and society in Germany. Some of these points were touched on in considering the development of Gestalt Psychology, but these are expanded here, and in addition consideration is given to German Psychology during the period in which the National Socialist party was in power.

With regard to the areas of Psychology to be discussed, the main focus will be applied Psychology, since here the links between Psychology and society are arguably at their strongest. This is particularly the case in considering the effects of war on Psychology, a central theme of the chapter. However, many applications of psychology rely on an underlying theoretical orientation, and the effects of societal context on pure theoretical development will be considered. Given this focus, there will be some overlap between this chapter and Chapter 4. However, whereas Chapter 4 gives a more conventional historical treatment of the development of applications of psychology, focusing on what applications developed and when, this chapter concentrates specifically on how social context influenced the motivation for, and the nature of, the application of psychology. It also considers the effects of application on society, highlighting the reflexive relationship discussed above.

The chapter concentrates on the period 1880–1945. This fits with the time period covered by the preceding chapters, and covers the period when Psychology expanded into a wide range of areas. In addition, this period was a time of great social change, particularly in the USA. The further reading includes suggestions for reading covering later years.

PSYCHOLOGY AND SOCIETY: A REFLEXIVE RELATIONSHIP

As stated, a central argument of the chapter is that Psychology has a reflexive relationship with its host society, such that the development of Psychology is influenced by the society, but in addition Psychology itself influences the host society. Often this relationship is hidden, and sometimes this has been a deliberate act of historians. As an objective science, Psychology cannot be seen to be influenced by societal concerns, since this compromises objectivity. In presenting themselves as objective scientists, seeking knowledge for its own sake, psychologists often claim to have no agenda for influencing society. If the facts they find have a wider impact or are put to particular uses, then the blame should lie with those using the information, not with those discovering it – scientists should be allowed to pursue knowledge, while policy makers are responsible for controlling its use. This not always the case: many modern critical psychologists are explicitly political, while historically there have been psychologists who were prepared to admit to a societal agenda. However, old style histories have tended to suppress discussion of this relationship.

In the remainder of the chapter, we hope to show that this reflexive relationship does indeed obtain, by showing cases from the past where the relationship can be clearly demonstrated. As a prelude, we hope it is reasonable to suggest that psychologists are themselves members of their host societies, and will to some extent share the host society's concerns. In seeking to explain behavioural phenomena, psychologists need to choose which phenomena to explain, and this choice is likely to be a reflection of societal concerns. More particularly, the choice is likely to be influenced by the psychologist's own psychology – the beliefs a psychologist has will influence their priorities in pursuing research. In addition, and despite claims to objectivity, the beliefs a psychologist has will likely influence their interpretation of ambiguous evidence. This effect is discussed very well in Gould's (1996) *The mismeasure of man*, where he shows, for example, how the interpretation of results from factor analysis will depend upon what the interpreter wants to find. The general point, that psychologists are influenced by their own psychology, is well summarized in the oft-used phrase 'racist psychologists produce racist psychology'. Beyond the individual, however, there are a wide range of institutional factors influencing the direction of Psychology. The clearest example of this is the effect of funding and patronage on the choice of research topic, and possibly on the results of research. If a psychologist is being funded by a fascist organization to conduct research on racial differences, it is hopefully clear what kind of psychologist will be engaged, what kind of research will be produced and probably what the results of the research will be.

The case of race research is a good example of Psychology in turn affecting the host society, and again this is well described in Gould (1996). When Psychology produces claims, with the stamp of scientific authority, these claims affect people's perceptions. Thus if an article is published claiming to prove that there are racial differences in intelligence, or that there is a gene for sexuality, then this will affect the general public's view of race or sexuality. In part, the effects are mediated by language – Psychology may develop terms or concepts which achieve public currency, and enter the language. The use of this language will then affect the way we think about ourselves and about others, for example, when we talk about being 'conditioned'. The role of language in changing people's psychologizing is described in Richards (1996), and is discussed more fully in Chapter 11.

Psychology's effect on society does of course go somewhat beyond affecting individuals' psychology, in a range of ways. To focus on just one mechanism, psychologists may present themselves as sources of knowledge and expertise to policy makers. Clearly in this case, the theories and interventions suggested by psychologists will have an impact on policy, and thus on society. As an example, the development of the 11-plus examination to determine the degree to which British schoolchildren were to be educated was founded in apparently sound, but now rejected, psychological theory, and had an effect on the education of millions.

This reflexive relationship can be difficult to show, since it is often hidden, as discussed, and always subtle. We do not wish to imply in this brief overview that the relationship consists in unidirectional societal effects on Psychology, and unidirectional effects of Psychology on society. The relationship is interactive, cyclical and mediated through a wide range of mechanisms. Our intention in this chapter is to show through history some of the ways in which the relationship can be seen to hold.

THE USA

The history of the development of Psychology in the USA has been covered in Chapter 3. In this chapter we concentrate on highlighting the role of social context in shaping the development of Psychology. In doing so, we shall first consider the social and political climate in the USA around the turn of the twentieth century.

The Early Socio-Political Climate

The end of the nineteenth century in the USA was a time of growth, industrialization and attendant social change. The Civil War had finished some decades before, and considerable reconstruction was occurring in the Southern states. In addition, there was a push for westward expansion, increasing industrialization and considerable technological innovation. The rapid industrialization had the effect of increasing urbanization, with considerable migration to cities, particularly by newly emancipated African-Americans, and high immigration – the Immigration Act of 1864, designed partly to appease the big businesses then forming, permitted the entry of cheap labour to work in the new industries. The developing urban areas were characterized by overcrowding and a shortage of facilities, which in turn led to a range of social problems and disease. There were two main societal effects of these changes that were relevant to Psychology. First, there developed a view of the American national character that was to exert a great influence on views of society and, as we shall see, on the programme of the social sciences; and second, there developed a faith in the societal benefits of technological change.

The view of national character that formed towards the end of the nineteenth century emphasized individual responsibility, the potential for advance by individual effort, the value of competition, and the importance of considering the practical value of ideas. More widely, the notion that any individual could advance through their own efforts encouraged a view of the USA as the land of opportunity. This pragmatic individuality fitted nicely with the changing intellectual climate of the time. Darwin's exposition of the theory of evolution had changed views of human nature, and Spencer's formulation of Social Darwinism had direct political consequences, being used to justify laissez-faire economics, limited social intervention by the state and limited control of companies. The view that society was governed by the rule of 'survival of the fittest' was used to rationalize inequality – if people are poor or needy, it is because they are unfit, and if they are unfit, social intervention either cannot or should not (depending on how extreme one's views are) override nature's cardinal rule. Hence at the time of the development of scientific Psychology in the USA, there was an entrenched, a priori, view of human nature. The new scientific psychologists did not start with a theoretical blank slate in trying to explain human nature, but rather with a certain set of beliefs both about human nature, and about how society should be organized. As we shall see, these pre-existing beliefs were to have an effect on the development of Psychology in the USA.

The rapid technological change occurring at this time also had profound effects on the public's view of how society should be organized. In this case, it was apparent that the introduction of new technologies such as the telegraph and electric lighting were having beneficial effects on people's lives – at least those people who could afford such luxuries. These technological advances were seen as a gift of science, and science was seen in a sense as a public benefactor. Relating to the emphasis on the practical utility of ideas, a new science would need, in order to gain acceptance as such, to offer practical suggestions for improving society. Psychology was not immune from these forces, and psychologists soon realized that they too would need to start producing useful results. This is evident, for example, in Scripture's *Thinking, feeling, doing*, specifically targeted at explaining psychology to the general public, wherein he expressed the hope that Psychology's desire to serve humanity would be evident; and in Dewey's presidential address to the APA, wherein he warned of the dangers of concentrating on pure laboratory research. As we shall see, Psychology was soon offering itself as a technology for social change.

Evolutionary theory and Social Darwinism were not only used to justify economic inequality within society. At the same time, and particularly noticeably in the USA, evolutionary theory was being used as a new intellectual justification for the existence of qualitative differences between groups, whether groups were specified by gender, race or social class. Women were seen as inferior to men, the lower classes were seen as inferior to the middle and upper classes, and non-whites were seen as inferior to whites. The commonly held view amongst white, middle-class, male academics and policy makers was that different races were at differing stages of evolution, with white western civilization being at the pinnacle. A fuller coverage of Psychology's treatment of gender and race is given in Chapter 9.

As the nineteenth century drew to a close, the USA experienced a reaction to what might be seen as the excesses of unrestrained capitalism. Increasing social problems in urban areas, resulting from poverty, disease, poor housing, and social inequality, coupled with an increasing wariness of the power and suspected corruption of the 'robber barons' who had control of industry, led to demands for social change. These demands were addressed by a group of academics calling themselves the Progressivists. The Progressivists rejected Spencer's Social Darwinism, but still worked in an evolutionary framework. They advocated 'Reform Darwinism', interpreting evolutionary theory as meaning that humans could influence change, rather than being forced to passively adapt to the environment as suggested by Social Darwinism. The goal of Reform Darwinism was to adopt an empirical approach to political and social reform, by creating a scientific government machine made up of experts that could implement new political and welfare policy. The progressives were strongly influenced by James's pragmatism, and believed that the social sciences, including Psychology, offered the potential for a scientifically managed technological society. The many social problems arising from rapid urbanization were to offer Psychology plentiful opportunities for suggesting theory and intervention.

Functionalism and Application

The development of functionalism as an early school of Psychology is described in Chapter 3. To recap briefly, functionalism developed out of James's pragmatism, and adopted a broadly evolutionary framework. The emphasis in functionalism was on the evolutionary utility of mental function – the mind's evolutionary role was to adjust behaviour to suit the environment. Functionalism, by studying this adjustment, could act to improve the process, thus the approach was from the start intended to allow the application of findings. While functionalism is often (though decreasingly) presented as a unified school of thought, the public display of unity, fostered by the newly founded APA, actually hid considerable disagreement on a number of fundamental issues. These included methodological approaches, the relative value of pure and applied work, the importance of behaviour as well as consciousness, and the relationship between Psychology and philosophy.

Functionalism was a broad church, but it allowed for the application of psychology by those who wished. A number of broad strands of applied work can be identified under the functionalist umbrella, of which two are important in the context of this chapter. The first strand was that of mental testing, characterized by Cattell, Goddard, Terman and Yerkes. The development of mental testing is described in Chapter 4. In the context of this chapter, it is important to note that the mental testing movement was very much a response by Psychology to concerns raised by Social Darwinism, as should be apparent when you consider that mental testing developed out of the anthropometric measuring of Galton. The early developers of mental testing were very concerned about the effects of the feeble minded, and of continuing immigration, on the national bloodstock. Mental testing was developed in part as a technology for the pursuit of eugenicist programmes. This involved both finding support for claims of differences between groups, and developing techniques for the identification of those who could be seen as a threat to the well being of society. The mental testing movement represents a very clear example of Psychology being shaped by the general social climate, and in turn of Psychology contributing to the social climate and offering society solutions to its ills.

A second strand of applied work was related to the progressive project, and is best characterized by the work of Dewey. As stated previously, the progressivists rejected Social Darwinism and advocated a Reform Darwinism. As part of this, progressive psychologists attempted to apply Psychology in the service of liberalism. Social change, particularly through education, could be effected through the application of psychological principles. Dewey, the founder of progressive education, viewed education as the foundation of effective democracy, since it allowed genuine opportunity. The rapid growth in public education at this time created a demand for new approaches, particularly in educating immigrants and newly urbanized farm children. Schools had to become child centred, and indeed were viewed as providing a community for the child. The adults produced would then reform the American community. To an extent, education was a stalking horse for Psychology's involvement in the progressive project: the wider goal was for Psychology to play a role in the reconstruction of American society. Psychology applied in this way, said Dewey, was an 'alternative to an arbitrary and class view of society'. This view of a centrally managed society was somewhat at odds with traditional American individualism, which limited the effect of the progressive programme, although modern governmental bureaucracy is an enduring legacy.

There was a degree of overlap between the two strands identified here. Broadly, the progressives wanted to use science to advance society, and for some progressive psychologists mental testing offered such a useful science. The eugenics movement, covered further later in the chapter, seems from the present to be a conservative movement. However, many of the supporters of eugenics were progressives, and the programme crossed ideological divides. Nevertheless, mental testing tended to be used in support of racist inspired negative eugenic programmes, whereas progressives were more likely to support positive eugenic programmes. General social concern about declining standards in society was shared to an extent by psychologists across the ideological spectrum. The distinction between mental testing and progressive psychology is therefore an artificial one. A truer distinction would be between Social Darwinists and Reform Darwinists, but as a generality the former can be associated with mental testing, and the latter with the progressives. Ideological differences between Social Darwinism and Reform Darwinism – a socio-political debate – was played out (simplistically) in Psychology in the difference between mental testing and progressive psychology. Both approaches suggested technologies for social change, but differing ideological positions led to rather different views of the project of Psychology. For example, the role of mental testing in education was to identify the feeble minded so that society could be protected from them, whereas progressive education sought to reform education as a first step in the reform of society. The approaches differed in their effects also, for example, mental testing provided support for restrictive immigration policy, whereas progressivism suggested interventions to help immigrants to integrate into US society.

Ultimately, mental testing became independent of any particular theoretical school and continued to grow. It remains an important element in modern Psychology, although its ideological affiliation is often all too apparent, as in continuing attempts to support claims of racial differences in intelligence. Functionalism was replaced as the dominant American school of Psychology by behaviourism, but this change was strongly influenced by the progressive movement. The progressive project, in attempting to provide a technology of social control, found it necessary to concentrate on behaviour, since social control is ultimately the control of behaviour. However, a tension is apparent between attempting to change people's behaviour and attempting to theorize on behaviour in evolutionary terms. Ultimately behaviourism, with its strong environmental emphasis, provided a more amenable theoretical underpinning to attempts to provide a technology for social change. The desire for Psychology to provide such a technology was an important factor in the ongoing development of the discipline.

Psychology and War (1): World War One

During the period before World War One, psychologists were attempting to apply their theories and interventions to a wide range of social problems. However, these were on a limited scale, and had limited public exposure. The advent of war was to provide Psychology with opportunities both to broaden the scope of its project, and to increase public awareness of its potential. Undoubtedly, those psychologists who contributed to the war effort were driven by feelings of patriotic duty. However, it was a fortunate coincidence that their patriotic duty could also help effect an increase in the profession's status, and increased opportunities for application.

American Psychology's contribution to the war effort was organized by Robert Yerkes, President of the APA in 1918. Shortly after the USA joined the War, the APA created twelve committees devoted to different aspects of war. Of these, the most successful were Yerkes's committee devoted to using mental testing in the screening of recruits, and Walter Dill Scott's committee on classification of personnel. The two differed in approach, and given potential overlap in their activities – Yerkes believed his tests could be used for classification – tension between the two was inevitable, culminating in Scott accusing Yerkes of using the opportunity of war to advance his own interests in Psychology. Of the two, Scott's committee was the more successful, having developed proficiency tests for over 80 military jobs and having classified more than 3,000,000 men. In contrast, the information gathered by Yerkes's group was overlooked by the military. However, Yerkes's work was to prove far more important than Scott's in providing publicity and impetus to Psychology, and was to have a much greater societal impact.

Yerkes's committee concentrated on the administration of intelligence tests – the Army Alpha and Beta tests – to nearly two million recruits. These tests were intended to grade recruits into one of five categories of mental fitness, A–E, with the lower grades being rejected for service. However, Yerkes also believed that the categories could be used for the classification of personnel, although this was rejected by the army. In order to test such a large number of personnel, current intelligence tests had to be discarded, since they relied on being administered face to face. Instead, Yerkes and his team developed the first mental tests that could be administered to large groups, and used these to collect a large amount of data on intelligence. Both the group tests and the data were to prove to be influential. Yerkes was a vigorous promoter of his techniques, and following the War convincingly, if disingenuously, argued that the success of the project helped win the War. This justification of the group test gave Psychology a new, improved technology which was believed to provide a scientific basis for the investigation of individual differences, and which expanded the scope of psychologists's activities. This enhanced status for mental testing created a marketplace for psychological expertise following the War, and hence advanced professional Psychology. The data also had a role in this: as we shall see in the next section, the findings of Yerkes's project helped fuel public concern about the effects of immigration and the feeble minded, and Psychology readily positioned itself to address these concerns.

Psychology's efforts during the War were not limited to testing and classification. Before the War a limited mental hygiene movement had been established, arguing for the humane treatment of the mentally ill and work towards the prevention of mental disease, and promoting psychiatry. The trauma of the War produced thousands of psychiatric casualties, largely from shell-shock or war neurosis, and this overburdened the still nascent psychiatric profession. Psychiatric training was time consuming, and so clinical psychologists were recruited to assist the psychiatrists, although they were given a subordinate role – largely the administration of mental tests within psychiatric teams. However, clinical psychologists used the opportunity to gain field and research experience, and also enhanced their own, and the discipline's, reputation. The benefits of these efforts were to become apparent in the years following the War.

A final major area of activity for psychologists was in the field of propaganda. At the start of World War One, the majority of Americans were opposed to US participation, and the USA remained neutral. When the US government decided to join the War on the side of the UK and France, it realized it would need to persuade a reluctant public to support the war effort. In order to do this, the government established the Creel Commission, whose staff included hundreds of psychologists. Before the War, Psychology had proved effective in the field of advertising. Now, psychological techniques, founded mainly on behaviourism, were to be used to change public opinion. Chomsky observes that the Creel Commission succeeded, within six months, in 'turning a pacifist population into a hysterical, war-mongering population' (1995: 1). The work for the Creel Commission not only allowed ample opportunities for psychologists to research and develop psychological theory, it also allowed Psychology to develop its usefulness in policy making and other government issues.

World War One proved to be very beneficial to the discipline of Psychology. The work conducted by psychologists, together with considerable proselytizing following the War, established Psychology as a discipline that could provide useful expertise to policy makers, to business and to individuals. Psychology was to reap the benefits in the following years.

Eugenics and Immigration Control

The eugenics movement existed prior to World War One, and was a reflection of the Social Darwinist views discussed above. Before the development of mass intelligence testing, there was little doubt amongst many parts of society that intelligence differed between races and genders, and that civilized society, having suspended evolution, had allowed the unfit to survive, hidden, within the population. The data produced by Yerkes during the War provided an empirical basis to support such views. The relationship between eugenics and branches of Psychology following World War One is a clear illustration that Psychology is not insulated from the society within which it proceeds, and so has a section devoted to it. However, the coverage will be brief: for a fuller discussion, Gould's *The mismeasure of man* (1996) covers the army tests, and their wider impact, in some depth. This has been criticized (see the Introduction) for being presentist and revisionist, and there is no doubt that Gould's political views affect his interpretation of the past, but it is an excellent source. In particular, Gould discusses very clearly the substantial methodological limitations of early mental ability testing, which will not be covered here.

The collection of a large volume of data, based on mass intelligence testing, allowed more than the screening of army recruits. By recording demographic data along with intelligence scores, the testers were able to analyse the data to look for patterns. The patterns looked for were necessarily dictated by pre-existing views, and Yerkes happened to subscribe to a view of racial differences. Thus Yerkes's analysis of the army data looked for racial differences, and found them, not only between Caucasians and African Americans, but on a graduated scale depending on distance of racial origin from north-western Europe, with African Americans at the bottom of the scale. These findings supported the earlier testing, by Goddard, of newly arriving immigrants at Ellis Island, which also found racial differences in ability.

In addition to providing evidence for racial differences, the army data also showed that even for whites, the average level of intelligence was at an alarmingly low level. Indeed, whereas Terman had standardized, using the Stanford-Binet scale, the average American adult mental age to sixteen, Yerkes found that the average IQ in his study was only thirteen. The finding provoked considerable alarm about the state of American society. Together with the alleged racial differences, the data supported calls for action, in particular for immigration control, and for a programme of eugenics. It should be noted that these calls came from a large section of intellectual society, not only from psychologists, and there is some debate about the role evidence from Psychology played in the establishment of immigration controls and eugenics. The claim we make here is that the widely publicized findings of a certain group of psychologists, a group who shared pre-existing racist and Social Darwinist views, certainly had an impact on everyday conceptions of racial differences and mental fitness, by providing evidence in support of such views. In a sense, it is not important whether immigration controls, for example, were the direct result of the army tests, as has been argued. They were certainly an indirect result of the tests, in that the findings helped shape perceptions of racial difference.

Arguments for immigration control, pressed strongly by a number of notable psychologists (for example, Brigham: 'Immigration should not only be restrictive but highly selective', in Gould 1996: 260), led in 1924 to the introduction of the Immigration Act, which set quotas for immigration for different racial groups. It is, we suggest, no coincidence that the relative quota sizes for differing groups were closely related to the putative average intelligence for those groups.

Immigration controls were seen as a solution to the threat from outside, however concern remained about the threat from within: that the feeble minded within society would continue to breed and dilute the national bloodstock. To address this, a programme of eugenics was advocated, following the lead of Galton and the British eugenicists. However, whereas British eugenicists promoted a positive policy of encouraging the middle and upper classes to breed, with little success, American eugenicists promoted a negative policy of institutionalization and sterilization, Goddard being a prime mover in these efforts. Although such suggestions preceded the war by some 15 years, with limited success, in the 15 years following the war 30 states had instituted sterilization programmes. This proved to be the golden age for American eugenics: by the 1930s many had retracted their eugenicist views, including Goddard and Brigham, and support for racial differences was dwindling. Following the excesses of the Nazi eugenic programme – itself inspired by the success of American eugenics – eugenics quickly dropped out of favour.

A Boomtime for Psychology – the 1920s

Following World War One, the USA enjoyed a period of considerable optimism. Compared with Europe, the USA had survived major devastation, and showed considerable strength and wealth. Business boomed. The public became more aspirational, and an increase in free time led to increased interest in leisure activities. There was an increasing interest in the nature of the human mind, partly fuelled by the publicity the discipline garnered as a result of its war efforts. The apparent success of applied Psychology in some areas led to attempts to apply psychology to all areas of everyday life, sometimes with the most spurious of bases. Books published during this period included *The psychology of Jesus* and *The psychology of playing the banjo*, an illustration of the breadth of application. Society seemed to have an insatiable demand for psychological expertise, and psychologists were happy to respond. We can see in this the beginning of popular psychology, as people without formal training began offering psychological expertise in areas of popular interest, without any necessary foundation in disciplinary Psychology. As might be expected, this demand led to a surfeit of bogus tests and interventions, leading to calls for the certification of psychologists by the APA. An initial certification scheme set such strict criteria that it was almost impossible to gain certification, and was soon discontinued. However, a precedent was set for later certification schemes, and for the control of the application of psychology by the APA. Coinciding with the increase in attempts to apply psychology was an increase in applications for undergraduate and postgraduate courses in psychology, producing both an increase in Psychology's academic presence and an increase in the number of individuals who felt able to offer psychological expertise.

The promise of applied Psychology was that it would improve life, and this promise was keenly promoted in the area of mental health. Following the success of psychiatry during the War, there was a great increase in demand for psychiatric services. Given the lengthy training time for psychiatrists, however, supply was unable to keep up with demand, creating an opening for clinical psychologists to increase their expertise, their areas of practice and their reputation. This was to pay dividends during and after World War Two. In addition, the successes of the psychologists working for the Creel Commission led to increased opportunities in government and in business. The techniques of propaganda developed during the War were readily transferable to advertising and public relations management, and psychologists were ready to offer their expertise to these enterprises.

Despite the general mood of optimism and the great economic growth, the social problems that caused concern were still extant, with burgeoning inequality between the newly prosperous and the continuing poor. During the 1920s, psychologists tended to concentrate on serving the prosperous, and garnered wealth and reputation by doing so. Although some psychologists remained concerned with social issues, and advocated the development of a coherent social Psychology to address these, their concerns were largely overlooked. During the 1920s, rising prosperity detracted attention from continuing social problems. However, this prosperity was not to continue, and soon social problems were at the forefront of the nation's attention.

Psychology and the Depression

In October 1929, the Wall Street stock market experienced a catastrophic crash. Much of the wealth accumulated during the 1920s was wiped out, and the country faced severe economic and social problems. Psychology's response was generally uninspiring. Whereas in times of prosperity psychologists had offered advice on almost any social phenomenon, they had little to say about the Depression. One reason suggested for this (for example, Napoli 1981) was that psychologists quietly left it to economists and other social scientists to address the nation's problems. An alternative explanation (for example, Finison 1986) is that psychologists themselves suffered from the effects of the Depression, and found that they were not in a position to address these problems. Finison suggests that psychologists took one of two attitudes to the crisis: restrictivist and expansionist. Restrictivists argued that the situation would, through Social Darwinian selection, force the survival of the few and hence improve the quality of psychologists. The expansionists believed that there was scope for an expansion in psychological services, particularly to address the problems caused by the Depression. As might be expected, the restrictivists tended to be older, more established members of the profession, and remained largely inactive, whereas the expansionists tended to be younger, recently qualified and more vigorous in their approach.

The expansionists varied in their vigour, but one outcome of the movement was the formation of a number of groups, based on progressive ideals, dedicated to using Psychology to address social issues. While a range of groups had been formed in the 1920s, the Depression led, during the 1930s, to an increasing interest in social Psychology. The expansionists were leading proponents of such an approach, in part reflecting their strong political views (many were involved in either the socialist or communist parties). The most prominent organizations established at this time were the Society for the Psychological Study of Social Issues (SPSSI), founded by members of the Marxist New America movement, and the Psychologists League (PL), made up of members of the communist affiliated Pen and Hammer Clubs. The theoretical and practical orientations of these groups reflected their political affiliation, and influenced the development of social Psychology. However, even in the Depression, the American climate was not entirely favourable to such political positions. The SPSSI affiliated with the APA, but had to cease political involvement to do so. The PL did not seek affiliation with the APA precisely because they wished to maintain their political activities.

During the 1920s and 1930s, advances were made in the development of methods, particularly those of Thurstone and Likert, for measuring attitudes. This development created the potential for empirical social psychological research. At this time also, the Democratic Social Engineering (DSE) movement, which had begun following World War One, developed its principles for application to large groups. The Depression created the political and economic need for both new methodologies and new techniques of intervention, and these in turn assisted in the early development of social Psychology. The view that the Depression led to some growth for applied Psychology is supported by the establishment, in 1938, of the American Association for Applied Psychology (AAAP), a response to the APA's continued concentration on academic Psychology at the perceived expense of applied areas. This was a major step towards the professionalization of Psychology.

Psychology and War (2): World War Two

The Depression assisted the development of DSE, and of methodologies of attitude measuring, but it was the arrival of World War Two that gave

Psychology its chance, once again, to show its utility on a large scale. Space precludes a full discussion of the role of Psychology during the war. In the context of this chapter, the importance of War was to drive the professionalization of Psychology, and to increase the public awareness of the discipline.

War started in Europe in 1939, and at the end of 1940 American Psychology started its preparations for war with the establishment of an Emergency Committee by the APA. Following this, a Committee on Psychology and War was formed, to plan for war activities and for Psychology's postwar social role. It became apparent that Psychology should be unified as a discipline, and to assist this the Office of Psychological Personnel (OPP) was established to help in the allocation of psychologists of all stripes to war work. The establishment of the OPP acted as a catalyst for the reunification of Psychology and for the advancement of Psychology's societal role. In 1944, a number of groups representing psychologists, including the APA, the AAAP, the SPSSI, and the National Council of Women Psychologists, voted to create a new, federal APA with a constitution treating the various groups more equally. In 1945 a new certification scheme was passed, finally establishing Psychology as a recognized, independent profession.

The work carried out by psychologists during World War Two re-established Psychology as a valuable source of expertise. A considerable amount of work was conducted in the areas of industrial human relations, industrial management, training and productivity. This had the effect of convincing the business community of the utility of psychology, and boosted considerably industrial psychology following the War. As with World War One, psychologists were involved in war propaganda, both at home and abroad. However, perhaps the main beneficiary from Psychology's war work was clinical Psychology. During the War clinical psychologists were employed in their traditional role of testing as part of psychiatric teams, but again the psychiatric profession was overwhelmed by the demands on their services. This created an opportunity for clinical psychologists to provide psychotherapy, setting a precedent for postwar practice. In addition, veterans returning from the War created a demand for counselling services. This demand was met by psychologists, creating the role of the counselling psychologist.

The services provided by psychologists during and after the War did more than establish the professions of clinical and counselling psychologist. As well as reacting to the needs of veterans, psychologists were involved proactively in improving morale and motivation amongst soldiers. Given this range of services, millions of army personnel were exposed to psychology and convinced of its utility. Following the War, this increase in exposure and public esteem was to help create a strong marketplace for voluntary psychological services, and for psychological information that people could use for self-guidance. World War Two was instrumental in making the USA a psychological society.

COUNTERPOINT: GERMANY

As a contrast to the relationship between Psychology and society in the USA, we will look briefly at the relationship in Germany. Psychology in Germany is often seen as having been less influenced by its social setting than the USA, probably because early Psychology in Germany had a less applied focus. However, we shall see that this itself was a result of Psychology's relationship to its host society. The central argument of the chapter, that the development of Psychology is influenced by the host society, is strengthened rather than weakened by considering Germany. The contrast between the USA and Germany shows, more than anything, that different societies produce different Psychologies.

We will initially consider the social setting within which Psychology first developed, and then look at the influence of society on the development of Gestalt Psychology. Finally, we shall look at the relationship between Psychology and society in Nazi Germany.

Before Wündt: The German Academic Environment

German Psychology was as much a product of its environment as US Psychology. The intellectual environment of Germany during the nineteenth century was the result of a drive to modernize Prussia, and later Germany, by the German Emperor at the start of the nineteenth century. This modernization included the development of an intellectual elite, served by a new model of research university which concentrated on the production of knowledge, rather than training in the professions of law, medicine and church. The knowledge produced by these new universities, together with industrialization, was to be the driving force behind Germany's regeneration. The universities were charged with two tasks: the generation of new knowledge, particularly in the sciences (*Wissenschaft*), and the provision of a broad humanistic education (*Bildung*), this second task being designed to create a culturally educated elite. These apparently contradictory aims were to be reconciled through the mediation of philosophy, which had a central place in the new curricula. This latter task reflected the general belief system of the intellectual elite in Germany, the *Bildungsburger*. This belief system, rooted in Romanticism and Kantian idealism, rejected the atomistic reduction of society and emphasized the value of community, in part reflecting the wider German desire for unity. *Bildung* was intended to prepare individuals to participate in a German cultural community.

These goals were to have an important effect on the development of Psychology. The pursuit of knowledge encouraged the development of new sciences and specialisms, and over time the focus shifted to de-emphasize *Bildung*, and to emphasize *Wissenschaft*. It would seem that such an environment would aid the creation of a new specialism of Psychology. However, psychology first entered curricula as part of philosophy, which maintained a commitment to *Bildung*, and was hindered in its development, since it was not clear how psychology could contribute to *Bildung*. As Psychology developed, later psychologists attempted to separate Psychology from philosophy as a natural science, but maintained to some degree a commitment to the ideal of humanistic education. They wished to make Psychology a separate discipline in order to allow the generation of new knowledge, but this knowledge was to be pursued for its own sake, rather than for any applied purpose.

The tension between a desire for Psychology to be a natural science, and a belief in the German humanistic ideal, placed particular strains on German psychologists. This is apparent in the work of Wündt, who placed limits on the scope of a scientific Psychology, with human achievements such as culture and language being outside this scope. For Wündt, two forms of Psychology were necessary, with physiological Psychology looking to natural science, and a cultural Psychology looking to the social world. This two-part Psychology as a whole was conceived as a bridge between the natural world and the social.

The culturally maintained German belief system was to come under attack, from the effects of urbanization and industrialization, and from Germany's defeat during World War One. In response to this, a growing number of psychologists became eager for Psychology to become autonomous, and in some cases even for it to become an applied field, but the philosophy establishment resisted this. Unlike in the USA, there was no great move towards application within German Psychology. Leahey (2000) suggests a number of reasons for this. First, the adoption of an applied orientation ran counter to the prevailing emphasis on pure knowledge. Second, academics in Germany had considerable freedom to pursue knowledge, but were barred from interference in social or political matters, which as we have seen were fertile areas of application for US Psychology. Finally, German *Bildungsburger* psychologists rejected the Darwinian influenced reduction of mental processes to adaptational responses of a mechanistic organism. Despite this, there was some progress in applying psychology, but it was to take the social upheaval of Nazi rule to establish Psychology as an applied profession in Germany.

Gestalt Psychology: Defenders of Culture

The *Bildungsburger* mentality in the German sciences fundamentally influenced the knowledge products of those sciences. As we saw above, the initial development of German Psychology was constrained by the desire to make Psychology compatible with a humanistic cultural outlook, which in part meant that German Psychology remained the lesser partner of philosophy. The same effect can be seen in Psychology's later development, but during the first three decades of the twentieth-century German society was to see dramatic changes, which threatened the *Bildungsburger* basis of German science.

The *Bildungsburger* view saw the German character in somewhat nostalgic terms, emphasizing a community of a single people with common ties in language, culture and land. This community was seen as being essentially rural, with an emphasis on people's relationship with others and with the land they inhabited. However, increasing urbanization and industrialization weakened this view. The rise of new large cities changed people's relationships with each other and with their living space, and industrialization, and the aspirations it brought, led to a greater mood of individualism and an increasingly mechanistic worldview. For many ordinary Germans, defeat during World War One brought an end to dreams of a single community. The second *Reich* created by Bismarck disintegrated into chaos and revolution, and its replacement, the Weimar Republic, suffered from economic problems and a lack of popular support.

Despite this social upheaval German academics, from their insulated positions, maintained their *Bildungsburger* values. The social changes were to be resisted, and academia was to be part of the resistance. This stance was to affect the development of German Psychology. Given the importance of philosophy to the old order, this clearly was not a time for Psychology to be disputing the role or value of philosophy, and its emergence as an independent discipline was inhibited. More generally, theoretical positions were adopted in Psychology that emphasized the old values. During this period, a number of holistic theoretical approaches developed, emphasizing the wholeness of experience and the culturally situated nature of mental life, the most important of which was to be Gestalt Psychology. For a fuller discussion, Ash (1995) traces the development of Gestalt Psychology, and related holistic approaches, in its social and intellectual contexts.

Gestalt Psychology was fundamentally a rejection of the reductionism evident in other approaches to Psychology. Traditionally, histories ascribe this rejection to a need to explain perception of form, and particularly to explain why a whole form is consistently perceived despite variation in its constituent elements, as in Von Ehrenfehl's observation that we can recognize a tune despite changes in pitch or tempo. However, the rejection of reductionism went beyond explaining a limited set of phenomena: the Gestaltists rejected reductionism as a suitable framework for explaining the nature of mind. The Gestaltists, imbued with *Bildungsburger* values, saw reductionist explanations of human nature as demeaning human values, and proposed instead a holistic approach that would allow consideration of meaning and culture. Thus Gestalt Psychology was not only a theoretical approach, but part of the defence of *Bildungsburger* values against the social changes discussed above.

Nazi Germany: Psychology in Service to the State

Germany's social upheavals were to continue past the Weimar Republic. The onset of the Depression caused great unrest and political upheaval, resulting in the appointment, in 1933, of Adolf Hitler as German Chancellor. Hitler's programme was in some superficial ways similar to traditional German values, emphasizing unity and the strength of the German community. However, unlike the *Bildungsburger*, Hitler was not concerned by the effects of urbanization and industrialization, and was prepared to harness these to advance his aims. The Nazi regime was to have a dramatic effect on German Psychology, described in Geuter (1992).

Traditional coverage of the history of German Psychology following Hitler's rise to power provides a good illustration of the shortcomings of old style histories discussed in Chapter 1. Coverage has focused on the effects of the Nazi regime on Gestalt Psychology. Briefly, in the first few years of Nazi rule a number of prominent Gestalt psychologists were dismissed from their posts and emigrated to the USA, and it is generally claimed that this led to the demise of Gestalt Psychology. These dismissals and emigrations, together with some attacks on psychoanalysis, have led traditional historians to suggest that the Nazis were anti-psychological. However, Geuter (1987) shows that while a number of prominent psychologists were dismissed, this was because they were Jewish or were considered politically unreliable, rather than because they were psychologists, and that similar dismissals occurred in other disciplines. Although the loss of leading personnel led briefly to a decline in German Psychology, the period to the end of World War Two was to see growth overall, together with a change in the project of German Psychology. Arguably, it was this change in project that weakened Gestalt Psychology in Germany.

Previous sections have discussed the relationship between early Psychology and the political, social and intellectual context in which it developed. In particular, German psychologists rejected application, and had a close association with philosophy. The Nazi regime changed these contexts, and encouraged the application of psychology both as part of preparations for war, and in providing a scientific rationale for Nazi ideology. A considerable number of German psychologists adapted to these changes, for a range of reasons. Unquestionably, some psychologists shared Nazi ideology, while others may have adapted to advance goals of establishing Psychology as an independent discipline and of developing applications for psychology. Still others probably changed their approach out of fear for their positions, having seen the result of being considered unreliable. The lead was given by the German Society for Psychology under the leadership of Felix Kreuger, who in 1933 called on psychologists to join politicians in achieving the psychological renewal of the German people (cited in Geuter 1987: 169).

Contrary to traditional history, the Nazi period witnessed the institutionalization of Psychology within German universities. The central science administration was instrumental in establishing chairs of Psychology, and filling them with reliable psychologists. Psychology had previously been subsidiary to philosophy, but the Nazi administration acted to replace philosophers with psychologists. This support was the result of the Nazi leadership seeing the potential for Psychology of the right orientation, partly in supporting ideology but particularly in the application of psychological methods.

In terms of theory development, the main change in German Psychology during this period came with an increased emphasis on typology and characterology, an existing area of study that took on new importance when typology was merged with race psychology. Typology became used to support Nazi claims of racial superiority, the best-known example being in the work of Jaensch. Jaensch had written widely on typology before 1933, but following the rise of the Nazi party he incorporated anti-Semitism into his theory. Other psychologists sought only to show the compatibility of their theories with Nazi ideology, for example, Sander's formulation of *Ganzheits*-psychology and Metzger's formulation of Gestalt.

The major impact of the Nazi regime on German Psychology was in its application. Although there had been some moves towards establishing applied Psychology in the 1920s, mainly in engineering and teacher training, the Nazi military authorities greatly expanded the use of psychology in screening of officers and selection of specialists. The number of psychologists employed by the army expanded from 33 in 1933 to 170 in 1938 and 450 in 1942. The German military was instrumental in creating the profession of psychologist. As part of this, the nature of psychology teaching in universities changed. Until 1941 students could only complete PhDs in psychology, which did not consist of practical training and did not qualify graduates for the civil service, although the nature of the examination had been changed at the request of the military to emphasize psychology. Between 1940 and 1941, the German Society for Psychology established a syllabus and examinations for a professional degree in psychology. This established Psychology as an independent discipline with its own university departments, and with full professional status in society.

CONCLUSION

This chapter has surveyed the development of Psychology in the USA and Germany with particular regard to the socio-political contexts within which development occurred. The central claim is that Psychology has had a reflexive relationship with its host society, such that societal concerns affect the development of theory and application within Psychology, and Psychology in turn influences society. Prominent examples of this include eugenics in the USA, where a belief in eugenics influenced the work of psychologists, who in turn provided evidence in support of eugenics; and the development of Psychology in Nazi Germany, where the ideological stance of the ruling party affected the work of psychologists, who reoriented their theories to provide support for the ruling ideology. Such observations cast doubt on traditional claims within the discipline that Psychology is an objective science concerned only with advancing knowledge. Even where Psychology seems to be divorced from influence, as in pre-Nazi Psychology in Germany, we see that the cultural context affects the nature of psychological theorizing.

The chapter has also looked at the process of institutionalization and professionalization in Psychology. We have seen that both in the USA and Germany, the discipline has achieved institutionalization in part by developing applications, presenting itself as a practical subject with value to policy makers. This application has created tensions within the discipline, and required changes to education and to the discipline's organization. In both the USA and Germany, the result was the development of accredited programmes of instruction, completion of which entitled the student to become a member of a recognized profession. The status conferred by the establishment of professional Psychology allowed the discipline to grow, opening it to those who wished to pursue a practical career as well as those who wished to enter academia. This led to greatly expanded numbers of psychologists and increased public recognition.

A final observation we can make is that the development of Psychology, both in the USA and in Germany, has been greatly advanced by war. War has influenced theoretical development in the discipline, with psychologists directing their attentions to topics that seemed to most serve the national need, such as motivation and morale. Postwar, psychologists have attempted to explain newly observed psychological phenomena, such as battle fatigue and authoritarian personality. In addition, war has increased recognition for Psychology and convinced policy makers of Psychology's utility. This is apparent, for example, in the increased demand for psychological services in the USA post World War Two, and in the development of professional certification in both the USA and Germany during World War Two.

FURTHER READING

Ash, M. 1995: *Gestalt psychology in German culture 1890–1967: holism and the quest for objectivity*. Cambridge: Cambridge University Press.

Ash, M. and Woodward, W. 1987: *Psychology in twentieth-century thought and society*. Cambridge: Cambridge University Press.

Buss, A. (ed.) 1979: *Psychology in social context*. New York: Irvington.

Geuter, U. 1992: *The professionalization of psychology in Nazi Germany*. Cambridge: Cambridge University Press.

Herman, E. 1995: *The romance of American psychology*. Berkeley: University of California Press.

Leahey, T.H. 2000: *A history of psychology*, 5th edn. Englewood Cliffs, NJ: Prentice Hall.

7

THE DEVELOPMENT OF SOCIAL PSYCHOLOGY

INTRODUCTION

Throughout this book we strive to be reflexive. In this chapter this still remains important but it is worth recognizing that what I write in this chapter is part of a current debate. I still identify myself as a social psychologist, and align myself with that somewhat loose grouping of critical social psychologists. There are debates both between critical social psychologists and traditional social psychologists and between those who identify themselves as critical psychologists. The main discussion of these issues comes in Chapter 15, but even for the purposes of this chapter it is worth reiterating my position. I identify myself most closely with the ideas of critical poly-textuality as explained by Curt (1994) and Stainton Rodgers and Stainton Rodgers (1998) as a social psychologist. The chapter is informed by two main sources, Farr (1996) and Danziger (1997).

In this chapter we have two main aims that are consistent with the aims of this textbook, we will attempt to sketch a non-positivistic history of social psychology and to show how contingencies have affected the modern form of social psychology. There are a number of objectives that we hope will be met during this chapter. We will build on the discussion in Chapter 2 about how founding figures are constructed in historical accounts, examine the individualization of social Psychology and by concentrating on two case studies, the notion of attitudes and the work of G.H. Mead we hope to contextualize the otherwise abstract points that we are making.

We will begin by sketching an account of social psychology up until what has been called the era of crisis, although perhaps era of perturbations is closer to the spirit of what happened. That will take the account into the 1960s, the end of what has been regarded by traditional social psychologists as the 'golden age' of social psychology. To reinforce the ideas of that sketch, the notion of attitudes will then be examined. Here the contemporary developments of social representations and the influence of social psychological discourse analysis will be mentioned, although a full debate of those influences will come in Chapter 15 and a discussion of the ways that gender and ethnicity have been treated within Psychology, often as an aspect of social Psychology, will be delayed until Chapter 9. Following on the account of how a concept came to be created within Psychology the chapter will consider the ambivalent status of G.H. Mead. His relative neglect by social psychologists working in the experimental paradigm of social psychology may help in our understanding of the type of science that social Psychology was trying to become. The overview of the history of social psychology provides the major theme of the chapter with the later sections providing variations on that theme.

THE ROOTS OF SOCIAL PSYCHOLOGY

Social Psychology has always been a heterogeneous subdivision of two larger disciplinary enterprises, sociology and Psychology. There has been cross fertilization between social psychology and disciplines from neuroscience to anthropology and there have always been a variety of positions on questions, ranging from the correct research methods and the relationship between the pure and applied aspects of the discipline. In writing a history as just one section of a chapter of a book it is inevitable that some of this complexity will become lost. The focus here cannot be the correctness or otherwise of theoretical positions. Instead it is on the complex interactions between social psychology and the wider cultures that it is embedded within. We are mainly concerned here with what happened within the USA because it is the form of social psychology that has come to be predominant both within and outside of the USA.

In order to make a beginning it is necessary to define the topic and in this context we are using an introductory textbook for the definition, not because we believe those definitions are correct but rather because they are almost guaranteed to be a good reflection of the (worldwide) status quo.

Social Psychology is defined by Baron and Byrne (1984) in these terms:

> Social Psychology is the scientific field that seeks to comprehend the nature and causes of individual behavior (sic) in social situations.
>
> (1984: 6–7)

The key part of this definition is the focus on individual behaviour. Another part of the definition that is worth looking at is scientific field. Much of the early part of the chapter will be trying to answer the question why did social psychology become so individualized. Later we will investigate why one particular model of science became the way that social psychology is done, at least within the time frame that we have chosen.

The emergence of social psychology

The social psychology that we have characterized as traditional has a number of elements: it is seen as a scientific discipline; it is distinct from sociological forms of social psychology because of the focus on the individual and it is has a history that takes place within the USA. According to G.W. Allport (1954: 3–4):'While the roots of social psychology lie in the intellectual soil of the whole Western tradition its present flowering is recognized to be characteristically an American phenomenon'.

Before looking at this history of social psychology in the USA it is worth considering the European writers, despite the lack of continuity between them and what happened later.

Both of these ancestors of social psychology are not founding figures. Wündt's *Völkerpsychologie* was a monumental work, published in ten volumes between 1900 and 1920, involving issues around culture, language and the psychology of peoples. Unlike his better known *Physiologischen Psychologie* this work was not readily translated into English. Wündt, as explained in Chapter 2, was a useful father figure for experimental psychology, although little remained of either his system or his methodological strictures. For a scientific social psychology the *Völkerpsychologie* is an embarrassment, Wündt located it firmly as part of the humanities rather than the sciences, and saw it as the home of all the 'higher mental processes' as well as social psychological phenomena. Second, Titchener, who has been accused of systematically mistranslating Wündt's work, was less concerned with Völkerpsychologie as he tried to establish what he called structuralism as a science in the USA. Finally Wündt's strong nationalism during World War One may have isolated him even further from his former students in the USA. Wündt may have had an indirect influence on those aspects of social psychology that use discourse analysis, as according to Blumenthal (1973) Wündt influenced linguistics including de Saussure. However, we are not going to claim that Wündt was some sort of ancestral discursive psychologist, as has recently been done for example with Bartlett and his cultural interests in cognitive psychology.

A second failed founding figure is Gustav Le Bon, although unlike Wündt, Le Bon, a political and social pundit as well as a popular science writer, was not trying to establish a psychological system. Despite this Le Bon, as detailed by Richards (1996), had a certain amount of influence, not just on psychologists but also practically in terms of influencing propaganda techniques. Writing at the time of one of a series of crises caused by, it was supposed, unruly mob behaviour (the Paris Commune of 1871 being one in a long line of incidents since the French revolution) Le Bon was writing about something close to French political life. He strove to explain the rules of crowd behaviour and saw the crowd as a distinct entity.

One of Le Bon's avowed aims was to help teach leaders how to use and harness the laws of crowd behaviour in order to rule more effectively. Le Bon used ideas from hypnotism (and its earlier incarnation mesmerism) which were scientifically credible within France (and elsewhere), particularly the idea that there is a primitive state that is more suggestible once the veneer of civilization has been stripped away. *The crowd* uses ideas that are in their time scientifically credible, and at least some of the ideas are taken up by Psychology's repressed sister discipline, with Freud's later cultural writings taking up the idea of the leader-follower relationship being similar to the hypnotist-subject relationship. Moreover these ideas are framed in a way that is consonant with (then) current ideas in Social Darwinism and carried with them ideas of race ideals a fashionable idea. Despite the later accusations (Allport 1924) of mysticism Le Bon's ideas were psychological, and scientific.

The crowd also influenced social psychologists both in the USA and Britain. Although the influence in the USA was one of strong condemnation, with the thorough repudiation of the idea of group minds existing beyond the individual. It is this development that ultimately leads me not to see Le Bon as either a founder or ancestor of social psychology, although the idea of understanding what happens in crowds and other groups has been central to at least some social psychology.

Le Bon's work also influenced Freud's ideas on culture and group psychology which Freud developed after World War One. Freud's notions were in turn influential on the theorizing of British psychoanalysts when they faced what was then the unique challenge of group psychoanalysis. Those developments are considered in Chapter 5.

Thus we are refraining from answering the potential question of who founded social psychology. The when question is easier to answer. Social psychology has shown a remarkable continuity in form, theory and method since the late 1940s. The 'who' question, however, is misguided, and goes back to the positivistic concerns with naming a founding figure. Modern social psychology emerged out of World War Two and has its roots in the inter-war period in the USA and Germany. Much of what emerged was based initially on the concerns of the US government and army during wartime. There is, however, some influence on the form of what emerged from some of the concerns of emigré Gestaltist psychologists.

During World War Two the US army commissioned a vast research programme for an interdisciplinary team of social scientists. They were interested in, amongst other things, the adjustment of soldiers to army life, their participation in combat and its aftermath, effective briefing of troops, in solving technical problems of the measurement of attitudes and predicting behaviour. *The American soldier*, a series of volumes on these topics, was published after the War under the general editorship of Stouffer, a sociologist. Many of the research teams formed in this period remained active post World War Two. One at Yale, under the direction of Hovland, involved the experimental study of mass media. The wartime experience also led to founding of a number of doctoral programmes in social psychology, based at Harvard, Yale, Michigan and Columbia; although these all begin as interdisciplinary enterprises they all eventually split across disciplinary lines.

World War Two left another legacy, returning military personnel who wanted to finish their degrees, begin degrees after a prewar profession or whatever. This led to an immense influx of extremely talented students, some of whom went on to become the social psychologists of the golden age of experimental social psychology (the 1950s and 1960s).

Given the relative recent emergence of social psychology it is difficult to get enough of a historical perspective on modern social psychology, per se, so like Farr does I will talk about the roots. The roots go a long way back, and given the constraints of time I will concentrate mainly on the inter-war period.

The institutional dominance of social psychology in the USA led to the exporting of this tradition throughout the English speaking world. Thus, to understand how social psychology became a discipline of the individual, rather than the social, we need to understand the individualization of social psychology in the USA.

Individualism

At least since the Renaissance individualism has been a key component in the western intellectual tradition (Burkhardt 1860). The philosophical tradition of Descartes (1637) reinforced this notion. Hegel ties this rise in individualism to the rise of the merchant class, and it is possible to sketch a picture of individualism in line with the economic developments within Europe. The Reformation and the invention of the printing press hastened the cause of individualism, as those who dissented from the church's reading of the Bible were labelled and persecuted in the Old World. Some of these non-conformists escaped Europe and went to colonies in North America and their concerns influenced the culture of what came to be the USA. However individualism is often not seen as influential. Part of the reason is that when individualism becomes a dominant ideology within a culture it becomes invisible to those affected by the ideology. Ideology as a term is often equated with holding collective beliefs. When the collective belief is a celebration of the individual, this, ironically, is no longer seen as a collective belief.

The roots of individualism are in the soil of the whole western intellectual tradition, but its flowering is a characteristically US phenomenon. Given this then it ought to be possible to understand the individualism of social psychology in the USA against this cultural backdrop. Two forms of psychological understanding appear to have particularly influenced the individualism of social Psychology.

The Influence of Behaviourism and Gestalt Psychology

F.H. Allport wrote a textbook, *Social psychology* in 1924, after noting that up until then most of the social psychology textbooks had been written by sociologists. This can be seen as a manifesto for a certain type of social psychology consistent with behaviourism.

There is no psychology of groups which is not essentially and entirely a psychology of individuals. Social psychology must not be placed in contradiction to the psychology of the individual.

> It is part of the psychology of the individual, whose behaviour it studies in relation to that sector of his environment comprised by his fellows . . . There is likewise no consciousness except that belonging to individuals. Psychology in all its branches is a science of the individual.

(Allport 1924: 4)

This statement can be seen as a direct contradiction of social psychology of G.H. Mead and the *Volkerpsychologie* of Wündt. F.H. Allport's methodological commitments also led him towards a methodological individualism. His prime method was the laboratory experiment. This commitment can be seen further in his definition of public opinion.

> The term public opinion is given its meaning with reference to a multi-individual situation in which individuals are expressing themselves, or can be called upon to express themselves, as favoring or supporting (or else disfavoring or opposing) some definite condition, person or proposal of widespread importance, in such a proportion of number, intensity or constancy, as to give rise to the probability of affecting action, directly, or indirectly, toward the object concerned.
>
> (Allport 1937: 23)

This position is of course at odds with the notions of social representation first defined by the sociologist Durkheim and carried into the work of Moscovici, a European social psychologist.

Allport wrote an astonishing account of the effect of institutions on people, concluding with the idea that, 'Our most vexing dilemmas arise not from the fact that we lack the right institutions but from the fact that we have institutions at all' (Allport 1933: 411). In this book, *Institutional behaviour*, he focused on institutions such as the family, the church, government, schools, politics, etc., and argued that they rob the individual of their autonomous moral authority. According to Farr, this illustrates how a core societal belief, individualism, can be seen as affecting Psychology and the psychology of those in that society, although those so affected have lost the understanding of how that may happen to them.

Although behaviourism is one factor affecting the individualization of social psychology it is not the only one. For example, F.H Allport's younger brother, G.W. Allport, had a more cognitive orientation, but still persisted in defining the discipline in terms of the individual, and, according to Jasper and Fraser (1984), defined attitude in individualistic terms by editing out the social parts of other definitions. So the turn to a more cognitive orientation does not by itself denote a major shift in the overall paradigm of social psychology.

This more cognitive orientation comes from Gestalt Psychology. The lead up to World War Two, and the exodus from Nazi Germany of a large group of Gestalt psychologists also had a direct effect on the individualization of social psychology. Although the Gestalt tradition was cognitive, the Gestalt psychologists found that social psychology was the best niche in the behaviourist US university departments. Later this cognitive social psychology, which predates the general rise in cognitive psychology by almost two decades, was to have an indirect influence on the forms that cognitive psychology was to take. However, the Gestaltist tradition, while more concerned with process than behaviourism, was much more strongly individualist than the French traditions of a more group orientated social psychology.

Asch, whose work is strongly influenced by the Gestaltist tradition, wrote (in 1952) a very influential textbook called *Social psychology*. This book is described by Farr (1996), as being as influential to modern US social psychology as Allport's (1924) textbook was for prewar social psychology. There are however clear differences between a Gestalt tradition and a behaviourist tradition. Individualism, as a core cultural concept remains extremely important to both conceptualizations of social psychology. The rise of the Cold War influenced further this individualization of social psychology. During this era in the USA, social scientists began to call themselves behavioural scientists as individualism as an ideology came to be contrasted to (so-called) communism as an ideology. Farr suggests that this was a successful ploy because the politicians who vote on funding may have confused socialism with the social sciences. When the balance between individualistic and social understandings of human beings becomes biased to just one pole it may have a very distorting influence on both the discipline of social Psychology and on Psychology as a whole.

ATTITUDES

There are a number of reasons why I have chosen attitudes as the case study. One is very pragmatic. There is an excellent chapter on attitudes in Danziger's *Naming the mind*. The second is that the history of attitudes is representative of the individualization of the social. The third is that attitudes, along with psychometrics, show that the schools of psychology notion was never monolithic. The final one is that it is a case study of methodology and theory construction interacting with each other.

The prepsychology of attitude

The term attitude did not emerge within Psychology, or sociology, but has an earlier aesthetic dimension. The concept of attitudes emerges in social psychology in the 1920s. Krauss (1995) reports that during the previous 20 year period over 34,000 published studies addressed attitudes in some way.

The technical use of attitude first emerges in discourses about visual art and the theatre. The posture of a figure, in a painting, sculpture or of an actor is seen as being expressive of an inner (emotional) state, and this is seen as an attitude. So a figure has an attitude. I feel that it is this meaning that has survived when people talk of someone having an attitude. In the original usage the inner and outer states in this discourse are seen as an inherent unity, rather than the outer expression being caused by an inner state.

Attitudes in Psychology

The term, like intelligence, comes into Psychology originally via biology. To some extent Psychology has always borrowed heavily from biology although part of the reason for this may be an attempt to gain scientific prestige by doing so. Darwin (1872) in the book *The expression of emotions in man and animals* while not defining it as a technical term uses it extensively, referring to the pattern of motor activity which constitutes the overt expression of an emotion. The technical term 'emotional attitudes' was used by Dewey (1894) and Angell (1904). The term, however, began to be used in other biologically related areas, the term 'motor attitudes' referring to reflex postural adjustments on the part of animal. This meant that the term is acceptable to behaviourists like J.B. Watson (for example 1919) who wanted to establish Psychology as a purely biological science. The term thus had a respectability. However none of these attitudes seem to have an obvious connection with the later social psychological use of the term.

Social Attitudes in Sociology

My analysis of this differs sharply with Danziger. He assumes that the addition of 'social' to attitudes comes out of the previous psychological use, whereas I see the term as coming originally from a separate strand of usage.

So, in order to understand how the technical concept 'attitude', as it is used within Psychology, came about I propose to look at what I think is a quite separate strand of usage. Durkheim, the French sociologist, uses the term in 1898, referring to social attitudes, as representations held by groups of people. This usage continues in sociology. Thomas, the Chicago sociologist, defined social psychology as the study of social attitudes in the 1920s. This object, social attitudes, is used to differentiate between different groups of people, not individuals. Social attitudes, within sociology are seen as a group, not individual, phenomena. This notion, if not the term, continues with Moscovici's theory of social representations. La Piere (1934), mentioned in many social psychology textbooks as an early attitude researcher, was a sociologist rather than a psychologist, which may help explain his methodology because he was more concerned with people as representatives of groups rather than individuals.

By the 1920s there are two separate 'attitudes' within Psychology, one with a biological orientation, the other with a sociological orientation. Social psychologists were probably aware of both uses and this may in itself help explain what emerged.

Bringing the terms together

The person probably most responsible for bringing these two notions together is G.W. Allport. In the first handbook (PhD guide) for social psychologists, published in 1935, he gives the following definition:

> A mental and neural state of readiness, organized through experience, exerting a directive or dynamic influence upon the individual's response to all objects and situations with which it is related.

(Allport 1935, 1954)

This definition preserves the biological component of the concept of attitude and the link with the social (objects and situations) and individualizes the sociological notion.

Attitudes and measurement

While looking at these internal developments is interesting, it is too easy to over state the case, since the individuals had profound influence on the discipline when there were other influences internal and external. Before looking at the external influences I want to look at the influence of the technology of testing. Gould, Richards and Danziger (for example) all regard the technology of testing as being influenced the psychological concept of intelligence. Along with Richards and Danziger I want to extend this argument to attitudes. The most common method of testing attitudes today is the Likert scale, relatively easy to construct and administer compared with its direct ancestor, the Thurstone scale. The Lickert scale became accepted, at least in part, because the values it measured correlated well with the values on the Thurstone scale. So I shall concentrate on the development of the Thurstone scale, taking this analysis from Danziger.

According to Thurstone (1952) his entry into attitude scaling came about after correspondence with F.H. Allport into the measurement of opinions. In 1925 Allport and Hartman had published a paper on opinions towards Prohibition, a hot topic of the time. Allport and Hartman had adopted a method, constructing statements and asking respondents to select the one that they most agreed with, already widely used in public opinion polling in the USA. While some psychologists treated opinions and attitudes as synonyms, others, including Thurstone, treated attitudes as underlying people's opinions. He proposed to measure underlying attitudes by the use of surface opinions. To some extent this project was going to give opinion polling a scientific basis.

Thurstone (1928) recognized that there would be differences between attitudes, the things that people had, and what he called attitude variables, the things that psychologists measured using his technique. The technique itself was based, by analogy, within an area of psychology with long rooted scientific credentials, psycho-physics.

One task in psycho-physical research is the classic comparison of pairs of weights, resulting ultimately in calculating the just noticeable difference. Thurstone decided to adopt this procedure to measuring between, for example, pairs of criminal offences (Which is worse, murder or rape?) and pairs of nationalities (Who would you prefer to associate with, an Italian or a Pole?).

Cumbersome though it is, it is possible by this method of comparing pairs of statements to come up with a graduated list of statements using a pool of judges to see if they agreed with the differences: 'The separations between the statements in the scale may be ascertained by psycho-physical principles on the common assumption that equally often noticed differences are equal' (Thurstone 1959: 237).

What Thurstone appears to have overlooked in his work is that difference between one individual noticing a difference (the classic psycho-physics method) and a group of individuals noticing a difference. However, noticing a difference is a behaviouristic way of measuring anything, and neatly sidesteps the issue of what the difference may mean to the respondent.

Likert's much more simple way of measuring attitudes pushes these concerns even further into the background, and the notion that an attitude towards something can be operationally defined as the measurement on an attitude scale really takes off. These issues of measurement are explored again in Chapter 12.

The Social Context

The final thing to look at is the social context within which attitudes became established. After the initial optimism following World War One and a decade of psychology growing and becoming established within wider society as a useful discipline, things took a darker turn with the Great Depression. There were editorials in newspapers calling for psychologists to do something. After all, economists, sociologists and others had all offered solutions but, as a discipline, Psychology was quiet. While it was World War Two that really put attitude research on the map, with the establishment of an Information and Education Division by the US War Department to measure, and when appropriate change, attitudes, it was the rise in opinion polling in the 1930s that provided the entry point. In 1935 Gallup established the American Institute of Public Opinion, and before then President Hoover had established a government commission whose brief was to measure public opinions on a variety of topics including social attitudes.

Thus attitudes, which are one of the enduring concepts in modern social psychology have a somewhat confused genesis but provide social psychologists with something that can be measured in an objective fashion. Such measurement leads to potential of change, the adjustment of attitudes through propaganda campaigns, with the measurement technique allowing for an evaluation of how well the propaganda has worked.

G.H. MEAD (1863–1931)

When first teaching the material that this chapter is based on to a mixed group of third-year sociology and Psychology students I asked the group if they had heard of G.H. Mead. The Psychology students had not, whereas many of the sociology students had, and identified him as the instigator of symbolic interactionism. One purpose in this section of the chapter is to try to bring the work of Mead to a larger audience. Another is to use the account of G.H. Mead to explore the divergence between sociological forms of social Psychology and psychological forms of social Psychology. The final purpose is to consider the ways that 'dissident science' is treated with some prospect of looking forward to Chapter 15.

G.H. Mead was one of the many US graduate students in Germany before

World War One. As well as taking a course with Wündt at Leipzig he studied at the University of Berlin from 1889–91, leaving before completing his PhD for an appointment at Michigan University. He moved to Chicago University in 1894 with Dewey. Dewey was appointed to the Foundation Chair of Philosophy in a department that included education and Psychology as well as philosophy. Mead remained in the philosophy department after Dewey left Chicago for Columbia. However, the remaining psychologists, under Angell and including Watson, formed a separate department.

Mead did not publish much during his life time, although his publications did include reviews of the first four volumes of Wündt's *Völkerpsychologie* and he was one of the very few Americans to recognize the importance of this work at the time that it was published in German. In the earlier part of his career he often lectured without notes and so much of our knowledge of his work comes from posthumous publications of transcriptions of his lectures, *Mind, self and society: from the standpoint of a social behaviourist* published in 1934 and *The individual and social self* published in 1982. This in itself gives some indication of why Mead has been to some extent neglected by psychologists and many histories of psychology, but it is not the whole the story. Watson, writing candidly in a short autobiography published in *A history of psychology through autobiography* (edited by Murchinson) admits that he did not understand much of what Mead talked about in his lecturers and seminar series.

In order to understand both this and Mead's neglect by the psychologists of his own era, it is necessary to sketch out some aspects of his social psychology.

Wündt had attempted to deal with the problem of investigating mind scientifically by separating his limited project on the immediate contents of consciousness from his cultural appreciation of mind as a social phenomenon. Watson attempted to deal with the same problem by ignoring mind, although rather than solving this Cartesian dualism, this move ironically reinforces it just by focusing on the individual and ignoring the social. Mead attempted to solve the problem by synthesizing the individual and social through a sophisticated understanding of evolutionary biology. As with Wündt mind is constructed as an inherently social phenomenon but unlike Wündt, for Mead this did not mean that it could not be appreciated scientifically. Wündt showed little appreciation of evolutionary biology in his work, whereas Mead's work, involving comparative psychology as well as social psychology, fully appreciated evolutionary psychology. Mead, a philosophical pragmatist, was also a realist, that is his philosophy was informed by findings in science.

For Mead language was essentially a social process. This non-Cartesian tradition of thought can be traced through Herder, Humboldt and Hegel and language is seen as a dialogue involving speaker and listener cooperating, rather than a monologue where the speaker attempts to transmit information to the listener. For Mead, unlike Wündt, mind is a product of language

Mind arises through communication by a conversation of gestures in a social process or context of experience – not communication through mind (Mead 1934: 50).

In conversation a person can only successfully communicate with another if one can take on to some extent the role of the other. Thus the speaker needs to be listener orientated and the listener speaker orientated. In addition when a person speaks they are simultaneously talking to themselves as they are to the other person. Language is at the heart of the self-reflexive nature of human intelligence.

Another aspect of Mead's social psychology involves his philosophy of the act. For all animals, including humans although for humans things get a little more complicated because of their species specific ability – language and social acts have a specific form for Mead. The act is a part action that others complete, or more fully others react to the start of an act in terms of its anticipated end and the self (originator of the act) then reacts to their reactions. The meaning of an act depends upon the reactions it elicits from others. The meaning is not to be equated to intentions, although an actor can and will adjust their actions according to prior experience and their anticipation of the reactions of others. For Mead, the beginning of an act is not necessarily the segment of the act that happens to be visible to an outside observer. It originates in the central nervous system of the actor. Neither though is the consequence of the act always predictable from the perspective of the actor. Both the observer and the actor have limited perspectives. The behaviourists were to concentrate just on the perspective of the observer. Some Psychology (for example, humanism) concentrates just on the perspective of the actor. For Mead the two need to be understood and interrelated. Earlier in his career Mead adopted the notion of taking the role of the other. Later, following his reading of Einstein, he replaced that notion with the idea of 'adopting the perspective of the other'.

Mead developed a philosophy, based on realist pragmaticism, through the medium of his lecture course on social Psychology. Ironically this was better received by sociologists than psychologists. Given that the three disciplines, Psychology, sociology and philosophy have been self-consciously maintaining their disciplinary boundaries it is perhaps not surprising that Mead's work, which transgresses these boundaries, is not fully appreciated even in a context when some parts of social psychology are reclaiming the social.

Mind, Self and Society: from the standpoint of a social behaviourist

Morris, a philosopher, had the task of editing a transcript of Mead's 1927 course of lecturers into a book. Mead had published little during his career and it was Morris who had the task of finding a suitable name for Mead's approach. He chose 'social behaviourism'. Mead's social behaviourism was of course a very different approach from either Watson's or Skinner's behaviourism. To begin with Mead was a much more consistent Darwinian than they were, and his appropriation of Darwin was not encumbered by the type of Social Darwinism that can be traced to Spencer, which to some extent the behaviourists were reacting against. This meant that Mead much more consistently used comparative psychology in an attempt to produce a science of social psychology, along with an appreciation of language and mind that behaviourism failed to have. However, it is probable that this title was misleading, and Morris had chosen it with a view towards some sort of reconciliation between Watson's behaviourism and Mead's approach. 'The judgement of time will perhaps regard Watsonism as behaviourism, methodologically simplified for purposes of initial laboratory investigation' (Mead 1934: xvii). This was an optimistic viewpoint, for while Mead was a positivist, seeing Psychology as a science, he dealt with the problem of mind by bringing it fully within science, taking the model of evolutionary psychology as his starting point. Behaviourism took its misunderstanding of physics as a model of science, decrying that which could not be directly observed as metaphysics and therefore to be ignored as not scientific.

Mead left no legacy of research findings. His work was theoretical, although his theories were based on research evidence and his reading of other scientists outside of Psychology. This also means that in a discipline that appears to favour the contribution of empiricists (hence the notion in some social Psychology texts that the discipline has a history that begins with the first social Psychology experiment) Mead was ignored. Indeed the only mention made of him by G.W. Allport (1954) in his history of social psychology is to criticise him for using imitation as a single explanatory principle in accounting for social phenomena. Hopefully, despite the brief sketch of Mead's social psychology I have been able to give here, the reader will appreciate how misfounded that criticism may have been. Skinner's (1957) work, *Verbal behavior*, in which Skinner, like Mead, wrote about language as expressive behaviour does not cite Mead. Unfortunately Skinner failed to understand that language is also a form of symbolic interaction, a lack of understanding that continued even after the cognitive revolution in language.

Finally Mead was misunderstood by the discipline, sociology, that at least part of his social psychology continued within. Following Mead's death, Blummer, a sociologist, took over Mead's social psychology course, and began the development of symbolic interactionism, based on the significance of language in the social psychology of Mead. There is little doubt that the sociologists at Chicago appreciated Mead's work. His course on social Psychology was a recommended ancillary course for graduate students in sociology. They also, probably, appreciated the criticisms of Watsonian behaviourism that Mead made. They appear to have misunderstood that Mead was working in a form of psychological social psychology, as a science. At the time of publication there were complaints that the contents of the book should have appeared in the order, 'society, self and mind', an order that many of the early symbolic interactionist texts appear. However the order 'mind, self and society' appears to be consistent across transcripts from Mead's course taken in 1927 and 1914, although society is dealt with at considerably more length in 1914. The other thing that appears not to have been fully appreciated by the sociological inheritors of Mead's work is the role that evolution played in his theories. By utilizing evolution Mead was able to fully naturalize mind. By ignoring this aspect of his work, mind for symbolic interactionists becomes something fully formed by the actions of society. This may be slightly more insightful than ignoring mind altogether as the behaviourists did, but it still appears to be inconsistent with what Mead was attempting to do.

As well as working on social psychology Mead also developed a philosophy of history. He was particularly critical of positivistic histories. However, it is a feature of those histories, especially in Psychology, to attempt to distinguish between philosophical speculation and true science. Mead may have fallen victim to that aspect of positivism because of his place in the philosophy department at Chicago. He also reminds us that all histories are written from the perspective of the present. It is at least a possibility that this reading of Mead's work appears to fit in neatly with some of the movements in social constructionist Psychology because that is the perspective that I adopt when doing social psychology.

CONCLUSIONS

The emergence of social psychology exemplifies a number of themes across this book: the influence of individuals, and their psychologies (for example, F.H. Allport's rabid individualism); the influence of internal debates and the influence of external forces. To try to isolate anyone of these things is to write a misleading history and it is only by attempting to look at them all together that we get an understanding of the history of psychology.

FURTHER READING

Billig, M. 1996: *Arguing and thinking: a rhetorical approach to social psychology.* Cambridge: Cambridge University Press.

Curt, B.C. 1994: *Textuality and tectonics: troubling social and psychological science.* Buckingham: The Open University Press.

Danziger, K. 1990: *Constructing the subject: historical origins of psychological research.* Cambridge: Cambridge University Press.

Danziger, K. 1997: *Naming the mind: how psychology found its language.* London: Sage Publications Ltd.

Farr, R.M. 1996: *The roots of modern social psychology, 1872–1954.* Oxford: Blackwell.

Ibanez, T. and L. Iniguez (eds) 1997: *Critical social psychology.* London: Sage.

Jasper, J.M.F. 1984: Attitudes and social representations. In: R.M Farr and S. Moscovici (eds), *Social representations.* Cambridge: Cambridge University Press.

Mead, G.H. 1934: In C.W. Morris (ed.), *Mind, self and society: from the standpoint of a social behaviourist.* Chicago: University of Chicago Press.

Mead, G.H. 1982: In D.L. Miller (ed.), *The individual and social self: unpublished work of George Herbert Mead*. Chicago: Chicago University Press.

Richards, G. 1996: *Putting psychology in its place*. London: Routledge.

Stainton Rogers, R. 1995: Q methodology. In: J.A. Smith, R. Harré and L.V. Langenhove (eds), *Rethinking methods in psychology*. London: Sage.

8

THE RISE OF COGNITIVISM

In this chapter, we look at the development of cognitive Psychology. Cognitive Psychology is characterized as an approach rather than a school, involving a commitment to a certain form of explanation within Psychology. Particular subject areas can be seen as fundamental to the approach, and certainly most amenable to the approach, including perception, learning, memory, reasoning, and language, and to many these topics define cognitive Psychology as a sub-discipline. However, taking a broader view the cognitive approach can be adopted for a range of areas of investigation within Psychology – thus there is a cognitive social Psychology, meaning an investigation of topics considered to be part of social psychology, adopting a cognitive approach. The cognitive approach has been dominant across a range of areas of psychology since the 1960s, particularly in North America and the UK. We distinguish between cognitive Psychology as a sub-discipline, with a particular range of topics of exploration, and a general cognitive approach to Psychology which we call cognitivism. This chapter will be concerned mainly with cognitive Psychology, since this provided the theoretical arena out of which cognitivism in general emerged.

The approach of cognitive Psychology is based on a particular set of theoretical assumptions. One of the purposes of this chapter is to show that these assumptions have developed contingent on a range of factors. To this end, we shall look at antecedents to cognitivism in Psychology and in other disciplines to see that despite a long tradition of cognitive discourse, the development of cognitivism as an approach was only possible in a particular context. We shall also look at the popular view of cognitive Psychology as a revolution overthrowing behaviourism, and at the main contribution of the cognitive approach that makes it distinct from previous cognitive discourse.

WHAT REVOLUTION?

We start by considering the historiography of the development of cognitive Psychology. By studying representations of the emergence of the discipline, we can at the same time both learn about how it emerged, and also about the nature of disciplinary history in Psychology. Greenwood (1997) identifies four common characterizations of the emergence of cognitive Psychology: as a Kuhnian paradigm shift; as a move from instrumentalist to realist conceptions of theories; as an evolution out of liberalized forms of behaviourism; and as a return to a form of structuralism. In this section, we shall look particularly at characterizations of the emergence as a paradigm shift. Claims that cognitive Psychology was evolutionary, or that cognitive Psychology represents a return to structuralism, are considered over the course of the chapter.

Our concentration on the notion of cognitive Psychology as a paradigm shift is because this is probably the most frequent representation, and also because this claim best characterizes the use of history to justify theoretical positions. The claim that there was a 'cognitive revolution' is based on Kuhn's work on scientific change, described in Chapter 1. In this characterization, psychologists became aware of anomalies in the theoretical bases of behaviourism, and responded by adopting new theoretical approaches based on a reacceptance of mentalistic concepts, which then displaced behaviourism as the dominant paradigm within Psychology. This makes for a pleasing narrative, for cognitive psychologists if not for behaviourists, and serves a celebratory role in legitimizing cognitivism. However, the view is probably best seen as a creation myth, since a considered analysis shows a number of weaknesses in the narrative.

Leahey (1992) identifies four reasons why the emergence of cognitive Psychology does not represent a Kuhnian paradigm shift. First, behaviourism was too diverse to be considered a paradigm. Consider, for example, the differences in the theoretical formulations of Tolman, Hull, and Skinner. Second, the shift from behaviourism to cognitive Psychology was too gradual to be called revolutionary. We shall see that there was a tradition of cognitive work in Psychology before the sub-discipline of cognitive Psychology was identified, and there is continuing work in the radical behaviourist framework, albeit with a restricted scope. Third, the early research in cognitive Psychology that was to define the new sub-discipline was not a response to weaknesses in behaviourism, but rather was carried out independently. We shall consider the origins of this early work later in the chapter. Finally, cognitive Psychology is itself too diverse to be considered a paradigm. We shall consider the varieties of, and debates within, cognitive Psychology in Chapters 13 and 14. It is true that some of the early cognitivists saw themselves as participating in a revolution, but this may have been as much a function of the social and intellectual contexts of the 1960s as of the work they were doing. During the 1960s political and social radicalism was in vogue, and the early cognitivists may have been responding to this Zeitgeist. In addition, Kuhn's work was published during the emergence of cognitive Psychology, and was immediately successful. Its publication may have created the suggestion that a revolution was underway, a suggestion that cognitive psychologists were happy to subscribe to.

With regard to the other traditional views outlined by Greenwood, the notion that cognitive Psychology represents a revolutionary shift from instrumentalist to realist conceptions of theory is dismissed by observing that behaviourists such as Tolman and Hull had realist views, while many early cognitivists were wary of such views. The claim that cognitive Psychology was an evolution from more mentalistic orientations in behaviourism falls down because there is clear difference between the views of mental states adopted by behaviourists and cognitivists. Finally, the view that cognitive Psychology represents a return to a form of Wündtian structuralism overlooks the fact that despite investigating similar topics, the theories generated, the investigative practices employed, and the data used by cognitive Psychology are very different from structuralism.

These traditional accounts generally share the feature that they are trying to explain the relationship between behaviourism and cognitivism, either in terms of replacement because of weaknesses, or a shift to a different view of theory, or as an evolution. What we hope to show in this chapter is that, while cognitivism replaced behaviourism as the most common approach in experimental Psychology, it arose independently of it out of a range of antecedents. The new cognitive approach offered a competing framework to behaviourism, and proved to be successful, mainly because it seemed to offer a sound framework for mentalistic constructs. The reason why cognitivism was successful in introducing mental constructs and other cognitive approaches were not is one of the focuses of this chapter.

PSYCHOLOGICAL ANTECEDENTS OF COGNITIVISM

Chapter 3 traced early theoretical developments in American Psychology, and showed that Psychology began as a science of conscious experience. We saw that in the USA, this science quickly adopted a functionalist perspective, and in response to a number of pressures began to concentrate on behaviour as the main source of data. This move to behaviouralism reached its logical conclusion in behaviourism, where perceived difficulties in scientifically investigating behaviour led to theoretical arguments that there was no need to investigate mental processes, since these were epiphenomenal, arising as a side effect of physiological association. However, while behaviourism became the dominant framework for American experimental Psychology, cognitive research continued in the USA, and more especially in Europe.

European Antecedents

As previous chapters have related, scientific Psychology has its roots in Europe. Initially, this scientific Psychology was structuralist, in a general sense, typified by the work of Wündt and Titchener. However, as described in Chapter 2, German Psychology quickly diversified, most notably with the research of Ebbinghaus and the Würzburg school. Ebbinghaus's work is often termed cognitive, in that he investigated a topic that is now considered a part of cognitive Psychology. However, he shared with the structuralists a commitment to associationist explanations, which are rather different to the explanations of cognitive Psychology. For cognitive Psychology, mental states are contentful and actively processed. Even in the case of Ebbinghaus, therefore, many early German psychologists were not pursuing cognitive research, despite similarities in topic area. An exception is the case of the Würzburg psychologists, whose studies of imageless thought and directed thought discounted association as an explanatory framework, showing that associative links could be overcome by directed thought. The Würzburg school emphasized the study of 'rule governed, intentionally directed and contentful representational activity' (Greenwood 1997) as fundamental to the investigation of thinking. The Würzburgers pioneered programmatic explanations of information processing, particularly in the work of Otto Selz with his 'thought-psychology', which had a major influence on Herbert Simon's work in problem solving (Bechtel, Abramsen and Graham 1998). Selz, Bühler and Külpe began a tradition of problem solving work which, through Duncker, Luchins and Wertheimer, informs cognitive research today.

The Würzburg school did not survive as a distinct school after the 1920s. However, it directly informed a number of diverse cognitive approaches in Psychology, which emphasized the active processing of mental content, often on the basis of rules. These approaches were somewhat hidden in Anglophone Psychology by the dominance of behaviourism, but represent a continuous cognitive tradition. More noticeable was the concurrent development of Gestalt Psychology. Gestalt was itself influenced by the Würzburg school, Wertheimer and Koffka both having worked with Külpe, which is particularly noticeable in Gestalt theories of problem solving. The concerns of Gestalt anticipated cognitive Psychology to some extent, including imagery, memory, unconscious processing, and the existence of an active processor, although they adopted a rather different theoretical orientation than the Würzburgers and their followers. Gestalt's influence on American Psychology is debatable, although Gestalt insights were adopted into the mainstream of American Psychology. Certainly, as we saw in Chapter 3, Gestalt was very visible in the 1930s, and Köhler worked to keep it so in the 1940s and 1950s. Perhaps Gestalt's greatest influence on future cognitive Psychology was to sustain the discussion of mental states during the domination of behaviourism. This influence was felt in American social Psychology more than experimental Psychology, but we shall see that the adoption of mentalistic concepts in social Psychology was to help their acceptance following the rise of cognitivism.

The contributions of these two schools are often overlooked. More often discussed are the contributions of three individuals – Piaget, Bartlett and Vygotsky. There is some irony in this, since these three arguably had less of an influence on the initial development of cognitivism than the Würzburg and Gestalt schools, although they had considerable influence on the later development of cognitive approaches in cognitive, developmental and social Psychology. These three are honoured post hoc as cognitive psychologists. As we shall see, it was common for early historical accounts to apply such labels, as a way of legitimizing the cognitive approach.

Piaget's early interests were in biology and epistemology, particularly on how we obtain knowledge of the world. He worked with Simon in Binet's laboratory in Paris, working to standardize a reasoning test developed by Burt. He found that he was more interested in how children answered questions than in their scores, and was especially interested in why children got answers wrong. He investigated this through interviews with children, and concluded that there were qualitative differences between adult and child thinking, which was to lead to his stage theory of cognitive development. In 1921 he established a research institute for the study of children in Geneva, developing observational methods for the identification of preverbal children. His focus was on how knowledge developed in children, which he explained in terms of children as active processors of knowledge stored in organized structures, called schemas. These schemas were irreducible wholes, and Piaget (1952) acknowledged his debt to the Gestaltists for legitimizing his holistic approach. Piaget's work had little influence in the USA, despite his participation in an international congress at Yale in 1929 (together with Lewin and Pavlov), and his award of an honorary degree from Harvard in 1936 (Goodwin 1999). The lack of influence was mainly due to a lack of English translations of his work and the dominance of behaviourism from the 1930s. This dominance may in part explain the lack of translation, the American audience being largely unreceptive to his ideas.

Bartlett was the head of Cambridge's psychology laboratory, one of the few centres for experimental Psychology in the UK. He is most noted for this 1932 book *Remembering: a study in social and experimental psychology*. In this work, Bartlett rejected Ebbinghaus' artificial approach to memory research and its associative theoretical basis. Rather, he argued that the memorizer actively organizes material into meaningful wholes, which he also called schemas, though independently of Piaget. These schemas, claimed Bartlett, affect people's perceptions and memory of events, and will differ in content depending on personal experiences. For Bartlett then, individual differences in perception arise from differences in existing knowledge, in comparison to Dewey's largely behavioural explanation (see Chapter 3). Bartlett followed *Remembering* with his 1958 book *Thinking: an experimental and social study*, and both *Remembering* and *Thinking* are notable for incorporating social contexts in cognition, although this element of his work is often overlooked. Bartlett was largely ignored in the USA, since by the time of his most productive work behaviourism was establishing its dominance, but his work was rediscovered in the 1960s. His central notion of the subjective, constructive nature of memory has influenced recent work in cognitive Psychology, for example that of Neisser and Loftus, but his main contribution to the early development of cognitivism was his training of Broadbent, whose research work incorporated some of Bartlett's insights.

Vygotsky is more marginal to cognitive Psychology than either Piaget or Bartlett, possibly because he adopted a strongly cultural and historical approach to cognitive and linguistic development. He emphasized the importance of interpersonal interactions, a view which remains unpopular with mainstream cognitive Psychology but which is increasingly appreciated in cognitive approaches to developmental and social Psychology. He produced productive work in collaboration with Luria, but his wider project was the creation of a unified science of mind. He was aware of all the major approaches in Psychology, but was most influenced by the Gestalt and Würzburg schools. As with Piaget and Bartlett, Vygotsky's work was largely unknown in the USA before the 1960s, in this case because of suppression of outside communication by the Soviet regime. His work has now been rediscovered, and is influencing cognitivism.

What these three cases share is a body of experimental cognitive work that was being conducted. They had limited influence in behaviourist America and they received belated recognition of their work in 1960s America, once the notion of studying cognition became acceptable again. This is interesting in that it shows the influence of a general intellectual climate on the acceptance or rejection of particular theoretical positions. The work of these three psychologists clearly did not have much impact on the development of Psychology in the USA before 1960, but arguably they have had considerable influence on the expansion and development of the new cognitive approach from the 1960s onwards. This later influence, together with the desire for legitimization mentioned above, goes some way to explaining why almost all histories of cognitive Psychology discuss their work as foundational.

American Psychology

It may begin to seem that Europe was a haven for mentalistic Psychology while American Psychology was dominated by behaviourism. However, behaviourism was never as dominant in the USA as is usually presented, with most psychologists adopting a more eclectic orientation, though still generally functionalist. Functionalism in general was not opposed to mentalism, and there was a continuing tradition of work in American psychology that used mentalistic concepts, in social and developmental Psychology and in psycho-physics. A part of this, as we saw in Chapter 3, was the influence of Gestalt Psychology in the USA.

The early development of social Psychology was shaped by Floyd and Gordon Allport. Floyd was instrumental in associating social Psychology with behaviourism within an experimental framework. Gordon, on the other hand, toured Europe and worked with Stumpf, Wertheimer, Köhler, and Bartlett. He retained an interest in Gestalt Psychology and imagery, and his social Psychology had a strong mentalistic element, particularly in his work on attitudes and personality. Following Gordon Allport, personality and attitudes became major areas of social Psychology. Attitude research in particular was necessarily mentalistic, and was strongly influenced by Gestalt Psychology. This is most evident in Lewin's work on social Psychology, but others working within a broadly Gestaltist framework included Asch, Festinger and Heider. Attitude research, and social Psychology in general, received a major boost during World War Two, with many psychologists being involved in attitude measurement and change within the military (see, for example, Herman 1995). By the 1950s, social Psychology, with mentalistic concepts, was a major area of American Psychology.

Personality and intelligence were major study areas within both developmental Psychology and applied clinical Psychology. Developmental Psychology was a diverse field, with some researchers adopting a behaviourist orientation, some adopting a descriptive approach, and others investigating the development of mental functioning. Good examples of early mentalistic developmental Psychology included Gesell's maturational approach and Werner's organismic-developmental psychology. Early clinical Psychology investigated a range of mentalistic topics, including personality, hypnosis, emotion and psychodynamics.

Social and developmental Psychology maintained a presence for mentalistic concepts in American Psychology. Of more direct relevance to cognitive Psychology however was research work in sensation and perception. Research in these areas preceded the development of scientific Psychology, and in the main continued to follow the methods and theoretical approaches laid down by Weber and Fechner. The main concern of psycho-physics was the investigation of the relationship between physical intensity and perceived intensity of stimuli, and through the first half of the century research focused on improving the methods of investigation and refinement of the laws describing the relationship. This is evident in the work of Stevens, who ran the psychoacoustic laboratory at Harvard. In 1956 he developed a new method of magnitude estimation and derived a new power law. Stevens's laboratory was to prove influential in the development of cognitive Psychology, providing PhD training for Miller, Neisser and Norman.

Given this brief survey, it would clearly be wrong to say that all of American Psychology was dominated by behaviourism, although most experimental work explaining cognition continued to be pursued within a behaviourist framework. Some of this work took on a more mentalistic character, based particularly on Hull's concept of intervening variables. This is true of most learning research during the 1940s, including verbal learning, which was explained in terms of chains of internal stimulus-response links. In the 1950s Skinnerian behaviourism, without intervening variables, became more prominent, but an increasing interest in the study of memory, language and visual imagery led to a revamp of Hull's mathematical modelling theories. This use of modelling was to prove important in facilitating the transition to cognitive Psychology.

Attempts to use mathematical modelling in a behaviourist framework proved unsuccessful, and during the 1950s a number of difficulties with behaviourism were becoming apparent. This left psychologists looking for an alternative approach. While the early behaviourists believed that modelling complex behaviours would be achieved in time, by the 1950s it was looking increasingly unlikely that this could be achieved. The serial order problem was the problem of explaining how complex sequences of behaviour could be the result of chains of links. At the end of the 1940s, advances in neurophysiology had suggested that the brain was too slow to do the necessary sequential processing in the required time. In addition, linguistic phenomena such as speech errors and use of syntax could not be explained in terms of sequences of links. A further problem was that new ethological research, for example that of Lorenz, was suggesting that there were biological constraints on the range of behaviours that could be learnt, and that some behaviours were innate. This brought into question behaviourism's extreme environmentalism.

ANTECEDENTS OUTSIDE PSYCHOLOGY

In response to the problems of behaviourism, some psychologists started looking for alternative frameworks for explaining cognition. However, the existing cognitive work discussed so far proved unattractive, because it did not agree with preconceptions about what the nature of an experimental Psychology should be like. Any alternative approach would need to be legitimized in some way to prove acceptable to mainstream experimental Psychology. Two developments were significant in establishing such an alternative. The first was the growth in interdisciplinary collaboration during the War, which brought psychologists into close contact with neuroscientists and engineers, and made them aware of new ways of conceptualizing cognition. The second was the development of the electronic computer, which provided a new metaphor for behaviour. During the 1940s and 1950s a number of psychologists continued to work collaboratively with neuroscientists and engineers, investigating the implications of the computer metaphor. These psychologists were to become the pioneers of the new cognitive Psychology.

Information Theory and Cybernetics

During the 1930s considerable advances were made in technology and engineering, which continued into World War Two. These advances depended heavily on the development of sophisticated calculating devices, and on the design and control of complex machines. As engineers and mathematicians began theorizing about these developments, they introduced new concepts that were to change the way people thought about cognition, providing a new language for psychologists to theorize in. The central ideas were information, feedback and programming (Richards 1996). The first two will be discussed here, and the last in the next section.

Feedback refers to the way in which information from the environment leads to an adjustment in a system. An example of this is in a heating system, where information from a thermostat is used to control whether the heating is on or off. This is negative feedback, because it returns a system to a desired state, thus if the room is too hot the heating is turned off, and if it is too cold the heating is turned on. Positive feedback occurs when information leads to the system diverging from an original state, as when a microphone picks up output from an amplifier leading to an increase in volume. Feedback has been used in the control of systems for centuries, for example in the design of release valves for steam engines, but it was introduced as a theoretical concept by Norbert Weiner. Weiner was initially trained as a biologist, and would have been familiar with the use of feedback in the functioning of homeostasis, but his use of the concept in engineering was based on his later training in mathematical logic. In World War Two Weiner worked on the design of anti-aircraft fire control systems, and realized that the system could be improved by using information about the results of one firing to control the aim of the next shot. From this pragmatic application Weiner developed the concept of cybernetics, as a theory of the control of both machines and animals. In a 1943 article for *Philosophy of Science* (Rosenblueth, Weiner and Bigelow 1943), Weiner and his collaborators Rosenblueth (a physiologist) and Bigelow (an engineer) proposed that the notion of feedback could be used to explain goal directed behaviour, a problem that had long eluded behaviourists. Weiner went on to establish a group from a range of backgrounds, including neurophysiology, engineering, mathematics, psychology (Lewin) and anthropology (Margaret Mead), to investigate the integration of neurophysiology and the engineering of artificial systems. The goal was to establish a new discipline for investigating mental phenomena. Although this failed (the last meeting of the group was in 1953) the cybernetics movement acted in a sense as a dry run for cognitive science.

The term 'information' is a common part of language. However during the 1940s Claude Shannon suggested a measurement for information, as being the amount of uncertainty that information eliminates. The need for such a definition had been driven by the development of the electronic computer, and Shannon's formulation was shaped by his own work on instantiating formal logic in electronic systems. In the seventeenth century Leibniz had suggested that symbols could be applied to concepts, and that formal rules for manipulating the symbols would also manipulate the concepts. In the nineteenth century Boole developed a system of formal logic that corresponded to Leibniz's rules. Boole's system was based on truth values (true/false) and logical operations (and, or, not) on those truth values. For Boole, these rules served as laws of thought. In the 1930s Shannon had shown how Boole's logic system could be realized in electrical circuits, a development which paved the way for electronic computers that manipulated binary information. When Shannon developed his information theory, he measured information in binary terms – uncertainty is eliminated by a series of true/false statements. The development of information theory gave rise to a new set of concepts, such as 'redundancy', 'storage capacity', and 'noise', that were quickly adopted by psychologists. Initially this was in the areas of psycho-physics and reaction time (for example, measuring reaction time as a function of the amount of information in a stimulus array), but the notion soon extended to the investigation of memory and other areas now termed 'cognitive'. This development was important in allowing cognition to be characterized as information processing.

Computers and Artificial Intelligence

The development of the electronic computer, using the principles of information and formal logic described above, had a major impact on Psychology.

A computer takes in information, processes it, and produces output. By analogy, the brain could be seen as doing the same thing. This metaphor, of the brain as a computer, was explicitly developed by Von Neumann at the interdisciplinary Hixon Conference in 1948, and its usage increased during the 1950s. By the 1960s, the comparison was commonplace, for example in information processing models of memory. Developments in computing provided a new set of terms to characterize cognitive processes, for example 'retrieval' and 'transfer'. Developments in programming, and particularly artificial intelligence, had a significant impact on Psychology.

The programming of computers – specifying information processing in terms of a series of discrete operations – seemed to offer an insight into the nature of cognition. In particular, a computer program was seen as being analogous to a plan of behaviour, showing how complex sequences of operations might be organized. Underlying the faith in the processing power of computers was Turing's mathematical formulation of the Turing machine. A Turing machine is a mechanism that can carry out a particular well-defined series of formal operations. Thus any decidable process can be implemented by a particular design of Turing machine. A Universal Turing machine is one that can instantiate any individual Turing machine, and so can implement any decidable process. The electronic computer, given an infinite memory, would be a Universal Turing machine. Hence, if we find the right program a computer can implement any decidable process. The importance of this is that if we assume that intelligence is a decidable process, then we can make computers intelligent (this assumption is debatable, as we shall see in Chapter 13). This led to the topic of artificial intelligence (AI), attempts to program computers to display intelligent behaviour. On one level, this was purely an engineering problem, though solutions found to problems in AI, for example breaking complex tasks down into sub-tasks, were to influence psychological theories. On another level, debate soon began about the relationship between artificial intelligence and human intelligence, with some believing that AI systems are qualitatively the same as human cognition. A middle ground was to use computers to model proposals for human cognition, although this involved a commitment to characterizing cognition in symbolic terms.

Neuroscience

The development of electronic computers created a view that information theory and computation provide the correct basis for understanding human cognition. Advances in neuroscience during the 1940s and 1950s added to this view, and neuroscientists soon found themselves collaborating with psychologists. For example, Hebb's 1949 *Organization of behaviour* attempted to synthesize behaviourism, Gestalt and findings in neurophysiology. The 1948 Hixon Conference, titled 'Cerebral mechanisms in behaviour', brought together Lashley, Köhler, Von Neumann, and many others to discuss the relationships between psychological phenomena and neural mechanisms.

Neuroscience had many contributions to make to the new study of cognition, based on several decades of research work. An important insight was the suggestion of modularity in the brain, claiming that the brain could be broken down into functional components. This functional decomposition was not new to Psychology, having been first suggested by Gall, and was not universally accepted, Lashley's concept of mass action providing the main opposition. However, studies of cognitive pathologies such as aphasia suggested there was some degree of localization, and the notion was to prove influential in guiding psychological models of cognition.

Studies of cognitive deficits had a long history in neuroscience, going back to the work of Broca and Wernicke, and these were augmented by stimulation studies such as those of Penfield. These studies allowed the development of detailed maps of the motor and sensory cortexes, suggesting new theories of sensation and action. More novel in the 1940s was the development of neural networks, computational simulations of brain functioning. In 1943 McCulloch and Pitts (1943) developed networks of binary neuron-like units connected together in a network designed to simulate brain architecture. These networks were equivalent to a Universal Turing machine, lending support to the analogy of the brain with computers. Later networks attempted to analyse more complex psychological tasks, using analogue computations based on statistical regularities rather than discrete logic. A notable contribution was from Hebb, who in 1949 proposed cell assemblies as discrete functional processors of information in the brain. However, there were important theoretical differences between discrete logic networks and statistical networks, particularly in their implications for Psychology. The later models were more neurologically plausible, but were running against the tide in favour of formal symbol manipulation. Between the late 1950s and the 1980s neuroscience had a limited role in the study of cognition, although through approaches such as cognitive neuropsychology it is becoming important once again.

Linguistics

Linguistics, and particularly the linguistics of Noam Chomsky, is often seen as a major factor in the development of cognitive Psychology. The traditional story is that Chomsky's revolutionary theory of language defeated Skinnerian behaviourism and set the agenda for cognitive Psychology, but this narrative is not entirely accurate. Chomsky's work depended in part on existing, though recent, theories in linguistics, and behaviourism's problems in explaining language were already established. As we shall see shortly, the seminal publications in cognitive Psychology came in 1956, preceding Chomsky's work. However, Chomsky helped bring about a revolution in linguistics, which fed into Psychology, and helped legitimize the new cognitive approach, increasing its appeal as a new framework for investigating cognition.

Roughly around 1953, linguistics was mainly concerned with the analysis of language into its component parts, such as morphemes and phonemes, in a largely descriptive behaviourist framework. Attempts to explain language use were mainly based on Hullian mediation theories, although briefly following information theory a statistical approach was used, particularly by Miller. However, in 1953 an eight-week seminar was established by the

Social Science Research Council, which set out an agenda for cooperative research and saw the application of continental structuralism to the psychology of language. The theories promoted at the seminar were short lived, but the goals suggested, such as establishing the psychological reality of theoretical constructs, and the methods to be employed, such as analysis of speech errors, continue. Soon however linguistics went through a theoretical transformation that was to establish psycholinguistics as a central part of cognitive Psychology. This began with the work of Zelig Harris at the University of Pennsylvania. Previously linguists had concentrated on phonology and morphology, but Harris emphasized syntactic analysis. To make this tractable, he introduced the notion of transforming complex sentences into simpler forms (kernel sentences) according to a set of transformational rules. This interest in syntax was pursued by Harris's student Noam Chomsky, whose first book, *Syntactic structures*, was published in 1957. This publication did not lead to an overnight revolution, having limited impact on contemporary linguists, but it strongly influenced later generations of linguists (Bechtel, Abramsen and Graham 1998). His key claim was that grammar was a generative system, and he described a novel mechanism by which this generativity is achieved. He proposed a transformational grammar that consisted of rewrite rules to generate a base structure, and transformational rules to generate derived phrase structures. To an extent this was an extension of structural linguistics, but Chomsky included the key concept of creativity – that novel language is generated through mental activity.

Chomsky's ideas had their initial impact on the new psycholinguistics, before influencing mainstream linguistics. His theory represented a move to rationalism and a mentalistic perspective, and was an explicit repudiation of behavioural approaches to language. This repudiation was based on the notion of creativity – language could not be a learnt response – and the poverty of stimulus argument. This argument claimed that language use was based on innate structures, since ordinary learning processes could not account for the rapidity of language learning, given the poverty of the stimulus. As an aside, presumably such 'ordinary learning processes' were conceived as behaviourist, even though Chomsky rejected behaviourism as an explanation for language. It is debatable whether the poverty of stimulus argument is as effective when different learning processes are suggested, as in cognitive linguistics. Chomsky's main impact for cognitive Psychology was to lend a suggestion as to what mental representations might be like. Before Chomsky, there was a reasonable quantity of research done on a statistical basis, for example Miller's analysis of speech perception. Chomsky's suggestion of a symbolic mental representation reinforced the symbolic approach to explaining cognition, at the expense of statistical approaches.

THE BEGINNINGS OF COGNITIVE PSYCHOLOGY

Cognitive Psychology was not an overnight revolution. Rather, it had a considerable gestation period. The elements that were foundational to it, described above, developed during the 1940s and 1950s, but the sub-discipline did not have a label until 1967. In between, it can be difficult to identify a particular starting point, but a commonly chosen year is 1956. This year saw the publications of a number of key articles that we would now say are identifiably cognitive Psychology. These articles synthesized the various elements into investigations of psychological phenomena, and showed what the new approach could offer to Psychology. With hindsight it is possible to identify similarities between these articles and previous cognitive work, but the articles were couched in the new information and computer-derived terminology and used the new concepts discussed above. The new approach won favour from sceptical psychologists because it maintained the methodological approach of behaviourism, and had its concepts legitimized by the demonstrable links with advances in computing, information sciences, neuroscience, and later linguistics. The leading lights in this new approach were Miller and Bruner, with a considerable contribution from Broadbent.

George Miller was a graduate of the Harvard psychoacoustics laboratory, and his training was in the techniques of psycho-physics rather than in behaviourism. His main interest was in speech perception, and during the War he conducted research on the jamming of speech. He found, contrary to accepted theory, that some messages were easier to understand in noisy environments than others. Initially he had no explanation for this, but a solution was to come when he applied information theory to the results – the signals that were easiest to understand were those that had the greatest redundancy. Miller introduced psychologists to information theory in a 1949 *Psychological Review* article, but his greater impact was to come in 1956, with the publication of 'The magical number seven, plus or minus two: some limits on our capacity for processing information'. This paper marked a return to the consideration of short-term memory within Psychology, and showed how concepts from information theory could be applied to the description of human information processing. To do so, he used the concepts of chunking and recoding, emphasizing the active role of the memorizer in reorganizing information to make it more memorable.

Also at Harvard in 1956 was Jerome Bruner, who was to work closely with Miller on establishing interdisciplinary links in cognition. In 1947 Bruner had introduced the New Look movement in perception, which emphasized the role of mental states, including social factors, in influencing perception, for example in showing that children's estimations of the size of coins was affected by the coins' value, and that the effect was greater for poorer children. The New Look movement believed categories to be central to perception, and soon Bruner turned to the investigations of categories more directly. This work resulted, in 1956, in the publication of *A study of thinking*, together with Goodnow and Austin. This work, based on a procedure of Vygotsky's, was an investigation into concept formation. The orthodox behaviourist view was that concept formation occurred through the reinforcement or otherwise of responses to aspects of the stimuli. Bruner *et al.*, however, characterized the subject as an active searcher for concepts, engaged in a process of hypothesis testing. Although cognitive in orientation, this book did not make much use of the new concepts. However, it was an important demonstration of the functional reality of mental representations.

Stevens's work in psycho-physics was also published in 1956, as was, Festinger's work on cognitive dissonance and Simon and Newell's AI logic theorist program. The logic theorist program was written to prove theorems from Russell and Whitehead's *Principia mathematica*, providing proofs of 38. This was taken as a powerful demonstration of the power of computer intelligence, and Simon and Newell believed that it was also a convincing demonstration of the nature of human cognition (Bechtel, Abrahamsen and Graham 1998). Key features of the system included the division of complex tasks into sub-goals, the representation of information processing as a sequence of programmed instructions (derived in part from Selz), and the use of heuristics as an aid to decision making.

Work in the emerging cognitive framework continued with Chomsky's *Syntactic structures* in 1957 and Broadbent's *Perception and communication* in 1958. Broadbent, together with Colin Cherry, reintroduced consideration of attention to Psychology through the design of dichotic listening experiments. This research was described in *Perception and communication*, together with a theoretical model of selective attention, wherein a perceiver actively screens out one of two signal streams according to the physical characteristics of the signal. Attention, one of the most mentalistic of concepts, had been neglected since Wündt. Broadbent's work made it acceptable again, and demonstrated the value of the new framework.

The final key early work in cognitive Psychology was published in 1960 as a result of collaboration between Miller, Galanter, a psychophysicist with interests in mathematical psychology, and Pribram, a neuroscientist. *Plans and the structure of behaviour* was an attempt to replace behaviourism with an overall framework based on the new cognitive concepts. The main argument of the book was that behaviour was organized according to plans – sequences of operations organized hierarchically, so that plans were nested inside plans and clustered together. These plans were conceived of in the same way as computer programs. Central to the operation of the plans was a decision mechanism termed the TOTE (test-operate-test-exit) unit. The TOTE unit used the notion of feedback from cybernetics, whereby the controller of the plan first tested a situation by gathering information, then carried out an operation to achieve a desired goal state. This was repeated until the desired goal state was reached, at which time the plan would exit, returning control to a potential higher order plan. Miller *et al.* used the example of hammering in a nail, whereby one tests to see whether a nail is in far enough in. If it is, then no further action is necessary and the TOTE exits. If it is not, then the TOTE operates by calling on a sub-procedure to test the state of the hammer: if the hammer is up, then it is brought down, and if it is down then it is brought up then down. This sub-TOTE then exits, returning to the higher level to test once again whether the nail is far enough in. The TOTE unit was intended to replace the reflex arc as the basic unit of mental activity, and proved to be very successful at modelling complex behaviours. For example, the authors showed how Chomsky's linguistic theory could be modelled using the TOTE framework. As a concept it did not catch on, but the book was influential in convincing psychologists that the cognitive approach was the best way to conceive of mental activity. Also in 1960, Bruner and Miller opened the Centre for Cognitive Studies at Harvard. This was an interdisciplinary initiative to establish collaborative research programmes, and proved influential in giving a focus to the developing area of cognitive Psychology.

Considerable advances were made in artificial intelligence during the 1950s and 1960s, helped by large research grants awarded by the US Department of Defense. Initially this research was carried out in both symbolic and neural network orientations, the two competing to some extent for status and research funding. This research was often linked to explicit claims about the nature of human cognition, increasing awareness of the cognitive approach. The symbolic approach fitted best with notions of cognition as being analogous to programs, whereas the neural network approach fitted best with arguments about the relationship between cognition and brain structure. In AI research, the symbolic approach came to dominate, and similarly program-like theories came to dominate cognitive Psychology, the two disciplines supporting each other to some extent. A consequence of this was that neuroscience became marginalized during this period, although more recently cognitive Psychology has integrated insights from neuropsychology into mainstream cognitive theories.

During the 1960s, an increasing amount of experimental research was conducted in the cognitive framework, and by 1967 Ulrich Neisser was able to produce a comprehensive textbook surveying research and theories in the field. The book, *Cognitive psychology*, both named the field and established the scope of the new discipline. Neisser had associations with the Harvard Centre, and had studied with Miller and Stevens, graduating from Harvard's psychoacoustics laboratory. Neisser also had sympathies with Gestalt, having studied with Köhler for a couple of years, and was influenced by Bartlett. He conceived of cognition in terms of the flow of information from the environment through to its storage and reconstruction, and included Broadbent's notions of attention and tripartite-partite memory structure. In his book he rejected any explicit correspondence between computer processing and human cognition – although this rejection was by no means universal – but acknowledged the role of computers in providing both a set of metaphors, and legitimization, for the new approach.

The Expansion of Cognitivism

Cognitive Psychology crystallized as a sub-discipline following the publication of Neisser's text. The normal processes of institutionalization occurred, as Psychology departments created specialized cognitive laboratories, hired cognitive psychologists and taught courses in cognitive Psychology. This institutionalization was supported by the establishment of dedicated conferences, the increasing acceptance of cognitive work in established journals, and the creation of new journals catering specifically to cognitive Psychology. Increasingly, behaviourism became marginalized, although not entirely eliminated, with remaining behaviourists restricting their research to a considerably more limited range of topics.

The cognitive approach soon spread beyond the set of cognitive topics associated with cognitive Psychology (for example, perception, memory, problem solving, language), as researchers in other areas attempted to apply what we broadly call cognitivism to topics in developmental, social, personality and abnormal Psychology. Developmental Psychology rediscovered the work of Piaget, stimulating a burst of research into cognitive development in children. Cognitive social Psychology had begun with Festinger's Gestalt-influenced cognitive dissonance theory, and soon extended into social cognition and attribution theory. As with Piaget, Vygotsky's work was incorporated under the cognitive umbrella. Cognitive theories of personality were produced by Mischel, Rotter and Bandura, and in abnormal Psychology Beck produced cognitive theories of depression, and cognitive-behavioural therapy was developed. Clearly, cognitivism proved to be a productive theoretical orientation for many topics in Psychology.

Unlike many previous approaches in Psychology, the development of cognitivism was driven by empirical work, often inspired by advances in related areas, and initially it did not have an analogue in philosophy. However, given the strong mentalist orientation of the approach it was clearly desirable, if not essential, for psychological theory to be supported by well founded philosophical argument about the nature of mind. Most extant theories of philosophy of mind adopted some form of materialism, the most notable for Psychology being identity theory and the work of Gilbert Ryle. Identity theory's argument that mental states could be directly identified with brain states supported the reduction of Psychology to neuroscience, but such a reduction had been strongly rejected by behaviourists. Ryle's suggestion that mental contents are propensities for an agent to behave in a particular way was compatible with behaviourism, but had problems with accounting for mental states that were not directly related to behaviour, such as emotions and sensations. Neither approach was compatible with cognitivism, particularly given that many cognitive psychologists wanted a common explanation for human and machine minds. However, Psychology was not alone in being shaped by advances in technology and artificial intelligence. Hilary Putnam proposed an alternative philosophy of mind which he called functionalism (unrelated to the earlier psychological school). For functionalism, mental states are defined by their typical causes and effects, and should be identified in terms of their functional role in mediating between sensation and behaviour. Such mental states were claimed to be multiply realizable, and could not be identified with any particular realization. This gave an alternative to identity theory materialism, and allowed for the possibility of machine minds. While the brain may provide one realization of mental states, those states could alternatively be realized by some other processor, provided the same functionality was achieved. This meant that cognitive psychologists could concentrate on giving functional descriptions of behaviour, without worrying about the underlying processing mechanism.

Functionalism was extended by Fodor, who in 1975 formulated the language of thought hypothesis. Fodor suggested that just as language consists of a system of symbols manipulated according to a set of syntactic rules, so too does cognition – cognition is, and only can be, the manipulation of discrete symbols according to syntax. This was a logical extension of the work of Leibniz and Boole, and of course compatible with advances in symbolic artificial intelligence. By this stage neural network AI research was largely dormant, and in any case the brain was conceived of as a Universal Turing machine that was solely manipulating symbols. The brain was important to Fodor in one sense however, since his position was strongly nativist. Faced with the difficulty of explaining how the brain develops the representational system necessary for interpreting symbols, Fodor claimed that the required system was innate. Fodor was explicit in saying that the language of thought was separate from, and preceded, natural language, but his ideas were clearly influenced by Chomsky's theory of language. For example, Fodor justified the emphasis on syntactic structure by pointing to the productivity and systematicity of cognition, as Chomsky had with language.

Functionalism provided a cognitivist solution to the mind-body problem, and particularly supported symbolic explanations of cognition. However, it has been strongly criticised within philosophy, and has difficulties in explaining some aspects of cognition. These debates will be considered in Chapter 13, which considers the adequacy of symbolic cognitivism, and in Chapter 14, which discusses the competing approach of connectionism.

CONCLUSION

We began by distinguishing between cognitive Psychology as a sub-discipline of Psychology, concerned with a particular set of topics, and cognitivism as a particular approach to Psychology that theorizes about the mind as an information processor. We saw that the shift from behaviourism to cognitivism as the dominant paradigm in experimental Psychology has been characterized in a number of ways, most notably as a revolutionary, Kuhnian paradigm shift. This notion of a paradigm shift is flawed, we argued, because cognitvism developed independently of behaviourism, and coexisted with it for some time. The shift from behaviourism to cognitivism as the dominant paradigm for experimental Psychology was gradual, and was the result of competition for perceived validity, rather than a direct replacement.

Having discussed the nature of the shift from behaviourism to cognitivism, we then went on to consider antecedents of cognitivism, both within Psychology and in other disciplines. Within Psychology, we saw that despite the popularity of behaviourism, there was an ongoing tradition of cognitive-style theorizing extending from the Würzburg school to the development of cognitivism, including the work of Gestalt psychologists in Germany, Bartlett in the UK, and Piaget in France. In America too, we saw that mentalistic concepts continued to be adopted in some areas of Psychology, particularly social and developmental Psychology, and psycho-physics. This work was considerably boosted by psychologists' contribution to the war effort, particularly in investigating sensation, perception, and instrument design, and in the measuring of attitudes. At the same time as this work was maintaining a tradition of considering mentalistic concepts, behaviourism was having difficulty in accounting for a range of higher level mental functions and instinctive behaviours, damaging its claims to be the only approach to Psychology necessary.

Much of the mentalistic Psychology conducted before the development of cognitivism differed from it in the nature of the theoretical structures used to describe cognition. These cognitive approaches were seen as relying on 'explanatory fictions', to use Skinner's term, in explaining mental events. However, the development of information theory and the electronic computer, and advances in neuroscience, lent support to the notion that information processing provided the basis of cognition. These developments, and particularly the production of programmatic specifications of apparently intelligent behaviour in computers, suggested the metaphor that the mind is an information processor that followed programmatic plans. The productivity of this metaphor was demonstrated in a number of key publications, including those of Miller, Bruner, Broadbent, and Chomsky, legitimizing the characterization of cognition in terms of information processing.

The sub-discipline of cognitive Psychology developed rapidly following the publication of Neisser's *Cognitive psychology*, and the approach was soon adopted in other areas of Psychology. Behaviourism can be seen as the last of the 'schools' of Psychology, current Psychology being better described in terms of competing approaches to investigating similar psychological phenomena. Cognitivism has proved to be a popular approach, supported in part by the development of functionalist philosophy, which emphasizes the functional role of mental states.

Despite the success of cognitivism, there is considerable debate about the adequacy of the approach. Philosophical debates include continued arguments about materialist versus functionalist philosophies of mind, and about the nature of folk psychology. There is dispute over the role of evidence from neuropsychology in the development of theories in cognitive Psychology, and over the adequacy of cognitivism to account for social phenomena. Finally, the dominant characterization of cognition in terms of symbolic processing is under attack from renewed research into neural network modelling. All of these debates will be considered in later chapters.

FURTHER READING

Bechtel, W., Abramsen, A. and Graham, G. 1998: The life of cognitive Science. In W. Bechtel and G. Graham (eds) *A companion to cognitive science*. Oxford: Blackwell.

Gardner, H. 1985: *The mind's new science: a history of the cognitive revolution*. New York: Basic Books.

Goodwin, C.J. 1999: *A history of modern psychology*. New York: John Wiley.

Greenwood, J.D. 1997: Understanding the 'cognitive revolution' in psychology. *Journal of the History of the Behavioural Sciences* 35(1): 1–22.

Leahey, T.H. 1992: The mythical revolutions of American psychology. *American Psychologist* 47: 308–18.

Murray, D.J. 1995: *Gestalt psychology and the cognitive revolution*. New York: Harvester Wheatsheaf.

Richards, G. 1996: *Putting psychology in its place*. London: Routledge.

Saito, A. 2000: *Bartlett, culture, and cognition*. Hove: Psychology Press.

9

PSYCHOLOGY AND 'MINORITIES'

In this chapter we are going to examine the relationship between Psychology and its host societies by examining the ways that Psychology has treated race and racism, and 'gender difference'. The interrelationships between Psychology and its host societies on these issues have been complex, with Psychology acting as both an agent for social change and upholding the status quo, and at times differing people within Psychology acting on behalf of different causes. Psychology, as Graham Richards points out, is also one arena where issues important to the host society are discussed and temporarily resolved. Thus, the aim here is to neither condemn Psychology as always acting as an instrument of the state, nor praise Psychology as acting positively to solve problems. Finally although we are of course concerned with Psychology within the context of this book we do not wish to over emphasize the importance of the discipline. It is one of the sites where issues such as race and gender is discussed, not the only one and often not the most important one.

One of the recurring themes in the history of Psychology is the interrelationship between it and peoples who have fallen outside of what Richards calls its key constituency. As this history has unfolded, so the people that make up the academics and practitioners of the discipline have changed and thus the relationships have changed. In this chapter, an attempt will be made to sketch this relationship. There has to be an obvious acknowledgement that each of the substantive topics, race and racism and the psychology of them merit books in their own right. Graham Richards's reflexive history of race and racism is an object lesson in just how complex the relationships are, and the care that needs to be taken with the broad brushstroke approaches being adopted here.

However, there does appear to be some commonality amongst the historical contingencies and I hope that there is more to this than the over optimistic projection of the current author.

In this chapter we will first examine the history of race and racism within Psychology before looking at gender. We will end both sections of this chapter reflecting on the current state of Psychology with regard to these issues and the broad similarities between the topics. We have omitted from this discussion the treatment of class differences by Psychology, which have been a peculiar feature of British Psychology. We have also omitted, due to word count and with some reluctance, work on sexuality. This chapter is also, to some extent, a crossover section of the present book. In Chapters 10 to 15 we shall investigate some aspects of the current state of Psychology. Up until this chapter we have been investigating the history of Psychology and in this chapter, perhaps more than elsewhere, we reflect on both in the hope of untangling some of the complexities of how modern Psychology has been shaped by the historical contingencies of its past.

All of these topics are stories of struggle against oppression. Psychology has at different times and sometimes at the same time been a part of the machinery of oppression and the attempts at liberation. Across Anglophone Psychology there have been sharp differences between British and US Psychology and across continental Europe these differences became alternatively more pronounced or more subtle.

Adopting Bhaskar's terminology the transfactual element here is that there have always been differences between people. However once these differences are ascribed to race, gender or sexuality there almost inevitably follows a story of one (the dominant cultural group within Psychology) being seen as superior and the others as inferior.

RACE, RACISM AND PSYCHOLOGY

As Howitt and Owusu-Bempah (1994) demonstrate much of current Psychology is unreflexively and uncritically Eurocentric. It is still common to write of the peoples of, for example, New Guinea as 'Stone Age', to refer to the peoples of Africa as 'tribes' with the associations of primitiveness that such discourses establish. While in agreement with much that they write, and the need to change, we are not going to write a story of Psychology as the site of unrelenting racism.

We have already discussed the racism of Francis Galton which Richards demonstrates is racism rather than the 'racialism' that was prevalent during the late Victorian age and his influence in terms of Psychological methods. Before we turn to what is a mainly US story it is worth considering the complexities of the position within Great Britain up until World War Two.

Britain up until World War One

Much of the history of Psychology is rooted in the USA because the USA has come to dominate the discipline. It is worth reflecting upon the British picture before turning to the USA in order to show how differences in host cultures may help explain differences in the discipline.

Britain was a colonial power, and in the Victorian age during which the discipline was founded the British Empire was at its peak. In the later Victorian period many eminent Victorians used a form of Social Darwinism to explain why they were at the peak of evolution and thus should rule over others who they saw as either savages, or at best, child like figures who did not know how to take care of themselves (the so called white man's burden). However, despite the scientific racism of figures like Galton and Spencer, and the slightly later racist writing of McDougall race was not high on the agenda of British Psychology. However, much of what was written was written, at least to some extent, within an intellectual framework provided by scientific racism.

These complexities can perhaps be highlighted by looking at the case study of the Torres Strait expedition mounted by a mixture of anthropologists and psychologists from Cambridge University in 1898. What follows is a brief summary of Richards's (1997a) work on the topic.

The expedition under the leadership of an anthropologist called Haddon consisted of a mixed group of anthropologists and psychologists; the psychologists were W.H.R. Rivers (1864–1922), C.S. Myers (1873–1947) and William McDougall (1871–1938). While Haddon's stance on race was informed by scientific racism, Richards, after considering Haddon's position suggests that it was not strictly a scientific racist project. Haddon's motivation for mounting the expedition had its roots in an earlier visit to the region in 1888–9 to study its natural history. Haddon developed an interest in the culture and the lifestyle of the people of the region, and given that this was about to change under the impact of trading and missionary activity, was in need of scientific study. Haddon, who before the 1888–9 expedition was a marine biologist, became interested in anthropological work because of that visit. The majority of his publications about the region after the first expedition were about ethnographic topics rather than the marine biology.

The psychologists on the expedition had an ambitious programme of study. They were mainly interested in psycho-physical phenomena to do with visual acuity, discrimination, visual illusions, colour perception, hearing and smell, together with cutaneous sensations and muscular sense. The scientific racist background to the work was the notion, put forward by Spencer, that more primitive people would perform better at basic sensory tasks than civilized people. While scientific racism provided an intellectual framework and possibly the only intellectual framework available for the studies, these three people seemed to have little personal investment in the position. They were, however, undoubtedly, scions of the British Empire and the modern reader would probably find it disturbing to read of the participants of the research in the Torres Straits being described as primitive, savage and uncivilized, especially as the researchers appeared to live amongst them on highly cordial terms. All of them seemed well versed in the paternalistic style of managing the natives and did not appear to rebel from the role of establishment figures on an imperial expedition.

Each of the researchers well understood the need for control subjects, and on their return from the Torres Straits they each carried out replications of their studies with a British sample, although the groups chosen for the repli-

cations are somewhat curious. Rivers, who was working on visual perception (although he also contributed to the anthropological studies) chose
undergraduate students, and people from the village of Girton. Myres used
people from a small village near Aberdeen and McDougall used working
class inmates of a Cheadle convalescent home. We shall deal briefly with
each set of findings in turn.

Rivers

Rivers's work was on perception, encompassing visual acuity, colour
vision, binocular visual space perception and visual illusions. In general,
the findings suggested that while there may be some differences they were
much smaller than traditional views would have suggested. For example,
with the studies of visual acuity Rivers finds some differences with his control sample but asserts that European islanders 'living an outdoor, seafaring
life do not differ very greatly in visual acuity from Papuan islanders' and in
general concludes that 'the visual acuity of savages and half-civilized people, though superior to that of the normal European, is not so in any
marked degree'. The research modified the scientific racist position, as
Rivers argued for an environmental explanation, but by invoking the idea
that primitive lifestyles require minute attention, and that this expenditure
of this energy inhibits intellectual growth, he maintained the framework
that he was working within. However, the findings of Rivers were widely
read as falsifying the notion of primitive superiority and this played a role
in removing psycho-physical phenomena from the attention of race differences research.

Myers

Myers's work on hearing was beset with methodological problems, not least
of which included the lack of control in the setting with interference from
background noise and the fact that some of the older participants had ear
damage caused by pearl fishing. Myers was very careful to hedge his findings appropriately, he found that the Murray Island adults were somewhat
poorer on auditory acuity tasks than his Aberdeen control sample and that
the children had a lower upper limit of hearing range than the control sample, although some of this difference was caused by ear damage in the
Murray Island children. Finally he found that Aberdeen subjects discrimi-
nated much finer intervals in pitch than the Murray Island group but he was
aware that these differences were probably caused by knowledge of
European musical styles.

Myers's work on the sense of smell was even more methodologically suspect, and he reports no control findings for this work. Finally he did work on
reaction times and again his work was beset by the lack of sophisticated
equipment. However he did find little difference between the Murray
Islanders on auditory and visual RT studies, while with choice RT studies the
educated English control group were much faster, although he speculated

that the Murray Islanders would have compared well with an English vil-
lager. The major lessons that Myers drew from his work were methodological. However the expected primitive superiority does appear to be notably
absent.

McDougall

McDougall studied topics to do with tactile sensitivity, discrimination of
weights, sensitivity to pain and variations in blood pressure in relation to
mental activity. The suppositions underlying the studies were as follows:
there would be primitive superiority in the discrimination findings, less pain
sensitivity, and a less active response to blood pressure. With the blood pressure research McDougall found no evidence at all. With the other research,
however, the findings were in the directions which supported scientific
racism, and indeed McDougall was the only member of the research team to
maintain a strong scientific racist position in later life, especially after emi-
grating to the USA.

In adult Murray Islanders, he found that they were twice as sensitive in a
two-point discrimination task, but only half as sensitive to pain. With regard
to the tasks involving weight the Murray Islanders were found to be rather
more delicate than Europeans, a result that McDougall couched in terms of
surprise because he felt that it was a task that they were totally unfamiliar
with, claiming that they lacked an abstract term for weight, while they were
more susceptible to the weight-size illusion (the illusion that larger objects
appear heavier than smaller objects of the same weight) a result that he
attributed to greater suggestibility.

The results were called into question, not least by Titchener (1916) who
reviewed all of the psychological studies carried out. Titchener was sceptical of the enterprise in general, and later Rivers would also doubt the utility
of using this type of psychological experiment in other cultures, but
Titchener was particularly scathing of McDougall's findings. With the two-
point discrimination task the Murray Islanders treated the task as something of a guessing game, and used stimulus magnitude as the basis of their
response, rather than only reporting when two distinct points were felt. The
pain sensitivity may reflect no more than different cultural norms in when
to use the 'pain' word, and may have been contaminated in any case
because the main way that participants were recruited for all the studies
was by being told that the researchers had come to see if they were better
than the white man at the tasks. With a judgement as subjective as pain it
would appear likely that such an appeal to vanity could lead to the results
that McDougall reported.

Summary

While the Cambridge Torres Straits expedition was probably a more important event in the history of anthropology that it was in the history of
Psychology it does give us some idea of the complexities of the position of

psychologists with regard to race. Although Rivers's and Myers's results were used to undermine the Spencerian hypothesis of primitive sensitivity at the time of the study, it was difficult for them to escape from the dominant scientific racism framework. Later both Rivers and Myers were to publish work that was more forthright in its rejection of scientific racism and it may have been that they could only reach that position after self-reflexive contemplation of the research that they carried out on the Torres Straits expedition. McDougall, by contrast, continued to regard his findings as robust despite the spirited attack upon the enterprise mounted by Titchener. After his emigration to the USA McDougall continued to concern himself with the eugenics programme that was initiated by Galton's speculations.

The Rise and Fall of Race Psychology

We have discussed at some length elsewhere the particular use of intelligence testing in relation to race difference research. We have also discussed some aspects of anti-racism, especially with regard to the authoritarian personality concept developed by Adorno and co-researchers at Chicago during his exile from the Frankfurt School. In this section we will concentrate instead on the social conditions within which this work took place, and speculate on the ways that psychological findings led to a reflexive shift within Psychology.

Race Psychology was a project undertaken by US psychologists between 1910 and 1940. Although it has some roots in scientific racism, the way that it developed was tied to the very specific historical and cultural circumstances of the USA before World War Two, the Negro education question and the immigration issue. In the first decade of the twentieth century, around thirteen million people migrated to the USA from Europe, the largest voluntary migration in history. Another resource available to psychologists at this time has its roots in the group approach to investigative practice that was becoming the predominant research technique across Psychology. We shall deal with each of these issues in turn.

The roots of the issues around education come out of the American Civil War (1861–5), following which the government embarked on reconstruction. While the constitution was amended to protect the rights of those slaves who had been freed the political momentum to continue the very considerable work necessary to ensure that Black Americans would be able to play a full role in the nation's socioeconomic life was soon lost. Many legislators in the Southern States of the USA found ways of evading and nullifying the effects of the newly amended constitution, and as White Americans sought reconciliation between North and South they often did so by sacrificing promises made to Black Americans. Despite the brief flowering of philanthropic and governmental support by the early 1880s, the White hegemony was firmly re-established and segregation rather than participation become the norm in the Southern USA.

With segregation the gulf in funding between White and Black education opened up, and by 1910 there was a dramatic gap in funding affecting everything: teachers' salaries, the amount spent on books and other materials, the length of terms, the condition of school buildings.

During the 1880s scientific racism was becoming the orthodox framework to understand differences between peoples, and even those involved in philanthropic work to raise money for Black schools began to conclude that there was little point in providing the same quality of education as White schools.

By the 1910s, the Negro education question was again on the agenda, but after the 30 to 40 years of broken promises and disillusionment deep frustration and pessimism had become endemic. When psychologists, who by this time were firmly allied with educators, entered the debate they did so with the promise of neutral scientific techniques to give a definitive answer to the question of whether it was worth educating Black children to a higher standard. They did so in alliance with a group of people who, while they held pro-segregationist views, were also paternalistic in that they desired improvement of the lot of the Negro.

Another area where eugenic concerns affected social policy in the USA (and these are not the only two, the USA had legislation ensuring that subnormal people could be sterilized without their consent) was immigration. The concerns here were with the preservation of the Nordic race and whether the migration of Slavs, Italians, Portuguese, Sicilians and Jews would affect the national character of the USA. After 1918 the issue was one of major concern in the USA, especially given the depredations in Europe following World War One, and had culminated in 1923 with the Immigration Restriction Act.

Finally, this was an era in which Psychology had established itself, at least to some extent as a marketable discipline. Part of the attraction of Psychology was the belief that because it was scientific it was neutral to ideological concerns and could find out the truth about issues around race through empirical work rather than armchair speculation. The historical contingencies that had led Psychology to throw off theoretical concerns for empirical ones helped to foster this illusion.

At the same time that this research began there was a reaction to it. As early as 1910 Woodworth discusses the problem of dividing 'men' into types when the variability within a group far exceeds the differences between the averages of these groups. Woodworth also raises a concern that is found in Titchener's critique of the Torres Straits work, the issue of culture fairness of tests. Although the work he produces throughout his lifetime is somewhat ambiguous, the main point that we want to make here is that these anti-racist sentiments were in existence at the start of the race psychology project and they continued throughout the period under question.

Amongst those publishing work during this period opposed to race psychology project were Margaret Mead (1926) and Otto Klineberg. The arguments that were made at this time will be familiar to most readers. The notion was that any differences which were found could be accounted for environmentally, and given segregation in schooling and the vast gap in funding this argument was quite powerful. In addition, there were arguments about whether the supposed race differences had in fact been proved, and whether it was in principle possible to demonstrate such differences. Finally, towards the end of this period as the science of genetics was more appropriately utilized to understand people, the notion that race was an unscientific category, a myth used for rationalizing oppression and injustice, was also developed.

Alongside these internal arguments, which to some extent demonstrated the way that Psychology is itself an arena where issues are debated, as well as a resource for policy makers, there were important external developments: migration from Nazi Germany of a number of academics, including psychologists and sociologists and the widescale rejection of eugenics in the period immediately following World War Two. The spectre of race difference research was to rise again, and still has not been completely vanquished, despite widespread acceptance of the central argument, that there is no biological reason to divide people into races.

Contemporary Psychology

It is worth reflecting on the impact of this on contemporary psychology. We do not wish to leave this topic on too upbeat a note. Although race difference research has for the most part faded, it still exists, although more now as isolated pockets of research than large-scale projects. While there may be few psychologists who are actively pursuing racist research there is still a Eurocentricism in psychological research, which when coupled with the idea that the Psychology that we produce is universal leads to implicitly racist assumptions. There is also a lack of anti-racism training in Psychology both at undergraduate and postgraduate level. As Howitt and Owusu-Bempah (1994) demonstrate we, as a discipline, are too quick too assert our few successes and too slow to acknowledge the history of racism within the discipline. Possibly, as long as Psychology attempts to be the science of the individual, we will all too often individualize social issues, and thus to some extent Psychology is a resource for the status quo within societies rather than for change.

PSYCHOLOGY AND WOMEN

The history of psychology in relation to women is also a complex one. There is some commonality with the race psychology project, because it was criticism of the quest for differences between men and women that allowed aspects of the discipline to change, just as the failure of the 'race psychology' project led to change both within individual researchers and across the discipline. However, many of the details are different beyond that initial similarity. With second-wave feminism and the emergence of feminist psychologies, the struggle against patriarchal psychology is perhaps more obvious, but with the subsequent marginalization of feminist voices within psychology and strong institutionalized sexism this issue seems less well resolved than race.

Richards (1996) divides research into the psychology of gender into two phases. First, from the 1850s–1950s gender was either ignored, or the psychology of gender was regarded as little more than a restatement of prevailing cultural stereotypes and assumptions. Non-psychoanalytical psychology paid little attention to gender during this era. The behavioural tradition had little to say and the early cognitive psychologists claimed to search for underlying functions that applied to gender. What was written (often in psychoanalysis and psychiatry) saw women as a deficient other to the male norm.

From the 1960s to the present day, gender was researched resulting from the revival in feminist writing in the 1960s (second-wave feminism) and the shifting male to female ratio of psychology undergraduates. This research took many forms, although most of it was in the quantitative tradition, and had many aims, for example:

- to show that pre-existing stereotypes were false (or true)
- to give a voice to the missing other
- to try to determine if there are essential differences in the psychologies of men and women
- to try to examine sex roles and how they develop
- to try to uncover the psychological and social sources of sexism.

Some of the research had a specifically feminist orientation, for example examining the psychological and social sources of sexism. Other research, for example, attempted to determine what the true, essential, psychological differences are between men and women which could be done from a feminist standpoint, but could be done equally from a sexist standpoint. The work on women, by women, to give a voice to woman (the missing other) is perhaps the most prototypically feminist work and the main thrust here was to attempt to counter the assumption that research work by men, using male participants, could be a universal psychology. We shall revisit this issue later in the section. We continue by examining the research that focused on differences between men and women before examining other work.

The Quest for Difference

Before we continue this section, it is worth exploring some issues of terminology with regard to the difference research. Much of this work was originally called 'sex differences' research, with a tacit or explicit notion that the psychological differences between men and women had a biological foundation. As feminist writing and psychological research began to explore the social differences between men and women, in, for example, the ways that parents and teachers treat boys and girls differently, at least some of these differences became known as gender differences, reflecting a social origin. This simple dichotomy is however problematic. There is a tendency amongst some researchers to use the term 'gender difference' while using an explicit biological framework to explain those differences. As with other instances of what is a nature-nurture distinction, there is also a growing realization that the debate is somewhat futile, most (if not all) psychological phenomena come about because of a complex series of interactions and transactions between the natural and the social, so the distinction is at beast blurred if not completely misleading. Finally, as some social constructionist orientated feminists (for example, Crawford 1995) have argued the more important distinction is between essentialist theories and constructionist theories. Throughout much of this section I shall use the two terms together. Later I shall explore the notion that sex and gender are things that we do, rather than things that are given which Crawford examines at length in her text *Talking difference*.

The investigation of psychological differences between men and women from approximately the 1960s onwards has not been a project in the same way that race psychology was a project just after the turn of the century. At least some of the work was inspired by the ideal of finding true differences in order to examine whether prejudices had any basis in reality. Other sex difference findings have come about because of the habit amongst some psychologists of including sex (or gender) as an additional variable, sometimes for no better reason than that it allows for more complicated statistical procedures, whereas other work appears to have had at its root the notion that women are intrinsically worse than men.

The areas in which difference research encompasses most of psychology are as follows: aggression, spatial ability, causal attribution, social influence, language use, sense of humour, mathematical ability, (various) attitudes, conformity, and just about every area of psychology amenable to examining differences between two groups of people.

A stereotypical experimental study of sex or gender difference takes some dependent variables of interest and measures men and women upon that variable. If differences are found then these are ascribed to sex or gender; often the term used depends on the dependent variable. The findings may be accompanied by a biological or social rationale about why the difference exists but often it is the 'fact' that men and women are different that underlies that explanation.

There are a number of problems with the single experiment that uses sex as an independent variable. Jacklin (1981) called the number of variables that interact with gender the most pervasive problem in sex and gender research. For example, in a unequal society men tend to earn more and have more powerful positions than women, so a group of men and women will tend to differ on socioeconomic economic factors as well as their biological sex. As well as these economic and status differences, there is the idea that men and women live in different social worlds. The way that a person is reacted to differs because of their gender. These interactions lead to confounding factors. It is difficult to know which factors need to be controlled or matched and which do not. Yet despite these objections, and the notion that all studies involving an independent variable that is not under the control of the experimenter are necessarily quasi-experiments, and thus strong claims of causality should not be made, research into sex differences continues. There are further issues, around who the participants are in these studies and who they can represent. This problem was labelled by Crawford as 'the problem of generic women'.

Generic Women

Crawford wrote in 1995 'It is a mistake to assume that all women necessarily have much in common simply because they are women'. If a research study does suggest that there is some difference between men and women Bohan (1993), reminds us it is important to ask, 'which women do we mean?'

We have already discussed the problem of the average person, and to some extent the criticism by Crawford of gender difference research echoes that criticism. When a study finds a sex difference, unless we have considerably more information about the participants than that normally provided for in experimental reports, it is very difficult, if not impossible, to work out what that sex difference might mean.

Often sex or gender differences are fairly small in these single studies, and that may explain some of the inconsistencies in findings because small, but reliable, differences may not be detected in typically small-scale psychological experiments. With the aim to surmount this problem and perhaps with the hope that larger sample sizes may make findings more representative there has been an attempt to use meta-analysis on sex and gender difference research. Meta-analysis is a statistical way of combining the results of a number of individual studies. There are various techniques of meta-analysis available, and according to Rosenthal and Rosnow (1991) the statistically best method is effect size combination.

Hyde (1986) argued against the narrative literature review as a way of combining studies. She claimed that meta-analysis has a twofold advantage:

1 It is a systematic and quantitative way to synthesize and integrate numerous studies.
2 By using effect size estimation it avoids some problems of hypothesis testing.

However not all meta-analyses of sex and gender have used effect size estimation. Maccoby and Jacklin (1974) used vote-counting methods. As a result some of their conclusions of no gender differences may be false, because small-scale studies finding no difference have as much weight as larger studies finding differences, while the converse is also true.

There are difficulties with even the best meta-analyses. Many of these are to do with the lack of agreement around the definition of topics such as aggression. For example, there is a debate whether there is a single psychological entity that deserves the label 'aggression' and whether or not it is sensible to attempt to combine studies that use different measuring techniques. There are also problems that derive from the generic women issue that Crawford raises. If the men and women are drawn from different sections of the population there is a question of whether like is being compared to like in the meta-analyses. There are also deeper problems. Often the effect sizes in gender research are very small, much smaller than the variation in the populations, yet the headlines from such research will tend to trumpet the difference, which tends to establish or reinforce stereotypes. There is also the problem that very often we do not know the *meaning* of these differences. Much psychological research tends to work within very sketchy theoretical frameworks, partly for reasons discussed in Chapter 12. The second reason is that many people who read research that includes effect sizes do not have any intuition for what effect sizes may mean in practice. While meta-analyses have advantages, they should not be seen as (yet another) empirical way to ignore thorny theoretical and metaphysical issues. Mary Crawford demonstrates this by examining the research on women's language and we will examine her argument on that topic below.

Women's Language

In 1973–8 Robin Lakoff published the claim that women's language differed from the language used by men on nine variables. In the following two decades her work has been cited over 350 times in published research papers. These nine variables were:

1 Specialized vocabulary: women have a different specialized vocabulary from men, with examples including women knowing more colour words, more food names, while men know more of the terminology for mechanical objects.
2 Expletives: women use fewer and milder forms of expletives than men ('sugar', 'dash', 'darn', etc.).
3 'Empty' adjectives: women include in their sentences more empty adjectives, (for example, 'That's absolutely fabulous').
4 Tag questions: women use tag questions more than men, turning statements into questions.
5 Intonation: women use more varied intonation than men.
6 Superpolite forms: women are more likely to use polite forms of speech.
7 Hedges: women are more likely to hedge and qualify statements.
8 Hypercorrect grammar: when speaking women are more likely to be grammatically correct.
9 Joke telling/humour: women are less successful at telling and remembering jokes.

Lakoff's work was not based on empirical research because in her words her publication was meant to function as a 'goad to further research'. It almost certainly did this. At the same time it spawned a cottage industry of self-help books, including the infamous 'Venus and Mars' series of books by John Gray. Before examining some of the empirical work, it is worth reflecting on the popular impact. Somewhat like the work on assertiveness training in the 1960s this work individualizes the issue of gender relations. Women and men fail to understand themselves because they talk a different language. If only individual men and women tried harder they could understand each other. With the implicit assumption that women might want to change their language to make themselves understood, they should attempt to understand how men talk (more psychological self-help books are bought by women than by men). To some extent it is likely that lay constructions have been more affected by popular self-help books than they have been by empirical research.

Even the easier to study variables (for example, tag questions) have led to very inconsistent findings, depending on who the men and women were. One study (Mulac and Lundell 1986) is even cited (by Zahn 1989) as showing 'no sex related differences' and (by Pearson *et al.* 1991) as showing differences. Elsewhere the findings are mixed, with differences sometimes falling in the expected direction and sometimes not. As Crawford points out, when the differences are against expectation the researchers will normally give elaborate explanations of why the study failed for those differences. When they are in the expected direction and the explanation given is often fairly simplistic, the differences exist, most often, because of cultural differences between men and women, without any attempt to elaborate how such mechanisms may work, or to examine the wider social impact.

After some meticulous work on each of the main variables highlighted by Lakoff, Crawford goes on to discuss how the number of variables explored has escalated over the last four decades, with over 35 possible variables having been examined, still with fairly inconsistent findings. As Crawford points out when an enterprise, after almost 30 years of asking the same question, appears no closer to reaching a conclusion it may be that the very question is incorrect.

There appear to be a number of stumbling blocks in the enterprise. We have already discussed the issues of generic women and the problems of using average findings when discussing very divergent populations. Added to this is the tendency to treat any findings of difference as complete without the need for further explanation of why such differences may occur. Another problem is how results are utilized.

Gender Development

Interest in developmental psychology began soon after the founding of Psychology. With the then prevalent notion of recapitulation (the idea that an individual in its lifetime repeats the development of the species) investigating how the child develops was a way of not only answering technical questions about schooling but also a way to understand the history of the species. Although this idea has long since been discredited the enterprise of developmental psychology still betrays its roots in that form of evolutionary thinking (for example, Morss 1995). As Burman (1998) discusses in an essay on the possibilities or otherwise of a feminist developmental psychology, there is a powerful appeal in using the rhetoric of the child that has to some extent inoculated developmental psychology from the same analyses that have been applied to gender, race, class and sexuality.

Gender development, despite the sometime unwanted conceptual baggage, has provided a resource for understanding the impact of society on how children understand themselves as gendered beings, and this has itself led to a wider discussion of those impacts. The notion that we react differently to newborn boys and girls, and that these differences in reaction continue throughout childhood and into adulthood comes out of research into gender development. The notion of gender roles as things that come out of expectations and are enacted by parents and later teachers has led to resources that liberal feminists, and others, can use to try to raise consciousness about the impact of child-rearing practices, educational materials and to change public opinion about accepted gender roles.

The role of this research into gender development may have had a similar effect to the race Psychology project we have talked about previously. The shift from describing how boys and girls develop to examining the social and cultural effects of gender roles may have contributed to an acceptance that there was a need for courses and modules on the Psychology of women, which may have helped in the struggles to establish the Psychology of Women's section within the BPS and its equivalent in other national psychology associations. However, at the same time, the politics of gender subjugation are not something that is seen as being of a psychology that is still projecting the image of being a value free natural science.

Feminist Psychology

Feminist Psychology can be identified with the cultural impact of second-wave feminism upon psychology. While there were occasional criticisms of the androcentrism in psychology prior to the 1970s for example, Horney countering the Freudian notion of 'penis envy' in women with 'womb envy' and the publication of de Beauvoir's *The second sex* (1949) there was little critical work in Psychology. Part of the reason for this may have been, as Sherif (1987) points out, the ways in which the topics that psychologists studied were often heavily funded by government agencies, and part of which may have been due to the concern that Psychology was a neutral, and therefore apolitical science. Another consideration is the relative lack of women in the discipline prior to the

1960s, due to institutional barriers and a general cultural sexism. From the late 1970s, through the 1980s and 1990s feminist critiques of Psychology have been growing and the impact of feminist Psychology has become more extensive.

The first place where this could be seen was probably the cross-cultural work on sex roles, which heralded work on the sources of sexism and culturally constructed gender differences. At this point, with the exception of some radical feminist voices, the approach was that of trying to understand how psychological differences are imposed upon boys and men, girls and women, through factors such as child rearing practice, culture in general and through social psychological processes. (See for example Carol Gilligan's *In a different voice: psychological theory and women's development* [1982].)

As this work was developing, and possibly because feminist work tends to be explicitly multidisciplinary, post-structuralism began to make an impact upon the debates. The publication by Henriques *et al. Changing the subject: psychology, social regulation and subjectivity* can be seen as one of the first instances when psychologists used post-structuralist arguments about psychology, rather than criticism coming from people who were regarded as being outside the discipline, and which clearly led on to further developments, unlike the 1970s work by, for example, Kenneth Gergen and Rom Harré. Part of the argument is whether the methods that Psychology uses are inevitably masculine, so for example Wendy Holloway (1989) *Subjectivity and method in psychology*, and Sandra Harding's *The science question in feminism* both argue from this perspective.

The argument over whether or not there are distinctive feminist methods has grown more complex with Peplau and Conrad (1989) arguing that there are no methods that can be guaranteed to produce non-sexist research. These arguments have become complex, with writers like Sue Wilkkinson (1997) arguing that given the priority that feminist Psychology gives to prioritizing the political then it follows that feminists should adopt whatever research methods work for a given topic. Many feminist writers (see, for example, Erica Burman 1999) have grave concerns that a position that is too social constructionist may undermine any points that could be made. However the style of research used in mainstream psychology (sometimes labelled male-stream as a reminder of just how androcentric it has been) is seen, at least by some feminist writers as an overwhelmingly masculine exercise, and the critiques of it often have their roots in social constructionism.

Feminist Psychology has had a range of impacts on Psychology as a whole and on how gender research is treated in particular. Throughout the section so far the critiques that we have highlighted have come from feminist psychologists. In Chapter 15 we will discuss the resources that feminist psychologists have made available to social constructionists and while in Chapter 10 we cite Danziger on the notion that psychology and politics are intertwined, it is important to make clear that this idea is very obvious in the writings of feminist psychologists.

Conclusions

It is not easy to try to summarize the current impacts of feminist psychology due to the multiple positions within feminist psychology. As we discuss in Chapter 15 feminist psychology has had a major influence on the social constructionist movement, and may in addition provide a valuable resource for those within psychology wishing to also pursue an agenda of political change. Feminist Psychology is no more a monolithic position than any of the other positions that we have examined in this book. Indeed one of the great strengths of feminist Psychology is the ability to switch between essentialist and constructionist arguments. To some extent it is necessary to argue with experimental psychologists in the language that they understand and as we discuss in Chapter 12 that is the language of variables and statistics. While it is always possible to reject another's position because of deep ontological or epistemological differences, very often such arguments are ignored. By rigorously applying the logic of experimental psychology it is possible to show how the quest for difference is in itself flawed. Meanwhile the more social constructionist focus of some feminist arguments gives us examples of how Psychology has been a product of its host societies. However, and despite the advances made in moving the psychology of women away from the margins of Psychology, the discipline as a whole continues to project an image of being a neutral, value free science and it is only if that representation is successfully challenged that it will be possible to talk in terms of a widespread acceptance of the insights from feminist Psychology.

FURTHER READING

Burman, E. 1998: Deconstructing feminist psychology, in E Burman (ed.), *Deconstructing feminist psychology*. London: Sage.

Burr, V. 1998: *Gender and social psychology*. London: Routledge.

Crawford, M. 1995: *Talking difference: on gender and language*. London: Sage.

Fox, D. and I. Prilleltensky (eds) 1997: *Critical psychology: an introduction*. London: Sage.

Gilligan, C. 1982: *In a different voice*. Cambridge MA: Harvard University Press.

Gould, S. J. 1996: *The mismeasure of man*. London: Penguin Books.

Henwood, K., Griffin, C. and Phoenix, A. (eds) 1998: *Standpoints and differences: essays in the practice of feminist psychology*. London: Sage.

Hollway, W. 1989: *Subjectivity and method in psychology: gender, meaning and science*. London: Sage.

Howitt, D and Owusu-Bempah, J. 1994: *The racism of psychology: time for a change*. Hemel Hempstead: Harvester-Wheatsheaf.

Ibanez, T. and Iniguez, L. (eds) 1997: *Critical social psychology*. London: Sage.

Kitzinger, C. 1995: *The social construction of lesbianism*. London: Sage.

Lakoff, R. 1973: 'Language and a woman's place'. *Language in society* 2: 45–79.

Morss, J. 1995: *Growing critical: alternatives to developmental psychology*. London: Routledge.

Nightingale, D.J. and Cromby, J. (eds) 1999: *Social constructionist psychology.* Buckingham: The Open University Press.

Richards, G. 1996: *Putting psychology in its place.* London: Routledge.

Whittle, P. 2000: W.H.R. Rivers and the early history of psychology at Cambridge. In A. Saito, *Bartlett, culture and cognition.* Hove: Psychology Press.

10

THE NATURE AND ROLE OF CONTEMPORARY PSYCHOLOGY

As we have seen in the previous chapters Psychology has never been a homogenous discipline. At the beginning of the twenty-first century the heterogeneity of Psychology as both an academic and professional discipline continues. In this chapter a number of themes are established which inform much of the second half of the book: the centrality of method in Psychology, the differences and commonalities between academic and popular psychology, the ways that psychological discourses inform everyday language use, and the ways that psychology at the same time is an influence on both regressive and progressive political impulses. Continuing the discussion in Chapter 6 this chapter questions the current impact of Psychology on society. It also speculates on the possible impact of recent policy within the British Psychological Society to establish a chartered professional status for all psychologists, professional and academic.

ACADEMIC PSYCHOLOGY

The largest single disciplinary employment opportunity for Psychology graduates in the UK is academic psychology, teaching and research in higher education, and teaching Psychology, mostly in further education. As a university subject, psychology is very popular within the UK, although the popularity of psychology degrees waned a little in the last half of the 1990s. This popularity has led to a situation where Psychology is often one of the most competitive disciplines, in terms of entry requirements, for potential students to find a place at university. Psychology at undergraduate level is dominated by female students as shown by UK national figures (however this is not reflected in postgraduate figures). A substantial psychological content is found in degrees such as business studies, sports science and medicine.

The dual nature of Psychology as an academic and professional discipline affects the content of psychology degrees in a way that is rare in academic disciplines, despite the fact that less than 20 per cent of Psychology graduates become professional psychologists.

The British Psychological Society (BPS)

All degree courses are affected by a number of factors in their content which include a number of effects of social context and new knowledge generated by the research community. However, at least within the UK, the largest single factor is the BPS.

Unlike, for example, the US model whereby all professional accreditation accrues with postgraduate qualifications, UK degrees in Psychology may carry graduate basis of registration accreditation (GBR). This level of accreditation is not itself a professional qualification, but is necessary for acceptance to postgraduate courses that lead, along with appropriate professional supervision, to professional status.

Increasingly, despite being divorced from the government led quality assurance mechanisms, GBR is seen as a quality kite mark. Despite only a minority of graduates becoming professional applied psychologists, the vast majority of applicants to Psychology degrees indicate in their personal statements an ambition to become a professional applied psychologist. Clearly a degree course without GBR standing is at a competitive disadvantage in recruiting undergraduate psychologists. Thus achieving and maintaining GBR standing has become an important factor in the planning of psychology degree provision within the British university sector. This has led to a uniformity in broad content areas within degrees in psychology, and has also given rise to this content being mirrored in academic courses at further education and school level.

The single largest part of an undergraduate Psychology degree is research methods, almost universally dominated by quantitative research methods and statistics. Including final year research projects, it is common for a Psychology graduate to have between 25 per cent and 33 per cent of their psychology teaching and learning in research methods. The effects of this for the discipline at a theoretical level are discussed in Chapter 12. However given this backdrop it is perhaps unsurprising that arguments against this methodological orthodoxy are met with little acceptance.

There are a number of benefits of this, however, some in a UK context and some more generally. Psychology graduates, whatever their future careers, have a level of familiarity with (albeit a restricted range of) statistical and numerical concepts and of different approaches to research, probably unequalled in any other disciplinary setting.

This high level of research methods training means that many Psychology degrees enjoy the funding arrangements from central government for science subjects. As discussed later, these important financial considerations mean that there are considerable restraints on Psychology departments from adopting any other model apart from Psychology as natural science.

The other, near, compulsory subject areas within Psychology are cognitive Psychology, social Psychology, individual differences, biological basis of behaviour and developmental Psychology.

Cognitive Psychology is second in importance to research methods, although with the cognitive approach dominating both social Psychology and developmental Psychology cognitivism may outrank research methods in some institutions. This reflects the dominance of the cognitive approach to Psychology. As discussed in Chapter 13, it would be a mistake to see cognitive psychology as a monolithic paradigm.

The biological basis of behaviour as a distinct topic within psychology reminds us of the historical roots of the discipline and the way that the BPS categorize psychology as both a biological and a social science. It also provides an entrée into the discipline for those wishing to pursue neurogenetic arguments. While it is possible to approach this area from a position of constraints and limitations on psychological functioning, all too often the argument is reductionist, with the biological level being constructed as more real than the psychological.

While there is no direct requirement for applications of psychology to be covered within a degree course, despite the GBR label, it is within the syllabus area known as individual differences that knowledge most directly applicable to professional practice is located. This is partly due to the popularity of standardized psychometric tests across psychological research practice, which is discussed in greater depth later in this chapter. At the same time this area is tied to the methodology of testing, with implications that are often ignored under the rubric of value free science.

Developmental Psychology, as Erica Burman (1998) pointed out, is the one area that seems to have remained aloof from the general critiques of developmentalism that have been seen throughout social theory. Developmental Psychology retains its links to the nineteenth-century notion that ontogeny recapitulates phylogeny, with the assumption that 'normal' development is inevitably a progression.

Social Psychology has been at the forefront of arguments about the nature of psychology. It is possible to study social Psychology without dealing with the issues and debates around social construction and critical Psychology. Indeed many of the US authored textbooks of social Psychology manage to do just that, with the research programmes set up by the US army during World War Two still dominating the field. It is within social Psychology, however, that there is an acute need to understand the interface between psychology and society. Given this it is perhaps not surprising that it is in this area of psychology that criticism of the natural science model of psychology has been most sustained.

Curious Omissions

If a psychology degree is to serve as the entry point into the discipline, it is perhaps curious that there is no requirement for equal opportunities training within the GBR syllabus. This omission becomes even more ominous given the lack of equal opportunities training in some of the professional postgraduate courses.

As an academic product the lack of a requirement for theoretical

Psychology is perhaps also curious, although given the lack of a theoretical Psychology specialism within the discipline perhaps not pragmatically surprising.

Other Aspects of GBR accreditation

As well as specified subject areas, which in itself may have a stultifying effect on developments within Psychology, perhaps leading to a pragmatic closure of the debate about the nature of the discipline at a time when the theoretical and philosophical arguments appear to be far from closed, there are other aspects to the GBR accreditation process that may also have a long term impact on the nature of developments within the field.

Laboratory provision

For a discipline that promotes itself as a science, and given the funding privileges accruing from central government regarding psychology as a science, it is perhaps unsurprising that laboratory provision has become one of the criteria for acceptance of a degree as leading to GBR accreditation. Reflecting the historical development of universities around departments such provision needs to be made exclusive for Psychology students and staff. This reinforces the disciplinary boundaries of the subject, again at a very pragmatic level, as heads of psychology departments need to make cases within institutions for the provision of resources. Thus, for example, both authors of this book have made arguments in favour of treating Psychology as a natural science within their institution, while at the same time being critical of this notion in teaching and discussions with colleagues. Once such resources are in place, with appropriate technical and academic staff to support them it becomes increasingly difficult to argue that Psychology is not a natural science, not least because colleagues' continued employment is dependent on such a view.

External Examiners

The external examining arrangements within the university sector are a way of sharing good practice across institutions and ensuring at least some commonality in standards of marking. For a degree to be accredited with GBR status the examiners must be either chartered psychologists or Associate Fellows of the BPS. As a consequence this increases the power of the BPS as an institution.

Consequences

There have been calls for a centralization of the examination of the core syllabus areas making up the GBR route in Psychology. This appeal, made on the grounds of the professional standing of Psychology, ironically undermines the professionalism of academic psychologists. It is also part of a broader movement where, under the guise of ensuring standards at university level, there has been a movement towards attempting to specify what precisely a degree in any academic discipline will have as its outcomes.

THE ROLE OF THE ACADEMIC PSYCHOLOGIST

Academic psychologists have at least three clearly defined roles: as the creators of new psychological knowledge through research, as educators and as consultants to industry and government. There are a number of other potential roles that academic psychologists have: appearing on television, radio and in print media as experts on particular topics. In this section we will focus on knowledge production.

Knowledge Production

It is the creation of new knowledge that is probably the most important role of academic psychologists. It is worth considering how this process generally occurs. We have discussed at length in earlier chapters the ways that historical and cultural contingencies affect what is researched and the processes that make certain types of psychological knowledge creation acceptable. It is worth reflecting on that process in the abstract and considering both the standard explanation of psychological knowledge creation and the explanation that we are utilizing, which is a combination of Graham Richards (1997) and some themes and ideas from more general work on social studies of scientific knowledge.

The standard story can be categorized as the 'up the mountain story' (Rorty 1980). In this story modern researchers are able to investigate problems in a progressively more successful way than previous researchers. The story can have one of two tropes, either the 'standing on shoulders of giants' or that modern research avoids the ignorance and prejudices of previous researchers.

Kitzinger's (1987) account of rhetoric in research on lesbianism and male homosexuality is an excellent example of the second of these two 'up the mountain' stories. In literature reviews, which almost invariably set the stage for research reports, the past research is either attacked as methodologically flawed, or contaminated by the prejudices of the previous researchers, or previous research is presented as being disadvantaged by the lack of access to current research understandings. In what might then be seen as a contradiction is the call for more social science research, in which presumably the investigators believe that they have overcome the methodological and theoretical difficulties, and that they, unlike their peers from previous generations, are able to rise above the prejudices of their age and be objective. As Kitzinger points out this notion reinforces the idea that social science research should be objective, and that we can do this by identifying the prejudices from previous generations of researchers, although it is unusual for an investigator holding to this story to be self-reflexive about their position towards what they are researching.

The other up the mountain of knowledge story is the notion that while previous research is not to be so badly condemned, some interesting variables have not been investigated and that current research can illuminate what has been a blind spot in previous research. As we discussed in the previous chapter this can be seen in the research on differences between men and women. The basic notion that there are psychological differences is accepted but then current research investigates new variables. As Crawford (1995) discusses in relation to research on differences in language use between men and women, the number of dependent variables investigated increased from an original list of nine types of speech to over 40 types of speech. The other way that this works is that the number of independent variables investigated within a specific area can increase. So, for example, in research on bystander apathy a wide variety of different situations have been used, varying the number of bystanders and varying the situation, followed by variations in the types of bystander. One of the things that appears to happen as research programmes mature is that the variables investigated become more obtuse and the concerns appear to become increasingly divorced from everyday Psychology.

What these stories under emphasize are any concerns beyond those of taking scientific knowledge forward. Graham Richards (1997) offers the following as a model of the process:

- Psychology as a discipline is a product of the 'psychologies' of those within the discipline. It is therefore necessarily reflexive in character. The Psychological knowledge that Psychology produces directly articulates and expresses the psychological character of the psychologists producing it – their ways of thinking, their priorities, attitudes, values, etc.
- Psychologists represent specific constituencies in the discipline's host societies. Until the mid-twentieth century these were predominately white, male and middle- or upper-class. While constituting a restricted sample of the psychological constituencies in society as a whole, there was always a degree of psychological heterogeneity within this group both within and between the sites where the discipline was practised.

The historical process of change within Psychology has thus been determined by several factors over and above any objective knowledge gains. These include:

> changes in the psychological character of its practitioners in the light of changed socio-historical circumstance (. . .), and broadening the range of psychological constituencies represented within the discipline. They also reflexively include the discipline's own previously produced 'knowledge'.
>
> (Richards 1997: 312)

In the previous chapter we have discussed how the range of constituencies represented have had an effect on issues around race and racism, gender and sexism, as well as sexuality and heterosexism. To some extent the discipline recognizes these issues, but in a somewhat limited way. As the up the mountain of knowledge stories illustrate it is likely that current researchers in some areas (more particularly those areas which more obviously have a connection with social issues) will identify biases and prejudices in previous researchers. The second way is the amount of instrumental control that psychologists strive for in the current incarnation of the laboratory experiment. However this is a somewhat limited recognition in two ways. It is rare for experimental psychologists to admit that when they undertake studies they may also be biased in the ways that their predecessors were, especially in their technical writing which draws heavily upon what could be identified as an 'empiricist repertoire' (Gilbert and Mulkay 1984). The other way is that, partly due to the heavy reliance on the up the mountain story and the empiricist repertoire, when potential biases are recognized by knowledge producers it is only in terms of what happens in the immediate experimental situation. It is rare for authors of research reports to consider either their personal stake in the issue (beyond the various techniques of minimizing it encouraged by the empiricist repertoire) or the wider issues of why particular research programmes become established.

One of the effects of the typical scientific writing used within Psychology is that it is quite possible for authors to hide behind scientific objectivity when putting across disgusting ideas. Thus, for example, those psychologists whose research on race differences was sponsored by the far right pioneer fund could state that they were just being scientists while denigrating their opponents as politically motivated.

Finally in the context of knowledge production it is worth reflecting on this process as a whole and the influence that it has on society. Danziger (1997) makes the point that psychological discourse is also, always, a political discourse. As Psychology establishes frameworks for understanding both ourselves and others it, inevitably, excludes other ways of understanding ourselves and others. While we will not claim that it is impossible to discuss things in ways other than the predominant discourses (for if it were discourses would be static instead of changing) it is certainly very difficult. As Danziger states, this is a strictly *public* phenomenon, and one that authors of texts are not unaware of. As we write we intend to accomplish something with our words, as other authors also do so. However, at the same time we are constrained in the ways that we can write and we are aware of the other sides of the argument that we are making, as well as being constrained in the ways in which it is acceptable to argue.

In creating knowledge and establishing dominant modes of psychological language, the ways that Psychologists describe things have both a descriptive but perhaps more importantly a normative role. Ways of describing human actions often provide resources for justifying particular forms of social arrangement, and legitimizing social practices, and this may be implicit when the discursive framework is both taken for granted and buttressed by scientists.

It is difficult to conceptualize this process as it takes place, and even the attempts by feminist psychologists, critical psychologists and some social constructionist psychologists to be reflexive may not go far enough.

However, as Richards points out, we should not ignore the political and moral dimension of psychological knowledge production, and with the historical writing of Richards and Danziger it appears difficult to ignore its importance.

Academic Psychology and the Media

It is in relationship to the media that psychologists perhaps show off their lack of understanding of social issues and how those will impact upon how findings are represented within the media. However the fault here is not necessarily with academic psychologists. For example, and despite the efforts of the BPS media unit who ask the authors of papers to clear all press releases, research that Adair and Elcock (1996) conducted on the discourses used by police officers about rave culture was presented as an attitude survey by newspaper conference reports. One other aspect of this is that research findings presented at conferences or in journal articles will only tend to get reported in the media when there is some form of news agenda and so findings are not received or reported neutrally, and within newspaper articles much of the detail of the study is not given.

Beyond this academic psychologists may get involved in the media because of their perceived expertise, so, for example, I (Elcock) was asked by a local radio station to be part of a mid-morning radio show, which ran for over a year. Others may be seen as an expert within one particular field, for example stress or gambling, and thus will often get asked for their opinion on that topic by national media, in the form of interviews with newspapers or the broadcast media or as guests in studio debates. Almost all of these forms of media do not allow for much in depth discussion of the issues, or the ways that research was conducted and how findings were derived. Thus even the best intentioned may slip into formulations that express things as scientific facts, rather than as research in progress and our best guesses about why things happen. All of this reinforces the notion that Psychology is a science, and a useful science able to commentate authoritatively on issues that matter to people.

One final topic that is worth touching on is how psychologists are represented within fiction. Perhaps the most well known of this was the British television drama *Cracker*, which was remade for US television under the name *Fitz*. Here the representation is not of a scientist but rather of an expert on human beings, a person who, usually, knows more about criminals than experienced police officers because of their background in Psychology. The character is also able to question witnesses and those accused with a deft touch, again due to their knowledge of Psychology. In keeping with most police dramas by the end of the story the correct person has been identified as the perpetrator and the implication given that they will be successfully prosecuted. While this television. show may have been wildly inaccurate in its portrayal of psychological criminal profiling which appears to have been the inspiration for the series, and while the psychologist in this case is not seen as a scientist, it nevertheless reinforces the notion that psychologists have hidden knowledge not available to everyday people. As an aside, while *Cracker* was showing on UK television, I was admissions tutor at Cheltenham and Gloucester College of Higher Education. During this time a large proportion of applicants put in their personal statements that they wished to become forensic psychologists. Although as academic psychologists we can be scathing of the way that psychologists are portrayed within the media that portrayal still has an impact on how we are represented in the social world.

ACADEMIC AND POPULAR PSYCHOLOGY

There is a major break point between academic and popular psychology that has been explored a little in Chapter 5 and which will be a focus of enquiry in Chapter 12, and is reflected on bookshop shelves across countries. Whereas academic psychology, no matter how ponderously and sometimes wrong-headedly, attempts to establish knowledge about the normal psychological functioning of human beings, much of the popular psychology literature is about self-improvement.

Much of this popular literature presents as fact issues that can be contentious within Psychology, or sometimes presents as fact things that the majority of psychologists would find difficult to believe. As there is a more extended discussion of this issue in Chapter 11, I will confine myself here to a few points.

Popular Psychology, especially in terms of offering expert help, is a part of the representation of Psychology as a discipline that has answers to profound questions. It is rare for academic psychologists to explicitly tackle the issue of why parts of popular psychology may be misguided or give false impressions (with the honourable exception of some work in feminist psychology). Part of the reason for that may be that it upholds our (academic psychologists') status as experts on human beings. Finally, as in the first half of the twentieth century, at least some of our students came into the discipline with the expectation that they too could learn answers to those sorts of questions. It is here that we invoke a rhetoric of science, perhaps in part to ameliorate the disappointment that at least some of our students must feel when faced with a typical psychology syllabus.

Academic and Professional Psychology

The majority of the chapter has examined the nature of academic psychology at undergraduate level within the UK. The aim of this second section is to question the role of professional psychologists and to examine the tensions between the academic and professional parts of the discipline.

There appears discontent amongst applied psychologists that their work is less valued than that of the pure scientist. This is curious given the history of the discipline, with the rise of certain models of investigative practice leading to the demarcation of the profession of psychology from competitors, such as psychoanalysis, and ways that the models of investigative practice developed in applied settings come to be regarded as the only legitimate ways to research psychology in academic settings. It may also be curious, in a more parochial UK setting, given that powerful lobbying of applied professional psychologists within the BPS has led to a strong level of control over what is taught as psychology and, with the chartering of academic psychologists, the possibility of controlling who is allowed to teach psychology.

In all this there remains the problem that, at least within the UK, the vast majority of people who graduate with Psychology degrees do not become professional psychologists. Compared with the professions that Psychology appears to be aspiring towards (law and medicine) this figure must be of some concern. In the USA current practice is not to give pre-professional recognition to undergraduate courses and it is in this issue that there are clear differences between the US university system and the UK one.

PROFESSIONAL PSYCHOLOGY

There are three major components to professional psychology: clinical Psychology, occupational Psychology (within which we include organizational Psychology) and educational Psychology. In addition there are forensic Psychology and counselling Psychology which are recognized as Psychology professions within the UK and the USA. Finally there is health Psychology, currently not recognized as a separate psychological profession within the UK (most are chartered clinical Psychologists), although there is strong lobbying in the BPS to separate this area from clinical Psychology, and sports Psychology, where the majority of professionals in the UK are chartered in another area of Psychology (for example, occupational) and some professionals receive their professional status through sports professional bodies.

While there are interesting stories around counselling Psychology, for example with the inter-professional conflict with counsellors and psychologists, health Psychology, especially with the questions around how this differs from Clinical Psychology, and the somewhat messy status of sports Psychologists, we shall concentrate in this section on the three major professions listed above. Again these sections will focus mainly on the context of the UK.

Clinical Psychology

Clinical Psychology has been identified as part of the 'psy-complex' the amalgamation of psychiatry and clinical Psychology which in turn is wrapped up in the legal codes that define the mentally ill and what rights they have. In the UK, and to some extent elsewhere the clinical psychology profession has been shaped in relation to the medical profession, especially psychiatry.

Clinical Psychology has probably led the way for professionalism within

Psychology, with moves in the UK to make the standard qualification for clinical Psychology a doctoral level rather than a masters level qualification, and to some extent pushing for the reform of the graduate basis of registration. While these developments are undoubtedly multiply determined one of the factors has been the need to come out of the shadow of psychiatry, and one way to do that has been to ensure a level of parity in education received and titles used.

Educational Psychology

Within the UK there is a statutory duty for education authorities to provide educational psychologists. In England and Wales there is currently a requirement for educational psychologists to have trained and worked as teachers before they enter training. In Scotland there is no requirement for this but it is not easy for an educational psychologist trained in one system to work in the other. There is currently a move afoot to change the standard educational psychology qualification from a Masters degree to a PhD and if this comes to fruition the requirement to train as teachers will no longer apply to England and Wales.

The role of the educational psychologist has changed quite dramatically over the last two decades. Currently the main statutory role for educational psychologists is to test children in order to decide if they should be given a statement of special educational needs by the local education authority. This has meant that the role of the educational psychologist has to some extent changed from that of someone who advised teachers and parents. Educational Psychology in the UK has recently mirrored clinical Psychology with a doctoral level qualification replacing the masters level one.

Occupational Psychology

Unlike the two categories of psychologist above, occupational psychologists overwhelmingly work either for large companies or as independent consultants. As a result there is little public funding for occupational psychology MSc courses (although occasionally universities do offer bursaries) and trainee occupational psychologists either fund themselves or are funded by their employers.

Unlike clinical and educational Psychology there appears to be little motivation within this profession for the doctoral level of qualification.

SUMMARY

Currently the major professions within psychology all share a deep interest in measuring people through the use of psychometric and other tests. Part of the claim to expertise that professional psychologists make is that they are trained to administer and interpret properly a range of tests and that they are able to design such tests themselves. Across all of these professions there is a vested interest in protecting the boundaries of their expertise in this matter.

Although of course all claim expertise in intervention after such testing, whether an active intervention in clinical and to some extent educational psychology, or as a recommendation as to which potential employee should be hired, or should be put on to a stress reduction programme. Historically the discipline has displaced others which have claimed knowledge in these fields on the basis that the knowledge that psychologists apply is scientific, and thus the advice given has a scientific backing. It is somewhat easier to claim to be an expert on human beings if the rhetoric of science is invoked, and while this has consequences that we examine in the final chapter of the book, being able to make that claim is of importance to psychology as an institution as well as psychology as an academic discipline.

FURTHER READING

Burman, E. 1998: Deconstructing feminist psychology. In: E. Burman (ed.). *Deconstructing feminist psychology*. London: Sage.

Crawford, M. 1995: *Talking difference: on gender and language*. London: Sage.

Curt, B.C. 1994: *Textuality and tectonics: troubling social and psychological science*. Buckingham: Open University Press.

Danziger, K. 1990: *Constructing the subject: historical origins of psychological research*. Cambridge: Cambridge University Press.

Danziger, K. 1997: *Naming the mind: how psychology found its language*. London: Sage.

Fox, D. and I. Prilleltensky (eds) 1997: *Critical psychology: an introduction*. London: Sage.

Gilbert, G.N. and Mulkay, M. 1984: *Opening Pandora's box: a sociological analysis of scientists discourse*. Cambridge: Cambridge University Press.

Kitzinger, C. 1987: *The social construction of lesbianism*. London: Sage.

Richards, G. 1996: *Putting psychology in its place*. London: Routledge.

Richards, G. 1997: *Race, racism and psychology: towards a reflexive history*. London: Routledge

11

EVERYDAY PSYCHOLOGY

We all psychologize, all of the time. In trying to find explanations of our own or others' behaviour, for instance, we are engaged in identifying the mental states and processes that give rise to that behaviour. Such activity seems to be vital in facilitating social interaction, as indicated by the problems in social interaction encountered by sufferers from autism, which is often characterized as an inability to do such psychologizing. This fundamental behaviour, the search for explanations of behaviour or ascriptions of personality characteristics, is variously termed 'common-sense psychology', 'folk psychology', 'lay psychology', 'everyday psychology', and any number of similar formulations. We prefer to use the term 'everyday psychology' because 'common-sense psychology' and 'folk psychology' also have specialist meanings, as we shall see.

In this chapter, we consider the status of such everyday psychologizing within professional and scientific Psychology. Clearly, there are differences between what people do every day and the discipline of scientific Psychology. If there were no such differences, there would be no need for the discipline. We start by considering these differences, and go on to look at attempts within social Psychology to describe everyday behaviour. We then discuss attempts within philosophy of mind and cognitive science to explain the mechanisms underlying such behaviour. These first sections of the chapter summarize briefly mainstream investigations of everyday psychologizing within disciplinary Psychology.

While disciplinary explanations of everyday psychologizing are interesting, they obscure the peculiar relationship between the discipline of Psychology and its subject matter. We have discussed this reflexive relationship in previous chapters, but it becomes most clear when considering the effects of the discipline on everyday psychologizing and vice versa. In the second part of the chapter, therefore, we consider this relationship more fully. We begin by suggesting that the mechanism that mediates this relationship is language, and that everyday psychology cannot be separated from psychological language. We consider the status and nature of this language, before looking more closely at the relationship between academic and everyday psychology. We end the chapter by considering the role of popular psychology, in contrast to academic Psychology, in shaping everyday psychologizing.

THE NEGLECT OF EVERYDAY PSYCHOLOGY

We began the chapter by claiming that we all psychologize. Such psychologizing is private to us, though we may choose to verbalize our reasoning processes or our conclusions. However, very often it is difficult to provide an accurate description of the reasoning involved, since we do not have conscious access to it. There is a long tradition of psychological discourse, preceding the development of the scientific discipline, that consists in part of attempts to establish explicit knowledge of the factors influencing our behaviour. The development of scientific Psychology attempted to improve on such discourses through the application of certain methods of reasoning, particularly empirical methods. However, if we all psychologize, then it is tempting to ask why we need a scientific Psychology. The problem is that everyday psychology is often inaccurate. It is inaccurate for many reasons, including a lack of knowledge to form a basis for psychologizing, and the fact that other people's behaviour is not necessary common sensical. More technically, everyday psychologizing is idiosyncratic – we all have a different set of ideas to base our psychologizing on; it is subjective – our psychologizing is based on our own viewpoint; and it is unreliable. In addition, everyday psychologizing is shaped by a range of biases and prejudices.

Psychology as a scientific discipline developed in part in response to these problems with everyday psychologizing. Psychological-type issues have been considered by (amongst others) philosophers and theologians for centuries, but this consideration has been subject to the same problems as mentioned above. Scientific psychology offered the promise of an explanatory framework that was objective, that was based on clear evidence, and that was publicly available. This in itself was a laudable objective, but in setting out a scientific Psychology a range of other factors came to bear to influence the nature of scientific Psychology, and hence of the kind of framework Psychology could produce. These factors included technologies (in the widest sense) available for use in investigation, including evolutionary thought, statistical analysis, and later the advent of computers the need to; clearly differentiate the new discipline of Psychology from philosophy; and the desire of psychologists to acquire the prestige of natural scientists. These mechanisms are discussed in previous chapters.

The impact of these various constraints on the development of scientific Psychology has been to limit the applicability of Psychology's theories to everyday life. Although a wide range of professional applications of Psychology have been developed, these require a considerable degree of training. Psychology has by and large failed to provide the lay person with the knowledge they need to improve their everyday psychologizing. Psychology's concentration on being scientific at the expense of being relevant has meant that Psychology has not had the expected impact on everyday psychologizing. Common sense has not been replaced by a scientific framework, but rather some theories of Psychology have been incorporated into everyday psychology. Less rigorous scientific approaches to the psychological have arguably had a greater effect, particularly psychoanalysis. Psychoanalysis has achieved its level of popular recognition, in part, because it addressed people's everyday concerns, even though it is often considered marginal by academic psychologists because of its lack of investigative rigour.

If the discipline's claims are to be believed, scientific Psychology has effectively created a social technocracy, where a privileged few are possessed of a body of scientific knowledge that can be used to explain behaviour. However, there is a considerable irony here. By and large, in our experience, psychologists do not replace their previous everyday psychologizing with their recently gained theoretical knowledge, although they may augment it a little. Often, outside their professional lives psychologists pursue everyday psychology in the same way as everyone else.

SOCIAL PSYCHOLOGY AND EVERYDAY PSYCHOLOGY

Everyday psychology is, above all, a means for facilitating interpersonal relationships. Being able to interpret and predict the behaviour of others is an invaluable tool for such a social species. Indeed, to a large extent, everyday psychology is only concerned with interpersonal relationships, it being relatively rare for lay people to discuss the mechanisms underlying perception or the processes of speech production. Given this, it should not be surprising that everyday psychology has been a topic of interest within social Psychology, particularly in the areas of attribution and personality judgements. It is perhaps more surprising that everyday psychology has not played a larger role within social Psychology. In this section, we survey investigations in social Psychology that seek to explain everyday psychology. For a fuller discussion of the development of social Psychology, see Chapter 7. There has also been work in individual difference Psychology, with some theories of personality attempting to incorporate people's everyday psychologizing.

Those portions of social Psychology concerned with everyday psychology use the metaphor of 'the person as psychologist' to motivate theory development. In this view, people are seen as naïve scientists, generating and testing hypotheses about people's behaviour in a logical and rational way. This commitment to rationality follows a common trend in philosophy and Psychology, and particularly reflects the postwar dominance of cognitivism. However, recently there has been doubt about whether people actually are rational in their interpersonal judgements, with increasing recognition that people's decisions are shaped by emotions and irrational prejudice. In response to this, recent approaches within social Psychology have concentrated on describing people's psychologizing rather than hypothesizing internalized processing mechanisms.

Social Psychology's interest in everyday psychology began with the work of Heider, who formulated a theory of what he called 'common-sense Psychology'. Heider attempted to apply Gestalt theories of perception to person perception, to explain how people make sense of behaviour. He introduced the notion of the naïve scientist, suggesting that people try to link observable behaviour to unobservable causes, these causes being seen as constituting the meaning underlying people's actions. The assignment of causes to behaviour was believed to be shaped by a set of basic assumptions, which were shared by members of a culture. Common-sense psychology thus formed part of a culture's belief system. Heider identified two basic sources of causes of behaviour, personal (internal) and situational (external), which were to be expanded on in later attribution theories within social Psychology. The acceptance of the role of culture was a departure for social Psychology, which often prefers to study individuals in isolation. The insight led to interesting developments in the field of attribution theory, but the basis of this culturally shared foundation of common-sense psychology was not fully examined. Later in the chapter we will see that considering every-day psychologizing to be mediated by language provides a mechanism for this shared knowledge.

Heider's explanation of how people acted as naïve scientists was limited, but it led to the development of attribution theory. This general term encompasses a range of approaches to explaining attribution, which lead to different specific theories of attribution. Here we will outline some general principles. For a fuller discussion of attribution, see Gross (1995). Underlying attribution theory is the belief that there is a pre-existing, culturally shared set of assumptions that are used for predicting and interpreting behaviour which is resistant to change. This body of knowledge is sometimes termed folk psychology. In the next section, we will look at debates about the nature of this body of knowledge and the mechanisms underlying its use – how we perform folk psychology. Attribution theories on the other hand attempt to describe what people actually do, the outcomes if you like of folk psychologizing. Following Heider, people are seen as using two sorts of construct in explaining behaviour, psychological and social, which correspond to internal and external causes.

The psychological constructs hypothesized in describing everyday psychology are predominantly desires and beliefs, wherein people are seen as behaving in a particular way because they believe that those actions will bring about a particular desire. Thus to attribution theorists, people interpret and predict the behaviour of others by explaining their behaviour in terms of beliefs and desires. Emotional reactions are seen as providing evidence by which we are able to judge others' desires and beliefs. Thus emotion is claimed to be the central construct everyday psychologists use for explaining desires, although thoughts and intentions are also accorded a role. Thus far then, we see that attribution theorists claim that everyday psychologists attempt to explain actions in terms of the desires and beliefs of the actor, desires being primarily caused by emotions. As well as single acts, however, everyday psychologists also try to explain patterns of behaviour. In this case, it is claimed that we identify and attribute personality traits to others, and use these to predict the beliefs and desires a person might have. To be successful as everyday psychologists therefore, we understand actions within a wider psychological context.

According to attribution theory, we explain the behaviour of others by assigning personality traits to others which allow us to first, generate expectations about their beliefs and desires, and second to use these expectations to interpret and predict their behaviour. However, we also recognize that the behaviour of others is often constrained by the situation they find themselves in. Another element of people's everyday psychologizing, then, is to use knowledge of norms of behaviour in particular situations, together with our beliefs about a person's psychological characteristics, to explain how that person will behave in a particular situation. Behaviour is thus caused by an interaction of personal psychology and situational context. This element of psychologizing is often summarized by describing people as 'situation theorists'. This ability to use knowledge of situations to explain behaviour is sometimes seen as a precursor to the development, in an individual, of a full theory of behaviour that underlies everyday psychological practice.

As part of the body of knowledge we use in our everyday psychologizing, it is suggested that we have implicit personality theories, that constitute a set of rules about how someone with a particular personality will behave. Part of forming an impression about someone is choosing the right personality theory to ascribe to them. In this, we make extensive use of stereotypes, which act as person schemas collecting together a body of knowledge which can be applied to an individual. These stereotyped representations are necessarily very generalized, and of course are often inaccurate, but they do allow us to make predictions about others with very limited information. This can of course be problematic. For example, judging someone solely on the basis of skin colour according to a racist stereotype is indefensible. This example suggests that perhaps Psychology should be concerned with showing the inadequacy of this approach to person perception, rather than just describing it. This constitutes part of the project of some forms of critical Psychology.

The theories discussed here about how we perceive others have wider implications. The examples show that how we perceive others is shaped by our implicit expectations. However, expectations do not only influence person perception, they also influence our perception of the world. This presents a problem for science, which relies on the assumption that the scientist is an objective perceiver. In practice, how data is interpreted depends on existing expectations, and this is a particular problem for Psychology where evidence is usually ambiguous and subject to interpretation. Although science relies on the falsification of theory, in practice experiments are designed to justify theories, and data is interpreted according to expectations. For example, on occasion, racial differences have been found in average group scores on IQ tests. These may be interpreted either as showing that there are racial differences in intelligence, or that the IQ tests used are biased in favour of a particular racial group. There is nothing in the results to decide between the two alternatives, so in practice those who want there to be racial differences conclude that there are, while those who do not want there to be such differences conclude there are not.

Clearly, there is a considerable body of work within social Psychology that attempts to explain everyday psychology. However, in general social

Psychology attempts to apply experimental methodology to the production of general laws of human social behaviour. As with most of Psychology, the emphasis is on objective measurement, the generation of hypothetical averages, and the ascription of generalizations to individuals. The emphasis on individuals is important, since much social Psychology, paradoxically, seeks to explain behaviour in terms of individual rather than social and cultural factors. This approach to social Psychology overlooks the insights captured in attribution theory regarding the importance of cultural factors. The alternative, discursive approach of social constructionism concentrates on people's psychology as being shaped by social context, seeing the person as part of a network of social, cultural and other forces. As such, it arguably provides a better framework for accounting for everyday psychology.

FOLK PSYCHOLOGY

Quite apart from attempts within social Psychology to explain everyday psychology, there is a theoretical area that can be seen as constituting a separate sub-discipline. We avoid using the term folk psychology to describe what people do because it has particular technical connotations within this approach, which attempts to explain the mechanisms underlying our use of everyday psychology. The more technical meaning of the term folk psychology refers to the repertoire of knowledge that people have underlying their everyday psychologizing. A related usage is in folk psychological practice, which refers to the deployment of this repertoire of knowledge. We prefer to use everyday psychology and everyday psychologizing because folk psychology and its variants may imply a commitment to a particular view of what everyday psychologizing is. Folk psychology, in this narrower sense, is an interdisciplinary area of study that particularly exercises philosophers and cognitive scientists. It parallels cognitive Psychology: while cognitive Psychology attempts to describe information processing, this approach to folk psychology attempts to describe person perception. However, as we shall see it is often difficult to draw a clear distinction between it and cognitive Psychology. It shares the theoretical orientations of cognitive Psychology, in that the mainstream orientation is to describe folk psychology in propositional, rational terms, while alternative orientations attempt to describe folk psychology in terms of neuroscience or connectionism. In general, the approach shares very little with approaches in social Psychology, attempting to explain the underlying mechanisms rather than the actual practice of everyday psychology. A better way of looking at it might be to see it as an expansion of cognitive Psychology, using the theoretical frameworks of cognitive Psychology to describe social interaction as well as information processing. In this sense, it is a merger of the 'person as psychologist' metaphor with the 'person as information processor' metaphor. Given this, the approach is susceptible to the same arguments levelled against mainstream cognitive Psychology, discussed in Chapter 13. Our purpose here is to give a brief overview of the area.

There are three main positions towards folk psychology, each of which casts everyday psychology in a different light:

- The 'theory' theory of folk psychology, which claims that folk psychology, as a repertoire, consists of a genuine theory: this theory includes concepts and laws just as a theory within scientific Psychology would. Within this, there is a view that our native folk theory should be eliminated by scientific Psychology (for example, Churchland 1989), and a view that our native theory can only be refined by scientific Psychology (for example, Fodor 1991).
- The 'simulation' theory of folk psychology: there are a number of sub-divisions, but all view folk psychology as a simulation of others rather than a theory.
- The 'language' theory of folk psychology: again there are two broad divisions, one that folk psychology is a language, but we (as psychologists) should ignore it, and the other that folk psychology is a language, but there is no scientific language that could act as a substitute.

The 'Theory' Theory of Folk Psychology

The broad position of 'theory' theory of folk psychology is shared by philosophers such as Fodor and Churchland, as well as some developmental psychologists. This view of folk psychology is inspired by approaches to symbolic artificial intelligence, which attempts to model cognition in terms of the processing of symbols in a syntactic framework. The position to a large extent rests on the notion that we make a division between our internal states and our conceptual response to them. It is the conceptual response that symbolic AI is attempting to model, and that is being referred to in the 'theory' theory. Folk psychology can be called a theory because it functions as one. We make predictions of the basis of it, we explain behaviour on the basis of it and it acts as a major resource when we describe what people do. We are seen as sharing a tacit understanding of a set of principles concerning the relationships between causes, psychological states and overt behaviour, and this understanding constitutes a theory of others' behaviour. After this general agreement the positions of Fodor and Churchland diverge considerably.

Fodor is claiming that the basic mechanism in folk psychology, which we can call the intentional stance (people behave because they intend an outcome) should be preserved in a scientific Psychology. At the same time Fodor is not suggesting that all that Psychology should be is a vague, pragmatic and context dependent use of belief and desires to explain or predict behaviour (what he calls granny psychology).

Churchland, however, has a very different position. For Churchland the folk psychology theory is just plain wrong. It can perhaps be best summed up in the words of Chater and Oaksford: 'A science of cognition must explain the basis of our folk theories and cannot use folk theories as its foundation' (1996: 253). Interestingly, here Chater and Oaksford are explicitly making the study of folk psychology the study of cognition, rather than of person perception.

Churchland argues for a science based on brain events as the way forward, and in some of their joint writings Churchland and Churchland advocate an extreme position that when such a scientific theory has been completed we should eliminate the use of folk psychology from common sense understandings.

The 'theory' theory of folk psychology comes down to the following:

- Folk psychology is a real theory.
- It has been a theory that has informed Psychology.
- We either need to sharpen up our theorizing, perhaps by using symbolic AI, or we should adopt a scientific approach to psychology, not based on folk psychology.

The 'Simulation' Theory

At the heart of the simulation theory is the position that we cannot separate knowledge of inner mental states and our conceptual response to them, in the way that 'theory' theorists suggest that we can. There is a highly technical literature within cognitive science about the divide between the 'simulation' theory and the 'theory' theory. What we intend to do is simply to present the conceptual history of the simulation theory and tease out some of its implications for Psychology.

The original psychological input comes from Kenneth Craik's (1943) *The nature of explanation*. Craik had been working, as many psychologists did, in applied problems for the Ministry of Defence. He was specifically working on problems associated with accurate firing of anti-aircraft guns. Part of the problem, as he saw it, was that human operators found it very difficult to predict where to aim so that AA fire hit aircraft. In his chapter 'Hypothesis on the nature of thought' he proposed that people run mental simulations of events in order to make predictions. By the early 1980s this idea, that people simulate events to make predictions, had begun to be applied to a number of domains including electrical circuits, control of thermostats and how Polynesian sailors navigate (Gentner and Stevens 1983). These simulations are seen as small-scale simulations about particular things, rather than theory-like representations of a whole domain. So, for example, Gentner and Stevens argue that people would understand some aspects of an electrical circuit (for example, resistances) in one way, while understanding batteries in a different way.

The simulation theory of folk psychology suggests that folk psychology works in a way analogous to folk physics. It is not a whole-scale theory, but rather a series of relatively independent models that we invoke when we want to explain a particular event. The 'simulation' theory, apart from aspects of the argument within cognitive science, makes less grand claims than the 'theory' theory of folk psychology. In the main it makes folk psychology a topic for Psychology to study, rather than suggesting it as something that either needs to be replaced or refined.

Language Theories

The language theory of folk psychology takes two forms, and the two forms are quite different. In one form folk psychology is 'just' the language we use when we are called upon to explain, predict or describe others. The language we use is, obviously, a social product, but it has no connection to what we actually do when we try to explain, predict or describe others. This position at least tacitly underlies a number of disparate areas of Psychology. For example, in Freudian Psychology, almost everything is subconscious. Our actual reasons for behaving are determined by our subconscious, which by definition we have no access to. (Of course a well-trained psychoanalyst can have such access). In Watsonian and radical behaviourism terms from language (for example, mind) are discarded as irrelevant. More recently Nisbett and Wilson (1977) wrote an article 'Telling more than we can know' in which the substantive claim was that participants in experiments make after the fact ad hoc rationalizations of why they behaved in the way that they did. This claim is supported by some of Jonathan Evans' work on the Watson selection task. All of this suggests that folk psychology is something that we had better ignore, although the grounds for doing so are slightly different to the eliminative materialists.

Graham Richards (1996b) take a very different approach to language. For Richards the language we use for psychological phenomena is part of the construction of those very phenomena. This argument has important implications for views of folk psychology, but also for the nature of scientific Psychology and its relationship to everyday psychologizing. Given the importance of these arguments, we discuss them in the next section.

PSYCHOLOGICAL LANGUAGE

Richards starts from the position of defending folk psychology from the eliminative materialism of Churchland. Briefly restating, eliminative materialism claims that folk psychology should be replaced by theories and language from cognitive neuroscience, which would allow us to transcend the prescientific frameworks of folk psychology. A true scientific understanding would allow us to replace primitive concepts such as belief and desire with more accurate language that reflects the underlying neurological reality of our experiences. There are a range of immediate difficulties with this, particularly as we have no direct access to our neurological states. The argument relies on there being an isomorphic relationship between brain states and psychological states, so that in experiencing a particular psychological state we would know the correct neurological label to assign. It is not at all clear that this direct correspondence obtains. Even if it does, it would take a considerable degree of education to equip the person in the street with the correct neurological terms, and it is not at all clear what the benefits might be.

Richards's defence of folk psychology is based on a different characterization of the status of folk psychology from the positions discussed above, according language a more central role. He begins by identifying four classes of phenomena that need to be considered:

1   Folk psychology as the subject matter that Psychology identifies. Folk psychology in this sense is used generally to describe people's psychological processes, which constitutes the subject matter of Psychology.
2   Folk psychological language (fpl), as the terms and expressions we use when talking about psychological matters.
3   Folk Psychology, as the generation of theories about psychology using everyday folk psychological language. This includes a range of discourses about everyday psychologizing including those produced by philosophers but also those produced by lay people. There is an inversion here compared with the discussion in previous sections, in that Richards sees folk psychological language as providing the resources to allow psychological discourse.
4   Psychology as a discipline that tries to produce a scientific theoretical understanding of psychology. As discussed previously, this is in part a response to perceived limitations in the discourses of folk psychology, and in part to the development of new concepts and technologies. One of the goals of Psychology is to provide better descriptions than Folk Psychology. This is clearly the case in Churchland's argument, where he suggests that instead of psychological discourses based on folk psychological language, we should have discourses based on the language of scientific Psychology.

Richards's central claim is that Churchland, and others, misunderstand the relationship between these classes. Richards identifies a number of aspects of misrepresentation. First, folk psychological language is seen as being distinct from psychology. Folk psychological language reflects people's attempts at theorizing about psychology. For Richards though, folk psychological language is only the means by which we achieve access to psychological states and processes, and functionally cannot be distinguished from psychology. The language we use both defines and creates the psychological phenomena that Psychology studies, and at the very least folk psychological language is a part of psychology.

Second, there is an artificial conflation of folk psychological language (fpl) and Folk Psychology, with fpl's function seen as being to allow Folk Psychology. Richards claims that fpl provides the resources for folk psychology but is not itself an instance of Folk Psychology; the language does not instantiate a theory. In support of this, he shows that there are many possible, and competing, psychological discourses that all rely on the same underlying language. Thus the language must be separate from the theories produced. While concepts in fpl may constrain the kind of theories that Folk Psychology can produce, people attacking theories from Folk Psychology should concentrate on the theories, not the language used.

Third, there is an over-differentiation between Folk Psychology and Psychology. As stated, Psychology is usually seen as a better replacement for Folk Psychology, with Folk Psychology seen as having a number of weaknesses. In fact, Richards claims, Folk Psychology and Psychology are interlinked. Folk Psychology changes as folk psychological language changes, and changes in fpl come from a variety of sources, including Psychology. Thus Psychology can introduce new terms and concepts that enter everyday fpl, for example IQ and extroversion. These terms then become available for a range of purposes, beyond Folk Psychology. Even if the terms do not provide an accurate description, in scientific terms, of psychological processes, they may be useful metaphorically for managing interpersonal interactions. Thus even though the term 'nervous' came from a now discredited theory of the operation of the nervous system, it remains useful in everyday descriptions of people's psychological states. Richards's final point is that there is a reflexive relationship between fpl and psychology. As the language we use to describe psychological states changes, so does our psychology. For example, the introduction of the concept of IQ into our language has changed the way we think about intelligence, and characterize it in ourselves and others. Given that Psychology introduces changes in folk psychological language, then the discipline of Psychology is itself involved in changing our psychology. The discipline then cannot objectively theorize about people's psychology, as it claims, because the act of theorizing changes the object of the theorizing.

In addition to Richards's arguments, it is also the case that folk psychological language affects the discipline of Psychology. In part, this is a logical consequence of the points outlined above, in that if fpl changes psychology then this necessarily changes the object of investigation for the discipline. This may be indirect, as Psychology finds itself chasing a moving target. It may also be more direct, in that observable changes in fpl suggest new topics for Psychology to investigate. We have seen a number of examples of this during the first part of the book, with theoretical developments in Psychology being shaped by changes in their host cultures, including changes in everyday discourses. This can be seen in Psychology's shift from trying to demonstrate racial differences to trying to understand racist personalities, and how following World War Two Psychology started investigating obedience, and looking at people's need to understand the excesses conducted during the war.

More recently, the introduction of the National Lottery led to a widespread interest in the psychological basis of gambling, which led to an increase in scientific research into gambling. Folk psychological language, then, continues to set an agenda for Psychology to follow. In addition however, as changes in fpl change psychology, then they change the psychology of psychologists. This will affect both the topics investigated by psychologists, and the kind of theories produced, since changes in psychologists' psychology will change their expectations and hence their interpretation of data.

To summarize Richards's claims regarding folk psychological language, at the core of his argument is the view that Folk Psychology is not a single theory, but rather the practice of producing theories of psychology. This may make use of fpl, but fpl has other roles to fulfil too. Given this, it cannot be replaced by a more scientific language because this would not be able to fulfil all the purposes of fpl. Folk psychological language has a very broad scope, from basic sensations to specific technical expressions, and it is continuously evolving while retaining terms that prove useful for particular purposes. Those theorizing about the nature of Folk Psychology concentrate on basic terms such as belief and desire, whereas the vocabulary of fpl is vast, allowing nuanced expression of psychological states. Richards draws a comparison between Churchland and J.B. Watson, who also wished to replace fpl. Just as Watson's attempt failed, Richards claims that Churchland's attempt will fail. A particular problem for Churchland's project is that the truth of psychological propositions is determined differently from propositions about the physical world, and this is particularly the case when the propositions relate to social interaction. You cannot reduce statements about social relations to statements about brain states because social relations are outside the brain. Folk psychological language is necessarily different from scientific psychological language because it includes an element of evaluation, and particularly moral evaluation, whereas scientific language is concerned with describing objective truths. For Richards, folk psychological language will endure, as it has done for centuries. The bigger question is whether scientific Psychology will prove adequate to the needs of everyday psychology.

EVERYDAY PSYCHOLOGY AND SCIENTIFIC PSYCHOLOGY

As the discussion so far indicates, the relationship between scientific Psychology and everyday psychology is difficult to describe. Scientific psychology has two approaches to everyday psychology. On the one hand, we have parts of social Psychology that attempt to account for people's everyday psychologizing. These attempts can be seen as a scientifically developed form of folk psychological explanations. On the other hand, there is an approach that merges philosophy of mind and cognitive science, that attempts to account for people's handling of concepts of beliefs and desires in a cognitive framework. This approach theorizes about a computational framework that acts on propositional attitudes, but strangely neglects insights from social Psychology.

Valentine (1996) has summarized the relationship between everyday psychology and scientific Psychology. Everyday psychology attempts to explain other's behaviour, and in doing so at the least provides hypotheses that scientific Psychology can investigate. In part, it defines the task of scientific Psychology. However, much scientific Psychology is still pursued using folk psychological language – it has not yet developed a complete technical vocabulary. There is some debate about whether fpl is suitable for scientific Psychology. For instance, Richards would seem to see it as inevitable that scientific Psychology will use fpl, whereas Churchland would prefer everyone, not only scientific psychologists, to adopt a new scientific vocabulary. However, given the scope of contemporary scientific Psychology it is unclear whether a single technical language is feasible. While memory may be describable in terms of neuroscience, it is unclear whether language production can be, given the many social roles language use fulfils, and even less clear that interpersonal relationships can be.

There is currently some overlap between everyday psychology and scientific Psychology, for instance in social Psychology. Scientific Psychology needs at least to give an account of everyday psychology, but as we have seen the attempts of social Psychology and cognitive science have given rather different results. It is debatable which form of description should be preferred, or whether both are needed. There is a widely held view that everyday psychology is doing the same thing as scientific Psychology, but badly. If this is the case, then it would seem that one of the purposes of scientific Psychology should be to give people the knowledge they need to engage in proper psychologizing rather than degenerate granny psychologizing. However, it is not clear how the kind of recondite theorizing we encountered earlier assists in this. In any case, everyday psychologizing has different purposes from scientific Psychology. Most critically, everyday psychology has to improve management of interpersonal relationships, and factual scientific knowledge may not be best placed to achieve this. Successful social relationships depend, for example, on tact, discretion and empathy, and reasoning about such relationships must include moral and possibly theological concerns. Scientific Psychology's focus on producing factual claims may be incompatible with this.

Everyday psychology also differs from scientific Psychology in terms of scope – most lay people are unconcerned with which brain structure mediates memory storage, for instance – and also in the focus of explanations. Everyday psychological explanations are concerned with the idiosyncratic actions of individuals in particular social contexts, whereas scientific Psychology tends to produce theories about hypothetical average people in isolation. Finally, our everyday psychologizing is necessarily constrained by our conscious awareness. While scientific Psychology can create artificial situations to investigate unobservable causes of behaviour, this luxury is rarely available in real life interactions.

In many ways, scientific Psychology has taken the wrong approach to everyday psychology. While there have been some attempts, such as attribution theory, to describe how we reason about others, scientific Psychology has generally attempted to replace everyday psychology, believing it to be degenerate for the reasons discussed in the first section of the chapter. The effect of this has been that scientific Psychology has limited relevance for people's everyday psychologizing. Although some elements of Psychology have entered into folk psychological language, elements of psychoanalytic theory being the most notable example, scientific Psychology has had a limited impact in general. The discipline's failure to engage with people's everyday psychologizing, and with people's everyday concerns, has left the way open for an alternative approach to psychology to influence folk psychological language.

POPULAR PSYCHOLOGY

Scientific Psychology has been very careful to use particular methods to investigate psychology, attempting to attain a desired state of scientific rigour. In addition, it has limited the scope of its investigations, and the theoretical frameworks it adopts, to those which are amenable to achieving this rigour. In many ways this is laudable, because its goal is to achieve a certainty of knowledge about mind and behaviour. However, in doing so it has made itself almost mystical, producing an arcane body of knowledge that requires considerable training to access. However, while Psychology has attempted to maintain its dignity, folk psychology (in Richards's terms) continues, and psychological discourses continue to be produced outside of the discipline. The most notable example of such discourses comes from what is generically termed popular psychology, where claims are produced about intra- and inter-personal psychology that are specifically tailored to a lay audience.

Popular psychology is difficult to define. There are a range of forms, which are best identified in terms of Wittgenstein's concept of 'family resemblance'. While it is difficult to say what popular psychology is, it is usually possible to recognize it. As an illustration of this, our local bookseller has two sets of shelves for psychology books, one labelled 'Psychology' and one labelled 'Popular Psychology'. It is very difficult to give definite criteria for what should be on what shelves, but we agree with the bookseller's classification in more than 95 per cent of cases. One way of describing popular psychology is in opposition to scientific Psychology, or perhaps more broadly academic and professional Psychology since not all forms of these adopt a scientific methodology. The points of opposition are in terms of methodological and theoretical rigour. Academic/professional works are more likely to be founded on empirical and theoretical evidence, whereas popular psychology often seems to be rather looser. Another way of characterizing popular psychology is that often it involves the application of principles from Psychology to topics that are marginal to the discipline, for example sex, religion and fame. These topics generally seem to be chosen to stimulate maximum interest, and hence of course maximum sales potential. Often topics seem to be dictated by fashion or trends in society. As a test of this argument, we speculatively searched the Internet for books on psychology and feng shui. Needless to say, we did indeed find books that merged the two. A final way of characterizing popular psychology is by example, and this approach gives an idea of the range of forms popular psychology takes. A perusal of the bestseller lists will generate plenty of examples. Our favourites include books about communication difficulties between genders, books that claim to teach you to read body language, and collections of sexual fantasies that apply a Freudian gloss to desire.

Some examples of popular psychology are little different from everyday psychology, the difference being that the authors have a publishing contract that allows them to present their everyday psychologizing to the public. This is relatively rare, but informally we can say that there seems to be a continuum between naïve everyday psychology and academic/professional psychology, in terms of rigour and language. At one end, there are works which are written almost entirely in folk psychological language, relying on anecdote and supposition as sources of evidence. At the other end are works which adopt theory and language from scientific Psychology, but apply it to marginal areas. These may have a reasonable theoretical foundation, but may be lacking empirical evidence. Towards this end of the continuum there may be some overlap between popular and professional/academic Psychology, and indeed the success of popular works may lead to more rigorous investigation within academic Psychology. An example here might be in the study of gambling, where widespread lay interest has led to academic research projects.

On the surface, popular psychology seems to be harmless. However, given the observations outlined above about folk psychological language this may be complacent. Popular psychology arguably has a greater effect on folk psychological language than scientific Psychology, and hence has a greater effect on our psychologies, on the ways in which we see ourselves and others. Scientific Psychology developed out of reservations about the nature of less formal psychological discourses. The constraints of the scientific method are in part designed to prevent unfounded speculation, and to prevent individual prejudices influencing claims about psychology. We have seen in earlier chapters that despite these constraints, scientific Psychology is often shaped by the prejudices of psychologists, and that the work of psychologists has often been used to support prejudices held more widely in society. The discussion of eugenics in Chapter 6 is a clear example of this. However, the checks and balances of scientific Psychology can ameliorate these effects to some extent; for example, evidence can be checked and reinterpreted. The claims of popular psychology are often untested, and it should be a cause of concern that our views of ourselves and others are shaped by such material. Unfounded claims about gender differences, or a genetic basis for some psychological characteristic, may be damaging and introduce or reinforce prejudice. Without alternative sources of information, people will tend to believe what they read, trusting the fact that because something has been published it must be true. The acceptance of such work is helped because in general, popular psychology presents simple arguments, for instance that men and women speak different languages, or that there is a gene for IQ, or that you can reliably interpret a particular bodily movement. Human psychology as represented in academic texts presents a rather more complex, and less easily digested, picture.

The argument we are presenting here seems to be that popular psychology is degenerate, echoing scientific Psychology's view of everyday psychology. However, earlier in the chapter we seemed to be writing in support of everyday psychology. Our view is that scientific Psychology needs to pay more attention to the needs of everyday psychology, and needs to produce well founded theories that will assist people's everyday psychologizing. As part of this, psychologists need to be aware of the nature of folk psychological language and its role in mediating human interactions. In order to aid everyday psychologizing, theories from scientific Psychology need to presented in a way that is accessible to a lay audience, but which retains theoretical and evidential rigour. If scientific Psychology pursues appropriate topics in a rigorous way, and presents its findings in an understandable form, then it can close the gap between scientific Psychology and everyday psychology that is currently inhabited by popular psychology.

CONCLUSION

We began the chapter by observing that we all engage in psychologizing, by virtue of reflecting on our own thought processes and participating in social interaction. We described everyday psychology as the psychological reasoning that we all participate in when interpreting and predicting the behaviour of others. One of the outputs of this everyday psychologizing is the generation of psychological discourses, that represent broad speculation about the nature of human psychology. There is a long tradition of such discourses, and we discussed the argument that scientific Psychology developed in part in response to reservations about the validity of such everyday discourses. While the replacement of ill-founded claims about human psychology with more rigorous, empirically based theories is laudable, theories in scientific Psychology have had a limited effect on everyday psychology.

Having introduced the notion of everyday psychology, we then examined attempts within social Psychology to account for people's everyday psychologizing. This work began with Heider's common-sense psychology, and developed into attribution theory. While social Psychology has made some attempt to describe the nature of everyday psychologizing, an alternative approach has been to hypothesize about the processes underlying everyday psychology. This approach to 'folk psychology' usually suggests that everyday psychology is the result of either an implicit theory of others' behaviour or the simulation of the mind of another, and there is considerable debate over which account is appropriate. An alternative is to account for everyday psychology in terms of language. This position is maintained by Richards, who argues that there is a folk psychological language that has a reflexive relationship with psychology, and that has an important role to play in mediating interpersonal relationships.

Following the discussion of psychological language, we returned to the relationship between everyday psychology and scientific Psychology. We saw that there were important differences between the two, and argued that scientific Psychology should attempt to be more relevant to people's everyday psychologizing. We finished by discussing the current popularity of popular psychology, suggesting that psychology's failure to engage with everyday psychology leaves a gap which is filled by psychological discourses that often have weak theoretical and empirical bases.

FURTHER READING

Churchland, P. 1989: Folk psychology and the explanation of human behavior. In: *A neurocomputational perspective*. Cambridge, MA: MIT Press.

Davies, M. and Stone, T. 1995: *Folk psychology*. Oxford: Blackwell.

Fodor, J.A. 1991: *The theory of content and other essays*. Cambridge, MA: MIT Press.

Greenwood, J. (ed.) 1991: *The future of folk psychology: intentionality and cognitive science*. Cambridge: Cambridge University Press.

Greenwood, J. 1992: Against eliminative materialism: from folk psychology to Völkerpsychologie. *Philosophical Psychology* 5: 349–67.

Gross, R. 1995: *Themes, issues and debates in psychology*. London: Hodder and Stoughton.

Haselager, W. 1997: *Cognitive science and folk psychology*. London: Sage.

O'Donohue, W. and Kitchener, R. (eds) 1996: *The philosophy of psychology*. London: Sage.

Richards, G. 1989: *On psychological language*. London: Routledge.

Wellman, H. 1990: *The child's theory of mind*. Cambridge, MA: MIT Press.

Wellman, H. and Woolley, J. 1990: From simple desires to ordinary beliefs. The early development of everyday psychology. *Cognition* 35(3): 245–76.

12

METHODOLOGICAL ISSUES

In the earlier part of this book we discussed the ways that methodology developed within Psychology. In part the types of methodology that Psychology favoured were due to the need to develop what Danziger (1990) called marketable methods, and the later methodological fetishism was perhaps due to an urge to maintain the construction of Psychology as a science. In Chapter 1 we discussed the philosophical underpinnings of our approach to science and to the history of scientific endeavours. Our argument there revolved around the notion that in order for a science to operate it is necessary that the object of study remains consistent across time. However, Psychology freed itself of such concerns with its historical rejection of metaphysics. In this chapter we discuss the consequences of those decisions on the discipline.

There has been a lot of work produced from within and from outside the discipline of Psychology that is critical of the way that it uses its methods. Yet despite this, much of the discipline appears unperturbed by the attacks. Some of the reasons for this are institutional and structural, as argued in Chapter 10. Another reason may be that as the most recent alternative approaches developed, discursive Psychology and critical Psychology could not, for different reasons discussed in Chapter 15, replace the academic and applied discipline that is modern Psychology. We shall not, ultimately, be calling for the abandonment of quantitative methods in psychology but rather an appreciation of their limits in understanding the complexity of minds in societies; which ought to be the subject matter of Psychology.

In this chapter we will explore the limitations quantitative and experimental methods impose upon the topics that it is possible to study within Psychology, the misuses (often unintentional, or perhaps subconscious) of data that are possible with the methods currently employed within the quantitative framework, and the problems of reification of the results of statistical analysis. We will then explore some of the ways that alternative methodologies are recuperated by the discipline so that potential perturbations are minimized.

DEFINING A DISCIPLINE THROUGH METHODS

One of the features of Psychology is the way that it is in part defined by its method. In many introductory textbooks, for example, Psychology is distinguished from common sense because of its use of the scientific method. Psychology employs a number of methods but the gold standard of methods is seen as the experimental method, which has its philosophical roots in J.S. Mill's method of difference. Sometimes this is confounded with the scientific method, although better contemporary accounts of research methods reflect that all science is founded on observation. Modern Psychology has at its core a modified Popperian stance to science, with the establishing of testable hypotheses, with one of the crucial ideas being that these must be stated in such a way that make falsification possible. The utility of observation as a method can be seen in, for example, evolutionary biology where many of the hypotheses developed are not open to experimental testing, but are open to refutation by observation. However the positivism of early psychology was not based on a science like evolutionary biology but rather, as is claimed below, the misreading of what happens in a science like physics.

At the same time that strong claims are made for methodology in establishing the credentials of Psychology as a science there is at least some recognition that this is not a sufficient condition. Thus many, or most, academic psychologists are sceptical of the claims of parapsychology, despite the methodological sophistication of some of the studies. As psychologists are not well versed in the discourses around philosophy of science their attacks are often in terms of bias of the researchers. Unfortunately it is doubtful that a Psychology so reliant on method in its self-construction as a science could itself withstand such attacks. It may have been an unfortunate contingency that Freud, who called himself a biologist of the mind, developed psychoanalysis as a discipline that was so heavily and explicitly dependent on the interpretation of cultural phenomena by an analyst. It is also an unfortunate contingency that G.H. Mead's social psychology was unappreciated and thus a social Psychology consistent with evolutionary biology was not developed further.

In order to develop the argument more fully it is necessary to examine in some detail aspects of the psychology experiment, in order to show both that these features are not natural aspects of science and to consider some of the consequences of them.

Operational Definition

This term was invented by a theoretical physicist called Bridgman, who in 1927 wrote a book on philosophy of science. His concern came out of new advances in physics around the problems of relativity and quantum mechanics. As a number of authors have noted, and as we discussed in the first half of the book, in constructing itself as a science Psychology adopted the model of physics, rather than biology, and adopting terminology within physics may have helped to reinforce the scientific credentials of the discipline at a time of expansion, when applied psychologists were competing for a market share with professionals from other disciplines.

One of the problems that Bridgman wanted to tackle was the way that 'data' was transformed into evidence. Bridgman introduced the term 'operational analysis' as a way of dealing with concepts across a range of sciences and thus it may have been appropriate to use his operational analysis within Psychology. Unfortunately Bridgman was used by psychologists whose epistemology, derived from behaviourism, was anti-metaphysics, derided the mental, and put the focus on measuring simple, 'objective', events. Bridgman was not anti-metaphysics. His theory of operational analysis put equivalent weight on mental as well as physical operations in turning data into evidence. Bridgman stressed the primacy of operations being someone's operations and as already stated he had an interest in those operations that transformed data into evidence. Operational definition, with the idea that all that needs to be done is to tell people how something was quantified, is all that the discipline of Psychology took on board. Now students are taught the importance of operational definitions, with no author attached, as if it were some form of commandment for scientists. At the same time the interesting step, how exactly that mark on a piece of paper comes to mean someone's score on a personality scale, or whatever, is ignored.

The hope is that specifying how data is collected will make for the collection of valid evidence, the difficulty is that without a theoretical level of operational analysis no such validity is ensured. Instead a simplification of complex phenomena, without the necessary theoretical justifications, is almost ensured.

The Social Construction of Variables

The next part of the argument is that the nature of Psychology is constrained by the meta-language used by (most) psychologists – the language of variables. Danziger traces the history of this change within Psychology. Psychology as a science managed for half of its history without the terminology that is now taught as if it were simply and neutrally a part of science. The terminology is so well-founded that recently some researchers have been writing about qualitative variables.

At the heart of the change in terminology that led to calling everything a variable is the British statistical tradition, already discussed at length in Chapters 2 and 3. However, as well as appreciating that this tradition influenced the ways that psychologists would conduct studies, it is useful to follow Danziger's analysis and consider the way that it affected the language that psychologists used. As noted above by creating (operationally defined) dependent variables and independent variables much of the meaning of complex phenomena is lost. Danziger (1997) argues that this leads to several problems. One of these is the conflation of instrumental control and conceptual control. Adopting the language of variables, which as stressed elsewhere helps psychologists to sell their services, as the sole language of theoretical exposition placed severe limits on what was seen as appropriate for psychological theorizing. Causality is reduced to a crude concatenation of antecedents and consequences, the complex patterns that psychology needed to deal with were reduced to lists of (logically and, necessarily for statistics) elements that were independent of each other. Part of the problem is a continuing expectation that single causes will be found for complex phenomena. It may also be the reason why psychology abounds with mini-theories rather than recognizable theoretical systems. Often a theoretical statement is little more than a hypothesis (X will affect Y).

Variable research in the social sciences, ironically given the incipient physicophilia, is one of the major breakpoints between the social sciences and the natural sciences. All too often the command to look for variables has gone hand in hand with a desire to investigate the objects of psychological research in terms of inter-individual variation. As Danziger somewhat curtly notes, if physicists had attempted to study the differences between falling bodies it is doubtful that they would ever have come across a theory of gravity. In physics at least there is a division between the theory necessary to understand the general principles of something and the theory necessary to explain variation of physical phenomena. In Psychology these are conflated, often leaving us with a theory that does neither successfully.

There is in Psychology an isomorphism between the practical activities of doing research and the types of theories that are seen as acceptable. Thus before they could become objects of scientific research for psychology, phenomena such as social action had to become responses to social stimuli (and thus decontextualized) and personality had to become personality variables.

Following the apparent theory wars in the early history of the discipline, and given the somewhat broad scope of Psychology degrees as discussed in Chapter 10, and the need to develop and maintain some facade of unanimity, it was variable talk that gave Psychology its paradigm. This may not be a paradigm recognizable in Kuhnian terms but it does allow the vast majority of psychologists to get on with doing something that appears to be normal science against a plurality of theoretical positions. When the degree that we teach on was designed just about a decade ago, the author of the validation document stated that Psychology at Cheltenham and Gloucester would take an eclectic approach with no one dominant theoretical approach. However that eclecticism was limited to Psychology as science, which appeared to mean in practice that as long as what was being talked about could be broken into independent and dependent variables the theoretical approach did not matter.

Probability Testing

After hypotheses have been established and data collected the next stage of the psychology experiment is statistical analysis. The reliance on the probability test as the main method of statistical analysis again constrains psychological theories. Imagining best practice for the time being, although later we discuss some of the casual misuses of statistics that permeate Psychology, the use of probability testing is still problematic. A test, such as the t-test or ANOVA, tests the probability that an experimental result could have occurred by chance and it is conventional to accept a result when this probability is less than 5 per cent or less than 1 per cent. However this is all that a probability test, by itself, can do and one of the serious problems when it comes to theorizing is that there is no account taken of the size of the effect that the independent variable has upon the dependent variable. This can be confounded by the statistical fact that the more subjects that participate in an experiment, all other things being equal, the more likely that a result will be accepted as not occurring by chance due to the higher the degrees of freedom. This is given by the formula:

statistical significance = size of effect × degrees of freedom

Thus it is possible, within large studies, to find non-random effects that nevertheless are extremely small.

There is one more snare of probability testing, the use of the word significant. While it is unlikely that academic or professional psychologists would confuse statistical significance with the everyday meaning of significance it is likely that others will. Given that the synonyms for significance include importance, consequence and meaningfulness, this may not be a trivial problem. Thus if a gender difference were found on some psychological phenomena and reported in the press and other media as 'significant' it should be no surprise if that finding is invested as having importance or consequence. The use of the shorthand 'significant' may also be the root cause of why psychology undergraduates are crestfallen when the results of a research project are not statistically significant and that may reinforce the tendency noted in research for people to search for confirmation of hypotheses, rather than disconfirmation.

Beyond the Experiment – Snares With Other Quantitative Methods

As every Psychology undergraduate appreciates, despite the prominence given to the experiment as a method in Psychology, much psychological research is based upon modern versions of the psychological survey discussed in Chapter 2, the personality inventory and the attitude scale, and some work is still done using the intelligence test. Sometimes the scores from these measuring instruments are compared against groups in the population, on an astonishingly wide variety of social variables and sometimes correlations, multiple regressions and factor analyses are used instead of difference tests. We have talked at length about some of the misuses of these techniques in earlier chapters, particularly Chapter 9. In this section we concentrate mainly on the lack of appreciation that psychologists appear to have of the limitations of these methods. Before moving into what is a technical discussion it is worth considering a few conceptual points, discussed by Richards (1996).

Cultural and Historical Specificity of Measures of Personality and Attitude

It should not be surprising that attitude tests are culturally and historically specific. They are created using a set of judges who indicate whether they think that specific items are negative or positive towards the 'attitude object' that they are describing. Such judgements may change with time, and almost certainly change with regard to the specific population that the judges are drawn from; this issue is discussed further in the section on gay, lesbian and bisexual psychology in Chapter 9. What might be more surprising is the way that personality tests are also tied to their cultural historical location.

Richards uses the concept of authoritarianism to illustrate this point. The work of Adorno *et al.* (1964 [1950]) has been discussed at some length in Chapter 5, one of the products of which was the Californian F (fascism) scale of authoritarianism. Authoritarianism, a particular cluster of personality traits, was constructed as a pathological personality type: close minded, intolerant of ambiguity, happiest in hierarchical institutions, obedient to higher authority and so forth. Working during the Nazi era Jaensch, a German psychologist, arrived at a very similar idea, however this was the ideal German citizen, strong willed, disciplined with clear unmuddled ideas. Working in the 1950s Eysenck's 1957 social attitude inventory attempted to distinguish between radicalism-conservatism and tough minded-tender minded, both to incorporate the idea that there could be left wing authoritarians and because the perceived threat was no longer extreme right wing beliefs but rather Stalinist communism. Later, during the Korean War with allegations of brainwashing of USA troops the ideal American soldier would be 'resistant to persuasion', with 'easily persuaded' being the opposite end of that scale. The general point here is that all of these scales carried with them an evaluative judgement, so that a person scoring at one end of the scale is necessarily better than a person scoring at the opposite end. By the time of the Korean war a good democratic soldier should either have been open minded and/or resistant to persuasion.

Similar examples can be found in the work on scales of masculinity, explored in some depth in Chapter 9, but here the picture is complicated because an ideal man should score at one end of the scale while an ideal woman should score at the opposite end, an idea that Sandra Bem's work on androgyny has partially subverted. However, as Richards points out, this is not the only problem with scales like the F-Scale. Not only do the evaluations attached to the overall score change with historical change, but so do the meanings of the items themselves. Thus an item from Eysenck's social attitude inventory 'Divorce Laws should be altered to make divorce easier' (with those agreeing scoring as 'radical') alters its meaning as divorce laws have been made easier. It would of course be possible to remove out of date items and replace them with items more relevant in the early twenty-first century, but then the problem arises of whether or not these new items measure the same construct. Indeed the list of personality traits that make up an authoritarian reads to my eyes somewhat like the stereotype of a sitcom 'jobsworth', unappealing, but without the threat of the early 1950s authoritarianism.

It is not only with such obviously politicized scales that such problems exist. Self-esteem scales, for example, explicitly carry the notion that high self-esteem is a good thing. While Robinson (1995) has done extensive work on the technical difficulties of measuring self-esteem, pointing out that too often self-concept and self-esteem get muddled, the general point is that self-esteem is only an obviously good thing in highly individualized societies. As Bond points out in some cultures, such as traditional Chinese societies, a student is encouraged to praise their teacher as well as themselves if they do well. Such a position would score low on a self-esteem scale. There is also an expectation that high self-esteem is in itself linked to good academic performance that permeates some educational theory, so raising self-esteem amongst pupils is seen as a practical intervention. This is an example of the individualization of a social problem, ignoring the idea that we live in an unequal society where some people have more access to material and/or cultural resources than others, and those with the most access to these resources tend to have both high self-esteem and good academic achievement. It seems that the truism that correlation does not imply causality is still to be fully accepted.

A final example, the locus of control scale, will serve to illustrate the point further, and being the third part of a three-point list may help to show that this is a general problem with personality scales. The locus of control scale, in its original form, has the two end points, internal and external. Those with an internal locus of control are evaluated more positively than those with an external locus of control. Again this ties into the USA myth of the 'rugged individual', the person able to make their own destiny without fate or government having a role.

Of course the cultural and historical specificity argument does not just apply to attitude scales and personality inventories, it also applies to intelligence testing. Briefly, because there are many excellent critiques of the whole IQ testing enterprise, the argument is that the notion of intelligence is tied to the education system. Thus what have been devised are tests that at best measure the educability of middle- and upper-class people within our current education system. This should come as no shock, since the tests were initially validated by comparing performance on tests with educational results. However, it is notoriously true that such tests are very culture and class bound, and that educational performance is affected by social circumstances that lie beyond the ken of some psychologists. The mistake is to believe that the psychological concept intelligence has much to do with everyday meanings of intelligence beyond academic ability.

The Illusionary Bell Curve

The whole individual differences enterprise has at its roots an evolutionary framework. It is true that for many physical traits that vary incrementally (for example, height and weight) it is possible to plot a normal distribution (or bell) curve. Raw scores on standardized personality and intelligence tests very rarely fit on a bell curve; in fact one product of the standardization process are techniques for converting raw scores to standard scores. This is taken from the analogy between physical and psychological traits that the evolutionary framework invites. Beyond that analogy there is no compelling reason to believe that the traits that populations of people have do form a bell curve, and if they did there would not be a need to convert raw scores in the first place. In societies where both educational achievement and intelligence test scores are standardized (for example, 10 per cent of a class achieve 'A', whatever their actual performance) not only will the correlations between the two scores increase but the illusion that one predicts the other will also be magnified.

Another part of this problem has already been mentioned in Chapter 2, with regard to Quételet and the later British statistical tradition – the notion that there is such a thing as an average individual. As we discuss in Chapter 13 there is no such thing as a typical Broca's aphasic because the constellation of symptoms found by looking at groups of people with this condition are never found in a single individual. A related but slightly different problem exists with attitude scales and personality tests, and is not unknown in intelligence tests as we discussed in Chapter 6. It is easier to use attitude tests as the example because the way that personality tests are standardized tends to push the problem further into the background without eliminating it. Imagine a ten item attitude scale, with each item being scored from one to five. A person could get a score of 30, a neutral attitude in a variety of ways. At the two extremes a person could mark three for every item or could alternatively score one and five for alternate items. Both final scores are 30, but the two people hold very different opinions about the attitude object. (The argument holds for so called forced choice scales with an even number of points, imagining a six-point scale a person who consistently ticked three and four could end up with the same score as a person who consistently ticked one and six.)

Before leaving this section for a more technical statistical discussion it ·is worth reiterating points made elsewhere by Richards and Billig, amongst others.

Measuring What Does Not Exist

It may be conceivable that everything which exists can be quantified (although this quantification may be problematic). However the opposite assertion, just because something can be measured means that it exists, does not hold true, at least within Psychology. Richards and Billig both give examples of attitude scales that could have been devised historically, Richards invites us to imagine a devoutness scale and Billig uses the example of our attitude to the proposition that rain is the urine of the gods (an early Greek belief). It is unlikely that a modern Psychologist would be particularly concerned to measure either today because of an a priori assumption that such things are ridiculous. We cannot be sure that some of the concepts that we try to measure today would not be written off as ridiculous by future generations of psychologists. The problem, as both Billig and Richards are aware, goes deeper. By developing a scale to measure locus of control, or stress, or attitudes towards joining a single currency we are to some extent in the business of constructing those psychological concepts as important. The problem can be magnified in market research. Once a person has agreed to fill in a questionnaire, or answer some questions, they normally do their best to complete it as this serves to give the illusion that the matter actually concerns them. Indeed this has been used, for example by Sandra Bem, to try to alter psychology, by introducing a concept, in this case, androgyny, that was seen as a corrective to earlier masculinity-feminity scales, and Marx developed a questionnaire as a consciousness raising instrument.

Questionnaires about many aspects of the service provided by businesses and public services are proliferating. These enable businesses to write in their annual reports that a certain percentage of their clients are satisfied and to make vague promises about how they will satisfy others. While it is doubtful that many of these measures reach even the limited validity of well-designed attitude scales it is not that technical problem that concerns me. Rather in all this business of public opinion polling I am still haunted by a description from *Internationale Situationniste*:

> a form of pseudodialogue . . . to elicit people's happy acceptance of passivity under the crude guise of 'participation'
> (Questionnaire, *Internationale Situationniste* 9 August 1964: 142)

Forcing Choice

Finally there remains the issue of whether a personality inventory or attitude scale can capture the complexity of a person's character or their opinions towards something. The individual items are a form of limited dialogue, where the researcher has created the only appropriate responses, whereas in conventional dialogues the potential for expressing positions is almost without limit.

The experimental approach, based on aggregate data, has certain limitations, but the psychological survey also suffers from limitations. Many of these are pushed into the background as psychologists routinely take the numbers generated by such measuring instruments and subject them to highly sophisticated statistical analyses.

STATISTICAL AND METHODOLOGICAL MISUNDERSTANDINGS

For a number of years now we have been running an advanced research methods module during which undergraduate students have to critique the method and results sections of recently published journal articles. Often the students are surprised at how badly authors of journal articles (and presumably their reviewers) misunderstand statistical analyses, and it is to these that we turn our attention next.

Quasi-Experiments

As every first-year undergraduate is taught, the only time that causality can be implied is when the investigator has control over the independent variable. However there are a range of phenomena salient to psychologists over which we have no control. These population and social variables include gender, age and class. As was discussed in Chapter 9 there has been a tendency, again explicable in terms of the nineteenth-century evolutionary roots of the discipline, to compare such pre-existing populations. Naturally it follows from the first line of this paragraph that such studies become quasi-experiments – they appear to be experiments but no strong conclusions about causality can be drawn. A quick glance through the last 30 years of sex and gender research unfortunately confirms that this necessary distinction is often not made. One possible reason for this is that the range of statistical procedures used, t-test and the ANOVA family of tests are those that have been designed for experiments. Another reason may be the tendency to call all such population variables independent variables regardless of whether or not they are pre-existing. This problem, confusion of experiment and quasi-experiment, can also be found when investigators split populations by using a personality inventory or attitude scale. Again such studies are quasi-experiments but the distressing trend of treating the results of such studies as if they can determine causality remains.

As discussed at some length in Chapter 9 with regards to gender, the reason why these studies must be treated cautiously with regard to causation is that noting a difference is not the same as finding a cause, and that population variables tend to be heavily confounded.

Multiple Regression

The confusion between experiment and quasi-experiment is a conceptual confusion. However, in an attempt to deal with the issue that a variable like gender may be confounded with a number of other variables investigators sometimes attempt to measure a whole range of variables simultaneously. In these circumstances techniques such as multiple regression (although there are alternatives such as partial correlation) become useful in order to look for patterns in the data. Naturally everyone knows that such techniques are ultimately based on correlation, and the old canard that correlation does not imply causality remains true for these techniques. However, the routine use of various forms of stepwise regression should serve as a warning about how difficult it is to use statistics. Rosenthal and Rosnow, in their excellent *Essentials of behavioural research* (1991) illustrate the problems of regression.

While multiple regression has a number of virtues it also has a number of often unrecognized problems. The multiple regression equation is an extension of the equation of a straight line that includes a number of χ, or predictor variables:

$$\gamma = \alpha + \beta_1\chi_1 + \beta_2\chi_2 + \varepsilon$$

When any new predictor variable is brought into the equation all the betas and the alphas change. The first thing that is too often not recognized is that the exact battery of tests used influences the outcome of the regression study, thus it is not easy to make straightforward comparisons between different batteries of tests even when several components are in common.

The problem with stepwise multiple regressions is that the predictors chosen by the algorithm that the statistical analysis software employs are a subset of the original predictor variables. The p values for any predictor are only accurate when the whole set of original predictors is used. As Moses (1986) comments, it is not a trivial matter to even begin to work out how accurate p values could be calculated for stepwise regression. Of course this would be unimportant if such stepwise procedures were only used in a sense of exploration, to be followed up by studies using a much more focused battery of tests. This best practice procedure is, however, rarely used, partially we suspect because of the pressure to publish research findings, linked in the USA to issues around tenure for staff and in the USA and UK to funding for universities based on research output.

There is, unfortunately, the well-recognized, by statisticians if not psychologists, phenomenon of shrinkage. When a follow-up study is carried out using the battery of tests indicated by the initial stepwise process the final r^2 is almost always smaller than that suggested by the stepwise procedure. Given that this is such a predictable phenomenon, that few psychologists appear to be aware of the problem when they report stepwise regressions without follow-up studies seems negligent. Again there may be a publication pressure at work here, as well as the recognized publication bias to mainly publish significant findings.

A FAILED DEFENCE

Capaldi and Proctor (1999) make an argument in favour of a philosophy of science called naturalism, especially the recent writing of a philosopher of science called Laudan. Capaldi and Proctor are both Psychology professors at Purdue University. As part of their defence of naturalism, they make an argument against contextualism, which they see as the philosophy of science behind social constructionism, postmodernism, constructivism and the operant conditioning approach popularized by B.F. Skinner. I am not going to examine their argument against contextualism at this point, although that will be part of Chapter 15. Rather I am going to examine the argument for naturalism.

Naturalism, especially Laudan's version which he calls 'normative naturalism' attempts to judge epistemology in terms of empirical evidence. If a science is being fruitful, that is if it is producing data and theories, then the normative naturalist's role is to describe what scientists do in order to proscribe what other scientists do. As a philosophical movement the claim is that whatever exists or happens in the world is susceptible to natural scientific methods. Amongst the features of normative naturalism that Capaldi and Proctor especially praise is the idea that it is not relativistic, and that it claims that questions of epistemology are best judged by looking at empirical data.

Now it probably surprises none of you that I do not agree with this approach, first with the claim that naturalism is a way out of the relativistic quagmire that some believe exists with the popularity of various social constructionist arguments. Unfortunately naturalism does no such thing. Most people recognize that as sciences change the methods and theorizing of scientists change. What counts as good methodology and theorizing in one era would not count as good methodology and theorizing in another era. Naturalism would have to recognize both as fruitful within their times, and it is relativistic in that the only criterion for good science is whatever the majority of scientists do.

The other thing that Proctor and Capaldi say is that most psychologists talk a language of data, as if that was in some way a neutral language, and that questions of ontology, that is, what the data might mean, are best downplayed (see, for example, Chapter 4 Mental Testing Movement). Needless to say this is very much at odds with how we see data. I feel that the problem Capaldi and Proctor just fail to see is the reflexivity problem in terms of the way that terms from Psychology interpenetrate lay psychology to such an extent that the subject matter of the discipline is changed with (at least some) psychological findings.

Perhaps the most annoying thing that Capaldi and Proctor repeatedly claim is that psychologists only recognize the language of data. While I would agree that variable talk has replaced theoretical discussion amongst psychologists, this has led to a restricted approach to the complexities of human beings. However, as the first half of this chapter illustrates, many psychologists do not appear to understand the language of data, especially when they analyse that data using statistical analysis.

META-ANALYSIS AND FINDINGS WITHIN PSYCHOLOGY

Ever since meta-analytical techniques have become available to academic psychologists they have been described as a way of getting to the truth of, for example, sex and gender differences, or findings on aggression and interpersonal attractiveness. There have been calls to use meta-analytical techniques across the whole range of psychological phenomena that are created in laboratories, field research and psychological surveys. There is some utility to this. As Rosenthal and Rosnow (1991) make clear, a focus on meta-analysis may mean that size of effect becomes a routinely reported statistic, something that may help psychologists produce more nuanced theoretical accounts. Rosenthal and Rosnow is also an excellent source for understanding the technical strengths and weaknesses of the variety of meta-analytical techniques that are now available to the community of psychologists. However, as we saw in Chapter 9, meta-analysis should not be seen as a panacea for the snags and weaknesses of probability testing that we have discussed so far in this chapter.

Curt (1994) remarks that when data is dirty then it is common to use statistics, and when it is really dirty it is time to call in a meta-analysis. Much of the data that psychologists collect as they create knowledge is dirty, due in part to the use of aggregate data that we have discussed in Chapter 3. However, simply applying a formula to a mass of findings will not lead to unambiguous findings for a number of reasons. The first revolves around the use of operational definitions. In aggression research, for example, there are a number of different measuring techniques that operationally define aggression. These span observational, survey and laboratory based methods and include behaviours such as the amount of electrical shock a person is willing to give another person, scores on scales saying how likely a person believes they are to engage in a range of behaviours, to hitting a Bobo doll. The difficulty is whether all of these behaviours or behavioural intentions are measuring the same underlying concept. This problem can be further aggravated when different theorists use different definitions of the term. While this is widespread in social phenomena such as aggression, the problem is not restricted to these. For example, in cognitive Psychology, the terms 'schema' and 'mental model' are notorious for the number of different definitions that exist.

Of course the problem of cultural and historical change in definition also exists, and this can augment the problem of differing operational definition. Thus, for example, schizophrenia as a diagnosis appears to be more readily given in the USA than the UK, so it becomes extremely difficult to combine findings from the two cultures about schizophrenics, as the people who attract that diagnosis may be very different types of people.

RESISTING CHANGE

In the last decade there has been a shift in investigative practice for some, mostly social, psychologists which has been characterized as the turn to the text. This has developed at the same time that social constructionism has become a metatheoretical approach adopted by the same loose group of, mostly, social psychologists. While discourse analysis is the methodology most often associated with this movement it is not the only one, as a number of qualitative and interpretative methods, including qualitative observation, Q-sort, and action research are also associated with it. The impact of feminist Psychology has also been profound in the acceptance of the methodology and theories that support and give a framework for the use of these methods. Whether or not this will lead to any lasting effect on either the discipline of Psychology or on social Psychology is obviously a moot point at this time. However there are a number of strong institutional factors that may limit that impact.

As Burman and Parker (1993) make clear, if discourse analysis is taught as just another method then any impact that it will have will be minimized. The recuperation of discourse analysis, and other interpretative qualitative methods, begins with the place they are given within the Psychology syllabus. Taught within a research methods course, especially when taught by those with little experience of discourse analysis, it is likely to be taught as a methodological alternative, without a supporting theoretical framework. Thus students may learn to look for three-point lists, or even to devise repertoires from a given text, but the end result, without a theoretical framework, would be closer to a form of content analysis rather than a qualitative approach. As universities and other higher education institutions become more aware of the need to have some equity in assessment across degree courses, so word limits and examination durations become a common currency. This, allied to increasing pressure of student numbers, especially in a UK context, has led to pressures to become more efficient in terms of the amount of marked assignments set. The worst case scenario is the use of multiple choice tests, which, while suitable for some forms of teaching and learning, are not a reasonable form of assessment for social constructionist and critical psychologies, where the answer would almost always be 'it depends on the historical, cultural and social setting under which the phenomenon is investigated'. The less worst case is pressure to shorten the word limits for assignments. However, a full qualitative report needs to have space for a critical analysis of the phenomena to be explored, the analysis of the findings (which often cannot be neatly divided into a results section and a discussion section), and critical self-reflection throughout. Such demands mean that qualitative reports tend to be longer than their quantitative siblings.

A second problem is the liberal pluralist ghetto discussed in Chapter 9. While, in the UK at least, Psychology departments attempt to get representatives of the various types of psychologists, this tends to mean that individual lecturers within departments who hold dissident views are marginalized within the predominately orthodox departments. This, of course, may just be a temporary problem but, as gender representation within departments illustrates, it is likely that the problem may last into the middle of the current century unless positive action is attempted.

Critical and Reflexive Psychology

Some of those Psychologists that we label as broadly social constructionist appear to adopt a stance that the only way to do academic Psychology is through techniques like conversation analysis. Most social constructionist psychologists, however, recognize that one of the problems of Psychology has been an over-identification with a limited set of methods and that there is no need to repeat that mistake again. We hope that they are not disappointed with the idea that it is possible to combine quantitative methods with a critical and reflexive approach to investigative practice. However, it is probably the existing quantitative psychologists that this chapter is addressed to and it is to them that we make a plea to consider allying existing skills and knowledge about quantitative methods with a more critical and reflexive approach.

Being critically aware in this context is an awareness that much of the knowledge that we produce is bounded in time and culture. That is not the same thing as saying such knowledge is not useful. Such knowledge is useful in present times and cultures, but how useful such knowledge remains beyond historical inquiry is, of course, an empirical question. Being critical in this respect is also an acknowledgement that the knowledge we produce and the expertise we sell has a political and moral dimension. Whether or not the individual psychologist is willing to admit it, we hope that the first half of this book, along with the work of Richards, Danziger, Farr, etc., has shown that Psychology has a political and moral role. As long as individual psychologists hide behind the crumbling facade that they are no more than humble scientists they ignore this political and moral responsibility. In the context of racism within Psychology as both Richards and Howitt and Owusu-Bempah (1994) point out, and as we discussed in Chapter 9, it has been those who have so assiduously clung to this illusion who have produced some of the most notorious work in that area. Part of this critical awareness, especially for those psychologists working within the fields of education and clinical practice, is being aware that not all problems can be solved at the level of adjusting the individual. While we, as psychologists, might not feel that it is within our ability to propose change at a societal level it would, at least, be more honest to admit the limits of our ability to intervene and we can at least suggest, for example, that stress might not be an individual problem but rather a problem of how workplaces and working practices are organized.

Of course, and fitting in with the broad idea of reflexivity, we should be aware that as we create psychological knowledge we are changing the ways that we talk of each other, and that such discourses can themselves have major political and cultural impacts. The other part of being critical is being aware of how, in our guise as experts, our judgements carry at least some weight within larger political debates.

There is of course another level of reflexivity that we should consider as psychologists, the way that we as individual, or groups of, researchers affect the research that we carry out. As we have indicated above part of this could be done by broadening out the concept of operational definition to operational analysis. However this may mean that we have to theorize in rather more sophisticated ways than saying that a change in X creates a change in Y, something that generations of psychologists appear to have been reluctant to do. In some statistical techniques the choices made by the psychologist are masked by the impression that results just appear as output from a statistics package. Again we should make these decision making processes clear so that people do not misjudge how much of a particular finding is just apparent in the data and how much is created by a certain approach to the data. Finally we should be aware of those human and institutional biases that mean that we tend to seek evidence confirming our positions; that we are under pressure to publish when we may have preferred to do a replication study; and that journals tend to prefer studies that show significant findings, so that we temper our claims about causality in the light of the limits of the techniques that we use to spot trends and patterns in our data.

CONCLUSIONS

In this chapter we have discussed some of the ways that the trend towards quantification, explicable by various contingencies within the history of Psychology, have affected the ways that psychologists theorize. We then went on to discuss the limitations of the statistical procedures used and strongly argued that it is a mistake to allow data collection and analysis to replace theorizing, especially given the problems of commonly used methods and analysis. We discussed the ways that Psychology resists change in its methods before offering suggestions as to how and when there is great utility in using quantitative methods, suggesting that if the critical and reflexive stance found in some qualitative work could be combined with quantitative reasoning then there may be even more utility in continuing to use the methods that most Psychologists are most comfortable with.

Whatever one's view on the utility of using quantitative methods within Psychology, and our position is that there is both pragmatic and theoretical utility for some aspects of Psychology, they need to be used with a full awareness of their limitations. It is distressing, especially in an age when it is as easy to get a computer statistical package to calculate a MANOVA as it is a t-test, that many psychologists at all levels appear not to recognize these limitations. It is not good enough for Psychology to base claims that it is a science on the use of inferential and descriptive statistics if the psychologists who claim to be scientists do not understand the tools of their science. While admitting that this conclusion is depressing we would challenge readers to take a selection of articles published in journals in the last year and look for themselves at the number of serious conceptual errors in the statistical analysis, especially when it comes to claims of causality from quasi-experiments, multiple regression and factor analysis. The more ambitious readers may also want to consider how well the operational definitions within these articles reflect anything more than a statement that measuring X in a certain way means that a true value of X was found without explaining how that transformation occurred. Once this depressing conclusion is out of date it will no longer be necessary to wonder if the majority of psychologists, while espousing that they are scientists because they use scientific methods, actually understand anything about the nature of quantitative analysis.

FURTHER READING

Bem, S. and de Jong, H.L. 1997: *Theoretical issues in psychology: an introduction*. London: Sage.

Burman, E. and Parker, I. (eds) 1993: *Discourse analytic research*. London: Routledge.

Capaldi, E. J. and Proctor, R.W. 1999: *Contextualism in psychological research? A critical review*. London: Sage.

Curt, B.C. 1994: *Textuality and tectonics: troubling social and psychological science*. Buckingham: The Open University Press.

Danziger, K. 1990: *Constructing the subject: historical origins of psychological research*. Cambridge: Cambridge University Press.

Danziger, K. 1997: *Naming the mind: how psychology found its language*. London: Sage.

Farr, R.M. 1996. *The roots of modern social psychology*. Oxford: Blackwell.

Moses, L.E. 1986: *Think and explain with statisics*. Reading: Addison Wesley.

Rosenthal, R. and Rosnow, R. 1991: *Essentials of behavioural research*. New York: McGraw-Hill.

Slife, B.D. and Williams, R.N. 1995: *What's behind the research: discovering hidden assumptions in the behavioral sciences.* London: Sage.

Thompson, B. 1999: If statistical significance tests are broken/misused, what practices should supplement or replace them? *Theory and Psychology* 9(2): 165–81.

13

COGNITIVE PSYCHOLOGY

In this chapter, we look at a range of issues in cognitive Psychology. There has been debate within the field about a range of fundamental issues regarding the nature of cognition since the early development of the approach. However, mainstream presentations of cognitive Psychology have tended to overlook these issues. The purpose of this chapter is to introduce some of these debates to a wider audience. In general, debates within cognitive Psychology are philosophical and technical, and can be difficult to follow. We have attempted to make them accessible, and this has necessarily meant omitting a lot of the detail from the debates. The selection of the debates that are covered is as much due to personal interest as to any relative importance.

We begin the chapter by outlining the basis of the information-processing paradigm within cognitive Psychology, the view that cognition consists of performing computations on symbolic representations, which has dominated most cognitive Psychology. However, recently cognitive Psychology has become more receptive to advances in neuroscience, and we look at how neuroscience can both challenge and support the information-processing approach. Following this, we consider the role of computational modelling within cognitive Psychology. This has been influential in cognitive science, but is often overlooked within Psychology. Having outlined the current status of the field, we then look at issues arising out of the philosophy of mind, out of the notion of representation within computational approaches, and out of the need to consider the environment.

This chapter relates to the discussion of folk Psychology in Chapter 11, but more directly to Chapter 14, on connectionism. Having considered the status of symbolic approaches to cognition in this chapter, the next considers sub-symbolic approaches. Some of the arguments started in this chapter continue in the next, so for complete coverage it is recommended that you read both chapters.

THE BASIS OF MAINSTREAM COGNITIVE PSYCHOLOGY

Underlying most theory development in cognitive Psychology is the notion of the Physical Symbol System (PSS). A physical symbol system consists of symbols (physical patterns corresponding to facts), expressions (structures of symbols), and processes (operations on symbols characterized by rules). Intelligent behaviour is seen as consisting in operations on symbols, with symbols forming the input and output of the system. The PSS organizes and reorganizes symbol structures, makes comparisons, and behaves contingently on the results of the comparisons. A symbol in a PSS is any kind of pattern denoting, or representing, something else. The symbols are not necessarily verbal. Indeed, the language of thought hypothesis (discussed in Chapter 8) specifies a symbol system (the 'language') that uses symbols that precede the development of language.

This is the way a computer works, and corresponds directly with the functionalist view of mind. It is related to the concept of the Universal Turing machine (UTM), also discussed in Chapter 8 – a UTM is a physical symbol system. The physical symbol system (PSS) hypothesis states that a PSS has the necessary and sufficient means for intelligent action, meaning that intelligence can only result from the operation of a PSS, and any PSS (or any PSS of sufficient complexity) has intelligence. A PSS thus provides a mechanistic but cognitive account of mental processes. In this view, humans are intelligent because they instantiate a PSS. However, while it may be reasonable to describe symbol systems as intelligent in some sense, there is debate about whether human brains do instantiate a PSS. A distinction may be drawn between brain intelligence and artificial intelligence, and the debate revolves around whether there are qualitative differences between brain intelligence and artificial intelligence. If there are, then a PSS may be sufficient for artificial intelligence, but not for brain intelligence, and a PSS may not be necessary to achieve intelligent action.

The Physical Symbol System view represents an application of the computer metaphor to human cognition, in a strong sense. The mind as computer metaphor can be taken in several ways, from a very weak sense of seeing cognition as the processing of information without specifying the form of that information or the nature of the processing, to the very strong sense represented by the PSS hypothesis. This specifies that information is symbolic and representational, and is processed according to a set of formal rules. The weak interpretation suggests that computer programs are metaphors of human cognition, giving ideas of how cognition may work at some level of abstraction. The strong interpretation suggests that computer programs in themselves instantiate theories of human cognition. Issues around computer modelling of cognition are discussed later in the chapter.

The degree to which cognitive psychologists support the PSS hypothesis varies, some taking a weak view and others taking stronger views. However, most subscribe to the hypothesis to some degree, if only implicitly, and also to a set of related assumptions. These include the philosophical position of functionalism, discussed in Chapter 8, the language of thought hypothesis, methodological solipsism, a representational theory of mind, and computationalism. Methodological solipsism is the concentration on the processing of information in the minds of individuals, without regard to the environment or the body within which the minds reside. This requires a representational view of mind, whereby cognizers form internal representations of the world, stored in symbolic structures. Once stored, these representations are then available to manipulation via computation. Computationalism is the strong view that mental processes are computations on formal, syntactical, symbols. This leads to the position of formalism, and a view of the mind as propositional.

The collection of views outlined above have a number of attractions for cognitive Psychology. We can develop an epistemology for computers, since we know how they work, and – if the mind is a computer – extend that epistemology to humans. Through functionalism, it is suggested that the PSS hypothesis provides a solution to the mind-body problem. This claim is discussed later. The information processing approach is also seen as overcoming the anti-mentalism of behaviourism and the anti-mechanism of Gestalt, justifying its replacement of these as the dominant approach to experimental Psychology.

This explanation of mind by metaphor to computer suggests that cognition consists in the flow of information between different processes, organized as a series of processing stages between input and output. Initially these stages were viewed as serial, although it has been necessary to concede a degree of parallelism in modelling cognition. The cognitive system is seen as being modular, a concept derived from programming that suggests that stages of processing take place in autonomous, functionally intact, modules. Modularity was originally proposed by Marr, who suggested that modules have the evolutionary benefit of allowing easy modification of single components without reorganizing the entire cognitive system. The notion was extended by Fodor (1983), who proposed four properties of modules:

- Informational encapsulation: the operation of each module is isolated from the operation of other modules.
- Domain specificity: each module processes one form of input or one souce of information.
- Mandatory operation: modules either operate or not, and if they do operate they complete their processing.
- Innateness: modules are innate, rather than being acquired developmentally.

There is some controversy over the last two of these, particularly innateness. The classic argument is that reading has developed as a cognitive skill too recently to rely on innate modules. This is supported by some cases of acquired dyslexia, where dysfunction arises following brain damage that is specific to reading. The counter-argument is that reading, and similar processes, reuse existing modules. This view is supported to an extent by developmental dyslexia, where children are born with a tendency to reading dysfunction. However, the first two properties are generally accepted, and foundational to much theory development in cognitive Psychology.

The computer metaphor gathered strength during the 1970s, but its hegemony within cognitive Psychology weakened after around 1985. Contemporary cognitive Psychology shows some heterogeneity in theoretical approach, with increasing interest in neurophysiology and ecological validity, but most psychologists remain committed to the central notions provided by the computer metaphor, those of representation and computation. However, these notions have been criticized, with debate about whether concepts are purely representational, and about whether computation is best conceived in formal terms. In addition, some psychologists believe that cognition cannot be investigated in isolation from affective (emotional) and conative (purposive or intentional) aspects of mental life.

COGNITIVE PSYCHOLOGY AND NEUROSCIENCE

Despite its important role in the genesis of cognitive Psychology, neuroscience was largely overlooked within the field during the 1960s and 1970s. To an extent, this was because neuroscience at the time was not asking the kind of questions that cognitive Psychology wanted answers to. In addition, however, this period represented the ascendancy of the information processing approach. If functionalism and the PSS hypothesis were true, then there was little point in studying neuroscience, the appropriate focus of cognitive Psychology being on the software – cognitive processes – rather than on the hardware of the brain.

From the 1980s, the computer metaphor began to lose its hegemony. In part, this was due to concerns about the adequacy of the strong PSS claim. The approach of connectionism, which had some impact during the 1940s and 1950s, became influential again. Given that connectionism emphasized the influence of architecture on processing, it suggested that there was a need to consider brain structure in theorizing about cognition. In addition, functionalist philosophy was coming under attack, from materialists who insisted that cognitive processes could be reduced to neurological descriptions. This development was helped by changes within neuroscience itself. New techniques of investigation were becoming available that allowed the examination of brain operation at the level of functional systems rather than the cellular level.

During the 1980s, there was increasing cooperation between cognitive psychologists and neuroscientists, for example in the work of Kosslyn, Posner and Gazzaniga. Using new scanning techniques such as PET and MRI allowed investigators to relate neurological processes to mental operations, while others investigated cognitive deficits arising from brain lesioning, for example Gazzaniga's work on split-brain patients. This new approach, often termed cognitive neuroscience, combined the methods of neuroscience with the analyses of cognitive Psychology. The approach became established during the 1980s with the establishment of specialist journals, societies and academic programmes – the usual mechanisms of institutionalization.

Cognitive neuroscience had important ramifications for cognitive Psychology and the philosophy of mind. Although still operating within a broad information processing framework, the reference to brain architecture challenged the functionalist separation of software and hardware, and was seen by many as supporting a materialist approach. Advances in cognitive neuroscience also supported, and in turn were supported by, increasingly sophisticated connectionist models of cognitive function. This challenge has led cognitive neuroscience to have a difficult relationship with cognitive Psychology, in that psychologists committed to an information processing view have been tempted to overlook advances in neuroscience. A more amenable approach, from the point of view of cognitive Psychology, was that of cognitive neuropsychology.

Cognitive neuroscience can be characterized as the neuropsychology of cognition, with an emphasis on neuropsychology and its methods rather than on cognition. Cognitive neuropsychology, on the other hand, is more closely related to cognitive Psychology, sharing the characterization of cognition in terms of functionally discrete modules. Underlying cognitive neuropsychology is a belief that the organization of the cognitive system can be understood by studying its failures, and particularly failures that arise as the result of brain lesioning. The analysis of errors in performance following brain trauma can assist in the identification of independent and dependent components of the cognitive system, this analysis being guided by the theoretical framework of cognitive Psychology.

A good example of the application of cognitive neuropsychology is in investigating the organization of memory. Atkinson and Shiffrin's model of memory structure posited sensory, short-term and long-term stores, and was characteristic of an information processing inspired cognitive model. Two key claims of the model were that the short-term store was unitary and verbal, and that information must pass through the short-term store in order to be registered in long-term memory. This model was supported by a range of experimental data, albeit data that often sought to confirm, rather than test, the model. It was also able to account for impairments of long-term memory in the presence of intact short-term memory, explained by selective damage to the long-term store. Indeed, the fact that amnesiacs generally have intact short-term memory supports the separation of short- and long-term stores. However, the discovery of a patient with relatively intact long-term memory but severely impaired short-term memory posed a great challenge for the Atkinson and Shiffrin model. Further, more detailed explorations of memory deficits following brain lesions have led to more sophisticated models of memory structure, such as Baddeley's working memory model.

Cognitive neuropsychology relies, as an approach, on the assumption of modularity, since its goal is to identify modules. Given the aim of identifying modules on the basis of brain lesioning, it also relies on the notion of neurological specificity. This is the assumption that different mental functions occupy different brain regions, and effectively that modules correspond to different brain regions. Damage to different brain regions can therefore be expected to separably disrupt cognitive functions, and the goal of the cognitive neuropsychologist is to identify patterns of disruption of function. Unlike cognitive neuroscience, there may be no concern with actually identifying the brain region corresponding to a given cognitive function, although some cognitive neuropsychologists do aim for this. In general however, dissociation studies are used to identify hypothetical modules and the relationships between them.

A dissociation occurs when a patient is impaired on one task, such as long-term memory, but intact on another, such as short-term memory. However, a single dissociation such as this is ambiguous, since the differential performance may be result of damage to separate, independent modules; to separate, dependent modules; or to a single module for which the impaired task is more difficult than the intact. This ambiguity is resolved if investigators find a double dissociation. Thus, if an investigator finds a further patient who is impaired on short-term memory and intact on long-term memory, then there is a double dissociation between the two processes, and the two processes must be independent. Such findings are the ideal. In practice, patients showing dissociation are rarely intact on the spared process. More typically, a patient will show pronounced impairment on one task relative to another, less disrupted, task. Such findings can make it difficult to be certain that two processes are indeed independent.

There is some methodological debate within the field of cognitive neuropsychology over the use of case studies versus group studies. Traditionally, neuropsychology has used groups of subjects sharing neuropsychological syndromes, with group results on tasks being averaged and used in statistical analysis, as in mainstream experimental Psychology. However, this can have the effect of obscuring differences between patients. If a group of patients is heterogeneous in terms of disruption, then a group average may obscure theoretically significant differences in performance. Traditional syndrome classifications tend to be quite broad. For example, Broca's aphasia (see, for example, Ellis and Young, 1996) incorporates a range of symptoms which co-occur for anatomical, rather than functional reasons, and a given sufferer will display some but not necessarily all of these symptoms. In response to this, many cognitive neuropsychologists prefer to concentrate on single case studies, that investigate individuals' deficits in depth. Generally, experimental Psychology has been against the use of single cases, since any findings may be due to idiosyncrasies on the part of the individual. Single case studies lead to problems in generalization, the response to which is usually to collate the findings from a number of single cases and show similarities.

The single case study approach, known as radical cognitive neuropsychology, rejects the hypothetical average that is fundamental to most experimental Psychology. Cognitive neuropsychology may in this way influence conceptions of methodology more generally within Psychology, but this remains to be seen. What is clear is that cognitive neuropsychology is proving to be a valuable addition to methodology within cognitive Psychology, providing evidence that tests existing theories and that suggests new phenomena and theories that can be tested experimentally.

COMPUTATIONAL MODELLING

As we discussed in Chapter 8, the development of cognitive Psychology depended in part of the production of a number of convincing computer models of cognition, for instance the general problem solver. Despite this, however, computer models have had limited impact on cognitive Psychology, most psychologists preferring to use techniques of experimentation and statistical analysis. Computer models of cognition continue to be developed within cognitive science more generally, however, and particularly in artificial intelligence research. Opinion varies as to the value and implications of such models for cognitive Psychology. The weak view is that computer models provide simulations of psychological processes, without necessarily replicating human cognition. The strong view is that computer models provide direct theories of cognition, provided they can be successfully tested against psychological data.

Strube (2000) advocates a strong view, suggesting that computer models provide valuable generative theories. He discusses the strengths and weaknesses of the approach, and concludes that computer modelling produces more rigorous theorizing than experimental research. Much experimental research focuses on the analysis of isolated effects, producing many demonstrations of effects but without an integrative theoretical framework. Such effect based research emphasizes generalization from robust effects, but this limits the scope of theorizing. As an alternative, Strube highlights the value of 'cognitive architectures', computer models of cognition such as SOAR and ACT. These architectures claim to be models of cognition at a functional level of description. They provide generative theories in that they generate the phenomena that they seek to explain. The data thus produced, suggests Strube, have the same characteristics as empirical data. In particular, generative models produce experimental effects. Unlike experimental research, which only allows us to say under which conditions effects occur, we can explain why effects occur. Models also allow the manipulation of the system, for instance by introducing lesions in connectionist models. Despite their advantages, however, computer models are subject to criticism, on the grounds of relevance, testability and completeness.

Relevance refers to the debate about whether artificial intelligence, as represented by computer models, is qualitatively equivalent to human intelligence. For example, computer chess programs are capable of very good performance, but seem to decide on moves in a very different way from that of expert humans. Humans consider a relatively small number of lines of play, and consider some in depth or rely on recognition. Computers however pursue all available lines of play, but to limited depth. The increasing ability of computer chess programs comes in part from the development of more powerful computers, which are able to increase the depth of decision making, rather than from more human-like play. To some, this is an indication of differences between artificial intelligence and brain intelligence. To others, however, human intelligence is seen as a special case of a general theory of intelligence based on PSSs. The argument about whether artificial and human intelligences are qualitatively equivalent is pursued further later in this chapter, and in the next chapter.

Testability refers to concerns about how we might test computer models for validity as psychological theories. One approach is to compare the outputs of computer models with the outputs of humans performing the same task. Equivalence of output is then seen as equivalence of process. Returning to the example of chess programs, however, a computer may be able to beat a human, showing equivalent performance, but using very different underlying processes. A more common source of evidence in testing models is the use of verbal protocols, whereby individuals give descriptions of the processes they follow when completing a task. If these correspond to the processing stages of the model, then the model is seen as equivalent. However, there are a number of problems with the use of verbal reports, particularly to psychologists who have previously rejected the use of introspection. People have limited access to the processes underlying their cognition, and even when they seem to have access they may be mistaken. Experts in a particular task will tend to produce, if asked, verbal reports that are rule based, specifying a set of processes to follow. However, if they then actually follow their verbal protocol in executing a task, rather than performing it as they normally would, their performance worsens. Despite this, it is generally accepted that if sufficient care is taken in the production of verbal reports, and if the scope of reporting is sufficiently limited, then they can provide useful evidence.

The final criticism of completeness reflects two sorts of omission in computer models. First, there is no distinction between conscious and unconscious processing, which is often a feature of everyday human cognition, if not in laboratory tasks. It is not at all clear how a computer simulation might begin to model such a distinction, although some have faith that they could. Second, in terms of Kant's specification of cognitive, affective (emotional), and conative (intentional) faculties, computer models only model the cognitive aspect. Again, it is unclear how affective and conative aspects might be modelled. A common response to these criticisms is to question the importance of consciousness to cognition, on the basis that if functional simulations without consciousness are effective at a particular task, then consciousness cannot be important to that task. Further, it is sometimes suggested that consciousness evolved for affective and conative reasons, separately and unrelatedly to cognition. This separation of cognitive, affective and conative components is investigated in a later section.

PHILOSOPHICAL ISSUES

This section looks at some of the issues around the philosophy of mind (PoM). This is a very broad area, as a glance at any PoM text will show. We shall concentrate particularly on the approach of functionalism described in Chapter 8.

The first question to ask is, 'What is mind?', or possibly, 'What comprises mental life?'. A reasonable starting point is to state that mind comprises sensations, emotions, beliefs and attitudes. Further, mind has no tangible physical reality: it is comprised of feelings that we metaphorically locate in our heads (previous generations have located it elsewhere). This lack of physical reality raises some issues, as we shall see shortly.

There is clearly a link between mind and consciousness. Naïvely, we could say that mind comprises what we are conscious of. An association is frequently made between mind and intelligence or rationality: many philosophers see mind as arising from intelligent action, and try to explain mind in terms of intelligent action. This follows to a large extent from the rationalistic tradition in western thought (such that only rationality is taken seriously, crudely stated). This view overlooks the role of affective and conative aspects of mental life. How important these aspects are in considering cognition is a matter of some debate. Possible positions are that affective and conative aspects have the same basis as cognitive aspects, and are amenable to the same forms of description; that affective and conative aspects are different from cognitive aspects, and are separable in that they do not affect cognition; and that affective, conative and cognitive aspects of mind are interrelated and cannot be separated. The first two positions are compatible with current approaches to cognitive Psychology, while the latter position challenges the theoretical bases of the approach.

Before proceeding, there are some terms that need to be defined.

- Attitudes (or propositional attitudes) are mental states with content, often reflecting beliefs about things. These are often characterized in terms of propositions, but whether propositional characterizations are reasonable is itself a matter of debate. For many, it is an accepted presupposition that attitudes are propositional.
- This property of content leads to the notions of 'intentionality' and 'semantics'. If mental states have content, then they have some inherent meaning (semantics). Further, such mental states are purposive, in that there is an inherent intention.
- Experiences are conscious mental events. Sensations and emotions are, in normal circumstances, necessarily conscious.
- Thoughts are attitudes with content, which may or may not be conscious. They include knowledge and beliefs.

The Relationship Between Mind and Brain

One of the most hotly contested issues is how the mind – our experience of a mental life – relates to the physical reality of the brain. There are a number of broad positions, which we shall only briefly skip over.

Dualism (sometimes known as Cartesian dualism, after René Descartes) is the position that holds that mind and brain are two different entities. A problem comes in explaining the apparent linkage between the physical (like someone stepping on your toe) and the mental (like feeling pain). One unsatisfactory (scientifically) explanation invokes divine intervention. An even less satisfactory explanation puts it down to coincidence. Dualism is not a commonly held position, but opposition to the other two positions often backs one into the corner of apparent dualism.

Materialism (or physicalism) proposes that mental events can be described entirely in terms of physical events (hence, this position is a form of monism). In theory, there should be an entirely physical description of any mental event, though philosophers leave it to neuropsychologists to find such descriptions. Three theses form the basis of materialism:

The identification thesis   Mental states are directly identified with physical states.

The explanation thesis   Behaviour is best explained in physical terms.

The exclusion thesis   Humans have no features which no physical object can possess.

Materialism has the clear advantage of not relying on mysticism to explain mind. It has its detractors however. A common attack is the access objection: we have access to, or know about, our minds in a different way from the way we know about our brains. But then, we can have knowledge about water without knowing about its chemical composition. A particular problem with materialism is that it leads to reductionism: the view that there is nothing interesting in the mental, so let us just talk about the physical (cf. the Churchlands). Reductionism is a commonly held stance in Psychology, but it has the danger that in reducing the focus of explanation important phenomena are missed.

Analogizing to computers, the materialist school says, 'Let us just talk about the hardware'. The functionalist school says, 'Let us just talk about the software'. Particularly, functionalism concentrates on the functional role of mental states, emphasizing inputs, outputs and the relationship between states. It is neutral regarding the underlying physical basis, suggesting that if you get the functionality right, then the mind will follow. Functionalism is currently a very popular approach within philosophy, and is closely related to the information processing paradigm for investigating cognition. The adequacy of functionalism as an explanation of mind has important consequences for mainstream cognitive Psychology.

Two Important Properties of Mind

Attacks on functionalism concentrate on two identified properties of mental life that functionalism has problems explaining – intentionality and qualia.

Intentionality is a property of content filled mental states, and can be crudely seen as saying that states have a purpose. Thus you may reach for a banana because you intend to eat it, or because you intend to give it to your pet monkey. Behaviourism's denial of the mental is in part a denial of intentionality: you reach for the banana because you have learnt to in response to some stimulus, rather than because you have some purpose. A range of arguments have developed around the issue of intentionality, mainly because materialism and functionalism have problems accounting for it. An extreme example is the claim that any remotely intelligent system has intentionality, including a thermostat.

The other important property of mind is the existence of qualia. This is a generic (and disputed) term for mental experiences, particularly sensation and emotion, but not exclusively. As an example, if you look at a red apple, you will have a certain sensation of seeing something red. There will be a sensation in your mind particularly related to perceiving the colour red. But how do you explain this in materialist, or (particularly) functionalist terms? Consider the following thought experiment:

Imagine a woman, Mary, who spends her life in an entirely grey room, filled only with entirely grey objects. There is nothing wrong with her colour vision, but there is no colour for her to see. In the room there is a very extensive library, including everything you could ever want to know about colour vision, and what is involved in experiencing colour. Mary has no television, so spends her time reading. She is particularly fascinated by colour vision, and reads everything there is to know about seeing in colour – the wavelengths of light, the operation of cones, the LGN, everything. One day, a handsome prince on a white charger (we are mixing fairy tales a little) rescues Mary from her room, and gives her a red apple.

The question is this: before receiving the apple, did Mary, with all her propositional knowledge of colour perception, know what it felt like to see the colour red? If she did, then functionalism has no difficulties. If she did not, then functionalism has a lot of explaining to do.

Computational Accounts of Mind

The functionalist view of the mind has some very important ramifications. In particular, it suggests that any system that has the functionality of human cognition will necessarily have a mind. Thus if human cognition comes simply from a computer program, then any computer running the same program will have a mind. This is the basis of some attempts at computational modelling in Psychology. The value of such models depends in part on the validity of functionalism.

It is important to note that symbol systems rely on syntax: the rules specifying processes upon symbols. The rules and symbols are context free – they have no meaning beyond themselves. But we talked earlier about mind involving semantics and intentionality. Where do these come from in a symbol system? To believers, they arise from the operation of the formal system. The formalist's motto is that if you look after the syntax, the semantics will look after itself. Further, if you have semantics, then you have intentionality.

In some senses, this seems a little weak. Particularly, it associates mind very directly with rational performance. Clearly, you can achieve some form of intelligent action using symbol systems, but perhaps mind involves more than this? Many criticisms of functionalism attack this notion of semantics and intentionality arising within syntactical systems.

Against Computational Accounts

One of the pioneers of artificial intelligence, Alan Turing, was interested in how we could decide whether computers were intelligent or not. He suggested a simple test, known as the Turing test.

Imagine you are sitting in a sealed, windowless room, with two computer terminals (and an oxygen supply). You know that one terminal communicates with a human, and the other with a computer, but you do not know which is which. In either case, your only communication is by typing messages on a keyboard, and reading replies on the screen. Your task is to ask questions of the two entities – any questions you want – and then decide on the basis of their answers which is the human. If the computer can fool you into thinking that it is the human, then the computer is judged intelligent.

This test reflects a number of biases. The bias of deciding on the basis of observed behaviour probably reflects behaviourism. The bias of relying on language reflects the centrality of language to western conceptions of intelligence. However, the test is generally accepted. Turing may have meant it as a quantitative, rather than qualitative test, and not as a test of mindedness. However, a further bias, linking intelligence to mind, has led to people ascribing mindedness to computers capable of passing the Turing test. This latter view has been attacked by John Searle in his Chinese Room thought experiment. The experiment was inspired by a computer system called SAM, which could read in a story about a trip to a restaurant, and answer questions about things that were not in the story. For example: John went into a restaurant. He ordered a hamburger. When the burger arrived, it was burnt. John stood up and left the restaurant.

If you were asked 'Did John eat the hamburger?', you would probably say no, even though there is no information about that in the story. SAM would give the same reply – apparently, intelligent, human-like behaviour that could pass the Turing test (though in the Turing test you can ask questions about anything). Does SAM have a mind? Searle (1984) does not think so.

We are playing 'let's pretend' again. This time, pretend you are sitting in a closed room (with an oxygen supply, and as much colour as you like. You can have a nice comfortable armchair if you like). In front of you, you have a book containing pairs of Chinese symbols. People outside pass counters in through a hatch which bear Chinese symbols. Your job is to look these symbols up in your book, and pass out counters bearing the corresponding Chinese symbols. Effectively, you are constituting a symbol system – you have symbols and rules. The people outside are dead impressed: 'Look,' they say, 'this room understands Chinese – it knows that Wang did not eat the noodles!' They ascribe to the room intentionality and semantics and all the rest of it. However, you actually have no knowledge of Chinese, and have no idea what these counters are on about. They could be talking about noodles, or they could be talking about feng shui. You, the symbol system, have no semantics, and no intentionality.

Searle explains this by distinguishing between real intentionality and as-if intentionality. Real intentionality is a feature inherent in the human mind – we have intentionality. As-if intentionality is intentionality ascribed to systems because they behave as if they have intentionality. Thus the Chinese room appears to have intentionality, but it is as-if intentionality not real intentionality. Thermostats also have as-if intentionality – they could be said to believe that a room is too hot, but that is anthropomorphism (ascribing human qualities) rather than any inherent quality of the thermostat. Searle's argument is that symbol systems can only have as-if intentionality, which is not sufficient for a mind. Real intentionality is a feature of the human brain, not yet explained.

As you can imagine, functionalists are not too happy with Searle's attacks. Perhaps they feel he is ridiculing a little. There have been three main responses to Searle. The first response is to say, 'Okay, the Chinese room has not got intentionality, but it is a pretty stupid system'. However, if we have a system clever enough, it will have intentionality. The argument is that there is some threshold of intelligence that must be crossed for intentionality to arise. The second common response is known as the Robot reply. This states that the Chinese room does not have intentionality because there is no direct link to the environment. Intentionality arises from receiving stimuli from the environment and interacting with the environment. Thus a robot which interacts with the world according to a symbol system will have intentionality. The argument gets a little unpleasant, involving disembodied heads and so forth, but seems attractive. However, it still relies on a belief that intentionality arises from the syntax of a symbol system. The final major response is a little controversial. The Churchlands, and Daniel Dennett, respond by saying that there is no such thing as real intentionality: humans too only have as-if intentionality. This is rather behaviourist, and does not explain why I believe myself to have intentionality. Actually, there is another response (or perhaps a null response). This is to ignore Searle's arguments altogether, and maintain that yes, thermostats really do believe that the room is too warm.

Those who agree with Searle see intentionality, and qualia, as emergent properties of the brain. This is related to materialism, though it does not necessarily support the reduction of mental states to physical states. While it is claimed that there is an important physical basis for mental events, things like consciousness, intentionality, qualia, etc. are seen as interesting in their own right, and are not to be reduced to a purely physical basis.

There is a strong relationship between the philosophy of mind and Psychology: popular notions within PoM inform the kind of theories Psychology produces, and advances in Psychology inform ideas within PoM. As an example of the former, the functionalist position lends support to the information processing paradigm. As an example of the latter, neuropsychology gives evidence for a physical basis of mind. In the next chapter, we shall see how connectionism informs PoM.

REPRESENTATION

The previous section discusses the view of the mind as a processor of symbolic information in terms of difficulties in accounting for intentionality and qualia. A further problem is in the account given of representation, that is in terms of what the symbols in a symbol system are supposed to represent. In this section we shall outline Bickhards's (1996) argument that the notion of representation underlying computationalism is false. His view is that accounts of mental representation need to account for the groundedness of such representations in interactions with the environment. This notion of grounding in the environment is expanded on in the next section, when we discuss the notion of the embodied mind.

Computationalism presumes that cognition consists of the manipulation of symbolic information, following the argument of Leibniz. In this view, perception consists of the encoding of stimuli into internal, symbolic representations. Once encoded, cognition proceeds entirely on the basis of these symbols, plus other internally generated ones. An alternative view is given by connectionism, whereby representations are not symbolic. However, these representations too are seen as arising from encoding of stimuli and internal generation. Bickhard attacks both for following what he terms encodingism, the presumption that representation is a particular form of correspondence between the symbol representing something, and the something that the symbol represents. Bickhard's claim is that basing all representation on correspondences is logically incoherent, and fundamentally flawed.

It is in no doubt that some forms of representation are indeed encodings, but Bickhard's claim is that other forms of representation are not only possible but necessary for cognition. Encodings carry representational content, in that they have the same content as the thing they stand for. Thus, the Morse code element ' . . .' has the same representational content as the letter 'S' – it borrows the representational content of the thing it corresponds to. Both ' . . .' and 'S' perform the same representational function, although they have a different symbolic form. However, encodings can only borrow representational content, in that they can only come to perform the same function as some other representation, or alternatively combine the representational content of other representations. In both cases, no new representational content is being created. This is not a problem for genuine encodings, for example, in inventing Morse code to represent the letters of the alphabet. However, it is a problem when we need to form representations of things for which we have no existing representation. Thus infants, in learning to perceive objects in the environment, cannot use encoding, since they have no pre-existing representations for the encoding to borrow from. For encoding to proceed, there must be some foundational set of representations to work off. The logical incoherence arises as follows. If these foundational representations are encodings, there is no way for them to have representational content. However, if they have no representational content then they cannot be representations, and hence cannot be encodings. Foundational representations cannot be defined in terms of other representations. One response to this (for example, Fodor) is to claim that the foundational representations are innate. However, this does not solve the logical problem: even if there are innate representations, they must have come from somewhere. This recourse to claiming an innate basis for elements of cognition is quite common when a theory has problems with accounting for the initial acquisition of such elements. While this may work, logically if not factually, for an individual organism, it cannot account for a species. At some point, such alleged innate components had to be acquired. In computer models, of course, the programmer provides the initial set of representations and assigns them semantic values, but as we saw previously it is debatable whether such representations have the intentionality that human representations seem to have.

Bickhard advocates an interactivist approach, whereby environmental stimuli induce internal state changes in a perceiving organism. Different environmental conditions lead to different final states of the cognizing system. Over time, a factual correspondence arises between environmental stimuli and internal states, out of which emerges a minimal representation. The set of primitive representations thus formed then forms the basis for further representations. This emphasis on the importance of the environment in shaping the elements of cognition is illustrative of a general trend to considering the cognizer as interacting with their surroundings, to which we now turn.

ECOLOGICAL VALIDITY AND EMBODIMENT

The conventional view of cognition arising out of the operation of a discrete, logical system has faced a number of challenges from those who emphasize the role of the environment and social interaction in shaping cognition. An early challenge came from J.J. Gibson, whose theory of direct perception claimed that the information necessary for perception is present in the environment as it impinges on the organism, rather than being the result of internal processing. This ecological approach suggested that an observer actively engages with the environment, sampling from it in order to pick up information from sensory cues. This approach was also adopted by Eleanor Gibson in investigating perceptual development in children, and was extended by Ulrich Neisser. Following the publication of *Cognitive psychology* in 1967, Neisser became increasingly dissatisfied with the narrow information processing focus of cognitive Psychology. In his 1976 book *Cognition and reality* he synthesized the Gibsonian and information processing approaches, and adapted Bartlett's notion of schema to provide an alternative explanation of the nature of perception. His theory of the perceptual cycle emphasized that cognizers actively gather information from the environment and use this information to modify schema based knowledge structures. These structures in turn influence future interactions with the environment. He criticised most laboratory based experimentation for a lack of ecological validity, overlooking the active role of cognizers and the kinds of information that they extract from the environment. He has continued to be active in calling for greater ecological validity in cognitive Psychology.

Another proselytizer for ecological validity has been Don Norman, who has emphasized how cognizers operate in real world environments, and how artefacts influence cognitive performance. For Norman, cognition is distributed between cognizers and constructed artefacts, a simple example being the use of a calculator to assist in solving mathematical problems. Norman (1980) proposed a radical reconception of the nature of cognition. The conventional view suggests that there are several separable systems, for example, perception, memory, motor control, which interact. Within these systems, processing is purely cognitive in the sense of operating solely on internal knowledge representations according to a PSS. However, while this may be a reasonable abstract characterization, alternative views are possible. These alternatives variously emphasize the roles of: interactions of the organism with the environment and other organisms, the influence of an organism's life history and cultural setting, and the needs of animate organisms. Cognitive Psychology has tended to ignore these factors, and even attempts at increasing ecological validity concentrate on testing models with more realistic problems, rather than fully incorporating such elements into a theoretical framework. The human organism investigated in cognitive Psychology is a being of pure intellect, communicating with logical dialogues and solving mathematically well-formed problems. This 'Mr Spock' characterization is rather different from our everyday experiences of how we and others behave within complex, changeable and poorly defined environments and interactions. The issue raised by Norman for cognitive Psychology is whether this characterization can later be extended to more realistic behaviour, or whether there are qualitative differences between the idealized intellect of cognitive Psychology and the human mind. In addressing this issue, Norman returns to the concept of feedback from cybernetics. Although cybernetics was influential in the establishment of cognitive Psychology (see Chapter 8), modern cognitive Psychology pays little more than lip service to the field. Feedback requires a system to produce output within an environment, and the feedback only has meaning and value to the organism within the context of that environment.

For Norman, social interaction is a cybernetic system that provides the right forum for considering human performance. People are responsive to both their physical and social environments, and their behaviour is the result of these environments, and of the behaviours of other participants. The lone intellect in a laboratory is thus a special case of cognition. A full theory of cognition should consider social and environmental influences as well as isolated cognition. Norman also points out the limited scope of cognitive Psychology, which overlooks subconscious processing, emotional influences, skilled performance, and language use in the context of social interaction. In particular, cognitive Psychology overlooks the fact that humans are biological organisms that have uniquely biological needs, such as survival, feeding, and reproduction. It seems reasonable to suggest that as cognition evolved, its evolution was driven by the need to satisfy these biological needs. Thus any theory of cognition needs to account for how these needs are best satisfied. This can be achieved to an extent by postulating a physiological regulatory system to maintain homeostasis and fulfil basic needs that is subsidiary to the purely rational cognitive system. However, a fundamental requirement of a system that ensures survival is that the organism should respond rapidly to perceived dangers. In the case of dangers that need to be interpreted, for example, in deciding whether a loud noise is a gunshot or a car backfiring, then the cognitive system needs to be marshalled to perform this interpretation immediately. This suggests to Norman that cognition is under the control of the regulatory system, rather than vice versa. This fits in with phylogenetic evidence, in that the parts of the brain that handle basic regulatory functions developed first. Logically, the regulatory system must have developed before complex cognition, so it seems more likely that cognition developed as a slave system rather than as a master system.

In addition to regulatory and cognitive systems, Norman suggests that emotional systems may act as an intermediary between the two, with emotional arousal being an alternative route to activating the cognitive system. Within this threefold hierarchy, the cognitive system is not seen as an isolated pure cognizer, but rather as being influenced by physiological and emotional inputs, and dependent on the physical make up of the brain in shaping the nature of cognition.

These approaches emphasize the need to consider cognition at the level of a complete system including the body housing the mind and the environment with which the body interacts. They represent the view that mind is embodied, and cannot be divorced from its physical basis. Logically, this view can be compatible with the view of the mind as a symbol system, albeit one that is not purely internalized. However, the notion of embodiment has also been extended to representation and the nature of meaning. Objectivist ideas of meaning claim that knowledge consists of statements with a truth value which encodes objects in the world. These objects have objectively given properties, and they stand in objective relationships with other objects, independent of people's knowledge of them. Categories, as collections of objects, are also seen as objective, and independent of the mind, suggesting that logical reasoning has a Platonic reality in the world. This objectivist philosophy is the basis of epistemology for cognitive Psychology. An alternative view, for instance that of Lakoff and Johnson (1980), is that concepts are ultimately based on the human body and its interactions, and that abstract concepts are derived metaphorically from spatial and physical concepts. The use of metaphor is seen as fundamental to concept formation and to semantics in language. Lakoff in particular concentrates on the embodied nature of semantics in natural language, arguing that meaning comes out of the nature of the body and of the world. The conceptual system is constrained by the nature of the body and of the perceptual system, by the architecture of the brain, and by social interaction. This last constraint suggests that meaning is not objective and universal, but rather will vary from culture to culture. Traditional conceptions of mental representation, relying on syntactical symbols, face difficulty in specifying how meaning is grounded in the world, as discussed previously. However, in viewing the mind as fundamentally embodied, meaning becomes grounded in the body and in interactions with the environment and with others. This view corresponds to the processing features of connectionist models, and also provides the basis for the programme of cognitive linguistics, both of which are discussed in the next chapter.

The notion that cognition can only be understood in terms of interaction with the wider environment is gaining ground within cognitive science, and is exemplified by attempts to model cognition using dynamic systems theory. In dynamical systems theory (Port and van Gelder 1995), cognition is modelled in terms of non-linear mathematical relations between parameters that characterize cognition, including parameters for environmental features. This approach emphasizes the stochastic nature of cognition, and often rejects the notions of representation, computation and modularity.

CONCLUSION

We began the chapter by considering the basis of the information processing approach in cognitive Psychology, seeing that the view of the mind as an information processor has been taken to mean that the mind is a Physical Symbol System, organized in a modular fashion. We then saw that this view, which assumes a separation between the functions of cognition and its physical basis, has been challenged to an extent by advances in neuroscience, but that evidence from neuroscience is also proving valuable in the development of theories within cognitive Psychology. This is particularly the case in the new field of cognitive neuropsychology, which analyses disruption following brain trauma within the theoretical framework of cognitive Psychology.

Computer modelling had an important role to play in the early development of cognitive Psychology, but such models are not widely used. We looked at arguments in favour of such models, in that they provide generative theories, but also saw reasons to question their validity. Following this, we considered arguments within the philosophy of mind, particularly in terms of the validity of functionalism. We saw that functionalism has some difficulty in accounting for certain aspects of mental life. If functionalism is proved to be false, then this has important implications for cognitive Psychology. We concluded by considering an argument against encoding based representations, which led to a wider discussion about the possible need to consider cognition in the context of environmental and social interactions.

Arguments about the need to consider the environment and social interaction in theorizing about cognition reflect a growing scepticism towards the value of the computer metaphor for cognitive Psychology. The view of the mind as an isolated information processor is increasingly seen as being insufficient to capture the richness of cognition, and the need to consider humans as humans is being emphasized. Attention is being directed to the importance of the physical makeup of the brain and of the social purposes of cognition. For some, the emphasis should be on cognition's role in facilitating life in the real world, allowing organisms to respond flexibly and appropriately in changing contexts.

FURTHER READING

Baumgartner, P. and Payr, S. (eds) 1995: *Speaking minds*. Princeton, NJ: Princeton University Press.
Bechtel, W. and Graham, G. (eds) 1998: *A companion to cognitive science*. Oxford: Blackwell.

Blakemore, C. and Greenfield, S. 1987: *Mindwaves*. Oxford: Blackwell.

Damasio, A.R. 1995: *Descartes's error: emotion, reason, and the human brain*. London: Picador.

Dreyfus, H.L. 1992: *What computers still can't do: a critique of artificial reason*. Cambridge, MA: MIT Press.

Gergen, K. and Gigerenzer, G. 1991: Cognitivism and its discontents: an introduction to the issue. *Theory and Psychology* 1: 403–5.

Guttenplan, S. 1995: *Companion to the philosophy of mind*. Oxford: Blackwell.

Hutchins, E. 1996: *Cognition in the wild*. Cambridge, MA: MIT Press.

Lakoff, G. 1987: *Women, fire and dangerous things*. Chicago: University of Chicago Press.

Lycan, W.G. (ed.) 1991: *Mind and cognition: a reader*. Oxford: Blackwell.

Neisser, U. 1976: *Cognition and reality*. San Francisco: Freeman.

Norman, D. 1980: Twelve issues for cognitive science. *Cognitive Science* 4: 1–33.

O'Donohue, W. and Kitchener, R.F. 1996: *The philosophy of psychology*. London: Sage.

Potter, J. 2000: Post-cognitive psychology. *Theory and psychology* 10(1): 31–8.

Shallice, T. 1988: *From neuropsychology to mental structure*. Cambridge: Cambridge University Press.

Still, A., and Costall, A. (eds) 1991: *Against cognitivism: alternative foundations for cognitive psychology*. Hemel Hempstead: Harvester Wheatsheaf.

14

CONNECTIONISM

This chapter discusses connectionism as an approach to modelling cognition. The approach has its origins in the 1940s, as described in Chapter 8,
and has recently become popular within artificial intelligence. It has had
less impact within cognitive Psychology, but in line with renewed interest
in neuroscience is attracting increasing attention. Connectionism uses the
principles of brain organization to inspire the design of computational
systems, drawing on theory from computer science, mathematics, psychology, and neuroscience. A range of terms are used to describe the approach,
including connectionism, artificial neural networks, and parallel distributed processing. We use connectionism, since connections are the unique
feature of the nets. The term (artificial) neural network implies a closer
relation to brain organization than actually obtains, although the term has
a simple appeal, while parallel distributed processing tends to reflect an
engineering bias, and is a bit clumsy for general use. Here, we describe the
approach, and discuss its potential as a framework within cognitive
Psychology. We illustrate its appeal by discussing how connectionism can
provide an explanation of language understanding, capturing a range of
aspects of language use that present difficulties for symbolic approaches.
We end the chapter by contrasting symbolic and connectionist approaches
to modelling cognition.

BIOLOGICAL AND ARTIFICIAL NEURONES

Biological Neurones

The brain is composed of networks of neurones. There are different types of
neurone for different jobs, but all share the features of having connections to
other neurones; of accepting input from them; and of producing output to
other neurones. A neurone has dendrites, a soma and an axon. The dendrites
are branching structures that synapse, or communicate, with other nerve
cells: they are the input mechanism. A cell may synapse with many other
cells through the dendrites. The soma is the cell body. It can also form
synapses. The axon is the nerve fibre that produces the output of the cell. It

may synapse with many other cells. Synapses may be either excitatory or inhibitory, wherein an excitatory synapse increases the likelihood that the target cell will fire, while an inhibitory synapse decreases the likelihood. Brain neurones function electrically and chemically. At a synapse, an axon comes very near a dendrite. If the axon belongs to a cell that is firing, it releases a stream of chemicals, called neurotransmitters. These cause a transfer of ions to the target cell. Neurotransmitters may be either destroyed or recycled. Narcotics work by affecting the uptake of neurotransmitters, so distorting brain functioning. After a neurone has taken up ions, the electrical balance within the cell changes. A potential difference results across the walls of the cell. When this difference exceeds a certain level, an electrical impulse is sent down the axon at speeds up to 100 metres per second. This is facilitated by transferring sodium ions between the inside and outside of the cell. When the impulse reaches points of synapse, neurotransmitters are released. In this way, impulses are passed around the brain.

Artificial Neurones

Artificial neurones are mathematical processing units based on biological neurones. An artificial neurone accepts a number of inputs, performs a calculation on their values, and on the basis of the net input outputs an activation value. The inputs are either external, supplied by an investigator, or internal, supplied by other units. Links between units are called connections, and have strengths, called weights, associated with them. The higher the weight value of a connection, the closer the relationship between the two units connected. Typically, net input to a unit is calculated by performing a dot product between the weights and the activation values of the source units. The activation value is calculated according to some function, typically either a threshold – if the net input is above a threshold then output 1, else output 0 – or logistic. The choice of activation function affects the characteristics of the network, as does the pattern of weights on connections. A number of units are combined in a network topology chosen to suit a particular task. Typically, the network formed is trained to produce some output given some input. This training consists of modifying connection weights. Connection weights store representations in networks, typically the relationship between an input set and an output set.

A BRIEF HISTORY

Before we consider connectionist architectures in more detail, we shall explain some of the history. Connectionist models were first suggested in the 1940s, but due to politics of research funding were dormant between the 1960s and the 1980s. The history of connectionist research gives a salutary example of the importance of funding biases to the progress of research.

The Perceptron

In 1943, McCulloch and Pitts described a processing paradigm based on the organization of the brain. They postulated a network of simple processing units receiving inhibitory and excitatory inputs from each other, and producing binary (on-off) outputs. Using these units, they demonstrated how various logical problems could be solved, and that if provided with large memory, the network could function as a Universal Turing machine. Much research was undertaken investigating what cognitive functions such networks could perform, particularly in pattern recognition. Rosenblatt extended the network model considerably, and coined the term perceptron to cover these models. He introduced continuously variable weight values and a training algorithm. He also emphasized the power of this kind of statistical model, compared with a Boolean model based on symbols. The advantages of network models for pattern recognition and memory modelling were soon established.

The Symbolist Tradition

While research into network models proceeded, an alternative paradigm was also being pursued. This school maintained that cognition was the result of symbol manipulation, that the brain acted merely as a computer running a Boolean program, and that if we could find that program, we could emulate human intelligence on a computer. Symbolic systems have a certain power: based on logic, they are very good at handling propositional knowledge and reasoning. Formal systems such as these are based on the premise that we need only consider the formal properties of a symbol; what it represents is unimportant. Western philosophy has a long tradition of treating the mind as a logical system. The physical symbol system hypothesis postulates that 'A physical symbol system has the necessary and sufficient means for general intelligent action'. Thus intelligence can only derive from a physical symbol system, and a physical symbol system must be intelligent. Computer programs are physical symbol systems; thus computer programs must be capable of intelligence. Chomsky's work on innate language ability was seen as supporting this case: if the brain comes with a system for handling symbols (i.e., language), then surely it is because the brain uses those symbols as the basis of its functioning?

Minsky and Papert

In 1969, Minsky and Papert, two eminent researchers in the symbolist tradition, published *Perceptrons*, an analysis of the capabilities of network models. Given their symbolist orientation they were not too kind, particularly since funding for AI research was tightening, and connectionist research was getting much of it. After the publication of *Perceptrons*, money for connectionist research dried up, and so did research in the area, though some workers continued their investigations. For 17 years, connectionism became a backwater, while symbolists made inflated claims for the future of their models which were never borne out. In *Perceptrons*, Minsky and Papert analysed the mathematical properties of network models, and showed that certain logical functions could not be performed without recourse to multilayer models, for which no reliable training procedure existed. Minsky and Papert judged connectionist research to be sterile – it would never be useful. A more general problem was that networks could only act as associators between input and output, conflicting with the physical symbol system hypothesis.

Rumelhart and McClelland

In the early 1980s, connectionist research began to be reported once more. Having licked their wounds, connectionist researchers were back with more powerful models and answers to old concerns. They were helped in this by the lack of progress in symbolist research, and by a growing interest on the part of cognitive scientists in neuroscience. A major breakthrough occurred with the publication in 1986 of *Parallel distributed processing* by Rumelhart *et al*. This collection of papers represented the current state of the art in connectionist research, and provided an accessible starting point for newcomers to the field. The initial run of 30,000 copies was sold before they were printed, and the twin volumes rapidly became the connectionists' Bible. Today, connectionism is very much in favour: symbolic research is suffering a backlash as people throw neural networks at any problem. However, this may create problems for connectionism in the future, as people use them for unsuitable tasks, and become disappointed by failure. Perhaps a more reasonable approach would be to try to build hybrid systems, incorporating features of symbolic systems in connectionist models; and features of connectionist models in symbolic systems. An example of the latter is Anderson's ACT model of a semantic network with spreading activation.

SEMANTIC INTERPRETATION OF CONNECTIONIST SYSTEMS

If a connectionist system models human performance in a particular domain, we need to consider how concepts in the domain are represented in the network. There are two approaches: localist networks assign concepts to units, while distributed networks represent concepts as a pattern of activation and connectivity across multiple units.

Localist Networks

Each unit in a localist network represents a property. For example, if a network is trained to make decisions about occupations, for example book, pusher and burglar, we may have one unit to represent each occupation. Localist nets have the advantage that it is easy to interpret network behaviour. However, it is important to remember that this identification of units with concepts is done by the investigator. The network itself sees no meaning in units. If a researcher is setting up a network in a localist manner, s/he must be very careful in setting up a correspondence between concepts and units. What concepts are necessary? How should they be connected? Despite this, localist nets are usually easier to set up than distributed ones. Distributed nets offer some unique features, but if they are not needed an interactive localist net will often do.

Distributed networks

In a distributed network each concept is represented by a pattern of activation across a set of units. Thus to represent occupations in a distributed net, we might keep three input units, but encode the concepts as a pattern of activation, thus:

I	I	I	= Burglar
–I	–I	I	= Bookie
I	–I	–I	= Pusher

Now there is no semantic interpretation of individual units.

Another approach is to extract features from a concept, and assign a unit to each feature. A concept is represented by the pattern of features it possesses. Now, the features have a localist representation (one unit for each feature), but the concept itself has a distributed representation. Thus in representing professions, Burglar, Pusher and Bookie would all share the feature illegal, and hence would have that unit active in input, but only Pusher would have the feature 'involves drugs'. Chemist would have the feature 'involves drugs', but not the feature 'illegal'. While the designer can decompose concepts into features for input and output, a net with hidden layers will perform its own decomposition in the hidden layer. The concept of microfeatures has been identified to describe the features hidden units become sensitive to.

Distributed representations have a number of advantages. For example, they are robust to noise and damage. Since representation is spread across a large number of units, some may malfunction and the net can still makes sense of the input. Thus in the profession example above, an input of 1 1 ? would be treated as if it were a burglar. Distributed representations are also easily extensible. Adding new input to a localist net involves adding units; in distributed representations it involves adjusting weights slightly, maintaining existing knowledge while assimilating new. Finally, distributed representations respond sensibly to novel input – given an input of –1 –1 –1, which it has not seen before, our profession net above will make a sensible generalization about what the input represents.

ATTRACTIVE PROPERTIES OF CONNECTIONIST MODELS

As has been hinted, connectionist models can be seen to exhibit properties of human cognition that are not shown in symbolist systems. These properties include: neural plausibility, satisfaction of soft constraints, utilization of regularities and prototype extraction, graceful degradation, content-address-able memory, and capacity to learn from experience. These are reviewed below.

Neural Plausibility

Connectionist models are neurally inspired. Although they are a long way from performing as the human nervous system does, they come far closer than do symbolic systems. For those unhappy with the strong AI hypothesis, connectionism offers a potentially more realistic paradigm for building intelligent systems. Of course, biological networks are far richer than artificial ones. Connectionist models come nowhere near to modelling the patterns of connectivity in the brain, and do not attempt to model the action of neurotransmitters. Artificial neurones do not even work like biological neurones – biological neurones either fire or do not, and have a complex system for determining whether to fire or not (analogous to activation rules). Connectionist models also depend on mechanisms with no parallel in the brain, for example, the back propagation learning algorithm. Connectionist models are however cognitive, rather than biological, and this rather coarse relationship between biological and artificial neurones may not be too much of a problem. What is clear is that brain functions depend on massively parallel and distributed processing: the brain is too slow to perform complex sequential instructions. It has also been seen that the connectionist paradigm produces human-like behaviours that are difficult to obtain from symbolic systems.

Satisfaction of Soft Constraints

Connections constitute constraints on processing: when two units are connected by an excitatory link, one is constrained to be active when the other is. Rules in symbolic systems also constitute constraints. However, rules are deterministic whereas connections are stochastic, since a unit receives input from many other units. Thus a network finds the best solution to a set of constraints, which is not necessarily compatible with all individual constraints. Constraints in a connectionist architecture can be said to be soft, in that they are not binding. Rules in symbolic systems form hard constraints, since each rule must be satisfied. Many cognitive processes seem more easily represented using soft constraints than hard, for example, decision making when conflicting demands have to be satisfied. Soft constraints are also more flexible when novel situations are encountered, and are better able to cope with exceptions to rules. Rather than having a set of rules to describe a system, and a further set of rules to handle exceptions, connectionist systems handle all with the same mechanism.

Utilizing Regularities and Prototype Extraction

In associating input and output, networks form internal representations of microfeatures of the input. The identification of such microfeatures allows the network to identify regularities in the input patterns. For example, without explicit coding a distributed network may identify a regularity between the three occupations listed above that we might label 'illegal' . The extraction of regularities, together with the probabilistic nature of the network's operation, allows the network to generate prototypes for categories in the input. The network can then use this information to make informed generalizations when presented with novel information.

Graceful Degradation

Like the brain, connectionist systems show a gradual reduction in performance when overloaded or damaged. This is graceful degradation. Again, it is a trait traditional symbolist systems do not share. Graceful degradation is shared by localist and distributed models, though distributed networks are more robust. Graceful degradation comes as an inherent feature of the model, rather than needing to be designed on an ad hoc basis by a knowledge engineer.

Content-addressable Memory

Human memory is content addressable – a number of aspects of an experience may trigger memory of it. Thus a meal might be remembered from sight, taste or smell. Content-addressable memory is difficult to achieve with symbolic systems, and requires work-arounds. Again, with connectionist models it comes as part of the package. Interestingly, in distributed systems there is no sense of retrieving a symbol: rather, a memory retrieval is the same as making an inference. This suggests that there is no clear distinction between a real memory and a plausible reconstruction. In considering bridging inferences in language understanding, or the work of Bartlett, we see that this is often the case in human memory.

Capacity to Learn from Experience

Connectionist models can learn from experience by changing weights. However, in human knowledge we can see two kinds of learning: some information is acquired gradually, and some is picked up very quickly indeed. Symbolic systems are good at modelling the latter, connectionist at the former. A unified account is needed.

CONNECTIONISM AND COGNITIVE SCIENCE

In this section, drawing heavily on Bechtel and Abrahamsen (1991), we discuss the implications of connectionism for cognitive science, and for a number of disciplines in Psychology.

Connectionism as a New Paradigm for Cognitive Science

Since the ancient Greeks, western philosophy has followed a rationalist tradition that has influenced all areas of study. In the realms of Psychology and philosophy, the influence has led to a symbolic paradigm for conceiving cognition. Mental processes, such as language understanding, are viewed as the result of symbol manipulation, and the mind as the product of symbolic processes, with thoughts and emotions being derived from atomic representations of experiences and knowledge. Connectionism provides an alternative paradigm for the cognitive disciplines, from the low level study of localization of functions in the brain to the high level study of thoughts and feelings. In the following sections, we will look at how this new paradigm might influence study in a number of the disciplines of cognitive science, concentrating on those of most relevance to Psychology.

Artificial Intelligence and Cognitive Psychology

Historically, traditional symbolic systems for modelling cognition were inflexible, and provided a poor model for learning and for pattern recognition. One answer to such problems was to develop new symbolic mechanisms that incorporated features such as constraint satisfaction and learning procedures. Such attempts proved successful at improving flexibility. The reborn field of connectionism provided a more distinct break, replacing hard rules operating on ordered strings with statistical analysis of distributed representations. At the end of the 1980s, both types of model exhibited flexibility, subtlety and ability to learn from experience. However, the distinction between operation on ordered strings, and on distributed representations, remained. At present, these two opposing paradigms compete for resources and recognition. How will this competition be resolved? The penetration of connectionism into these two disciplines will depend on whether it is characterized as a new paradigm, or just an extra tool for building systems. A number of conditions can be identified for connectionism to be firmly established as a tool or paradigm. First, a number of successful models must be demonstrated. Second, connectionist models must compete successfully with the non-traditional symbolic models discussed above. Partly, this will depend on the attractiveness of connectionism as a notion of the nature of mind. Third, large numbers of researchers have to work in connectionism. Fourth, postgraduates must also be tempted, since these will influence the course of research in the future. Fifth, funding needs to be expanded. And finally, researchers may have to move, at least in the interim, towards hybrid models using both symbolic and connectionist techniques.

Artificial Intelligence

A number of successful programs have been developed in the symbolic paradigm. These have been in domains where symbolic representation of knowledge is sufficient: here, there is little to attract workers to connectionism. Further, many AI models represent high level reasoning, areas that have not yet been tackled successfully by connectionist models. However, all symbolic systems have certain problems. They tend to be domain-specific, brittle and context-insensitive. Further, they cannot learn, and so each has to be hand crafted into a domain by a knowledge engineer. Some domains have proved less amenable to a symbolic approach, for example, vision and speech. Many successful vision systems are based on connectionist models, and current speech recognition technology depends on probabilistic models that are mathematically equivalent to connectionist models. Most attempts to model language understanding still follow the symbolic approach, since language is seen as the paradigmatic symbol system, with limited success. We shall see later an alternative, connectionist approach to modelling language understanding that challenges symbolic models. Connectionist success in this domain, which should be most amenable to symbolic modelling, would pose a serious challenge to the symbolic approach.

Cognitive Psychology

Cognitive psychologists have a different goal to knowledge engineers. Rather than trying to solve a problem in a domain, they seek to model human behaviour. Connectionist models will become attractive if they provide a better account of behaviour than symbolic systems, if they can model behaviour that symbolic systems have been unable to do, and if they suggest new areas of study. Connectionist models can be seen to display aspects of human performance. However, they also have limitations. The critical question for cognitive psychologists is whether these limitations are due to specific models, or due to the inadequacies of connectionism as a paradigm. Some cognitive psychologists have argued that connectionist networks work only because of the encoding of input and output, and that this encoding is informed by past work in the symbolic tradition. While it is true that encoding schemes are almost universally derived from previous research, a connectionist network forms its own internal encodings, and these encodings dictate in large part the behaviour of the model. Besides, if the structure of a domain has been accurately described in the past, why not use this structure to influence coding schemes? It cannot be disputed that symbolic models describe the general character of a domain accurately. The claim of connectionists is that it is only through more finely detailed models, incorporating representation of a microstructure, that subtle and important behaviour can be captured. The central claim is that while much of cognition can be described at an abstract level in symbolic terms, such descriptions are simplifications, and unable to capture the mechanisms underlying cognition.

These are the disciplines where connectionism has already made an impact. In the next two sections, we look at other disciplines where connectionism has had a minimal effect, but may be more influential in the future.

Developmental Psychology

Developmental Psychology looks at changes in human development, for example, language acquisition in children. In some cases, such as language, it intersects with cognitive Psychology. Developmental Psychology can benefit from the advantages postulated previously for connectionist modelling, but there are also particular advantages in the developmental domain offered by a connectionist approach. Connectionist modelling can be applied in a number of areas of developmental Psychology, offering explanations of mechanisms of development, context effects, stage-like changes, and developmental and acquired disabilities.

Mechanisms of Development

Progress has been slow in understanding the mechanisms underpinning development. Mechanisms have been proposed that are vague or difficult to test. Two very general mechanisms that have been suggested are maturation and learning. Maturation occurs when developmental changes occur under genetic control. Learning occurs when changes are due to experience. These two processes are closely linked, making study difficult. Connectionism suggests a way of considering these processes. Maturation may be compared to changing the architecture of a network – the number of layers, number of units, number of connections, etc. Learning can be seen as changes resulting in a system of given architecture due to environmental input, akin to changing the weights in a network. These two can be linked by allowing architectural changes to be due to environment as well as to genetics. The richness of an environment can be seen to affect the rate of learning in children, and a similar effect is observed in connectionist models. Similarly, a process of pruning can be seen to occur in early development, when very general neurone organizations are refined in line with experience. Again, a similar mechanism can be modelled in connectionism.

Context Effects

Context effects prove disruptive for developmental research. A child, particularly if retarded, may be able to perform an experiment within the environment (room, experimenter) in which s/he is taught, but unable if the environment changes – the experiment is occurring in a disadvantageous context. A process of decontextualization has been suggested for development, whereby concepts are initially learnt in a specific context, and gradually the set of contexts in which the concept is understood is expanded. Thus a child initially learns only one use for a given word, but eventually learns how to apply it in different linguistic contexts. However, no mechanism has been suggested for this process. Connectionism offers potential to provide such mechanisms, and also to show the importance of context effects on adult behaviour, currently underrated in importance in cognitive Psychology. McClelland *et al.* (1986) have described a preliminary study in which the effects of context on learning were modelled by a connectionist network.

Stage-like Transitions

Development has been observed to proceed in stage-like steps, where in the long-term discrete states of development can be observed, whilst in the short term only gradual changes within a state are observable. A small number of connectionist models have been constructed that display similar stage-like development in learning. For example, Rumelhart and McClelland's model of past-tense acquisition shows a stage of over-generalization before exceptions are integrated into the mechanism, as occurs when children learn language.

Developmental and Acquired Disabilities

Cognitive functions may fail to develop properly (developmental disability), or may become disrupted through damage (acquired disability). Studying degenerate mechanisms can provide very useful data about the functioning of healthy mechanisms. Work on developmental disability within a connectionist framework has been slow in appearing. However, acquired disabilities have been modelled. Acquired dyslexia is a dysfunctioning of language mechanisms as a result of lesions (caused by head injury or stroke, for example) to certain brain areas. Previous studies of the patterns of damage and impairment have given information about localization of language function in the brain, and about how the various processes work together. Surface dyslexics can access the pronunciation, but not the meaning, of written words, and also tend to over-generalize pronunciations, suggesting they are processing words letter by letter, rather than as units. Deep dyslexics can access meanings, but have difficulties in pronunciation. They make semantic errors, and they make visual errors. Hinton and Shallice have reported a connectionist model of deep dyslexia that emulates normal behaviour until lesions are introduced by breaking connections in the network, at which time patterns of impairment typical of deep dyslexia are observed. They suggest that the mixture of errors displayed are a consequence of distributed representations. It is the first model of deep dyslexia that displays such a mixture of error types.

Linguistics

Chomsky viewed linguistics as one of the pillars of the symbolic approach. Language is believed to be represented and produced symbolically, so the brain is seen as working in the same way. While this does not necessarily follow, the claim is widely accepted, and today almost all work in linguistics is carried out in the symbolic paradigm. This conviction that language is, and can only be, symbolic is understandable given the way we seem to use language, and is supported by a long tradition in philosophy. For much of philosophy, language is a logical system operating on symbols, but this is not a universally held view. For example, the later work of Wittgenstein suggested a more flexible view of language use.

Despite the dominance of the symbolic view in this domain, connectionism has started to exert an influence on linguistics and psycholinguistics. The challenge to linguistics from connectionism can be illustrated by considering Rumelhart *et al.* (1986) model of past-tense formation of English verbs. This model spurned the linguistic approach of applying rules to words as symbols. Instead, past tense formation on a stem was seen as the result of statistical regularities in the behaviour of phonemes and phonemic features, a finer level of detail than allowed by linguistic theory. Representation was distributed across phonological units, rather than encoded symbolically in morphological units.

There have been three responses to the connectionist challenge: to reject connectionism; to embrace it as a complete paradigm for linguistics and psycholinguistics; and to accept it as a paradigm for psycholinguistics, but maintain a distinct symbolic theory of linguistics.

Connectionism Rejected

Under Chomsky's distinction between competence and performance, knowledge of competence is represented mentally. Thus linguistic competence is a part of cognitive Psychology, whilst linguistic performance is a part of psycholinguistics. Followers of this view reject the claim of connectionism that explicit rules are not represented mentally, and that they do no more than approximate the more detailed analyses of connectionist models. In the pure connectionist paradigm, there is no rule-based competence, and thus no linguistics at a level above psycholinguistics. Performance is the direct result of language processing mechanisms, and the only area needing to be studied. Thus linguistic rules lose their causal role in cognition. Many Chomskian psycholinguists reject this, and their objections are beginning to be shared by Chomskian linguists, who had previously ignored the connectionist challenge. They maintain that linguistic theory does indeed specify mental processes.

Connectionism Championed

Despite Chomskian claims that linguistic theory specifies mental processes, no attempt has been made within that framework to incorporate psychological data. They do not suggest a mechanism that results in performance not matching competence. A body of researchers now argues that we must consider psychological processing before we can suggest models of language use. A new programme of cognitive linguistics has been suggested which denies the autonomy of syntax suggested by Chomsky, and regards semantics as fundamental. Further, they reject semantic analysis in terms of propositions and truth conditions, and argue that grammar and meaning are grounded in knowledge and mental representations. For cognitive linguistics, language depends on the same processing mechanisms as other aspects of cognition, rather than being represented in a separate module. Reasoning and rule application are not the central processes of language understanding. Rather, understanding is based on extraction of prototypes and identification of metaphors. Linguistic expressions are solutions to multiple soft constraints. This point of view rejects linguistics, as currently understood, as being irrelevant – merely an abstraction of what is really happening. This programme wholeheartedly embraces connectionism as a tool for implementing theories. However, it is still a very new area. One example of work in this paradigm will be considered later.

A Compromise

The theories being suggested by cognitive linguistics can be seen as compressing linguistics and psycholinguistics into a single area that is strongly psycholinguistic. Some however accept the view that connectionist-type processes underpin psycholinguistics, but maintain that a separate theory of linguistics is needed, albeit watered down. Thus linguistic theories are abstractions that specify well-formed utterances within a language, but do not specify the nature of the psychological processes underpinning language use. Grammars, in this view, are descriptive rather than prescriptive. They provide a competence theory for those interested only in how people communicate, but also inform the construction of a performance theory, for example, by guiding the construction of connectionist models.

CONNECTIONISM AND COGNITIVE LINGUISTICS

In this section, we will consider Catherine Harris's discussion of connectionism and cognitive linguistics (in Sharkey 1992), which clearly describes the advantages of connectionism for language understanding, and also details a study which used a connectionist model to capture the many senses of the word 'over'.

The Cognitive Linguistics Agenda

Cognitive linguists reject the two central tenets of Chomskian linguistics, that language is in some way innate and special, and that linguistic knowledge is organized in a modular way in the brain. Rather, they assert that language is a product of the same cognitive processes that underlie other aspects of human performance. An extreme view is that all human cognitive processes depend on the mechanism of pattern processing, even though higher processes can be abstractly described to some degree of accuracy using symbolic models. A critical argument of cognitive linguistics is that language can only be understood by considering its relationship to the range of knowledge stored in the brain: encyclopaedic knowledge, mental models, the processes of concept mapping, and the use of soft constraints to integrate multiple sources of information. The cognitive linguistic approach seems to be particularly amenable to connectionist modelling.

The Concepts of Cognitive Linguistics

Cognitive linguists view language as a system for understanding communication, in which linguistic forms appear on a continuum of regularity, from the highly specific (and unproductive) forms of idioms, to the highly regularized and productive structures identified in a conventional grammar. All these forms, it is argued, should be handled using the same mechanism. A mechanism powerful enough to process idioms and exceptions to regularities should have no problem handling regular forms. Thus cognitive linguists reverse the focus of investigation. While Chomskian linguistics focuses on regular forms, and suggests extra exception handling mechanisms, cognitive linguistics emphasizes the important role irregularities play in communication. The search for such a holistic mechanism requires abandoning the hypotheses of autonomy of syntax and compositionality of semantics.

Schematicity

Forms of language can be described at varying levels of specificity. Single utterances, such as 'John kicked Mary', are very specific, while the general form 'NP V NP' is abstract, and infinitely productive. The latter is an instance of a schema: a description of a language form that can describe a number of utterances. Schemas (or pedantically, schemata) can be derived at various levels of abstraction. Chomskian linguists look at language in terms of a small number of levels of abstraction, and only consider schemas that fit these levels. Cognitive linguists argue that instead, schemas should be considered as the central representation, and that a given schema should be looked at using whatever level of abstraction is required to explain it. Thus an idiom, for example, 'not in a million', cannot be abstracted further, while a regular form can be considered in terms of an abstract structure, for example, 'NP V NP'. A cognitive linguistic mechanism will handle all schemas on the continuum of abstraction. Meaning, for cognitive linguists, is a culturally shared schema. Communicating meaning involves invoking in the audience the schema that the speaker has in mind. Misunderstandings occur when the wrong schema is invoked. Schema formation in the listener is viewed as being a process of extracting invariances in a set of words – a general cognitive ability that does not require innate structures.

Non-autonomy of Syntax

A cognitive grammar is specified as a pairing of utterances and their meanings, where meaning is viewed in the way noted above. Meaning schemas are fundamental to language. All forms have a conceptual basis, though it may be very abstract. In this view, there is no place for separate syntax, semantics and pragmatics: all are captured in a schema. Competence is now viewed as including the handling of irregular or idiosyncratic utterances, which for Chomskians are ignored as being merely aspects of performance. Indeed, cognitive linguistics does not allow for a separation between competence and performance. This may be sensible. If competence, in Chomskian terms, is encoded in structures in the brain, it is difficult to see a cause for widespread performance errors. An occasional error may be explained as a glitch in the system, but spontaneous speech often falls short of competence.

Non-compositionality of Semantics

Compositionality of semantics suggests that the meaning of an utterance is composed of the individual meanings of words. However, such an approach depends on identifying primitive features for words, which is only practicable for nouns and some verbs. Polysemy is also badly represented in such a view. Cognitive linguists, in contrast, see the meanings of words as specifying conditions for use, rather than giving inert features to be combined. Each word in a sentence has a number of different meanings, and thus a number of conditions of use. Utterances tend to have a single meaning. This single meaning is derived by a process of soft constraint satisfaction on the constraints specified by the meaning of words.

As an example of constraint satisfaction, consider the pair of sentences 'The plane flew over the mountain' and 'The hare flew over the mountain'. We understand different things by these two sentences. In the first, a literal sense of 'to fly' is invoked, and there is distance between the plane and the mountain. In the second, a metaphorical sense of 'to fly' is invoked, suggesting that the hare is running quickly, and is in contact with the mountain. This difference is explained in that each of the words in the sentence imposes constraints on its use. 'Flew' could be interpreted either literally or metaphorically, while 'over' has a range of slightly different meanings. The word 'plane' could be an aircraft, a tool for smoothing wood or a level geometric construct. Only the first sense is compatible with a known sense of 'flew' and 'mountain' – the most likely interpretation is of an aircraft in flight above a mountain. In 'The hare flew over the mountain', the constraints imposed by the word 'hare' suggest that a metaphorical interpretation of 'flew' is most likely, although of course the hare could be sitting in an aeroplane. As a further example, the sentence 'The plane flew over the plank', while odd, would suggest a most likely interpretation of a tool moving quickly over a piece of wood.

Such an approach to conceiving the meaning of words was pursued by Brugman, who analysed the polysemes of the word 'over' in terms of what constraints each polyseme imposed on its use. Which polyseme of over is invoked in a sentence depends on the relationship between the arguments of the preposition – what kind of nouns and verbs the preposition is acting on. Thus the meanings of the nouns and verb in the sentence are critical to determining which polyseme of the preposition to use. The meanings of nouns and verb specify constraints on the preposition: the resolution of these constraints specifies which schema the preposition induces.

Modelling Polysemy

A number of features of connectionist models appear appealing to the cognitive linguist, including prototype extraction, representation of rules and exceptions in the same mechanism, generalizing to new forms, and constraint satisfaction. Harris uses a connectionist model to learn form-meaning pairs for sentences using polysemes of 'over'. After training, generalization performance was checked, and found to be very good. Novel utterances were understood correctly, using a process comparable to analogy, a feature of sophisticated language use. Harris further analysed the representations formed within the network, by examining activation of hidden units for given inputs. Patterns of activation were identified that can be seen as giving constraints for words akin to those suggested by Brugman. These constraints can be seen in semantic terms. Despite the fact that no semantic input was given to the network, words with semantic similarities were grouped together, resulting in shared constraints between those words. Thus nouns specifying objects that fly provoke similar patterns of activation in hidden units. The network, in producing its own encodings of words on the basis of their context, seemed to be developing a representation of semantic meaning.

CONNECTIONISM AND MODELLING INTELLIGENCE

In this section we look more closely at the implications of connectionism for modelling intelligence. In part, this results in connectionism presenting a challenge to the prevailing functionalist philosophy of mind. This has been discussed in its own terms in the previous chapter. Here we look at an alternative view of mind based on connectionism. The central argument is that while some degree of intelligence can be modelled symbolically, symbolic systems have shortcomings that make it difficult to account for all aspects of intelligence. A sub-symbolic approach, on the other hand, may prove to be more successful at providing a complete view of mind and cognition.

Chapter 13 has already discussed the Turing test, as a test of machine intelligence, and John Searle's Chinese room argument. For Searle, a machine that passes the Turing test may be quantitatively equivalent to humans in intelligence, but they are qualitatively different – artificial intelligence is not the same as brain intelligence. Searle's view is that there is something special about the biological nature of the brain that gives rise to conscious experience. His argument has been supported by Penrose (1999) who suggests that consciousness arises from quantum events within the brain. That argument is beyond the scope of this chapter. Here we will concentrate on the limitations of symbolic systems, and alternative methods of modelling cognition.

Modelling an Intelligence Using a Symbol System

We start by briefly recapping the place of symbol systems in traditional AI. A symbol system is a logical system that uses symbols to instantiate a formal representation of the world, and a set of rules to manipulate these symbols. Such a system may receive input, in the form of symbols, and produce output, in the form of symbols. Symbols store knowledge, and knowledge is conceived of as being atomistic and reducible. Intelligence is seen as the use of a symbol system. In simple terms, 'good old fashioned AI' (GOFAI) sees the human brain as a computer running a particular program, and believes that if we can find the same (or an equivalent) computer program, then we will have an intelligence the equal of human intelligence. Newell and Simon hypothesized that the computer and the brain had a common functional description.

This belief is derived, we suggest, from the rationalistic tradition in western philosophy. The tradition of rationalism and logical empiricism can be traced back to Plato, and has been very effective in informing study in the physical sciences, and particularly in mathematics. It reached a peak in the philosophy of mind around the 1940s, when Wittgenstein, in his *Tractatus*, described the world in terms of a totality of facts that could be reduced to primitive objects, or atoms of thought. Wittgenstein believed the mind to represent these atoms and facts, and logical relations between them – in short, he viewed the mind as a symbol system.

Wittgenstein's views drew on previous work by Frege and Russell, and by Husserl. Husserl, termed the 'grandfather of AI' by Dreyfus and Dreyfus (1988), embarked on a project to identify the facts and atoms represented in the mind. He was joined on this enterprise by Heidegger, who soon decided that the project was unsound. Husserl was forced to agree with him at the age of seventy-five, when he described phenomenology as 'an infinite task'. Wittgenstein too changed his mind, abandoning rationalistic philosophy, and in his *Philosophical investigations* criticized both his own early work, and the work that had gone before it. Ironically, it was at this time that AI took on board the atomistic, rationalistic tradition, with workers like Minsky beginning their own phenomenology. In Fodor's language of thought hypothesis (Fodor 1975), the 'words' in the language are equivalent to atoms in previous phenomenologies.

The Intellectual Limitations of a Physical Symbol System

Recent attempts at a phenomenology for AI have had some limited successes, such as Winograd's SHRDLU system. In such systems, the domain of knowledge is strictly limited to that which can be represented in atomistic terms. There can be no doubt that symbol systems can display intelligence in these limited domains, but can the domains be slowly extended to encompass the breadth of human experience? Good old fashioned AI believes they can be, with more time and more research money, but there are good reasons to believe that this is not the case.

We have already mentioned one reason why GOFAI may be doomed: all previous efforts at phenomenology have proved to be unsuccessful. An alternative view is that human intelligence does not derive from a symbol system, and that no amount of looking for atoms of thought will succeed, since they do not exist. A second reason is that humans do not seem to behave like symbol systems. Dreyfus and Dreyfus (1988) analysed human expertise, and suggested five stages of skill acquisition:

Novice

Advanced beginner

Competent

Proficient

Expert

Now, GOFAI reduces all skill to the level of declarative knowledge – 'knowing that', rather than 'knowing how'. In Dreyfus and Dreyfus's analysis of skill acquisition, they found that only the first three levels could be characterized in this way. Proficient and expert performers used instead procedural knowledge, based on experience and recognition of similarities between a current problem and previously encountered problems. Competent performance is rational; proficiency is transitional, and experts act arationally. The expert recognizes thousands of special cases, appraised as wholes. The trouble with GOFAI is that there is no room for the non-analytic aspects of intelligence which are so important in human intelligence. There is no intuition and there is no experiential 'know how'. Briefly stated, symbol systems deduce, while expert humans induce. Interestingly, if an expert is asked how they perform, as in the verbal protocols used to verify symbolic models, they will tend to produce a list of rules to follow. However, if they actually follow these rules their performance tends to worsen – they no longer act as experts.

A final reason for doubting symbol systems is that they are inherently limited. As demonstrated by Gödel, rule systems are necessarily incomplete. Any rule system has statements in it that cannot be proven within the rule system. A meta system is necessary to cope with this. However, this meta system also requires a meta system, and so on. The result is an infinite regress of rules. The implications of this are discussed in Penrose (1999).

Modelling Human Intelligence Sub-symbolically

We have talked about the difference between 'knowing that' and 'knowing how'. Ryle saw knowing how as primary to human intelligence, providing a basis for thought that then allowed the luxury of knowing that. Early GOFAI systems knew that, but did not know how. The importance of knowing how has only slowly been addressed. GOFAI attempts at modelling procedural knowledge have involved converting propositional representations of declarative knowledge into rules, for example a set of steps that describe how to serve a tennis ball. We have seen though that expert human performance goes beyond such rules.

One of the many attractions of connectionist systems is that knowing how comes for free. When an input is applied to a connectionist network, it knows how to respond – knowing how is the basis of connectionist operation. In the connectionist paradigm, knowing that is a special case of knowing how, not vice versa, echoing Ryle. Related to this, knowledge in connectionist networks is not stored in symbolic form, but is encoded as a pattern of weights across the network. Such a representation is non-propositional, and sub-symbolic, and this seems to offer more flexibility in processing, and more human-like intelligence. Connectionist networks behave as Dreyfus and Dreyfus suggest proficient and expert humans behave – they recognize a situation, and know how to respond.

Beyond this, we have already seen that connectionist systems seem to have a number of features that are apparent in human cognition, including the satisfaction of soft constraints, graceful degradation, prototype formation, and generalization. In addition, connectionist models are ecologically economical. It may be possible to build rule-based systems that exhibit all these features, but they would need to go beyond straightforward rules, for example, by utilizing 'fuzzy' logic, or by weighting rules according to confidence levels. However, connectionist models show these features as inherent aspects of their operation. This can be taken as suggesting that the functionalist separation of 'hardware' and 'software' is misplaced, and that there are important effects of the hardware of the brain on the nature of human cognition.

CONNECTIONISM AND SYMBOLIC PROCESSING

Localist networks show that connectionist architectures can be used to do symbolic manipulation. Beyond this, however, distributed networks also show, at a level of abstraction, symbolic processing. At no point in a distributed network is a symbol instantiated directly, but in associating input and output such networks can be seen to be manipulating symbolic information. However, by decomposing the symbolic information into internally determined micro-features, distributed networks display a range of attractive properties. We looked at these, and saw that distributed networks showed neural plausibility, the satisfaction of multiple 'soft' constraints, graceful degradation, content addressable memory, and the capacity to learn from experience. Ellis and Humphreys (1999) suggest that satisfaction of multiple constraints, in particular, is a ubiquitous feature of human cognition, and very difficult to achieve using physical symbol systems. Such satisfaction is, however, a fundamental operating feature of connectionist models.

The ability of connectionist models to utilize regularities is akin to the use of rules. In connectionist systems, however, rules are not specifications to be followed in all circumstances, but rather probabilistic statements capturing the most likely behaviour of the network. In language, for instance, a network will learn that for most language use there are regular rules influencing how language is used. However, these rules can be 'broken', in that some forms of language do not show such rule-based behaviour. In connectionist models, the same mechanisms handle both regular and irregular processing. Again, such flexibility is difficult to achieve in symbolic systems. The important lesson here is that to the outside observer, a connectionist model will show symbolic, rule based behaviour in certain idealized circumstances, but such behaviour is a special case of more generalized underlying processing mechanisms. We can compare the observer of the behaviour of a connectionist model with the observer of a human using natural language. It seems as though language is a paradigmatic symbol system, but it may be, as cognitive linguists suggest, that underlying such apparent regularity are processing mechanisms that are common across cognition, and are based on the probabilistic satisfaction of soft constraints.

The observation that connectionist models can show the features of symbol systems, but also show more generalized probabilistic reasoning, and the fact that such features are an intrinsic feature of the processing architecture, or 'hardware', present a challenge to symbolic conceptions of cognition in at least two ways. First, they suggest that symbolic processing is a special case of cognition rather than its fundamental basis, and second they suggest that the separation of cognitive function from brain architecture is false. The cognitive linguistics programme in particular, in attempting to demonstrate that language is not symbolic, suggests that cognition needs to be recharacterized.

The argument presented here seems to support a form of materialism, and possibly the reduction of cognitive Psychology to neuropsychology. However, this is not our intention. Although the nature of cognition may be strongly influenced by the architecture of the brain, there is a need to explain cognition in its own terms, at a level above that of the processor. Using the analogy of the computer – only as an analogy, and without claiming that the brain is a computer – a piece of software is best understood, for a range of purposes, in terms of the functions it fulfils. Similarly, there is a need for cognitive Psychology to describe the form of information processing that humans produce, but recharacterizing this information processing in probabilistic, rather than rule based, terms. Pragmatically, this suggests a form of 'materialistic dualism', which recognizes the basis of cognition in the brain, but which also recognizes the need to describe cognition in its own right.

CONCLUSION

We began the chapter by outlining the basis of connectionism, as the modelling of networks of artificial neurones, and we discussed the differences between localist and distributed representations. Localist representations are more readily understood, but distributed representations display more flexible processing. In considering the implications of connectionism, we began by looking at connectionism as a paradigm for AI and cognitive Psychology, where the approach has already had some influence, but also looked at the role of connectionism in developmental Psychology and linguistics. In each of these, we saw that connectionist models had attractive features that suggested solutions to continuing issues in these fields. We continued the discussion of linguistics by looking at the approach of cognitive linguistics, which rejects the claim that language is mediated by separate and specialized brain systems, arguing instead that language uses the same mechanisms of satisfying soft constraints as other aspects of cognition. We saw that features of connectionist systems match the claims of cognitive linguistics for the nature of language processing. We then briefly compared symbolic and sub-symbolic approaches to modelling intelligence, seeing that symbolic systems have limitations in capturing the nature of human intelligence that can be overcome, to an extent, by modelling cognition in sub-symbolic terms. Finally, we considered the view that connectionist models can model symbolic processing at a certain level of abstraction, but that their underlying processing mechanism allows for a richer conception of cognition.

FURTHER READING

Bechtel, W. and Abrahamsen, A. 1991: *Connectionism and the mind*. Oxford: Blackwell.
Bechtel, W. and Graham, G. (eds) 1998: *A companion to cognitive science*. Oxford: Blackwell.
Clark, A. 1989: *Microcognition*. Cambridge MA: MIT Press.
Ellis, R. and Humphreys, G. 1999: *Connectionist psychology*. Hove: Psychology Press.
Graubard, S. (ed.) 1988: *The artificial intelligence debate*. Cambridge, MA: MIT Press.
Lakoff, G. 1987: *Women, fire and dangerous things*. Chicago: University of Chicago Press.
Penrose, R. 1999: *The emperor's new mind*. Oxford: Oxford University Press.
Sharkey, N. 1992: *Connectionist natural language processing: readings from connection science*. Oxford: Intellect.
Ungerer, F. and Schmid, H-J. 1996: *An introduction to cognitive linguistics*. London: Longman.

15

SOCIAL CONSTRUCTIONISM

Throughout this book we have used social constructionist arguments and critiques, and across most of the human sciences it is almost a given. However within Psychology, despite the availability of social constructionist discourses, this does not seem to apply. A personal example may help illustrate the point. Early in the summer of 2000 I was introduced, while in a pub, to a psychology graduate from a traditional university (it would be churlish to name it). My friends introduced me as a psychology graduate and this graduate's first question to me was what type of psychology I lectured in. My reply was social constructionist psychology and there then followed a lengthy conversation. I came away with the impression that they had never heard of social constructionism and what I did could not be psychology because I did not treat it as a natural science. Although we, as authors, assume that social constructionism has had an impact, in parts of the USA, the UK and Spain, on Psychology it may be that from within, so to speak, we overestimate this reaction.

In this chapter, we are going to examine social constructionism as it applies to Psychology. As we have made clear throughout this book our historical approach to Psychology belongs to that family of approaches that can be regarded as social constructionist, and as is also clear it is only within Psychology of the human and social sciences that there is a need for using the label of social constructionist. That is because elsewhere in the human and social sciences social constructionism is almost a given of disciplinary approaches.

In this chapter we will first consider what social constructionism consists of, as it is applied to Psychology and will draw on Burr's (1995) notion of family resemblance (what some AI orientated cognitive psychologists would call fuzzy sets). Then we will briefly review some of the previous approaches within Psychology that had social constructionist elements, before moving on to consider what historical contingencies led to the current social constructionist movement within Psychology and speculate on whether or not it is going to be any more successful than earlier approaches. Finally, we will consider the varieties of social constructionism that are available as resources for students and researchers.

It can be somewhat vexing to write about social constructionism within

Psychology as there is a realization that what we write is, of course, itself a social construction with its political, cultural, immediately contingent and pragmatic aspects. We also acknowledge that we cannot be aware of the impact of all of these forces upon us. Perhaps they are working subconsciously, and in any case it is probably best to read this in terms of its impacts than any intentions that we may state.

It can also be disturbing to read about social construction because although the authors who write about social constructionism no longer as natural scientists and many have given up writing in the third person, passive sentence style, there is still considerable terminological over-sophistication (or big words, Kemeny 1959) to wade through. We to some extent follow Burr here, in that we are using the label social constructionism for psychologists who may choose to label themselves as critical psychologists, discursive psychologists, postmodern psychologists, critical polytextualists and a variety of other labels not referred to here.

We will try to avoid the tendency to classify people in ways that they would not accept, but occasionally for the sake of clarity in writing we may do just that. We also acknowledge that for the majority of those that we label as social constructionist that would not be their primary self identification as psychologists, and some would wish to contest to some extent the idea that psychologist is a primary self-identification.

WHAT IS A SOCIAL CONSTRUCTIONIST PSYCHOLOGY?

Kenneth Gergen (1985) described four key assumptions that defined the social constructionist movement in modern psychology, which Burr uses as her starting point in describing the family resemblance between different psychologists. We will follow her approach here.

A Critical Stance Towards Taken-for-granted Knowledge

The critical here is quite definitely with a small 'c'. When taking a social constructionist approach there is a wariness about the view that we are able to obtain direct information about the world through unbiased observation. In terms of Psychology there is a considerable scepticism about treating the categories through which we understand people as 'natural' or 'pre-given'.

Historical and Cultural Specificity

The categories which are used when understanding people, the types of research questions asked, the methodologies employed, are all seen, to some extent, as historically and culturally specific. This of course applies to our ways of understanding the world now as to others ways of understanding the world now and then. To some extent the ways that we created and reproduce knowledge are grounded in particular social and economic processes and these have their own histories.

Knowledge is sustained through social processes

All knowledge is sustained through the myriad transactions that we have with people, social institutions and the (constructed) natural and social worlds. This is not a doctrine of 'anything goes' because what counts as justifiable and valid knowledge is a social process to which we may not have much access.

Knowledge and social action go together

As Danziger (1997) discusses, psychological categories have political dimensions because they are not only descriptive but they are also normative. The ways that we, as academic psychologists, categorize behaviour and experience becomes part of what Rose (which one) has described as the psy-complex, that mesh of the psychiatric, psychological and state within which things that we do are either normal, in need of self-help, psychological or medical intervention, or legal sanction. This, as Danziger suggests, may go even further. Our notions of what it is like to be a person may also be shaped by Psychology as well as other social institutions. It is very difficult to distance ourselves from the idea that we have quantifiable personalities, a level of intelligence falling somewhere on a bell curve, discrete attitudes to a variety of things because these are predominant discourses at this time and in this culture. So not only are the ways that we are constructed by others part of the way that knowledge and social action go together but also the ways that we construct ourselves, and of course in all this there is an issue of power, because not all constructions have, in this time and place, equal validity.

Different psychologists using social constructionism may differ to the extent that they prioritize these features of the family resemblance, but to some extent these are the features that distinguish social constructionists from the psychologists who construct themselves (and simultaneously are constructed) as natural science psychologists.

There are also distinctions between social constructionist psychologists and humanist psychologists, and social constructionist psychologists and psychoanalysts on the basis of these four features that are rarely found in these non-traditional approaches. The main one comes from the anti-essentialism of social constructionist approaches.

It is possible, on the basis of this notion of family resemblance, to review briefly some of the approaches within Psychology that could be described as social constructionist. None of these approaches is seen as an ancestor or a founder figure, however, because they had little, if any, direct impact on the current social constructionist psychology. Hopefully this is more than an exercise in historical imperialism or a Whiggish history and is more an invitation to reconsider the notion that some of the concerns of modern social constructionist psychologists have also been the concerns of other psychologists in the past, and to consider whether or not they had viable solutions to some of the problems that we face as social constructionist psychologists.

VÖLKERPSYCHOLOGIE AND BEYOND

It would probably be a mistake to overstate the case for Wündt's *Völkerpsychologie* being part of a heritage that led to psychological forms of social constructionism. For reasons discussed in Chapters 2 and 5 Wündt's collective psychology did not have a great impact, but still had some influence. Wündt in his *Völkerpsychologie* depicted minds, at least in their higher processes, as dependent upon society. However he did to some extent presuppose the existence of mind, which G.H. Mead criticized him for and which shows a demarcation between the work of Wündt and most modern social constructionists. He did however influence de Saussure, whose work on semiology is important in understanding linguistic construction and Durkheim, whose work on social representations was later taken up by Moscovici. G.H. Mead also influenced Blumer, the instigator of the sociological, social psychological approach social interactionism, and Vygotsky whose work on mind is often cited by social constructionists. It appears to be churlish to underestimate the influence that Wündt has had on this strand of psychology, and while Freud's influence on aspects of discourse analysis may be underestimated because of the hermeneutics of suspicion that have grown up around Freud, it is quite possible that Wündt's mythical status as the founder of experimental psychology may mean that he is overlooked in accounts of the precursors within Psychology to social constructionism.

Wündt also clearly bracketed off all but a few aspects of psychology as belonging to the *Geiteswissenschafenten* rather than the natural sciences, and while modern social constructionists may be wary of his limited natural science project it may be worth considering that even at its (mythical) outset Psychology was not constructed as just a natural science. Wündt was insistent that even his natural science project could not be reduced ultimately to physiology. Wündt was also insistent that theoretical questions needed to be considered before it was possible to create an applied discipline. Modern social constructionists are sometimes accused of writing too much about ontology and not with getting on with Psychology (for example, contextualism), and that may be because we do not consider that those theoretical questions have ever been fully explored by the discipline as a whole.

We have also discussed the work of G.H. Mead at some considerable length earlier in this book. In this context his work is not directly influential, as Billig (1987) cites him, if only to describe the difference between Billig's notion of 'taking the side of the other' and Mead's 'adopting the perspective of the other'. Elsewhere Mead, although he is co-opted by Samson as support for his dialogic approach, is an invisible figure in the writing of social constructionist psychologists. There is some indirect influence because sociologists working in the symbolic interactionist tradition influencing aspects of the social sciences take on social constructionism.

For Mead mind was a product of society, and language played a crucial role in the ways that minds were formed. His theory of the act, the notion that any act is a product of the immediate social environment as the actors react to the (constructed) reactions of others is reminiscent of the ways that Conversation Analysts write about Goffman's work. Finally that Mead also utilized comparative psychology may help in reminding us that we have (human) bodies with a variety of shapes and forms but with language as a species-specific attribute which means that human-made societies have a great impact upon our minds.

One of the things that Farr (1996) discusses is the way that Mead was potentially misunderstood by both psychologists and sociologists. As far as psychologists were concerned this was because of his critique of what he called Watsonism. He would not leave the philosophy department (and that is at least symbolic of not breaking from metaphysics) because a comparative approach was not in keeping with the potentially optimistic view that biological inheritance is unimportant. Sociologists possibly misunderstood him, as Farr suggests, because his critique of Watson was taken to be a critique of positivism in general whereas Mead was suggesting that a broadly biological approach could be used. While it may difficult for any of us for whom positivist is an insult, and in an intellectual environment where biological approach is almost synonymous with some form of genetic determinism to appreciate Mead's work may offer some avenues that are worth exploring today.

Vygotsky

Vygotsky's project was to develop a Psychology that was consistent with the writings of Karl Marx. Unlike some psychologists in the Soviet Union he did not attempt to do this by picking appropriate quotes from Marx and littering his work with them, but rather by considering how dialectic materialism could be applied to Psychology. Vygotsky's legacy has been somewhat confused, first because the initial translations of his work in the USA either ignored or obliterated the references to Marx and Marxism and second, because his work was thoroughly Marxian and at times in the Soviet Union, during Stalin's reign, that was seen as counter-revolutionary. Third, he is often regarded as a developmental psychologist, and his insights translated into the dominant cognitive paradigm within developmental psychology.

Bartlett

Bartlett, and ways that his work has been used, illustrate just how problematic it can be to use historical figures without enough sense of their positions. Bartlett has been hailed both as a proto-cognitive psychologist and a proto-social constructionist psychologist. His book *Remembering* (1932) has been interpreted in both ways. Bartlett, as Richards points out, originally had interests in both anthropology and psychology, but ended his career as the head of the experimental psychology department at Cambridge, which at that time was one of the most strident in a view of Psychology as natural science. Again, like the figures above there was no immediate impact of his social constructionist views on the ways that Psychology developed.

Summary

To some extent it is often rhetorically advantageous to package something as new. In the 1880s the new Psychology was represented as a revolutionary break from the past, and in this case the past was mental and moral philosophy. Of course, those who manufacture more mundane products, such as soap powder, toothpaste or shampoo have long used the idea that new brand is better than old brand. Acknowledging that there have been varieties of Psychology in the past that have consonance with social constructionism may mean that we have more difficulty in packaging it as a radical break from what has gone before. However, an understanding of why these approaches did not leave much of a legacy may provide resources for those who want to develop a Psychology that utilizes some aspects of social constructionism.

With Wündt we have discussed at some length in previous chapters his lack of impact, within Psychology. This was partly because his later work was not translated into English, and his splitting of Psychology between natural and human sciences in part led to his repudiation both in his native Germany and in the USA. Mead published little during his lifetime and at the end of his life was the head of a philosophy department. This outsider status, especially as a head of philosophy at a time when many psychologists announced that they had left metaphysics behind, probably contributed to his lack of impact. Although, somewhat paradoxically, he is often credited within sociology as being the founder of symbolic interactionism, the name that he used for the approach that he developed by removing from Mead's work the idea that human beings could be understood scientifically. Vygotsky was isolated by global politics and although he has been (re)discovered mainstream developmental textbooks conceptually translate his work to be consistent with the dominant cognitive paradigm. Bartlett, heralded in the 1970s as a proto-cognitivist was heralded in the 1990s as a proto-social constructionist. Richards (1996) suggests that his position as head of the experimental psychology department at Cambridge, and the lack of cross fertilization between the two disciplines that Bartlett combined earlier in his career (anthropology and psychology), meant that he did not develop his social constructionism further.

With two of these figures (Bartlett and Mead) part of the reason why their work was not developed further was because the interdisciplinary alliances which were part of it later dissolved. With all of them, Vygotsky as a partial exception, the work that they did was out of step with the self-construction that Psychology has as a certain type of natural science. Richards suggests that part of the reason why Psychology developed as something analogous to natural science is that scientific reason was a dominant (although never uncontested) theme of the late nineteenth and twentieth centuries. In the arena of producing work constructed as useful by policy makers this remains a powerful force. Social constructionist explanations tend to be (necessarily) complex and we have not yet won the (political) battles for these to be seen as more acceptable than other arguments. With some varieties of social constructionist work within psychology we may be explicitly denying ourselves the possibility of ever winning such political battles.

It may be a cliché, but one reason for understanding the history of Psychology is so that we do not make the same mistakes as our predecessors.

The Crisis in Social Psychology

Many accounts of the way that social constructionism came into psychology begin with the crisis in social Psychology. In Chapter 7 we discussed the history of social Psychology up until the end of World War Two. At that time many of the main research programmes of social Psychology had been established during the War and the issues that social psychologists researched were often of direct relevance to the US and UK governments. Before the crisis, experimental social Psychology had what is sometimes called its golden age. Research programmes which had been developed to answer fairly specific applied questions began to investigate more variables, often in a laboratory-based environment. Meanwhile the social scene in the USA was slowly changing. By the late 1960s and early 1970s the civil rights movement and second-wave feminism were having an impact on US society. Then as the Vietnam War continued there was a wave of protest at the continued involvement of the USA. Social Psychology was seen as curiously disengaged from these issues (although as Richards shows with regard to racism that is not the whole story), and the liberal left generation of postwar psychologists became increasingly uneasy at the identification of Psychology with the state.

The crisis identified in many accounts was a crisis at many levels, the methodological, with Harré's (1974) ethogenic attack on mainstream methods and the ways that the principal models of humans removed the agency of people (Shotter 1975). Whether natural science was the appropriate metaphysical approach (for example, Kenneth Gergen's 1975 call to adopt a historical perspective) and the attendant problems of a natural science approach. This may have led to the links between psychology and other disciplines being rediscovered, and thus influences from areas such as sociology, social theory, psychoanalysis and linguistic philosophy enriched debate about social Psychology. However, despite the fact that many of the individual critics remained active the nascent momentum did not lead to any major alternative movements. Ethnogenics, for example, did not become a research tradition within social Psychology.

Today experimental social Psychology textbooks talk of the crisis in social Psychology as something that was resolved by social Psychology becoming more orientated to problems in modern society, and developing (quantitative) non- laboratory based methodologies. In addition, they tend to highlight the ways that ethical sensitivity has increased in social Psychology. This strategy, ignoring the social issues that led to the crisis, was successful in its time as the experimental mainstream was effectively unchallenged by the crisis.

Influences From Outside

The 'turn to the text' marked the probable beginning of social constructionist psychologies and this appears to have been (or can be knowledged as being) heavily influenced by a number of academic trends from outside Psychology. There are a number of accounts given of these influences else- where and so we shall only briefly summarize them, focusing first on devel- opments in linguistic theory, then on the work of Foucault and finally considering situationism and postmodernism. In this we are omitting a lot, ethnomethodology, the sociology of scientific knowledge, Wittgenstein's philosophy and Derrida's deconstruction (to name the most important omis- sions). This is because we want to tell more of a political and cultural story than an academic and intellectual story.

While Psychology developed behaviouristic and cognitivistic approaches to language, there developed outside Psychology an altogether different approach to language. Semiotics (sometimes called semiology) is the major structuralist account of language outside cognitive psycholinguistics. There is some dispute as to whether semiotics is a sub-branch of linguistics, or lin- guistics a sub-branch of semiotics.

Semiotics and meaning

A good way to introduce this is to look briefly at how semiotics handles meaning. It is a slight, but only a slight, over simplification to say that mean- ing within psycholinguistics (the study of meaning) is associated with the study of word meaning. The idea here is that the word represents things in the world (including things in our heads), and that we use words to build sentences. This can be summarized as:

SYMBOL (word) = THING

In contrast to this there are two moves that are commonly made. The first is to point out that in everyday conversation meaning becomes an 'issue' when there is some type of breakdown in an interaction. The second is that the problem simply cannot be as simple as that, even if we allow a cognitive get out clause.

Frawley (1992) defines semiotics as the discipline that studies all meaning- ful (human) signal exchange. This includes culture, as sets of rules for accept- able behaviour, talk, text, the visual media, and literature and art as conventionalized aesthetic meaning. The study of meaning becomes the study of the process of signification. The nature of the signs themselves is, or can be, somewhat tributary.

Frawley (1992) provides a fairly succinct semiotic definition of meaning:

> To say that something has meaning is to say that it is a *sign*, a composite unit consisting of a relation between an overt signal, called the *signifier*, and

the information that this overt signal evokes, called the *signified*. The signifier, signified and the relation make up the sign, Sign = Signifier/Signified.

De Saussure developed his general science of signs at the turn of the century, which was published in English in 1974, and his main target was the idea that words derive their meaning by standing for things in the world.

> Everything that has been said up to this point boils down to this: in language there are only differences. Even more important: a difference generally implies positive terms between which the difference is set up; but in language there are only differences without positive terms.
>
> (de Saussure1974: 120)

De Saussure's argument is that we cannot understand descriptive language of any kind through a consideration of just the words that have been uttered, written down or whatever. Semiology is primarily concerned with understanding what is present by understanding what is absent. You need to understand the underlying system that gives the words their full sense, and this system is only realized through the whole set of possible utterances. For de Saussure the aim of semiotics is to elucidate the underlying system of differences that gives sense to any domain of meaning, whether it is language, architecture or road signs. One of the problems of structuralism was its avowedly ahistorical approach. Within a structuralist semiotics it is not possible to ask questions about how words change their meanings, or why some terms are evaluated more favourably than others.

Post-structuralist linguistic theory makes the argument that meanings are never fixed, but are always contestable and so open to question. To some extent it tries to add to semiotics by adding a historical and political dimension, unlike postmodernism which can be claimed to make a distinctive break with modernism. Post-structuralism is an addition to structuralism not a decisive break with it.

Foucault, who denied that he was a post-structuralist (possibly because of unease with the structuralist roots that would imply), is often portrayed as one. Certainly the notions of Foucault have been taken up by (some) social constructionist psychologists because they allow for an analysis of power and subjectivity. The usefulness, or otherwise, of Foucault's work is hotly contested within the disciplines of history and sociology and here we limit our discussion to the ways that his work has been appropriated by social constructionist psychologists.

Summary

While these disparate areas have not, and probably never could be, welded into one approach, social constructionist work within psychology may show features of some of them. All of these areas have their own contestations in disciplines other than psychology and sometimes it can be very frustrating for undergraduate students who find that they need to learn another set of discourses beyond those of psychology in order to employ these notions with any confidence. Using resources such as this may be necessary as the mainstream of psychology has lost (if it ever had) its own language to deal with the social. However there is much more to this account than a tracing of intellectual changes within philosophy, social theory and sociology, as we attempt to explain in the next section.

The Influence of Feminist Psychology

If changes in Psychology are, as Danziger suggests, also political changes, then it would not be too unexpected that in order to change Psychology political battles will be fought. To some extent, as Richards suggests, the nature of Psychology changes as the constituency of psychologists change. However, as the political battles continue to be fought by feminists, Black psychologists and gay, lesbian and bisexual psychologists, such changes do not just happen. They only happen because of these political battles. In examining the way that social constructionism has come into the discipline in this section we shall argue that feminist Psychology, and of course feminist psychologists who fought for recognition both nationally in the APA and the BPS and locally within universities, created a conceptual space which was exploited by social constructionists.

Not all feminist psychologists are social constructionists, and those that are to some extent tend to be ambivalent about it, because of the possible relativistic morass whereby all discourses are seen as equally constructed and so there is no way to argue that one discourse is better than another.

VARIETIES OF SOCIAL CONSTRUCTIONISM IN PSYCHOLOGY

Throughout this chapter we have made it clear that there are different ways psychologists employ social constructionism within their Psychology. It is tempting at this point to write of schools of social constructionism, but much like the historical discourse on early schools to do so would be to possibly oversimplify the variety of social constructionist work. It would also be tempting to divide the various forms of social constructionism along a single dimension. So, for example, Kurt Danziger (1997) divided social constructionism into 'light' and 'dark' forms. The light form was the work and theorizing derived from speech act theory with ethnomethodology and deconstruction, being more concerned with language than other social practices, and tending to be practised by those with an interest in discursive psychology and conversation analysis. The dark form tended to be derived more from the work of Foucault and concentrating on investigating other social practices as well as language (although acknowledging that it needs to use language to do this) and having more interest in issues of power and subjectivity. Erica Burman (1999) resists this classification because of its inflections of Enlightenment discourse, and because such visual descriptions evoke a response against a long history of colonialism and racism. However others appear to enjoy the descriptions, perhaps because dark evokes responses that have to do with the mysterious and the occult, whereas light has synonyms that include unsubstantial and frivolous. The realism-relativism debate, which Derek Edwards redescribes as a division between ontological and epistemological constructionism tends to over polarize the positions, which we attempt to explain below. A similar division between soft and hard forms of social constructionism would have some overlap with dark (soft) and light (hard) as softer forms of constructionism admit some level of realism here. However, the evaluative poles may be at the opposite ends to the dark and light division. Ian Burkitt (1999), writing in the same volume as Burman, suggests a blending of the dark and light versions of social constructionism which he claims may also rescue social constructionism from the dualism between the social and the material that sometimes affects social constructionist writing. Mike Michael (1999) also writing in the same volume suggests that it may be fruitful to follow the feminist analysis of Hilary Rose (1993) that the either/or antagonism between constructionism and realism is itself a product of patriarchal preferences, with academic debate becoming some form of argument with a winner and loser rather than a discussion, and that it is possible to replace either/or with both/and. While we admit that our form of social constructionism when doing history of psychology has more in common with critical realism, within this section we will attempt to describe not two competing camps but rather a fairly complex clustering of positions.

IS THERE A LIMIT TO SOCIAL CONSTRUCTIONISM?

In the first chapter we discussed critical realism as an approach to the philosophy of science in the natural sciences. Although we think that, because of the nasty reflexive twist within Psychology, it is not fully appropriate as a philosophy of science. For historians of Psychology it may have a role as a philosophy of knowledge for psychologists. In brief, and we have explained this in some depth in Chapter 1, critical realism assumes that the products of science are human constructions. However these constructions interact with a transfactual real world. The transfactual real exists independently of the scientists who are attempting to create theories. While this transfactual realm is never fully knowable it has an effect upon the scientific theories that are developed, which however imprecisely need some features that successfully explain aspects of the transfactual. Turning to Psychology, critical realism can be used to provide a limit to social constructionism. Some things are real, independent of our actions. The debate here is twofold. Is there anything that we should take as not constructed and if there is how does this affect our Psychology? There are a number of takes on these issues.

One is the position taken by Potter (1996: 41) in his book *Representing reality*:

> In this book the consequences of a strong notion of rhetoric will be explored where nothing (the data, the sides in the controversy, the text I am currently writing) is excluded a priori from being considered as a rhetorical construction.

One is the position taken by a number of authors in the booked edited by Nightingale and Cromby (1999) *Social constructionism psychology* that some of these consequences, which Potter does not explore, include the inadequate consideration of issues such as embodiment, materiality and power.

Another is the position that some feminist psychologists hold (for example, Wilkinson 1997) that while they will strategically use social constructionist arguments they will also use essentialist arguments, or neither, when it suits their political purposes.

Yet another is the critical relativism described by Curt (1994) and two of her component parts (W. Stanton Rodgers and R. Stanton Rodgers 1997). This is a complex position and not open to simple summary, although the quote below gives quite a good feel for the general tenor of the argument:

> The opposition to 'critical realism' is not mere 'relativism' but '*critical* relativism'. It is not a position in which 'everything goes' but one in which 'nothing goes' (Sawicki 1991) – where all discourses must be made open to critical challenge, including our own (and others') moral and ideological readings. Thus while we *risk* a criticality that perturbs foundation, we do not read into it the same sense of *hazard* (or 'danger') that critical realists detect. Our argument is that we are aware of the traps of naïve relativism and the enchantments of carnivalism – and have adopted a more manifold working of concern to counter them.
>
> (Stanton Rodgers and Stanton Rodgers 1997: 71–2, italics in the original)

Those who adopt this position do not deny their political concerns and do not focus so much upon linguistic construction as may happen with Potter's position, especially when participants' concerns are represented as the only allowable level of analysis.

Thus some readings of social constructionism will explicitly set boundaries and a level of realism. The reason for this is the possibility of a relativistic morass in which no argument is possible because all positions are mere constructions, none with more force than another. This reading is consistent with some postmodern positions that have given up on trying to effect political change because of the power of the (capitalist) system to recuperate and make safe all revolution. It is also the charge levelled at (especially) Edwards, Ashmore and Potter in relation to their treatment of the 'death and furniture' argument.

We will not attempt to close the argument here, although as we have made clear we find the position of Curt amenable when we 'do' social Psychology, and a form of critical realism amenable when we 'do' history. We have also talked about the usefulness of using quantitative methods, despite the pull towards essentialism, when we are doing other things with our academic work. It may be that these debates, which can be very difficult to follow for readers new to the field, are a part of what keeps social constructionism from being easily recuperated back into the mainstream of psychology. Despite the frustration that they occasion, if that is true, long may they continue.

Recuperating Social Constructionism

Social constructionism, as a form of Psychology, is more successful than some other historical alternatives and part of the reason for this is that PhD students are learning both the techniques of and the philosophies and metaphysics behind those techniques; thus new generations of social constructionist psychologists can emerge. It is also having an impact in applied areas of psychology, and while social constructionist applied psychologists are very much in the minority there are some reasons for optimism that the impact may broaden. That applied psychology has, historically, been the domain where both theoretical and methodological innovation have entered the discipline (making the applied-pure dichotomy appear somewhat false) it may be that the task of further expanding social constructionist psychology's application may be important. However this is not the first time that alternatives to the experimental and quantitative mainstream psychology have emerged and the discipline retains that as part of its official description. In this section we will briefly review the threats to social constructionism.

Method as Theory

The major threat is that the relatively new (to Psychology) methods used by social constructionists, in particular discourse and conversation analysis, will come to be seen as just methods. In the UK at least qualitative methods, following the examples in the text by Bannister *et al.* (1995), are being taught on Psychology research methods courses. Thus, for example, Curt (or rather the authors who make up Curt) resisted the idea of writing a book just about Q methodology because that the product would not capture the multiple complexities that surround their use of Q methodology with a critical relativist framework. Burman and Parker (1993) make clear their unease that discourse analysis will become just another method without a framework, thus increasing the possibility that interview transcripts and the results of analysis will become reified.

One of the problems is that methods are often taught just as a 'given'. There is little attempt to show that methods have a history and an (often) implicit metaphysics, and if qualitative methods were taught in a similar way they too would become just alternative ways of doing mainstream psychology. Although it is not often made explicit, the argument that social constructionists should just get on with doing Psychology and let the data decide, if the approach is fruitful, is one that we feel that many mainstream psychologists would endorse. At the same time it would probably lead to all the critical bite being lost and herald the end of social constructionism (in whatever variety) as an alternative to quantitative and experimental Psychology.

Marginalization

The apparently liberal eclecticism of Psychology (which we have questioned in Chapter 9) could be welcoming for alternative approaches. However it is far more likely that the limited eclecticism (eclectic as long as people are willing to use variable talk) will result in departments having 'a social constructionist' with a small range of courses to teach.

Psychology as Science

There is, at least in the UK with direct government funding, a price to pay for a Psychology that takes social constructionism seriously, for then it would be somewhat difficult to argue that Psychology departments should receive the same level of funding as the natural sciences.

CHAPTER SUMMARY

Whether or not social constructionist psychology continues to have an impact within Psychology, whether it is recuperated back into the mainstream, or whether it becomes the new status quo against which a new generation of critical psychologists react, are questions that can only be left to historians of the future. What we have attempted to show in this chapter is that in its current incarnation social constructionist psychology has come into existence against a backdrop of cultural and historical particularities and contingencies. In keeping with the notion that changes in psychology are also political changes, we have attempted to show that for social constructionism to happen there have to have been political struggles, although these have not necessarily been instigated by constructionists. We have attempted to acknowledge the influence of feminist psychology, and the wider struggles of feminism, and hopefully have done this in a way that does not just recuperate feminism for the purposes of our argument. We considered the varieties of social constructionism and briefly considered the apparent major theoretical arguments within social constructionism and critical psychology. Finally we considered possible threats to social constructionist psychology. All of this has been done against an acknowledgement that we welcome many of the changes to Psychology that taking social constructionism seriously would entail. When Boring wrote his *History of experimental psychology* (1950) he did so in part to justify an independent discipline of Psychology. In writing this chapter, and this textbook, we do so in part to justify a Psychology that is more fully part of the human and social sciences.

CONCLUSION

One of the intriguing things about Psychology is its reflexive nature, and in this context we are referring to the way that Psychology affects psychology. Although it needs to be acknowledged that it is not the only impact upon psychology, we would need to understand no more than the history of the discipline to understand psychology. If social constructionist Psychology does have an impact at that level (which will inevitably be a political as well as an academic move) the affects upon psychology could be very confusing. What would a conversation analysis of someone who self-consciously utilizes rhetorical features and acknowledges their use look like? What would a discourse analyst do with a discourse full of participants talking about their subject positions and acknowledging their use of discourses? Such changes if they were to happen probably would not happen quickly, and would possibly signal a wider change in the individualistic societies that Psychology inhabits than can be imagined.

FURTHER READING

Banister, P., Burman, E., Parker, I., Taylor, M. and Tindall, C. 1995: *Qualitative methods in psychology*. Buckingham: Open University Press.

Billig, M. 1987: *Arguing and thinking: a rhetorical approach to social psychology*. Cambridge: Cambridge University Press.

Billig, M. 1991: *Ideology and opinions*. London: Sage.

Burr, V. 1995: *An introduction to social constructionism*. London: Routledge.

Capaldi, E.J. and Proctor, R.W. 1999: *Contextualism in psychological research? A critical review*. London: Sage.

Crawford, M. 1995: *Talking difference: on gender and language*. London: Sage.

Curt, B.C. 1994: *Textuality and tectonics: troubling social and psychological science*. Buckingham: The Open University Press.

Danziger, K. 1997: *Naming the mind: how psychology found its language*. London: Sage.

Farr, R. 1996: *The roots of modern social psychology*. Oxford: Blackwell.

Frawley, W. 1992: *Linguistic semantics*. Hove: Lawrence Erlbaum Associates.

Gergen, K.J. 1975: Psychology as history. *Journal of Personality and Social Psychology* 26: 309–20.

Gergen, K.J. 1985: Social constructionist inquiry: context and implications. In: K.J. Gergen and K.E. Davis (eds) *The social construction of the person*. New York: Springer-Verlag.

Harré, R. 1974: Blueprint for a new science. In: N. Armitead (ed) *Reconstructing social psychology*. Harmondsworth: Pelican.

Ibanez, T. and Iniguez, L. (eds) 1997: *Critical social psychology*. London: Sage.

Kitzinger, C. 1995: *The social contraction of lesbianism*. London: Sage.

Micheal, M. 1996: *Constructing identities*. London, Sage.

Nightingale, D.J. and Cromby, J. (eds) 1999: *Social constructionism psychology*. Buckingham: The Open University Press.

Plant, S. 1992: *The most radical gesture*. London: Routledge.

Potter, J. 1996: *Representing reality*. London: Sage.

Rose, H. 1993: Rhetoric, feminism and scientific knowledge: Or from either/or to both/and. In: R.H. Roberts and J.M.M. Godd (eds), *The recovery of rhetoric*. Charlottesville: University Press of Virginia.

Sawicki, J. 1991: *Disciplining Foucault*. New York: Routledge.

Shotter, J. 1975: *Images of man in psychological research*. London: Methuen.

Wilkinson, S. 1997: Prioritizing the political: feminist psychology. In: T. Ibanez and L. Iniguez (eds) *Critical Social Psychology I*. London: Sage.

CONCLUSIONS

We have written this textbook in an attempt to make the insights of critical historians of Psychology more accessible to students and practitioners of Psychology. It was not an attempt to write a full history of Psychology from a critical position, not least because we wanted to show how the positions that we adopt can be utilized in understanding current issues in Psychology, but also because of our own strengths and interests, with Dai having strengths in cognitive psychology while Jonathan pursues interests in social psychology.

We are, of course, aware of the argumentative context of this book, an ongoing argument about what Psychology is and what Psychology should be. We have argued consistently that Psychology should not be regarded as a natural science, and we will summarize those arguments here. We have, however, also argued that that does not mean that we should abandon quantitative methods, although we do believe that those methods should be combined with some critical understanding of what it means, both to investigate isolated psychological functions and to attempt to explain psychological functions on the basis of aggregate data.

In this final chapter we also intend to suggest ways that individuals could utilize the arguments that we present in their own work. Although we fall far short of attempting to proscribe the way that psychological research should be conducted, psychological theory be written and psychological interventions be carried out. In the first section of this conclusion we shall briefly review what we have done.

REVIEW

In the Introduction and Chapter 1 we attempted to make our approach clear, the notion that a historical approach can be used as a way of understanding current theories within Psychology, and the idea that we cannot treat Psychology as a natural science were explored.

We then examined a number of instances from the history of Psychology. The work of Wündt was considered. It has become a psychological fact for most psychologists that Wündt is the founder of the discipline, we explored

272 HISTORY AND THEORIES OF PSYCHOLOGY

why this myth may have endured and what its purpose may have been. We also considered, through exploration of Wündt's social psychology what legacies he may have had outside of Psychology and how some of his ideas, modified by a hundred years of scholarship, can be found within the approach we label as social constructionism. In addition, we considered the nexus of social and cultural forces that coalesced to make a science-like discipline of Psychology viable towards the end of the nineteenth century.

We then considered the forms of Psychology that prospered as the centre of gravity for Psychology switched from Europe to the USA. We discussed how the notion of schools of Psychology helped to preserve a continuity across a fledgling discipline where much, the underlying metaphysics, the most suitable methodological approaches and what should be studied, was in dispute. This led to a discussion of how the application of Psychology was, perhaps paradoxically, a powerful impetus to the methodology and broad theoretical approaches adopted by Psychologists. Curiously Psychology as a discipline has been application driven, although subtle re-presentation often suggests that in Psychology, like the natural sciences, theory drives application.

We also considered a number of specific developments. The ways in which psychoanalysis and Psychology overlapped, with ultimately psychologists claiming that we, being scientists, should be the ultimate arbiters of the correct approach, while at the same time adapting many psychoanalytic ideas to fit into scientific Psychology. Within the sub-disciplines of social Psychology and cognitive Psychology we considered the many contingencies that led to the ways that they were shaped, with not least amongst these being the funding given to Psychologists by the military and over agencies of government to solve specific problems on their behalf.

The first eight chapters of the book formed the distinctly historical component of the book, and although we did speculate on how some of these historical contingencies have left enduring legacies on the shape of Psychology, we somewhat self-consciously left our considerations of modern psychology to Chapter 9 and beyond.

Chapter 9 considered specifically race and racism, together with gender and sexism within Psychology, and led from consideration of the past to consideration of the present. While there may no longer be a sub-discipline of Psychology entitled race Psychology we still have to face the racism that exists within the discipline. However consideration of this topic demonstrates just how complex the relationships between Psychology and its host societies can be, with race Psychology acting to some extent as an arena in which psychologists could question, and ultimately reject, the arguments of scientific racism. With gender the issues are even less resolved, although there are powerful arguments against simple minded gender difference research. Such research continues, perhaps because of the availability of another independent variable to make our statistical procedures more complex. Feminist Psychology, as a political force, was considered, along with some of the difficulties of promoting political change within a discipline that still represents an objective science.

With Chapter 10 we took a somewhat parochial look at the role of Psychology in a UK context. We considered how the syllabuses of degrees, to some extent regulated by the British Psychological Society, helps to buttress the claim of Psychology as a science as well as aspects apart from the syllabus that help to maintain that position. We considered Psychology the science in relation to some aspects of psychology the institution, and how in wider society we, as psychologists, strive to retain our scientific credentials, often by attacking enterprises such as 'pop psychology' for not being scientific enough.

We then considered folk and everyday psychology including the role of popular psychology, and their relationship to Psychology. In examining folk psychology we saw how current cognitive concerns mirror the investigation of folk understanding of scientific debate disciplines. Unfortunately this approach has tended to get bogged down into discussions of how scientific folk understandings of Psychology are, or can be, and philosophical discussions which given that Psychology is a science debate whether folk understandings should be replaced or augmented. In keeping with the approach that we have followed throughout this book that Psychology is a discipline that alters its subject matter through the knowledge it generates we feel that the cognitive approach to folk psychology will in principle fail and in practice has led to a failure to recognize the multiple roles that folk psychology plays. Our approach to everyday psychology is one in which it is regarded as a set of discourses that people use. These discourses are public phenomena and the key idea is that these discourses are not mere reflections of underlying cognitive processes but rather part of a discursive system. This discursive system has been formed by many contributions, Psychology only being one of them. Nevertheless, for many people, the discursive system whereby they have attitudes, motivation and motives, intelligence, and the various other formulations from Psychology, is one that is inescapable as they understand their own subjectivity and the reasons why they and others act in the ways that they do. However the majority of mainstream Psychology has paid little attention to this part of people's psychology thus leaving a gap for popular psychology. While many academic psychologists abhor popular psychology to a large extent it is our neglect of lay psychology, and wrapped up with this our general disregard of 'giving psychology to the people', that gives popular psychology its space in bookshops and people's lives.

In the latter quarter of the book we considered some current issues within Psychology, methodological issues, arguments within cognitive Psychology, discussions of whether connectionism is a new form of cognitivism and the rise of social constructionism. With each of these we attempted to show how these current debates are influenced by both by current concerns as well as historical legacies. Within these chapters it is clear what our preferences are. If we are to continue to use quantitative methodologies we need to do so in a much more transparent way rather than just representing them as a scientific necessity. If it is plausible to talk of cognitive structures then we need to consider carefully how we model these, with 'black box' cognitive psychology the less viable alternative. Finally we considered the potential impact of social constructionism, and acknowledged the role of feminist Psychology in making that, limited, impact viable.

PSYCHOLOGY AS A SCIENCE

One of the overwhelming messages of this book has been that we do not see Psychology as a natural science. We are not, however, proposing a wholesale abandoning of quantitative methods and it is worth re-presenting our arguments again here, along with our, very speculative, alternatives. Some psychological phenomena, especially those that can be labelled 'psycho-physics' are probably best investigated utilizing laboratory techniques, and it is in studies of these phenomena that investigative practices similar to those used by Wündt still continue. Some applications of Psychology, where there are groups of people who are exposed to different interventions, akin to the randomized placebo control group trials in medicine, are probably best investigated using what has become the standard investigative practice across the whole of Psychology. Elsewhere there is a need for systematic, critical, methodological eclecticism. During the course of this book we have demonstrated that while Psychology continues to have an eclecticism towards theory, it is a discipline that has adopted a monoculture with regard to method. Whatever the methodology chosen we firmly believe that allied to it should be a critical approach to the psychological phenomena being studied. This would allow for an understanding of the cultural role of the phenomena and may help us, as psychologists, to understand psychological phenomena without excessive individualizing.

Possible Futures

Of course speculation about the future is much more the role of the science fiction author than the textbook author. In the context of this book such speculation has to be written within a framework of, 'it all depends upon future social trends'. However, there do appear to be a number of possibilities that are close, each of which draws upon differing views of the role of psychology.

Potential Splits

There have always been fault lines within Psychology and it has survived for over a hundred years as an apparently unified discipline despite of these. However there does seem to be some potential for splits developing within the discipline.

Cognitive Science versus Social Science

In both the USA and the UK there have been some institutions where the cognitive aspects of psychology have joined natural science faculties while the rest of psychology has joined social science faculties. Part of the reason for this is the recent interest in the multidisciplinary discipline of cognitive science. This leads to a potential disengagement between the various current sub-disciplines of Psychology, which we believe will ultimately impoverish Psychology.

Psychology versus Psychological Studies

Within the UK there has recently been a rise in the number of undergraduate courses with titles such as psychological studies. Often these degrees do not carry full British Psychological Society recognition. We suspect that this may reflect ongoing concerns with keeping the image of Psychology as a natural science untarnished. As we discussed in Chapter 10 we believe that these concerns may act as a brake on future critical developments within Psychology, moving from a marginalization of critical voices to a rejection of critics who may find themselves not just outside the mainstream of Psychology but in fact outside of the discipline altogether. Given our critical historical position we find this trend worrying.

Academic Psychology versus Professional Psychology

This has been almost a perennial concern within Psychology, and in different countries there have been different solutions to the tensions between the academic aspects of the discipline and the professional aspects of the discipline. Within the UK the trend towards three-year taught doctoral programmes, first in clinical psychology but also beginning in educational psychology, may make a divorce between these two aspects of Psychology easier. The worrying aspect of this is, again, the disengagement that would result.

OUR VISION OF PSYCHOLOGY

Finally, we probably owe our readers an explanation of what our vision for Psychology may be. To some extent this is a compromise between both our hopes and we are aware of the balance between stating blandishments and being overly prescriptive.

An Engaged Psychology

We believe that Psychology, as an academic discipline as well as a profession, should be a discipline actively engaged in the societies that it is within. We believe that such an engagement would encourage psychologists to have a more thorough understanding of how psychological phenomena relate to larger societal issues. We also believe that it would be beneficial if more academic and professional psychologists wrote about the issues that are important to people and in a language that they can understand. It has been a long time since Miller, the APA President, urged that Psychology should be given away to the people. An engaged Psychology ought to be able to do that.

A Critical Psychology

Coming from this interest in engagement is a need to be critical, and at times critical. As we hope to have demonstrated, changes in psychological discourses are political changes. Psychology in this sense remains a moral science, and we as psychologists need to show some sensitivity towards the moral outcomes of our models of people.

We want Psychology to remain scholarly and systematic but to recognize that it is not a natural science. This may, in the short term, cause us some problems as part of our moral authority has come from the rhetoric of science but we believe that it will open up more possibilities to us as psychologists than the alternative.

We believe that there can be no final words on Psychology for as people change so does their psychology; as psychology changes so does Psychology.

APPENDIX: USEFUL RESOURCES

This appendix gives information about useful resources in the history of Psychology and theoretical Psychology. It includes details of organizations, journals, archives and museums, on-line books and other web resources, and a selected bibliography. Many of the resources are listed with relevant web addresses. For more on using the Internet to find resources in Psychology, consult:

Stein, S. 1998: *Learning, teaching and researching on the internet*. London: Longman.

ORGANIZATIONS

There are a range of professional societies and other organizations which organize conferences, publish journals and facilitate communication and collaboration. Many offer reduced subscriptions for students. Here we give web addresses for a number of such organizations, which are subject to change, although correct at the time of writing (September 2000).

National Psychology Societies

American Psychological Association Division 26 – History of Psychology – http://www.yorku.ca/dept/psych/orgs/apa26/
American Psychological Association Division 24 – Theoretical and Philosophical Psychology – http://www.yorku.ca/dept/psych/orgs/apa24/apa24.htm
British Psychological Society History and Philosophy of Psychology Section – http://www.chelt.ac.uk/ess/soss/hps/
Canadian Psychological Association History and Philosophy of Psychology Section – http://www.yorku.ca/dept/psych/orgs/cpahpp/index.htm

Societies for the History of Science

British Society for the History of Science – http://www.man.ac.uk/Science_Engineering/CHSTM/bshs/
Centre for the History of Psychology, Staffordshire University – http://www.staffs.ac.uk/schools/sciences/psychology/chop/chop.html

Cheiron: The International Society for the History of Behavioral and Social
Sciences –
http://www.yorku.ca/dept/psych/orgs/cheiron/cheiron.htm
European Society for the History of the Human Sciences –
http://psychology.dur.ac.uk/eshhs/
History of Science Society – http://depts.washington.edu/hssexec/

Societies for Theoretical Psychology

International Society for Theoretical Psychology –
http://www.yorku.ca/dept/psych/orgs/istp/
Society for Philosophy and Psychology –
http://www.hfac.uh.edu/cogsci/spp/spphp.html
Society for the Psychological Study of Social Issues –
http://www.spssi.org/

Other Professional Societies

http://www.yorku.ca/dept/psych/orgs/profsocs.htm

JOURNALS

Journals in the History of Science

British Journal for the History of Science –
http://www.man.ac.uk/Science_Engineering/CHSTM/bshs/bshsbjhs.htm
History and Philosophy of Psychology –
http://www.chelt.ac.uk/ess/soss/hps/journal.htm
History and Philosophy of Psychology Bulletin: Official Bulletin of CPA
History and Philosophy of Psychology Section –
http://www.yorku.ca/dept/psych/orgs/cpahpp/bulletin.htm
History of the Human Sciences –
http://www.sagepub.co.uk/journals/details/j0051.html
History of Psychology: official journal of APA Division 26 –
http://www.WPI.EDU/~histpsy/
Journal of the History of the Behavioral Sciences –
http://www.interscience.wiley.com/jpages/0022-5061/

Journals in Theoretical Psychology

Feminism and Psychology –
http://www.sagepub.co.uk/journals/details/j0191.html
International Journal of Critical Psychology –
http://www.l-w-bks.co.uk/cp-announce.html
Journal of Constructivist Psychology – http://www.tandf.co.uk/journals/
Journal of Social Issues – http://www.spssi.org/jsi.html
Journal of Theoretical and Philosophical Psychology –
http://www.yorku.ca/dept/psych/orgs/apa24/journal.htm

Radical Psychology: A Journal of Psychology, Politics, and Radicalism –
   http://www.yorku.ca/faculty/academic/danaa/
Theory and Psychology – http://www.psych.ucalgary.ca/thpsyc/

Philosophy

Cogito – http://www.tandf.co.uk/journals/
Mind – http://www.oup.co.uk/journals/

ARCHIVES AND MUSEUMS

Archives of the American Psychological Association –
   http://www.apa.org/archives/
Archives of the History of American Psychology –
   http://www.uakron.edu/ahap/
Barnard College History of Psychology Museum –
   http://www.columbia.edu/barnard/psych/b_museum.html
Centre for the History of Psychology Collection, Staffordshire University –
   http://www.staffs.ac.uk/schools/sciences/psychology/chop/catal.html
Museum of the History of Psychological Instrumentation –
   http://chss.montclair.edu/psychology/museum/museum.html
University of Toronto Museum of Psychological Instruments –
   http://www.psych.utoronto.ca/museum/

ON-LINE BOOKS

On-line books page – http://www.cs.cmu.edu/books.html
Project Gutenberg – http://www.promo.net/pg/index.html
Classics in the history of psychology –
   http://www.yorku.ca/dept/psych/classics/
http://www.usca.sc.edu/psychology/histor~1.html

OTHER WEB RESOURCES

York University in Canada maintains a number of useful collections of
   links, including:
   http://www.yorku.ca/dept/psych/orgs/onlinebj.htm
   http://www.yorku.ca/faculty/academic/christo/webreview/index.htm
   http://www.yorku.ca/dept/psych/orgs/archcoll.htm
Critical psychology web ring home page –
   http://www.sar.bolton.ac.uk/Psych/Main/WebRing.htm
Founders of neurology – http://www.uic.edu/depts/mcne/founders/
History of American education web project –
   http://sun1.iusb.edu/eduweb01

History of influences in the development of intelligence theory and testing –
  http://www.indiana.edu/~intell/
History of psychology archives –
  http://muskingum.edu/~psychology/psycweb/history.htm
Human science – http://www.human-nature.com/
Library guide to the history of psychology –
  http://www.slu.edu/colleges/AS/PSY/510Guide.html
Social psychology network's history of psychology links –
  http://www.wesleyan.edu/spn/history.htm
Women in psychology –
  http://teach.psy.uga.edu/dept/student/parker/PsychWomen/wopsy.htm
Women's intellectual contribution to the study of mind and society –
  http://www.webster.edu/~woolflm/women.html

Selected Bibliography

Bem, S. and Looren de Jong, H. 1997: *Theoretical issues in psychology*. London: Sage.
Benjafield, J.G. 1996: *A history of psychology*. London: Allyn and Beacon.
Brennan, J.F. 1995: *Readings in the history and systems of psychology*. Upper Saddle River, NJ: Prentice-Hall.
Bringmann, W.G., Lück, H.E., Miller, R. and Early, C.E. (eds) 1997: *A pictorial history of psychology*. Chicago: Quintessence Publishing.
Buxton, C.E. (ed.) 1985: *Points of view in the modern history of psychology*. New York: Academic Press.
Carruthers, P. 1996: *Language, thought, and consciousness: an essay in philosophical psychology*. Cambridge: Cambridge University Press.
Corsini, R.J. 1994: *Encyclopedia of psychology*, 2nd edn, 4 vols. New York: Wiley.
Flanagan, O. 1992: *Consciousness reconsidered*. Cambridge, MA: MIT Press.
Fuller, R., Walsh P.N. and McGinley, P. (eds) 1997: *A century of psychology*. London: Routledge.
Geirson, H. and Losonsky, M. 1996: *Readings in language and mind*. Oxford: Blackwell.
Graham, G. 1993: *Philosophy of mind: an introduction*. Oxford: Blackwell.
Guttenplan, S. 1995: *A companion to the philosophy of mind*. Oxford: Blackwell.
Hock, R.R. 1999: *Forty studies that changed psychology*. London: Prentice-Hall International.
Kimble, G.A. and Wertheimer, M. 1998: *Portraits of pioneers in psychology*, vol. 3. Washington, DC: American Psychological Association.
Kimble, G.A., Boneau, C.A. and Wertheimer, M. 1996: *Portraits of pioneers in psychology*, vol. 2. Washington, DC: American Psychological Association.
Kimble, G.A., Wertheimer, M. and White, C.L. 1991: *Portraits of pioneers in psychology*, vol. 1. Washington, DC: American Psychological Association.
Kusch, M. 1995: *Psychologism*. London: Routledge
Leahey, T.H. 1992: *A history of psychology: main currents in psychological thought*. Englewood Cliffs, NJ: Prentice-Hall.
Leary, D. 1990: *Metaphors in the history of psychology*. Cambridge: Cambridge University Press.
Lycan, W.G. 1990: *Mind and cognition: a reader*. Oxford: Blackwell.

MacDonald, C. and MacDonald, G. 1995: *Philosophy of psychology*. Oxford: Blackwell.

Maiers, W., Bayer, B. *et al.* 1999: *Challenges to theoretical psychology*. Ontario: Captus University Publications.

Nunn, C. 1995: *Awareness*. London: Routledge.

O'Connell, A.N. and Russo, N.F. 1990: *Women in psychology: a bio-bibliographic sourcebook*. Westport, CT: Greenwood.

Robinson, D.T. 1995: *Intellectual history of psychology*. London: Macmillan.

Root, M. 1993: *Philosophy of social science*. Oxford: Blackwell.

Slife, B.D. and Williams, R.N. 1995: *What's behind the research: discovering hidden assumptions in the behavioral sciences*. London: Sage.

Sokal, M.M. and Rafail, P.A. 1982: *A guide to manuscript collections in the history of psychology and related areas*. Milwood, NY: Kraus.

Soyland, A.G. 1994: *Psychology as metaphor*. London: Sage.

Stich, S.P. 1983: *From folk psychology to cognitive science*. Cambridge, MA: MIT Press.

Stich, S.P. and Warfield, T.A. 1994: *Mental representation: a reader*. Oxford: Blackwell.

Tolman, C.W., Cherry, F. *et al.* 1996: *Problems of theoretical psychology*. Ontario, Captus University Publications.

Trigg, A. 1993: *Rationality and science*. Oxford: Blackwell.

Viney, W. and King, D.B. 1998: *A history of psychology: ideas and context*, 2nd edn. Boston: Allyn and Bacon.

REFERENCES

Ackerman, N. and Jahoda, M. 1950: *Anti-Semitism and Emotional Disorder: A Psychoanalytic Interpretation*. NY: Harper.

Adair, Y. and Elcock, J. 1996: *Pushers and victims: police discourses of rave culture*. BPS Annual Conference: Brighton.

Adorno, T.W., Frenkel-Brunswik, E., Levison, D.J. and Sanford, R.N. 1964 [1950]: *The authoritarian personality*, 2 vols. New York: Science Editions.

Allport G.W. 1954: The historical background of modern social psychology. In: G. Lindzey (ed.), *Handbook of Social Psychology*, vol. 1. Reading, Mass.: Addison-Wesley.

Allport, F.H. 1924: *Social psychology*. Boston, MA: Houghton Mifflin.

Allport, F.H. 1933: *Institutional behavior*. Chapel Hill, NC: University of North Carolina Press.

Allport, F.H. 1937: Towards a science of public opinion. *Public Opinion Quarterly*, 1, 7–23.

Allport, F.H. and Hartman, D.A. 1925: The measurement and motivation of atypical opinion in a certain group. *American Policy Science Review*, Vol. 19 No. 4.

Allport, G.W. 1954: The historical background of modern social psychology. In: G. Lindzey (ed.), *Handbook of social psychology*, vol. 1. Reading, MA: Addison-Wesley.

Angell, J.R. 1904: *Psychology*. New York: Henry Holt.

Angell, J.R. 1911: Usages of the terms mind, consciousness and soul. *Psychological Bulletin* 8: 46–7.

Asch, S.E. 1952: *Social psychology*. Englewood Cliffs, NJ: Prentice-Hall.

Ash, M. 1995: *Gestalt psychology in German culture 1890–1967*. Cambridge: Cambridge University Press.

Ash, M.G. and Woodward, W.R. (eds) 1989: *Psychology in twentieth-century thought and society*. Cambridge: Cambridge University Press.

Atkinson, R.C. and Shiffrin, R.M. 1968: Human memory: a proposed system and its control processes. In: K.W. Spence and J.T. Spence (eds), *The Psychology of Learning and Motivation (Vol. 2)*. London: Academic Press.

Baddeley, A. 1986: *Working Memory*. Oxford: Oxford University Press.

Bakan, D. 1966: The influence of phrenology on American psychology. *Journal of the History of the Behavioural Sciences* 2: 200–20.

Banister, P., Burman, E., Parker, I., Taylor, M. and Tindall, C.1995: *Qualitative methods in psychology*. Buckingham: Open University Press.

Baritz, L.J. 1960: *The servants of power: a history of the use of social science in American industry*. Middletown, CT: Wesleyan University Press.

Baron, R.A. and Byrne, D. 1984: *Social psychology*, 3rd edn. Boston, MA: Allyn and Beacon.

Baron, R.A. and Byrne, D. 1998: *Social psychology: understanding human psychology*, 9th edn. Boston: Allyn and Bacon.

Bartlett, F.C. 1932: *Remembering: a study in social and experimental psychology*. Cambridge: Cambridge University Press.

Bartlett, F.C. 1958: *Thinking: an experimental and social study*. London: Allen and Unwin.

Bechtel, W. and Abrahamsen, A. 1991: *Connectionism and the mind*. Oxford: Blackwell.

Bechtel, W., Abrahamsen, A. and Graham, G. 1998: The life of cognitive science. In: W. Bechtel and G. Graham (eds) *A companion to cognitive science*. Oxford: Blackwell.

Bem, S. and de Jong, H.L. 1997: *Theoretical issues in psychology: an introduction*. London: Sage.

Bem, S.L. 1985: Androgyny and gender schema theory: a conceptual and empirical integration. In: T.B. Sonderegger (ed.) *Nebraska Symposium on Motivation, 1984: Psychology and Gender*. Lincoln, NE: University of Nebraska Press.

Benjamin, L. 1997: *A history of psychology: original sources and contemporary research*. New York: McGraw Hill.

Benjamin, L., Durkin, M., Link, M., Vestal, M. and Accord, J. 1992: Wündt's American doctoral students. *American Psychologist* 47: 123–31.

Bettleheim, B. and Janovitz, M. 1950: *Dynamics of Prejudice: A Psychological and Sociological Study of Veterans*. NY: Harper.

Bhaskar, R. 1991: *Meeting of minds. Socialists discuss philosophy*. London: Socialist Society.

Bhaskar, R. 1997: *A realist theory of science*. London: Verso.

Bickhard, M. 1996: Troubles with computationalism. In: W. O'Donohue and R.F. Kitchener (eds) *The philosophy of psychology*. London: Sage.

Billig, M. 1987: *Arguing and thinking: a rhetorical approach to social psychology*. Cambridge: Cambridge University Press.

Billig, M. 1991: *Ideology and opinions*. London: Sage.

Blumenthal, A.L. 1973: Introduction. In: W. Wündt, *The language of gestures*. The Hague: Mouton.

Boring, E.G. 1950: *A history of experimental psychology*, 2nd edn. Englewood Cliffs, NJ: Prentice-Hall.

Bramel, D. and Friend, R. 1981: Hawthorne, the myth of the docile worker, and class bias in American psychology. *American Psychologist* 36: 867–78.

Bridgman, P.W. 1927: *The Logic of Modern Physics*. Chicago: University of Chicago Press.

Broadbent, D.E. 1958: *Perception and communication*. London: Pergamon.

Brugman, C. 1981: *Story of Over*. MA Thesis, University of California, Berkeley.

Bruner, J. 1995: Meaning and Self in Cultural Perspective. In: D. Bakhurst and C. Sypnowich (eds), *The Social Self*. London: Sage Publications.

Bruner, J., Goodnow, J. and Austin, G. 1956: *A study of thinking*. New York: John Wiley.

Burkhardt, J. 1860: *The civilisation of the renaissance in Italy*, 1958. English translation of German original. New York: Harper.

Burman, E. 1997: Differentiating and de-developing critical social psychology. In: T. Ibanez and L. Iniguez (eds) *Critical social psychology I*. London: Sage.

Burman, E. 1998: Deconstructing feminist psychology. In: E. Burman (ed.), *Deconstructing Feminist Psychology*. London: Sage.

Burman, E. 1999: Whose construction? Points from a feminist perspective. In: D. J. Nightingale & J. Cromby (eds) *Social constructionist psychology: a critical analysis of theory and practice*. Buckingham: Open University Press.

Burman, E. and Parker, I. (eds) 1993: *Discourse analytic research*. London, Routledge.

Burr, V. 1995: *An introduction to social constructionism*. London: Routledge.

Burr, V. 1998: *Gender and social psychology*. London: Routledge.

Burrkitt, I. 1999: Between the dark and the light. In: D. J. Nightingale & J. Cromby (Eds) *Social constructionist psychology: a critical analysis of theory and practice*. Buckingham: Open University Press.

Capaldi, E.J. and Proctor, R.W. 1999: *Contextualism in psychological research? A critical review*. London: Sage.

Cattell, J. 1890: Mental tests and measurements. *Mind* 15: 373–81.

Chater, N. and Oaksford, M. 1996: The falsity of folk theories. In: W. O'Donohue and R. Kitchener (eds) *The philosophy of psychology*. London: Sage.

Chomsky, N. 1957: *Syntactic structures*. The Hague: Mouton.

Chomsky, N. 1995: Media control: the spectacular achievements of propaganda. *Open Magazine Pamphlet* Series 10: July 1995.

Churchland, P. 1989: Folk psychology and the explanation of human behavior. In: *A neurocomputational perspective*. Cambridge, MA: MIT Press.

Cohen, J. 1994: The earth is round (p<.05). *American Psychologist* 49: 997–1003.

Craik, K. 1943: The nature of explanation. Cambridge: Cambridge University Press.

Crawford, M. 1995: *Talking difference: on gender and language*. London: Sage.

Crews, F. C. (ed.) 1998: *Unauthorized Freud*. London: Viking Penguin.

Curt, B.C. 1994: *Textuality and tectonics: troubling social and psychological science*. Buckingham: The Open University Press.

Danziger, K. 1990: *Constructing the subject: historical origins of psychological research*. Cambridge: Cambridge University Press.

Danziger, K. 1997: *Naming the mind: how psychology found its language*. London: Sage.

Darwin, C. 1872: *The expression of emotions in man and animals*. London: Murray.

De Beauvoir, S. 1949: *The second sex* (1984 edition). Harmondsworth: Penguin.

De Saussure, F. 1974: *A course in general linguistics* (W. Baskin trans.). London: Fontana.

Dennett, D.C. 1992: *Consciousness explained*. London: Penguin.

Descartes, R. 1637: *Discourse on the method of rightly conducting reason and seeking the truth in the sciences*, 1912 edition. London: Dent.

Dewey, J. 1894: The theory of emotion I. Emotional attitudes, *Psychological review*, 1: 553–69.

Dewey, J. 1896: The reflex arc in psychology. *Psychological Review* 3: 357–70.

Dobles, I. 1999: Marxism, ideology and psychology. *Theory and Psychology* 9(3): 399–406.

Dreyfus, H.L. and Dreyfus, S.E. 1988: Making a mind versus modelling the brain: artificial intelligence back at a branchpoint. In: S. Graubard (ed.) *The artificial intelligence debate*. Cambridge, MA: MIT Press.

Dryden, W. and Feltham, C. (eds) 1992: *Psychotherapy and its discontents*. Buckingham: Open University Press.

Edwards, D. 1997: *Discourse and cognition*. London: Sage.

Edwards, D., Ashmore, M. and Potter, J. 1995: Death and Furniture: the rhetoric, politics and theology of bottom line arguments against relativism. *History of the Human Sciences*, 8: 25–29.

Ellis, A.W. and Young, A.W. 1996: *Human cognitive neuropsychology: a textbook with readings*. Hove: Psychology Press.

Ellis, R. and Humphreys, G. 1999: *Connectionist psychology*. Hove: Psychology Press.

Ettorre, E. 1980: *Lesbians, women and society*. London: Routledge.

Eysenck, H.J. 1971: *Race, Politics and Education*. London: Temple Smith.

Farr, R.M. 1996: *The roots of modern social psychology, 1872–1954*. Oxford: Blackwell.

Finison, L. 1986: The psychological insurgency 1936–1945. *Journal of Social Issues* 42(1): 21–33.

Fodor, J. 1975: *The language of thought*. Cambridge, MA: Harvard University Press.

Fodor, J. 1983: *The modularity of mind: an essay of faculty psychology*. Cambridge, MA: MIT Press.

Fodor, J.A. 1981: The present status of the innateness controversy. In: J. Fodor, *RePresentations*, pp. 257–316. Cambridge, MA: MIT Press.

Fodor, J.A. 1991: *The theory of content and other essays*. Cambridge, MA: MIT Press.

Fox, D. and Prilleltensky, I. (eds) 1997: *Critical psychology: an introduction*. London: Sage.

Frawley, W. 1992: *Linguistic semantics*. Hove: Lawrence Erlbaum Associates.

Freud, S. 1937: Analysis terminable and interminable. In: *Standard edition of the complete works of Sigmund Freud*, vol. 23. London: Hogarth Press.

Frost, S. 1999: *The politics of psychoanalysis*. London: Macmillan.

Galton, F. 1962: *Hereditary genius*, 2nd edition. Cleveland, OH: World Publishing

Gentner, D. and Stevens, A.L. (eds) 1983: *Mental models*. London: Erlbaum.

Gergen, K.J. 1975: Psychology as history. *Journal of Personality and Social Psychology*, 26, 309–20.

Gergen, K.J. 1985: Social constructionist inquiry: context and implications. In: K.J. Gergen and K.E. Davis (eds) *The social construction of the person*. New York: Springer-Verlag.

Geuter, U. 1987: German psychology during the Nazi period. In: M. Ash and W. Woodward *Psychology in twentieth-century thought and society*. Cambridge: Cambridge University Press.

Geuter, U. 1992: *The professionalization of psychology in Nazi Germany*. Cambridge: Cambridge University Press.

Gibson, J.J. 1979: *The Ecological Approach to Visual Perception*. Boston: Houghton Mifflin.

Giddens, A. (ed.) 1974: *Positivism and Sociology*. London: Heinemann.

Gilbert, G.N. and Mulkay, M. 1984: *Opening Pandora's box: a sociological analysis of scientists discourse*. Cambridge: Cambridge University Press.

Gilligan, C. 1982: In: *A different voice*. Cambridge MA: Harvard University Press.

Goodwin, C.J. 1999: *A history of modern psychology*. Chichester: John Wiley and Sons.

Gould, S.J. 1991: *Bully for brontosaurus*. London: Penguin Books.

Gould, S.J. 1991: *Wonderful life: the Burgess shale and the nature of history*. Harmondsworth: Penguin.

Gould, S.J. 1996 revised: *The mismeasure of man*. London: Penguin.

Greenwood, J.D. 1997: Understanding the 'cognitive revolution' in psychology. *Journal of the History of the Behavioural Sciences* 35(1): 1–22.

Gregory, R.L. 1981: *Mind in science*. London: Penguin Books.

Gross, R. 1995: *Themes, issues and debates in psychology*. London: Hodder and Stoughton.

Hacking, I. 1995: *Rewriting the Soul: Multiple Personality and the Sciences of Memory*. Princeton: Princeton University Press.

Hacking, I. 1995: *Rewriting the soul: multiple personality and the sciences of memory*. Princeton, NJ: Princeton University Press.

Halperin, D.M. 2000: 'How to do the history of male homosexuality. *Journal of Lesian and Gay Studies* 6(1): 87–123.

Hamilton, W. 1863: *Lectures on metaphysics*. Boston, MA: Gould and Lincoln.

Harding, S. 1986: *The Science Question in Feminism*. Ithaca, NY: Cornell University Press.

Harris, B. 1979 Whatever happened to little Albert? *American Psychologist* 34: 151–60.

Harris, B. 1997: Repoliticizing the history of psychology. In: D. Fox and I. Prilleltensky *Critical psychology: an introduction*. London: Sage.

Harré R. 1974: Blueprint for a new science. In: N. Armitead (ed.) *Reconstructing social psychology*. Harmondsworth: Pelican.

Harré, R. 1993: *Social being*. Oxford: Blackwell.

Hebb, D.O. 1949: *The organisation of behaviour*. New York: Wiley

Hedblom, J.H. 1973: Dimensions of lesbian sexual experience. *Archives of Sexual Behavior* 2: 329–41.

Heider, F. 1958: *The Psychology of Interpersonal Relations*. New York: Wiley.

Hempel, C.G. 1946: *Aspects of scientific explanation*. New York: Free Press.

Henwood, K., Griffin, C. and Phoenix, A. (eds) 1998: *Standpoints and differences: essays in the practice of feminist psychology*. London: Sage.

Herman, E. 1995: *The romance of American psychology*. Berkeley, University of California Press.

Herman, E. 1996: *The romance of American psychology*. London: University of California Press.

Hinton, G.E. and Shallice, T. 1991: Lesioning an attractor network. Investigations of acquired dyslexia. *Psychological Review*, 93, 411–28.

Hollway, W. 1989: *Subjectivity and method in psychology: gender, meaning and science*. London: Sage.

Howitt, D and Owusu-Bempah, J. 1994: *The racism of psychology: time for a change*. Hemel Hempstead: Harvester-Wheatsheaf.

Hyde, J.S. 1986: Meta-analysis and the psychology of gender differences. *Signs* 16(11): 55–73.

Ibanez, T. and Iniguez, L. (eds) 1997: *Critical social psychology*. London: Sage.

Jacklin, C.N. 1981: Methodological issues in the study of sex-related differences. *Developmental Review* 1: 266–73.

Jahoda, M. 1977: *Freud and the Dilemmas of Psychology*. London: The Hogarth Press.

James, W. 1890: *Principles of psychology*, 2 vols. New York: Henry Holt.

Jaspars, J. M. F. and Fraser, C. 1984: Attitudes and social representations, In: R.M. Farr and S. Moscovici (eds), *Social Representations*. Cambridge: Cambridge University Press.

Kamin, L.J. 1974: *The science and politics of IQ*. Potomac, MD: Lawrence Erlbaum Associates.

Kemeny J. 1959: *A Philosopher looks at science*. Princeton: Van Noustrand.

Kitzinger, C. 1987: *The social construction of lesbianism*. London: Sage.

Knorr-Cetina, K. 1983: The ethnographic study of scientific work: towards a constructionist interpretation of science. In: K. Knorr-Cetina and M. Mulkay (eds) *Science observed*. London: Sage.

Koffka, K. 1922: Perception: an introduction to Gestalt-theorie. *Psychological Bulletin* 19: 531–85.

Krauss, S.J. 1995: Attitudes and the prediction of behavior: a meta-analysis of the empirical literature. *Personality and Social Psychology Bulletin* 21: 58–75.

Kuhn, T.S. 1962: *The structure of scientific revolutions*. Chicago: University of Chicago Press.

Kuhn, T.S. 1970: *The structure of scientific revolutions*, 2nd edn. Chicago: University of Chicago Press.

Kusch, M. 1999: *Psychological knowledge: a social history and philosophy*. London: Routledge.

Köhler, W. 1959: Gestalt psychology today. *American Psychologist* 14: 727–34.

La Piere, R.T. 1934: Attitudes versus action. *Social Forces* 13: 230–37.

Lakoff, G. 1990: *Women, fire and dangerous things*. Chicago: University of Chicago Press.

Lakoff, G. and Johnson, M. 1980: *Metaphors we live by*. Chicago: University of Chicago Press.

Lakoff, R. 1973: Language and a woman's place. *Language in Society* 2: 45–79.

Latour, B. and Woolgar, S. 1979: *Laboratory life: the social constitution of scientific facts.* Beverly Hills, CA: Sage.

Le Bon. G. 1896: *The Crowd*, London: Fisher Unwin.

Leahey, T.H. 1992: The mythical revolutions of American psychology. *American Psychologist* 47: 308–18.

Leahey, T.H. 2000: *A history of psychology*, 5th edn. Upper Saddle River, NJ: Prentice-Hall.

Maccoby, E.E. and Jacklin, C.N. 1974: *The psychology of sex differences*. Stanford, CA: Stanford University Press.

Maslow, A.H. 1954: *Motivation and Personality*. New York: Harpers Press.

May, T. 1997: *Social research: issues, methods and processes*. Buckingham: The Open University Press.

McClelland, J., Rumelhart, D. and the PDP Research Group 1986: *Parallel distributed processing: explorations in the microstructure of cognition*, vol. II. Cambridge, MA: MIT Press.

McCulloch, W. and Pitts, W. 1943: A logical calculus of the ideas immanent in nervous activity. *Bulletin of Mathematical Biophysics* 5: 115–33.

Mead, G.H. 1934: In: C.W. Morris (ed.) *Mind, self and society: from the standpoint of a social behaviourist*. Chicago: University of Chicago Press.

Mead, G.H. 1982: *The Individual and the Social Self: unpublished work of George Herbert Mead* (ed. D.L. Miller). Chicago: University of Chicago Press.

Mead, M. 1926: The methodology of racial testing, its significance for sociology. *American Journal of Sociology* 31: 657–8.

Mead. G.H, 1934: *Mind, Self and Society: from the standpoint of a social behaviourist* (ed. C.W. Morris). Chicago: University of Chicago Press.

Michael, M. 1996: *Constructing identities*. London, Sage.

Michael, M. 1997: Critical social psychology: identity and de-prioritization of the social. In: T. Ibanez and L. Iniguez (eds), *Critical Social Psychology*. London: Sage.

Miller, G. 1956: The magical number seven, plus or minus two: some limits on our capacity for processing information. *Psychological Review* 63: 81–97.

Miller, G. and Frick, F. 1949: Statistical behaviouristics and sequences of responses. *Psychological Review* 56: 311–24.

Miller, G., Galanter, E. and Pribram, K. 1960: *Plans and the structure of behaviour*. New York: Holt.

Minsky, M. and Papert, S. 1969: *Perceptrons*. Cambridge: MA: MIT Press.

Morgan, C.L. 1968: Lloyd Morgan's Canon. In: R.J. Herrnstein and E. Boring (eds), *A Source Book in the History of Psychology*, pp. 462–8. Cambridge, MA: Harvard University Press (original work published 1894).

Morss, J. 1995: *Growing critical: alternatives to developmental psychology*. London: Routledge.

Moses, L.E. 1986: *Think and explain with statisics*. Reading: Addison Wesley.

Mulac, A. and Lundell, T. 1986: Linguisitic contributors to the gender-linked language effect. *Journal of Language and Social Psychology* 5: 85–102.

Murchison, C. (ed.) 1930: *Psychologies of 1930*. Worcester, MA: Clark University Press.

Napoli, D. 1981: *Architects of adjustment*. New York: Kennikat Press.

Neisser, U. 1967: *Cognitive psychology*. New York: Appleton-Century-Crofts.

Neisser, U. 1976: *Cognition and reality*. San Francisco: Freeman.

Newell, A., Shaw, J.C. and Simon, H. 1958: Elements of a theory of problem solving. *Psychological Review* 65(3): 151–66.

Nightingale, D.J. and Cromby, J. (eds) 1999: *Social constructionist psychology*. Buckingham: The Open University Press.

Nisbett, R.E. and Wilson, T.D. 1977: Telling more than we can know: verbal reports on mental processes. *Psychological Review* 84: 231–59.

Norman, D. 1980: Twelve issues for cognitive science. *Cognitive Science* 4: 1–33.

Palmer, S. 1995 Gestalt psychology redux. In: P. Baumgartner and S. Payr (eds) *Speaking minds*. Princeton, NJ: Princeton University Press.

Pearson, B.A. 1991: Discourse structure of direction giving – effects of native non-native speaker status and gender. *TESOL Quarterly* 26: 113–27.

Penrose, R. 1999: *The emperor's new mind*. Oxford: Oxford University Press.

Peplau La, Conrad E. 1989: Beyond nonsexist research – the perils of feminist methods in psychology. *Psychology Women Quarterly* 13(4): 379–400.

Peplau, L.A. and Gordon, S.L. 1983: The ultimate relationships of lesbians and gay men. In: E.R. Allegeirier and N.B. McCormick (eds) *Changing boundaries: gender roles and sexual behavior*. Palo Alto, CA: Mayfield Publications.

Piaget, J. 1952: Jean Piaget. In: E. Boring, H. Langfeld, H. Werner and R. Yerkes (eds) *A history of psychology in autobiography*, vol. 4. New York: Russell and Russell.

Plant, S. 1992: *The most radical gesture*. London: Routledge.

Port, R. and van Gelder, T. (eds) 1995: *Mind as motion: dynamics, behavior and cognition*. Cambridge: MA: MIT Press.

Potter J. 1996: *Representing Reality: Discourse, Rhetoric and Social Construction*. London: Sage.

Putnam, H. 1960: Minds and machines. In: S. Hook (ed.) *Dimensions of mind*. New York: New York University Press.

Richards, G. 1989: *On psychological language*. London: Routledge.

Richards, G. 1996: *Putting psychology in its place*. London: Routledge.

Richards, G. 1996b: On the necessary survival of folk psychology. In: W. O'Donohue and R. Kitchener *The philosophy of psychology*. London: Sage.

Richards, G. 1997: *Race, racism and psychology: towards a reflexive history*. London: Routledge.

Richards, G. 1997b: The presence and absence of race as a topic in British Psychology 1913–1940. In: M.C. Chung *Psychological concepts from philosophical and historical perspectives*. Leicester: The British Psychological Society.

Robinson, D.N. 1995: *An intellectual history of psychology*. London: Arnold.

Romanes, G.J. 1977: *Animal Intelligence*. New York: University Publications (original work published 1883).

Rorty, R. 1980: *Philosophy and the mirror of nature*. Princeton, Princeton University Press.

Rose, H. 1993: Rhetoric, feminism and scientific knowledge: Or from either/or to both/and. In: R.H. Roberts and J.M.M. Godd (eds), *The recovery of rhetoric*. Charlottesville: University Press of Virginia.

Rosenblatt, F. 1962: *Principles of Neurodynamics: perceptrons and the theory of brain mechanisms*. Washington DC: Spartan Books.

Rosenblueth, A., Weiner, N. and Bigelow, J. 1943: Behaviour, purpose and teleology. *Philosophy of Science* 10: 18–24.

Rosenthal, R. and Rosnow, R. 1991: *Essentials of behavioural research*. New York: McGraw-Hill.

Rumelhart, D., McClelland, J., and the PDP Research Group 1986: *Parallel distributed processing: explorations in the microstructure of cognition*, vol. I. Cambridge, MA: MIT Press.

Sawicki, J. 1991: *Disciplining Foucault*. New York: Routledge.

Searle, J. 1984: Minds, brains and science: the Reith Lectures. London: Penguin.

Sharkey, N. 1992: *Connectionist natural language processing: readings from connection science*. Oxford: Intellect.

Sherif, C.W. 1979: Bias in psychology. In: J.A. Sherman and E.T. Beck (eds), *The prism of sex: essays in the sociology of knowledge*. Madison: University of Wisconsin Press.

Shotter, J. 1975: *Images of man in psychological research*. London: Methuen.

Simon, H.A. 1992: What is an explanation of behavior? *Psychological Science* 3: 150–61.

Skinner, B.F. 1957: *Verbal behaviour*. New York: Appleton-Century-Crofts.

Slife, B.D. and Williams, R.N 1995: *What's behind the research: discovering hidden assumptions in the behavioral sciences*. London: Sage.

Sokal, M. 1997: James McKeen Cattell and the failure of anthropometric mental testing. In: L. Benjamin (ed.) *A history of psychology: original sources and contemporary research*, 2nd edn. Boston, MA: McGraw Hill.

Sokal, M.M. 1981: *An education in psychology: James Mckeen Cattell's Journal and letters from Germany and England: 1880–1888*. Cambridge, MA: MIT Press.

Spencer, H. 1855: *Principles of psychology*. London: Smith and Elder.

Stainton Rogers, R. 1995: Q methodology. In: J.A. Smith, R. Harré and L.V. Langenhove (eds) *Rethinking methods in psychology*. London: Sage.

Stainton Rogers, R. and Stainton Rogers, W. 1997: Does Critical Psychology Mean the End of the World? In: T. Ibanez and L. Iniguez (eds), *Critical Social Psychology* London: Sage.

Stearns, C.Z. and Stearns, P.N. 1988: *Emotions and social change: a psychohistory*. New York: Holmes and Meir.

Sternberg, R.J. 1993: *Psychologist's companion: a guide to scientific reading for students and researchers*. Cambridge: Cambridge University Press.

Strube, G. 2000: Generative theories in cognitive psychology. *Theory and Psychology* 10(1): 117–25.

Thompson, B. 1999: If statistical significance tests are broken/misused, what practices should supplement or replace them? *Theory and Psychology* 9(2): 165–81.

Thurstone, E.L. 1928: Attitudes can be measured. *American Journal of Psychology* 33: 529–54.

Thurstone, E.L. 1952: Autobiography. In: E.G. Boring, H.S. Langfelt, H. Werener and R.M. Yerkes (eds), *A history of psychology in autobiography*, vol. 4. New York: Russell and Russell.

Thurstone, E.L. 1959: *The measurement of values*. Chicago: University of Chicago Press.

Titchener, E.B. 1898: Postulates of a structural psychology. *Philosophical Review* 7: 449–65.

Titchener, E.B. 1916: On ethnological tests of sensation and perception with special reference to tests of color vision and tactile discrimination described in the reports of the Cambridge anthropological expedition to Torres Straits. *Proceedings of the American Philosophical Society*, 55, 204–36.

Tuing, A.M. 1950: Computing machinery and intelligence. *Mind*, 59, 433–60.

Valentine, E. 1996: Folk psychology and its implications for cognitive science. In: W. O'Donohue and R. Kitchener (eds), *The philosophy of psychology*. London: Sage.

Von Ehrenfels 1890: On Gestalt qualities. In: T.H. Leahey (2000) *A history of psychology*. Englewood Cliffs, NJ: Prentice-Hall.

Watson, J.B. 1913: Psychology as a behaviourist views it. *Psychological Review* 20: 158–77.

Watson, J.B. 1919: *Psychology from the standpoint of a behaviourist*. Philadelphia: Lippincott.

Weiner, N. 1948: *Cybernetics: or, control and communication in the animal machine*. New York: Wiley.

Wertheimer, M. 1968, originally published 1912: Experimental studies on the perception of movement. In: W.S. Sahakian (ed.) 1968 *History of psychology: a source book in systematic psychology*. Itasca, IL: Peacock.

Whittle, P. 2000: W.H.R. Rivers and the early history of psychology at Cambridge. In: A. Saito Bartlett *Culture and cognition*. Hove: Psychology Press.

Wilkinson, S. 1997: Prioritizing the political: feminist psychology. In: T. Ibanez and L. Iniguez (eds) *Critical social psychology I*. London: Sage.

Winograd, T. 1972: *Understanding Natural Languages*. New York: Academic Press.

Woodworth, R.S. 1918: *Dynamic psychology*. New York: Columbia University Press.

Woodworth, R.S. 1931: *Schools of contemporary psychology*. New York: Ronald Press.

Woolgar, S. 1988: *Science: the Very Idea*. Chichester: Ellis Horwood.

Wündt, W. 1916: *Elements of folk psychology: outlines of a psychological history and the development of mankind*. London: George Allen and Unwin.

Zalin, C.J. 1989: The bases for differing evaluations of male and females speech: evidence from ratings of transcribed conversation. *Communication Monographs*, 56, 59–74.

INDEX